HTML5 Game Development with GameMaker

Experience a captivating journey that will take you from creating a full-on shoot 'em up to your first social web browser game

Jason Lee Elliott

[PACKT]
PUBLISHING

BIRMINGHAM - MUMBAI

HTML5 Game Development with GameMaker

Copyright © 2013 Packt Publishing

All rights reserved. No part of this book may be reproduced, stored in a retrieval system, or transmitted in any form or by any means, without the prior written permission of the publisher, except in the case of brief quotations embedded in critical articles or reviews.

Every effort has been made in the preparation of this book to ensure the accuracy of the information presented. However, the information contained in this book is sold without warranty, either express or implied. Neither the author, nor Packt Publishing, and its dealers and distributors will be held liable for any damages caused or alleged to be caused directly or indirectly by this book.

Packt Publishing has endeavored to provide trademark information about all of the companies and products mentioned in this book by the appropriate use of capitals. However, Packt Publishing cannot guarantee the accuracy of this information.

First published: April 2013

Production Reference: 1150413

Published by Packt Publishing Ltd.
Livery Place
35 Livery Street
Birmingham B3 2PB, UK.

ISBN 978-1-84969-410-0

www.packtpub.com

Cover Image by Suresh Mogre (suresh.mogre.99@gmail.com)

Credits

Author
Jason Lee Elliott

Reviewers
Dave Hersey
Chris Sanyk

Acquisition Editors
Antony Lowe
Grant Mizen

Lead Technical Editor
Mayur Hule

Technical Editors
Saumya Kunder
Amit Ramadas

Project Coordinator
Arshad Sopariwala

Proofreader
Bernadette Watkins

Indexer
Hemangini Bari

Graphics
Ronak Dhruv
Aditi Gajjar

Production Coordinator
Arvindkumar Gupta

Cover Work
Arvindkumar Gupta

About the Author

Jason Lee Elliott is a digital media expert with a passion for game design. He started his career as an all-purpose Artist at Konami, working his way up to the position of Lead Artist on Spawn for the Game Boy Color. Jason then returned to school to study film at the Vancouver Film School, where the shot he wrote, directed, and produced was selected as a finalist for the BC Film Director Internship Program. Games were never far away from his thoughts and with his new cinematic skills in hand, Jason returned to the industry as a Level and Game Designer at Radical Entertainment. While there, Jason became a proficient scripter, working on several acclaimed titles including Hulk, Hulk Ultimate Destruction, and The Simpsons: Hit & Run. Since 2005, Jason has been a teacher at the Art Institute of Vancouver, and is currently a senior faculty member in the Game Art and Design program. In his spare time, he develops indie games, dabbles in web and graphic design, is the webmaster for the Vancouver chapter of ACM SIGGRAPH, and occasionally blogs at jasonleeelliott.com.

> I would like to thank my wife Su and my daughter Pixel, for allowing me the time to write this book. I would also like to give a shout out to Bert Dennison for his help with the artwork, and Brian Werst for all of his music and sound effects used in this book.

About the Reviewers

Dave Hersey has over 35 years of experience in Apple software development, dating back to the Apple II personal computer in 1977. In 2000, after more than six years in software engineering at Apple, Dave started Paracoders, Inc., focusing on custom Mac OS X-based application and driver development. In 2008, Dave's company expanded into iOS (iPhone) mobile applications, followed by Android applications soon after. Some bigger named clients include Paramount Home Entertainment, Lionsgate Entertainment, Seagate, Creative Labs, and Kraft Foods. Most recently, Dave's business expansion has included additional mobile and server-side platforms as well as support services. As a result, the custom software development division of Paracoders now operates as torchlight apps (http://www.torchlightapps.com).

Dave was also a technical reviewer for *Creating Games with cocos2d for iPhone 2* by *Packt Publishing*, and stays busy with his wife raising 3 children, 3 dogs, 2 parakeets, and about 25 ducks, at the last count.

Chris Sanyk is a life-long videogame enthusiast, whose love affair with gaming started in the early 1980s with the Atari 2600 and the golden age of the arcade. He began designing his first videogame on paper at age six, and has been using GameMaker since 2010. He is an active member of the Cleveland Game Developers, the International Game Developers Association, and is a regular participant in Global Game Jam and Ludum Dare. He blogs and releases his game projects at `http://csanyk.com`, and his Twitter handle is `@csanyk`.

Chris is the coauthor of *Wireless Reconnaissance in Penetration Testing* by *Matt Neely, Alex Hammerstone*, and *Chris Sanyk*, published by *Elsevier Press*.

> I would like to thank Mike Substelny, for providing me with my first introduction to GameMaker; my many friends at the Cleveland Game Developers, for their continued support and camaraderie; the communities of indie game developers around the world who put together Global Game Jam, Ludum Dare, and similar events; and the many designers, engineers, programmers, and artists who've inspired me over the years and provided me with endless hours of entertainment, challenge, and frustration, and everyone who has ever played one of my games.

www.PacktPub.com

Support files, eBooks, discount offers and more

You might want to visit `www.PacktPub.com` for support files and downloads related to your book.

Did you know that Packt offers eBook versions of every book published, with PDF and ePub files available? You can upgrade to the eBook version at `www.PacktPub.com` and as a print book customer, you are entitled to a discount on the eBook copy. Get in touch with us at `service@packtpub.com` for more details.

At `www.PacktPub.com`, you can also read a collection of free technical articles, sign up for a range of free newsletters and receive exclusive discounts and offers on Packt books and eBooks.

PACKTLIB®

`http://PacktLib.PacktPub.com`

Do you need instant solutions to your IT questions? PacktLib is Packt's online digital book library. Here, you can access, read and search across Packt's entire library of books.

Why Subscribe?

- Fully searchable across every book published by Packt
- Copy and paste, print and bookmark content
- On demand and accessible via web browser

Free Access for Packt account holders

If you have an account with Packt at `www.PacktPub.com`, you can use this to access PacktLib today and view nine entirely free books. Simply use your login credentials for immediate access.

Table of Contents

Preface	**1**
Chapter 1: Getting to Know the Studio with Your First Game	**7**
Making HTML game development easy	**7**
Setting up the software	**8**
Our first look at the Studio	**10**
The Menu	10
The Toolbar	11
The Resource tree	11
The Workspace	11
Exploring the resource editors	**11**
Loading your art assets with the Sprite Properties editor	12
The wall sprite	12
The player sprite	13
Creating game objects with the Object Properties editor	14
The Wall object	16
The Player object	16
Creating worlds with the Room Properties editor	20
Running the game	23
Introducing code with the Script Properties editor	23
Filling the scene with the Background Properties editor	24
Bringing noise with the Sound Properties editor	27
A little background music	28
Controlling the game with the Overlord	28
The collectible	29
Writing text and the Font Properties editor	32
Creating complex movements with the Path Properties editor	35
Using the Time Line Properties editor to spawn collectibles	38
Tools for debugging your games	**41**
Using the HTML5 DEBUG console	42

Table of Contents

Using the Windows version debugger	44
Taking a look at the JavaScript code	45
Summary	**47**
Chapter 2: Triple 'A' Games: Art and Audio	**49**
Manufacturing art assets	**49**
Understanding the image file formats	50
Importing sprite sheets	**51**
Introducing the image editor	**53**
Creating backgrounds with tilesets	54
Animating and creating sprites	**65**
The illusion of action	65
Maximize the sprite space	66
Looping an animation	66
Manufacturing audio	**71**
Understanding the audio file formats	71
Using the GM:S Audio engine	**72**
Raising the quality bar	**74**
Consistency	74
Readability	75
Polish	76
Summary	**76**
Chapter 3: Shoot 'em Up: Creating a Side-scrolling Shooter	**77**
Coding conventions	**78**
Building the player	**79**
Setting up the player sprite	80
Controlling the player object	82
Building the bullet	85
Firing the bullet	87
Removing bullets from the world	88
Constructing three little enemies	**88**
Making the enemy parent	88
Building the FloatBot	91
Creating the SpaceMine	93
Making the Strafer	97
Controlling the game with the Overlord	**100**
Spawning waves of enemies	100
Building the Overlord	102
Dealing with the life and death of the player	**104**
Setting up the win condition	105
Respawning with a Ghost object	106

Drawing the user interface	**109**
Adding the finishing details to the game	**113**
Adding the game music	113
Making the background move	114
Creating the explosions	115
Summary	**117**
Chapter 4: The Adventure Begins	**119**
Creating animated characters	**120**
Simplifying the character movement	120
Implementing a melee attack	124
Navigating between rooms	**126**
Setting up the rooms	126
Creating Room Portals	129
Teleporting a persistent player	132
Bringing enemies to life	**133**
Summoning the Ghost Librarian	133
Building a wandering Brawl	140
Creating the Coach	146
Adding finishing details to the game	**157**
Summary	**159**
Chapter 5: Platform Fun	**161**
Structuring systems-based code	**161**
Creating gravity	162
Building an animation system	163
Creating a collision forecasting system	166
Checking the keyboard	169
Building the player	**169**
Setting up the room	**177**
Building a boss battle	**179**
Creating the indestructible Gun	179
Constructing the first phase: The Cannons	184
Building the second phase: The giant LaserCannon	190
Setting the final stage: The shielded Boss Core	195
Winding it up	**200**
Summary	**201**
Chapter 6: Toppling Towers	**203**
Understanding the physics engine	**203**
Activating the world	204
Defining properties with fixtures	205
Connecting objects with Joints	210

[iii]

Table of Contents

Applying forces to objects	214
Building a tower toppling game	**219**
Constructing the Pillars and Debris	219
Breaking the Pillars into Debris	224
Adding in the collision sounds	**229**
Building the demolition equipment	**232**
Creating a Wrecking Ball	232
Making a Magnetic Crane	235
Completing the game	**239**
Setting the win condition	240
Creating the Equipment Menu	245
Constructing the towers	250
Summary	**253**
Chapter 7: Dynamic Front Ends	**255**
Setting up the rooms	**255**
Initializing the main menu	257
Selecting levels with 2D arrays	259
Preparing the Shop using data structures	266
Rebuilding the HUD	**272**
Adding risk and reward to destruction	**279**
Adding introductory text to each level	**286**
Saving the player's progress	**290**
Understanding local storage	290
Writing to local storage	291
Saving multiple game profiles	294
Summary	**297**
Chapter 8: Playing with Particles	**299**
Introducing particle effects	**299**
Understanding particle systems	299
Utilizing particle emitters	300
Applying particles	301
HTML5 limitations	302
Adding particle effects to the game	**302**
Creating a Dust Cloud	302
Adding in Shrapnel	306
Making the TNT explosion	309
Cleaning up the particles	313
Summary	**314**

Chapter 9: Get Your Game Out There — 315
Releasing a game on your own site — 315
Creating the application — 315
Hosting the game — 317
Uploading the game with FTP — 318
Integrating with Facebook — 321
Adding a Facebook login button — 325
Tracking the game with Flurry Analytics — 329
Setting up Flurry Analytics — 330
Tracking events in the game — 332
Sending the data to Flurry — 334
Understanding the Analytics — 335
Making money with your games — 337
Summary — 338
Index — 339

Preface

The introduction of HTML5 has revolutionized the web browser as a legitimate gaming platform with unlimited potential. Making games for the browsers has never been simpler, especially with GameMaker Studio.

HTML5 Game Development with GameMaker will show you how to make and release browser-based games using practical examples. This book utilizes GameMaker's powerful scripting language allowing you to create your first game in no time. With this guide you will develop a thorough skill set and a coherent understanding of the tools to develop games of increasing complexity, gradually enhancing your coding abilities and taking them to a whole new level.

This book guides you on how to use advanced features easily and effectively, including, data structures and demonstrating how to create rigid body physics with simple explanations and visual examples. By the end of this book, you will have an in-depth knowledge of developing and publishing online social browser-based games with GameMaker.

What this book covers

Chapter 1, Getting to Know the Studio with Your First Game, will help you in making your own game. You will have an opportunity to explore the GameMaker: Studio interface. In this chapter, we will be creating and implementing every type of resource available while utilizing all the various resource editors.

Chapter 2, Triple 'A' Games: Art and Audio, will help you understand how art and audio work in GameMaker: Studio. It will cover the acceptable image formats and how to import a sprite sheet. In this chapter, we will be creating a tile set that will make better use of computer memory and allow for large unique worlds, and understand how to control sounds and the direction they are heard from.

Chapter 3, *Shoot 'em Up: Creating a Side-scrolling Shooter*, will help you in creating your first side-scrolling shooter. In this chapter, we will be applying all three methods of movement: manually adjusting the X and Y coordinates, and setting the speed and direction. We will be able to add and remove instances from the game world dynamically.

Chapter 4, *The Adventure Begins*, simplifies the player controls by placing the keyboard checks and collision forecasting into a single script. It covers several ways to deal with Sprite animation from rotating the image to setting what sprites should be displayed. We will be dealing with artificial intelligence through the use of proximity detection and path finding.

Chapter 5, *Platform Fun*, delves into systems design and creating some very useful scripts. We will be building an animation system that most objects in the game utilize and forecast for collision, and apply our own custom gravity to the player. Lastly, we will be creating a three-phase Boss fight utilizing all our previous knowledge along with our new systems.

Chapter 6, *Toppling Towers*, covers the basics of using the Box2D physics system. We will be learning how to assign Fixtures to objects and different properties that can be modified. We will be creating a Chain and Wrecking Ball that utilizes Revolute Joints, so that each piece would rotate with the one preceding it. Also, the chapter covers Draw GUI events and the difference between a Sprite's location as represented in a Room versus the location on the screen.

Chapter 7, *Dynamic Front Ends*, consists of adding an entire frontend, including a Shop and unlockable levels. We will be dealing with Grids, Maps, and List data structures to hold a variety of information. We will be rebuilding the HUD, so that we could display more buttons, display only the available equipment, and build a basic countdown timer. Lastly, we will add a save system that teaches us about using local storage and allows us to have multiple player saves.

Chapter 8, *Playing with Particles*, will show you how to add some spit and polish to really make our game shine. We will be delving into the world of particles and create a variety of effects that will add impact to the TNT and Pillar destruction. The game is now complete and ready to be released.

Chapter 9, *Get Your Game Out There*, will help us in uploading a game to a web server using an FTP client. We will be integrating Facebook into the game, allowing players to log in to their account, and post level scores to their walls. It also covers analytics using Flurry to track how players are playing the game. Finally, we will briefly learn about making money off our games through sponsorship.

Appendix, *Drag-and-drop Icons to GameMaker Language Reference*, will help us in understanding what each icon does, as each icon is often more than a single function. The appendix provides a thorough reference of the code equivalent to all the drag-and-drop icons.

You can download this Appendix from `http://www.packtpub.com/sites/default/files/downloads/4100OT_Appendix_Drag_and_drop_Icons_to_GameMaker_Language_Reference.pdf`.

What you need for this book

This book requires GameMaker: Studio Professional with HTML5 export module, and an HTML5-compliant browser (Google Chrome works the best).

Who this book is for

This book is for anyone with a passion to create fun and action packed web browser games using GameMaker: Studio. This intuitive practical guide appeals to both beginners and advanced users wanting to create and release online games to share with the world, using the powerful GameMaker tool.

Conventions

In this book, you will find a number of styles of text that distinguish between different kinds of information. Here are some examples of these styles, and an explanation of their meaning.

Code words in text, database table names, folder names, filenames, file extensions, pathnames, dummy URLs, user input, and Twitter handles are shown as follows: "Create a new Sound and name it `snd_Collect`."

Preface

A block of code is set as follows:

```
mySpeed = 4;
myDirection = 0;
isAttacking = false;
isWalking = false;
health = 100;
image_speed = 0.5;
```

When we wish to draw your attention to a particular part of a code block, the relevant lines or items are set in bold:

```
isWalking = false;
if (keyboard_check(vk_right) && place_free(x + mySpeed, y))
{
    x += mySpeed;
    myDirection = 0;
    sprite_index = spr_Player_WalkRight;
    isWalking = true;
```

New terms and **important words** are shown in bold. Words that you see on the screen, in menus or dialog boxes for example, appear in the text like this: "clicking the **Next** button moves you to the next screen".

[Warnings or important notes appear in a box like this.]

[Tips and tricks appear like this.]

Reader feedback

Feedback from our readers is always welcome. Let us know what you think about this book—what you liked or may have disliked. Reader feedback is important for us to develop titles that you really get the most out of.

To send us general feedback, simply send an e-mail to feedback@packtpub.com, and mention the book title via the subject of your message.

If there is a topic that you have expertise in and you are interested in either writing or contributing to a book, see our author guide on www.packtpub.com/authors.

Customer support

Now that you are the proud owner of a Packt book, we have a number of things to help you to get the most from your purchase.

Downloading the example code

You can download the example code files for all Packt books you have purchased from your account at http://www.packtpub.com. If you purchased this book elsewhere, you can visit http://www.packtpub.com/support and register to have the files e-mailed directly to you.

Errata

Although we have taken every care to ensure the accuracy of our content, mistakes do happen. If you find a mistake in one of our books—maybe a mistake in the text or the code—we would be grateful if you would report this to us. By doing so, you can save other readers from frustration and help us improve subsequent versions of this book. If you find any errata, please report them by visiting http://www.packtpub.com/submit-errata, selecting your book, clicking on the **errata submission form** link, and entering the details of your errata. Once your errata are verified, your submission will be accepted and the errata will be uploaded on our website, or added to any list of existing errata, under the Errata section of that title. Any existing errata can be viewed by selecting your title from http://www.packtpub.com/support.

Piracy

Piracy of copyright material on the Internet is an ongoing problem across all media. At Packt, we take the protection of our copyright and licenses very seriously. If you come across any illegal copies of our works, in any form, on the Internet, please provide us with the location address or website name immediately so that we can pursue a remedy.

Please contact us at `copyright@packtpub.com` with a link to the suspected pirated material.

We appreciate your help in protecting our authors, and our ability to bring you valuable content.

Questions

You can contact us at `questions@packtpub.com` if you are having a problem with any aspect of the book, and we will do our best to address it.

Getting to Know the Studio with Your First Game

Welcome to *HTML5 Game Development with GameMaker*! You are about to enter the exciting world of game development for the web. If you have never used **GameMaker: Studio** before, this book will show you everything you need to know about using the software, making games, and getting them up on the Internet. If you have previous experience with GameMaker: Studio, but this is your first foray into HTML5, this book will give you a better understanding of the differences between developing stand-alone games and browser-based games. Feel free to skim through this chapter and move onto the projects.

Now if you are still reading this, we can assume that you want to know more about this software. You might be asking yourself, "Why should I use GameMaker: Studio? What features does the HTML5 module give me? For that matter, what is HTML5 and why should I care?" All of these are good questions, so let's try to answer them.

Making HTML game development easy

GameMaker: Studio is an incredibly powerful and easy to use development tool for making games. The software was originally designed to be used in a classroom setting as a way for students to learn basic programming concepts, understand game architecture, and create fully featured games. As a result, the development environment is very intuitive for first time users due to the drag-and-drop system of coding. Unlike many other competing development tools with similar functionality, GameMaker: Studio has a very robust scripting language that allows users to create almost anything they can imagine. Add to this the fact that you can easily import and manage graphics and audio resources, the integration of the fantastic Box2D physics library, and built-in source control, why wouldn't you use it? Up until now, making games generally meant that you were creating a stand-alone product.

The Internet was not really a consideration as it was fairly static and required a slew of proprietary plugins to display dynamic content, such as games, movies, and audio. Then HTML5 came along and changed everything. HTML5 is an open-standards collection of code languages that allows anyone and everyone to develop interactive experiences that will be able to be run natively on any device with a modern browser and an Internet connection. Developers are now able to use cutting edge features, such as WebGL (a graphics library that allows for 3D rendering), audio APIs, and asset management, to push the boundaries of what you can do in a browser.

> Not all browsers are equal! While the HTML5 standards are set by the W3C, each vendor implements them differently. Also, not all the standards have been set at this time, which means that some things may not work in certain browsers. For example, there are multiple audio APIs competing to become the standard. As the standards become locked down and as the browsers become more compliant, these issues should go away. To see how well your preferred browser supports HTML5, go to http://html5test.com.

Normally, developing a game for HTML5 would require a working knowledge of three different coding languages: **HTML5 (Hypertext Markup Language)**, the code language that creates the structure of a web page, **CSS3 (Cascading Style Sheets 3)**, that determines the presentation of the site, and **JavaScript** that actually makes the magic happen. The GameMaker: Studio HTML5 export module makes all of this simple by allowing developers to work in an integrated environment and export to these languages with the press of a button. Beyond just being a game engine, the HTML export module includes specific functions for dealing with URLs and browser information. It also comes with its own local server software that will allow you to test your games as if it were up on the Internet live. Finally, you can extend GameMaker: Studio even further, because it allows you to import external JavaScript libraries for any functionality you may need or want. Sounds great, doesn't it? Now let's get the Studio up and running.

Setting up the software

In order to use this book, we need to have a few pieces of software. Firstly, we need an HTML5 compliant browser, such as Mozilla Firefox, Microsoft Internet Explorer 9.0, or for the best results, Google Chrome. Secondly, we need to purchase and install GameMaker: Studio Professional with the HTML5 export module. Once we have all of that we can start making games!

> Please be aware that GameMaker: Studio Professional and the HTML5 export module are two separate items, and you will need to own both in order to create games for the web.

1. Purchase and download GameMaker: Studio Professional and the HTML5 export module from `https://www.yoyogames.com/buy/studio/professional`.
2. Once they have been downloaded, run the program `GMStudio-Installer.exe`.
3. Follow the onscreen instructions and then launch the program.
4. Enter your license key. This will unlock the software and the modules that have been purchased.

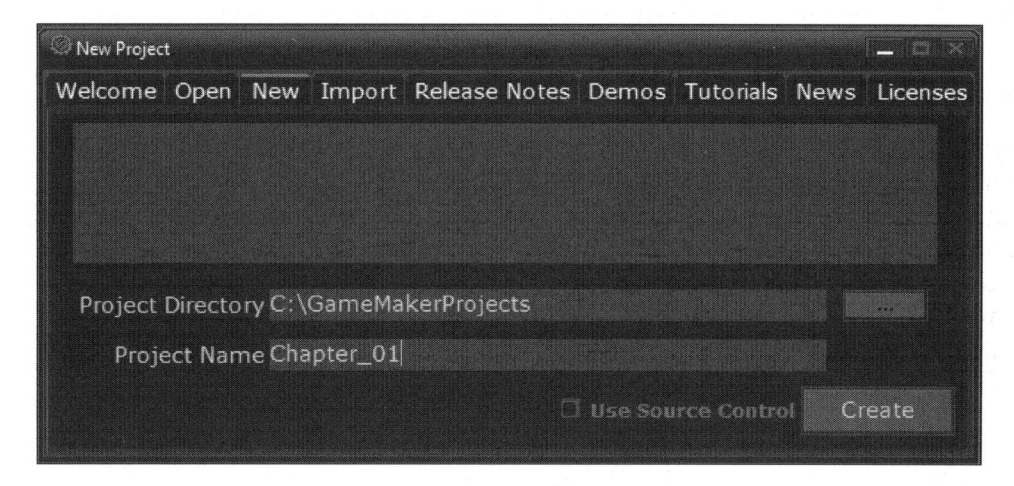

GameMaker: Studio is ready to go, so let's start a project!

1. In the **New Project** window, select the **New** tab. It should look like the preceding screenshot.
2. GameMaker: Studio manages projects by creating folders for each resource along with a project file. For this you will want to specify a directory where the game files are to be stored. Set the **Project Name** field to `Chapter_01` and click on **Create**.

Getting to Know the Studio with Your First Game

Our first look at the Studio

Now that we have the software up and running, let's take a look at the interface. The basic layout of GameMaker: Studio can be broken down into four components: the Menu, the Toolbar, the Resource tree, and the Workspace. We will be exploring these components throughout this book, so don't expect a breakdown of each and every item. Not only would that be incredibly boring to read, it would delay us from making games. Instead, let's just focus on the stuff we need to know right now.

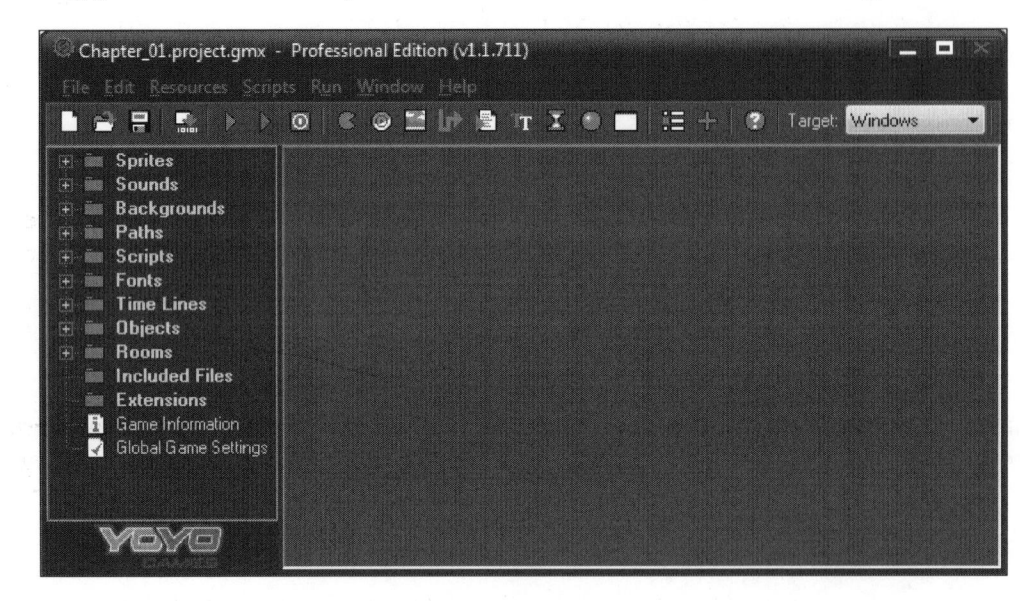

Firstly, as with most complex software, each of these components has its own way of allowing users to do the most common tasks. For example, if you want to create a Sprite you can navigate to **Menu | Resources | Create Sprite**, or you can click on the **Create a Sprite** button in the Toolbar, or you can right mouse click the **Sprites** group in the Resource Tree, or you can use *Shift + Ctrl + S* to open the **Sprite Editor** window in the Workspace. There are actually even more ways to do this, but you get the point.

While there is a lot of overlapping functionality, there are also many things that can only be done in each specific component. Here is what we need to know.

The Menu

The **Menu** is where you will find every editor and tool you will need. There are a few very useful tools, such as the ability to **Search in Scripts** and **Define Constants** that are only found here. Why not just spend a moment and take a look at each menu option so that you have an idea of all the things you have available to you. We'll wait.

The Toolbar

The **Toolbar** uses simple graphic icons for the most common editors and tools we will be using. These buttons are the easiest and quickest way to create new assets and run the game, so expect to be using these often. There is one very important, unique element on the Toolbar: the **Target** drop-down menu. The **Target** determines what format we will be compiling and exporting to. Set this to **HTML5**.

> The default setting for the **Target** menu is **Windows**, so make sure you change it to **HTML5**.

The Resource tree

The **Resource tree** shows and organizes all the assets that have been created for the game. Keeping a project organized won't affect the performance of the software, but it will save us time and reduce frustration in the long run.

The Workspace

The **Workspace** is where all the various editors will open up. When the game is run, the **Compiler Information** box will appear at the bottom, and will show everything being compiled when the game is run. There is also a tab for **Source Control**, which can be used if you have an SVN Client and repository for working in groups.

> If you want to know more about Source Control, check out the following GameMaker: Studio wiki page: `http://wiki.yoyogames.com/index.php/Source_Control_and_GameMaker:Studio`

Exploring the resource editors

In order to create a game in GameMaker: Studio, you need a minimum of three types of resource assets: a **Sprite** (what you see), an **Object** (what it does), and a **Room** (where it happens). On top of these, you can also have **Scripts**, **Backgrounds**, **Sounds**, **Fonts**, **Paths**, and **Time Lines**.

Each resource that you can bring into GameMaker: Studio has its own properties editor. In order to get acquainted with each of them, we are going to build a very simple game of cat and mouse. We will create a player character (a mouse) that can move around the room, collect items (cheese), and avoid an enemy (a cat). Let's dive right in by creating some sprites.

Getting to Know the Studio with Your First Game

Loading your art assets with the Sprite Properties editor

Sprites are bitmap images that are intended to be used for the graphical representation of an object. These can be a single image or an animated sequence of images. GameMaker has its own image editor to create these, but also allows JPG, GIF, PNG, and BMP files to be imported.

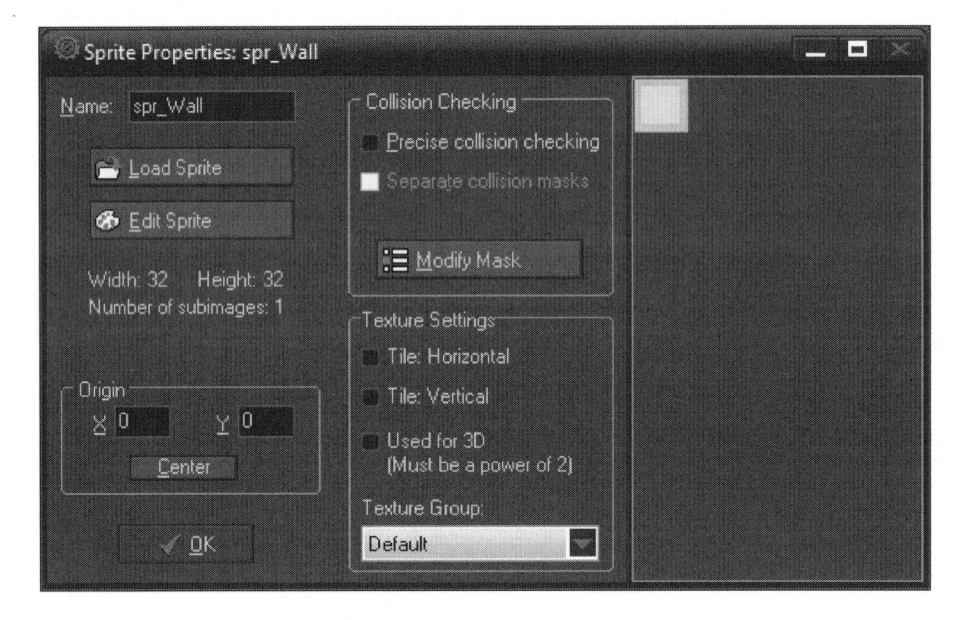

For our example, we are going to start by creating two sprites; one for a wall and one for a player character. If you have downloaded the support files, we have supplied image files for this in the `Chapter_01` folder.

The wall sprite

We will start with a simple Sprite that will represent the walls of our game.

1. Create a new Sprite by navigating to **Resources** | **Create Sprite**. This creates a Sprite in the Resource tree, and opens up the **Sprite Properties** editor.
2. Name the sprite `spr_Wall`.

3. Click on **Load Sprite** to open a Sprite image. On the side of this window there is an **Image Information** section, where we can see a preview of the selected image and choose to activate several options. **Make Opaque** will remove all transparency from the selected sprite. **Remove Background** will remove all pixels with the color found in the pixel in the lower-left corner of the image. **Smooth Edges** will smooth the transparent edges of an image and is very useful when importing animated GIF files to get rid of the hard edges.

4. With none of the options checked, open Chapter 1/Sprites/Wall.png and click on **OK**.

5. As you can see in the following screenshot, it has a width and height of 32 pixels and has one subimage. Nothing else needs to be changed, so click on **OK**:

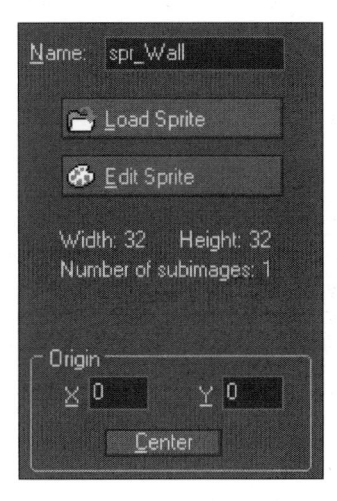

The player sprite

The player in this game is going to be a mouse and the Sprite consists of two frames of animation.

1. Create a new Sprite.
2. Name the sprite spr_Player.
3. Click on **Load Sprite** and select Chapter 1/Sprites/Player.gif. Check the box for **Remove Background and Smooth Edges**. Click on **OK**.

Getting to Know the Studio with Your First Game

4. Once again, it has a width and height of 32 pixels, but this has two subimages as shown in the next screenshot. This means it has animation! Let's see what each frame looks like by clicking on the arrow beside **Show**. It is useful to do this when loading animated images to ensure that all the frames are in the appropriate order and are aligned properly.

5. Set **X** in **Origin** to 16 and **Y** to 16, or you can just click on the **Center** button.
6. Click on the **OK** button.

Congratulations! You have created your first sprites. We will be going deeper into the creation of art assets in the following chapter, so let's move onto Objects.

Creating game objects with the Object Properties editor

This is where the real power of GameMaker: Studio truly shows itself. **Objects** can be thought of as containers that hold the properties, events, and functions that we want each item in the game to do. When we place an object into the game world, it is called an **instance** and it will operate independently from all other instances of that object.

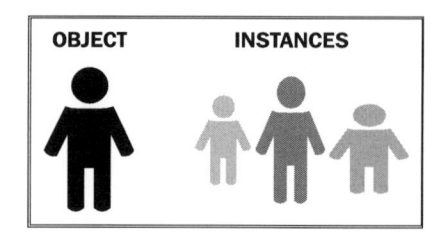

Chapter 1

Before we move on, it is important to understand the difference between an **object** and an **instance** of that object. An object is a set of rules that describe something, while an instance is a unique representation of that something. A real-world example would be *you* are an instance of a *human* object. A *human* is something that has arms, legs, speaks, sleeps, and so on. A *you* is the unique interpretation of these elements. An example of this concept can be seen in the preceding diagram.

The reason this is important is because depending on the functions being used, the effect will be applied either to all of the items of that type or to the individual item. Generally you wouldn't want to shoot an enemy and then have all the enemies in the world die, would you?

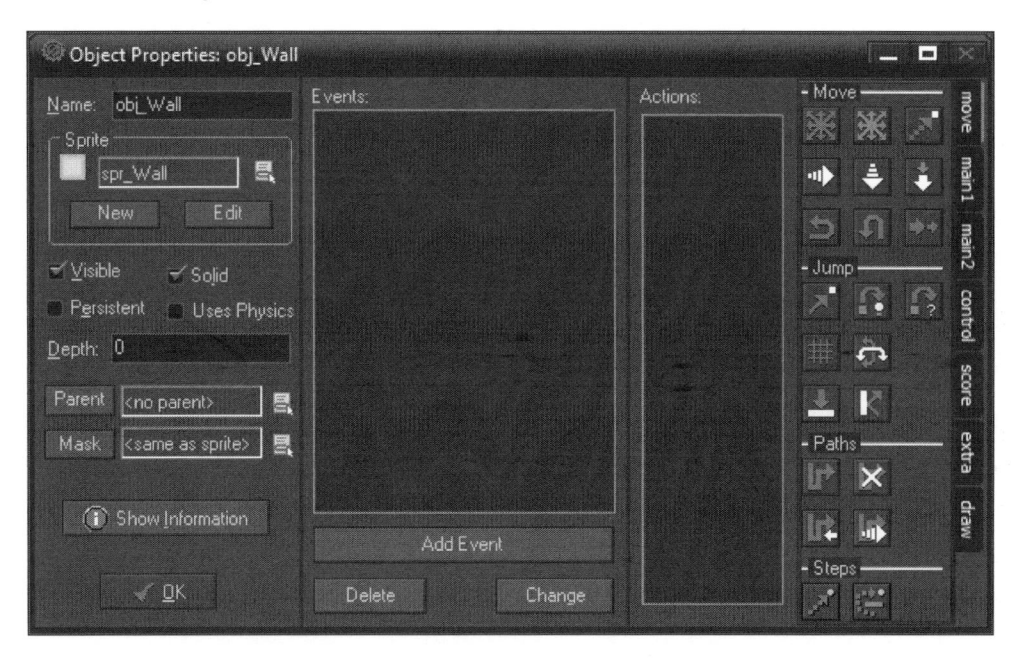

Continuing with our example, we are going to create a Wall object and a Player object. The Wall is going to be a stationary obstacle, while the Player is going to have controls allowing it to move around the world and collide with the Wall.

[15]

The Wall object

We will start with the solid Wall object that we can use to create a maze for the player.

1. Create a new Object by navigating to **Resources | Create Object**. This will create a new Object in the Resource tree and open up the **Object Properties** editor.
2. Name this object `obj_Wall`.
3. Click on the input box in **Sprite** and select `spr_Wall`.

   GameMaker treats collision with solid objects differently than non-solid objects. If a solid object and a non-solid object collide, GameMaker will try and prevent them from overlapping by moving the non-solid object back to its previous position. Of course, in order to do this properly, the solid object has to be stationary. Therefore, we should add the solid property to the Wall.

4. Click on the **Solid** checkbox and then click on **OK**.

> The **Solid** property should only ever be used with objects that do not move.

The Player object

The Player object will introduce us to using **Events** and **Actions** for things, such as movement and collision.

1. Create a new Object and name it `obj_Player`.
2. Select `spr_Player` as the Sprite.

   GameMaker's power comes from its event-driven system. Events are moments and actions that occur during the running of a game. When you add an Event to an Object, you are asking the item to respond to that action when it occurs, and then apply the assigned instructions.

Sounds fairly straightforward, doesn't it? Well it can be a bit confusing when it comes to the order of events. GameMaker breaks down the game into steps (finite moments of time), which run the events many times every second. Some events happen in a preset order, such as Begin Step, which always starts at the very beginning of the step. Other events happen whenever they are called, such as Create, which is run immediately when an instance of an object is created, to check whether that code occurs at the start or end of the step.

> Go to http://wiki.yoyogames.com/index.php/Order_of_events to learn more about GameMaker: Studio's order of events.

3. In the **Events:** area, click on **Add Event** and navigate to **Keyboard | Left**. This event will run code each step that the left arrow key is held down.

   Events need **Actions** to be applied for them to do anything. GameMaker: Studio uses a **drag-and-drop (DnD)** system where icons representing common behaviors can be easily implemented. These have been separated into seven different tabs based on functionality. For the vast majority of this book we are going to use only the Execute Script icon found in the **Common** tab, as we will be writing code placed into **Scripts**. In this chapter, however, we will use the DnD Actions, so that you get an understanding of what they do.

Getting to Know the Studio with Your First Game

4. From the **Move** tab, select and drag the Move Fixed icon into the **Actions** area of the Left Key event.

The Move Fixed icon

5. In the **Move Fixed** options box, there is an option for what object this action is to be applied to. We want this to be set to **Self**, so that it is applied to the instance of the player.

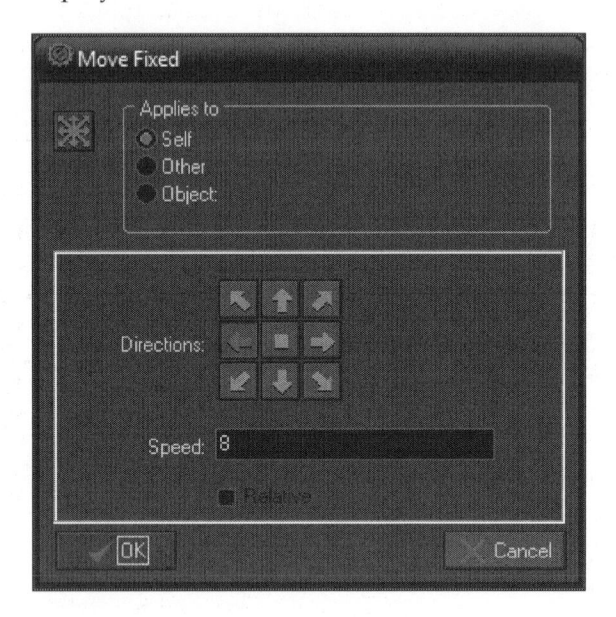

6. Click on the left arrow to indicate the direction we want the movement to go.
7. Set the **Speed** field to a value of 8. This will apply a velocity of eight pixels per step.
8. Ensure that **Relative** is *not* checked. Relative will add the value to whatever the current value is.
9. Click on **OK**.
10. Repeat steps 4 to 9 for the other keyboard arrows (right, up, and down) with the same **Speed** and the appropriate direction.

Now we have an object that will move around the world when the arrow keys are pressed. However, if we were to run this, once we started moving, we would be unable to stop. This is because we are applying a velocity to the object. In order for us to stop the object, we need to give it a velocity of zero.

Chapter 1

11. In the **Events:** area, click on **Add Event** and navigate to **Keyboard | No Key**. This is a special keyboard event that will only happen when no keys are being pressed.
12. Select and drag the Move Fixed icon into the Actions area.
13. Set the direction to be in the center and set the **Speed** field to 0.

    The last thing we need to do is to add our collision detection. Collision in GameMaker: Studio is a single event comprising two instances. Each instance is capable of executing an event call on this single collision, though it is generally more efficient to put the code on only one of them. In our case, it makes sense to put a Collision Event on the Player for when it collides with a Wall, as the Player will be the instance that does something. The Wall will remain where it is, doing nothing.

14. Click on **Add Event** and navigate to **Collision | obj_Wall**.
15. Drag the Move Fixed icon into the **Actions:** area.

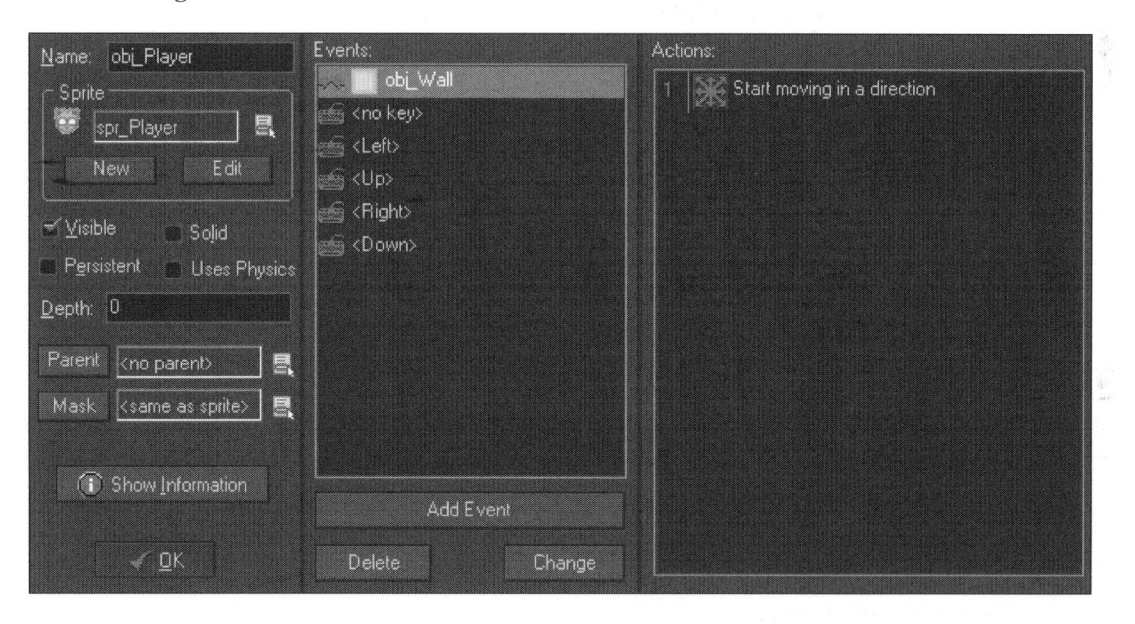

16. Set the direction to be in the center and the **Speed** field to 0. Click on **OK**.

The actors are ready; we have some objects that can be seen and do something. Now all we need to do is put these into a room.

[19]

Creating worlds with the Room Properties editor

Rooms represent the world in which the instances of our objects live. Most rooms you create will likely be used as various levels, but rooms can also used for:

- Frontend menu screens
- Non-interactive scenes
- Any self-contained environment you need

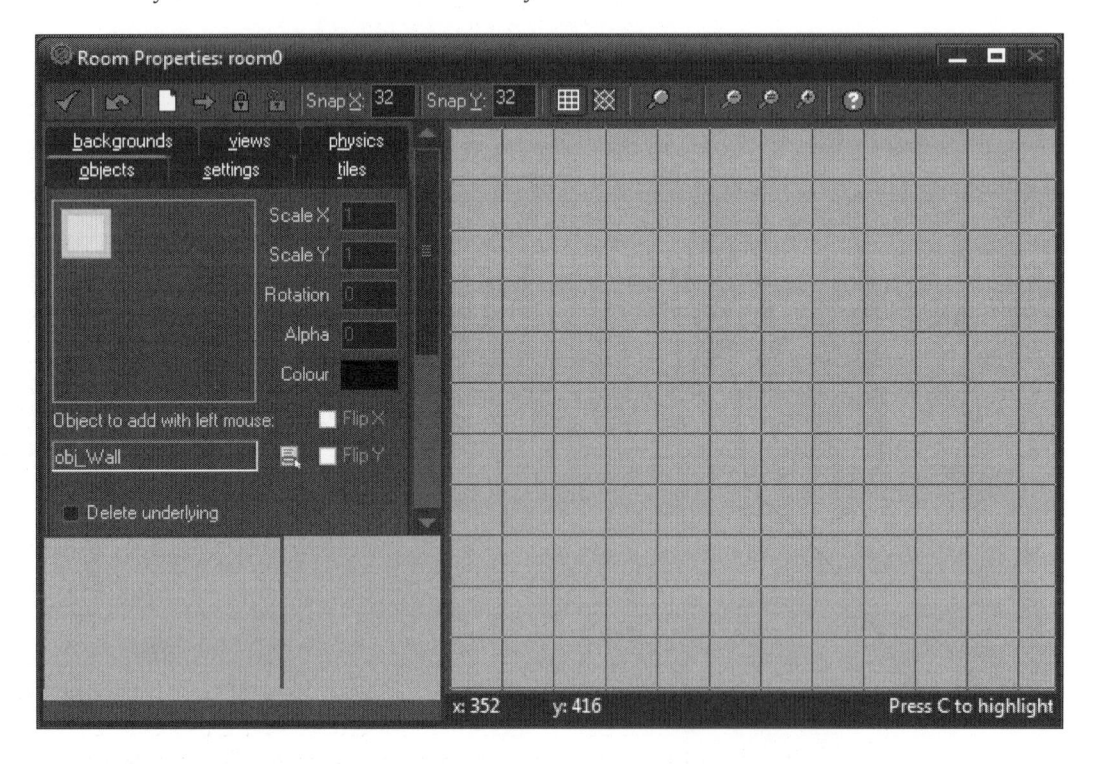

We want to lay out a world that will contain the player as well as presenting some obstacles. To do this, we are going to place down wall objects around the outer edges of the room and place a few lines in the center.

1. Create a new room by navigating to **Resources | Create Room**. This will create a new room in the Resource tree and open up the **Room Properties** editor.

Chapter 1

2. To make placement a bit easier, set the **Snap X** and **Snap Y** fields to 32. This will create a placement grid with snapping points every 32 pixels.
3. Select the **settings** tab. Here we can change the basic room properties, the size, steps per second, and the name of the room.
4. Name the room as `rm_GameArea`.
5. We will leave the room **Width**, **Height**, and **Speed** fields at their defaults as seen in the following screenshot:

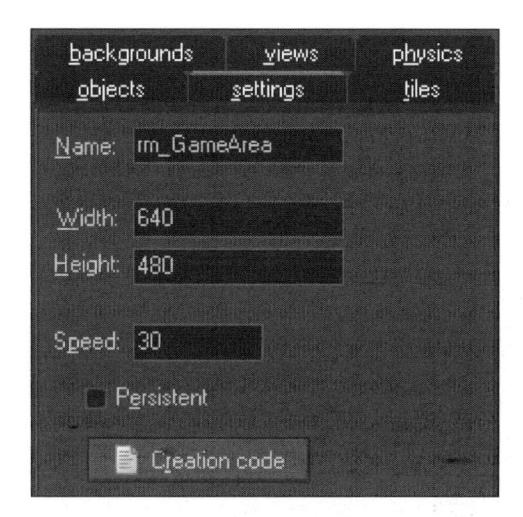

```
backgrounds      views        physics
  objects       settings       tiles

Name:  rm_GameArea

Width:  640
Height: 480

Speed:  30

   ■ Persistent

        Creation code
```

6. Select the **objects** tab, and under **Object to add with left mouse**, select `obj_Wall`.
7. In the upper-left corner of the room, click with the left mouse button to place an instance of the wall.

   Now you might be thinking that this is going to take a painfully long time to build the room, click by click. Don't worry, there is an easier way. If you hold down *Shift + Ctrl*, you will be able to paint the world with the instances. If you make a mistake and want to remove an instance, just right mouse click to delete one instance, or hold the *Shift* key to de-paint the instances. If you just want to move the instance a tiny bit, as in not a whole grid unit, hold the *Alt* key down.

[21]

Getting to Know the Studio with Your First Game

8. Holding down the *Shift* + *Ctrl* keys and the left mouse button, draw the perimeter walls. Also lay down two extruded sections as shown in the following example screenshot:

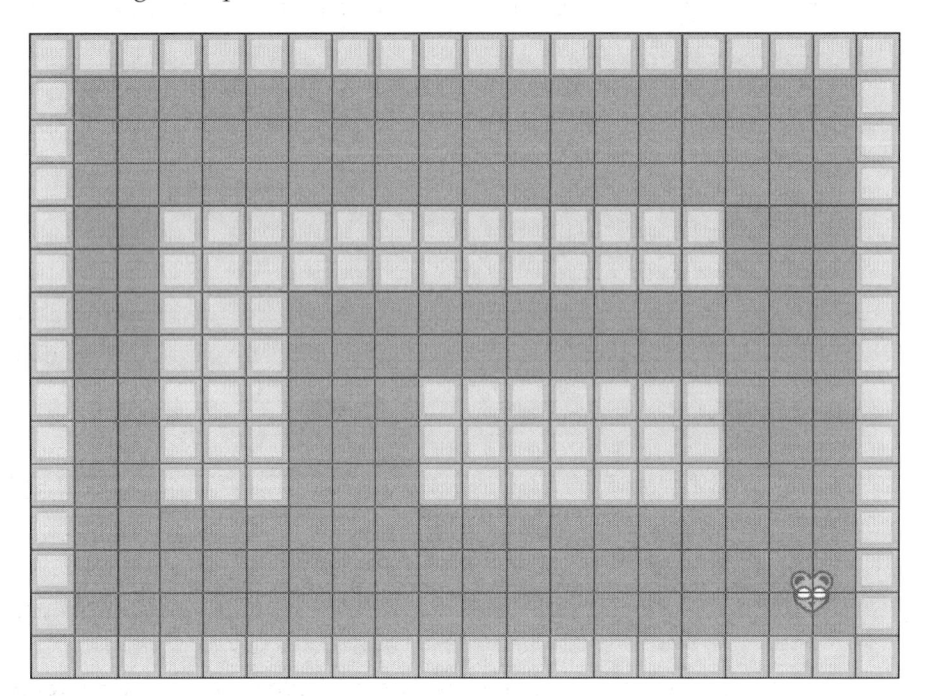

Don't forget to add the Player in!

9. In the **objects** tab, select `obj_Player`.
10. Place a single instance of `obj_Player` into the room in the lower-right corner of the room.
11. Close the room by clicking on the check mark in the upper-left corner of the **Room Properties** editor.
12. At this point, we have all the required elements necessary to run a game in GameMaker: Studio. Before we test the game out, we should save our work by navigating to **File** | **Save**.

Running the game

While creating a game, there are three different types of compilations that can be done. If the game is 100 percent complete, you can select **Create Application** for the target platform. If the game is still in development, there is **Run Normally**, which will compile and run the game as if it were an application, and **Run in Debug Mode**, which runs the debugging tools.

Let's not wait any longer. Run the game by navigating to **Run | Run the Game**, or by pressing *F5*.

If everything is working correctly, the player object should be able to move around the world using the arrow keys, but not be able to pass through any of the wall objects. However, there is something not quite right. The player object appears to be flickering due to it being animated. Let's fix this while taking a look at the Script Properties editor.

Introducing code with the Script Properties editor

GameMaker: Studio utilizes its own proprietary scripting language called **GameMaker Language**, otherwise known as **GML**. This language was developed to be very forgiving to the novice user, and utilizes some functionality you likely won't find in other scripting languages. For example, GML will accept the standard expression && to combine two comparisons, or alternatively the word and. GameMaker: Studio does a lot of hard work when it comes to creating games by giving the user a great set of functions, variables, and constants.

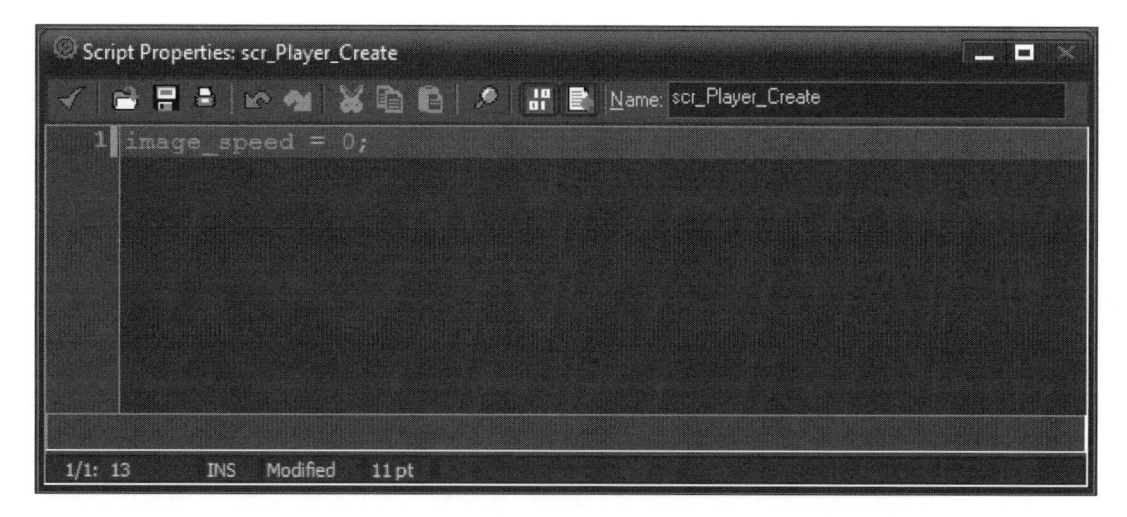

As previously stated, we want to stop the player object from animating. This is very easy to do using scripts.

1. Create a new Script by navigating to **Resources | Create Script**. This will create a new Script in the Resource tree and open up the **Script Properties** editor.
2. Name this as `scr_Player_Create`. Throughout this book we will be naming most of our scripts with the name of the event at the end of the name. In this case we will be placing this code into a `Create` event.
3. To stop a Sprite from animating, all we need to do is set the playback speed of the Sprite to zero. On line **1**, type the following:

   `image_speed = 0;`
4. Close the Script by clicking on the check mark in the upper-left corner of the editor.

   In order for the script to run we need to attach it to an object.
5. Reopen the **Object Properties** editor for `obj_Player`.
6. Add a **Create** Event.
7. Navigate to **Actions | Control**, and select and drag the Execute Script icon into the **Actions:** area.

The Execute Script icon

8. Select `scr_Player_Create` as the script to execute, and then click on **OK**.

We can now run the game, and we see that the player object is no longer animating.

Filling the scene with the Background Properties editor

Backgrounds are a special kind of art asset that come in two different types: background images and tilesets. Unlike Sprites, backgrounds never have any animation as a part of the art asset. **Background images** are mainly used as large backdrops of a room and are useful if you want the background to move. **Tilesets** are small slices of art that can be used to paint the background, are useful for creating large, unique worlds, and to keep the graphics cost computationally low.

> Use Background images if you want:
> - One large image in the background
> - The background to move

> Use Tilesets if you want:
> - Only a few art assets to create large worlds
> - To add unique details to the background

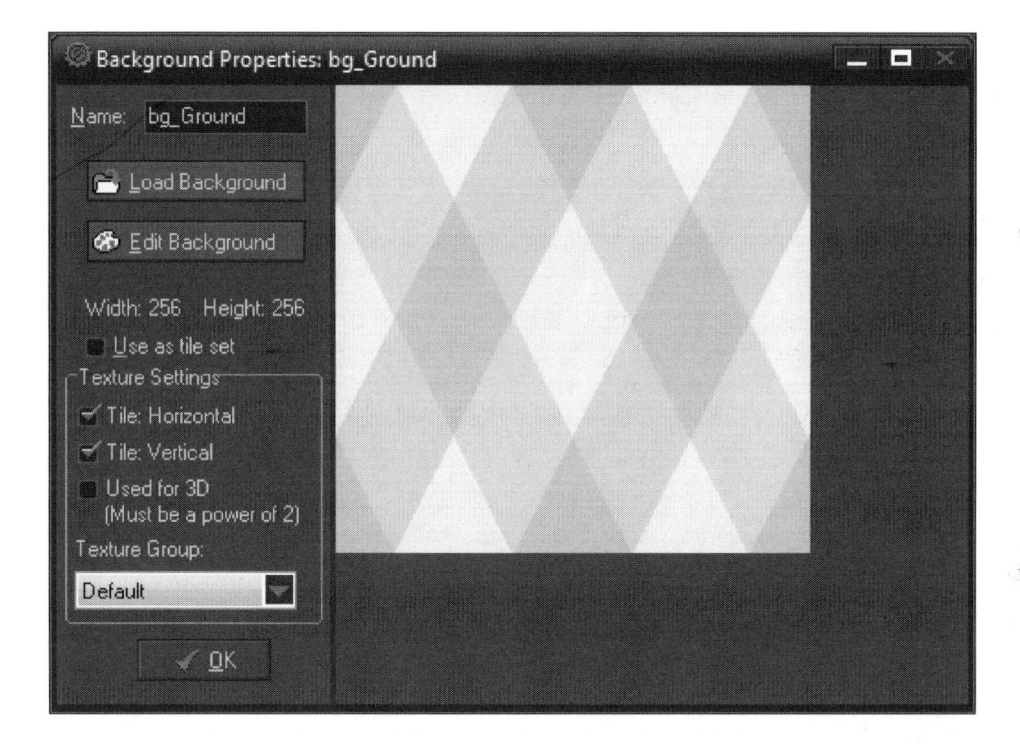

For this simple example we will just create a static background. We will look more into tilesets in the next chapter:

1. Create a new Background by navigating to **Resources | Create Background**. This will create a new background in the Resource tree and open up the **Background Properties** editor.
2. Name this as `bg_Ground`.
3. Click on **Load Background** and open `Chapter 1/Backgrounds/Ground.png`.

Getting to Know the Studio with Your First Game

4. Then click on **OK**.

    We now have the art asset ready to go, we just need to place it into the room.

5. Reopen `rm_GameArea`.

6. Click on the `backgrounds` tab.

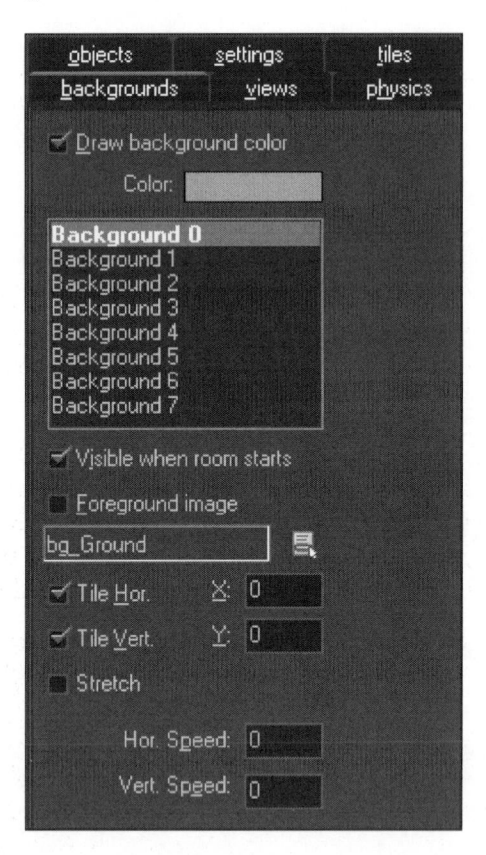

Each room allows up to eight backgrounds to be displayed simultaneously. These backgrounds can also be used as foreground elements. If no background is active, it will display a solid color.

7. Select **Background 0**, and then check the box for **Visible when room starts**. This has to be active in order to see the background during gameplay.

8. Select `bg_Ground` as the background to be displayed.

9. Everything else can remain at their defaults. **Tile Hor.** and **Tile Vert.** should be checked and all other values should be set to 0.

10. Close the room by clicking the check mark in the upper-left corner of the editor.

Chapter 1

Let's run the game again and we can now see that we have a background. Things are definitely looking better, but something is missing. Let's get some sound into the game.

Bringing noise with the Sound Properties editor

The Sound Properties editor is where you can bring in sounds to be used in your games. GameMaker allows you to bring in MP3 and WAV files only. There are two types of sounds that you can use:

- Normal sounds
- Background music

Normal sounds are all the small sound effects that you hear, such as gunfire and footsteps. These should generally be WAV files. Background music is for the longer sounds such as the game music, but also things such as spoken dialog. This should be in MP3 format.

When GameMaker: Studio exports the game audio for HTML5, all sounds will be converted to both MP3 and OGG format. This is due to the fact that different browsers use different audio file formats in their implementation of the HTML5 audio tag. Luckily for us, GameMaker: Studio automatically adds browser identification code into the game, so the game knows what files are being used.

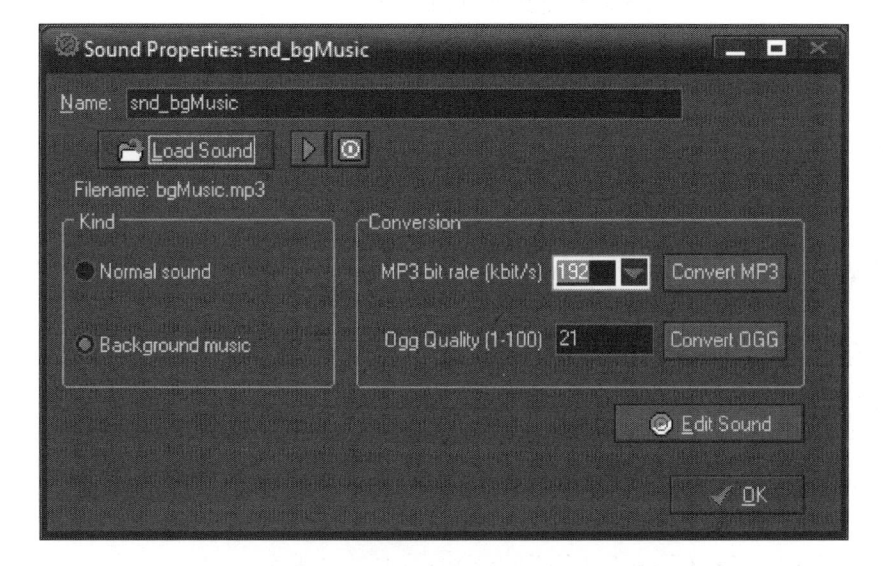

We are going to create two sounds for the game, some background music and a sound effect for a collectible object.

[27]

A little background music

Let's bring in some music to our game to help build some atmosphere.

1. Create a new Sound by navigating to **Resources | Create Sound**. This will create a new Sound in the Resource tree and open up the **Sound Properties** editor.
2. Name this as `snd_bgMusic`.
3. Load the `Chapter 1/Sounds/bgMusic.mp3` file. If you want to hear the music, just hit the play button. When you are done listening, hit the stop button.
4. Under **Kind** select **Background Music** as the type, and then click on **OK**.

We will want to have the music start right at the start of the game. To do this we are going to create a **data object** that we will call the **Overlord**. Data objects are generally not meant to be seen in the game, so we do not need to assign it a Sprite.

Controlling the game with the Overlord

We will be using an Overlord object to watch over the game and control things, such as the music and win/lose condition.

1. Create a new object and name it `obj_Overlord`.
2. Add an Event, and then navigate to **Other | Game Start**. This is a special function that will only be run when the game first starts.
3. Navigate to **Actions | Main1**, and select and drag the Play Sound icon into the **Actions:** area.

The Play Sound icon

4. Set the **sound:** field to `snd_bgMusic`, set **loop:** to `true`, and then click on **OK**.

[28]

Before we test this out, we need to make sure the Overlord is in the world. When you place it into a room, it will be represented by a little blue circle icon, as shown in the following screenshot:

5. Reopen `rm_GameArea`.
6. Select `obj_Overlord` from the **objects** tab and place a single instance in the room.

Let's run the game and listen. Music should start playing right away and loop infinitely. Let's move on to creating a collectible.

The collectible

We are going to create an object that the player can collect during the game. When the player collides with it, the sound will be played once.

1. Create a new Sound and name it `snd_Collect`.
2. Load the `Chapter 1/Sounds/Collect.wav` file and set it to **Normal Sound**, and then click on **OK**.

   We haven't created an Object for this, nor have we brought in a Sprite. Now is a chance for you to test your memory. We will only quickly go over what we need.

3. Create a new Sprite and name it `spr_Collect`.
4. With **Remove Background** and **Smooth Edges** selected, load the file `Chapter 1/Sprites/Collect.png` and center its origin.
5. Create a new Object and name it `obj_Collect`.
6. Assign `spr_Collect` as its **Sprite**.
7. Add a **Collision Event** with `obj_Player`.
8. Navigate to **Actions | Main1**, and drag the Play Sound icon into the **Actions:** area.
9. Set the `sound:` field to `snd_Collect` and set **loop:** to `false`.

   Now when the player collides with the object it will play the sound once. That's a good start, but why don't we give the player a bit more of a reward?

[29]

Getting to Know the Studio with Your First Game

10. Navigate to **Actions** | **Score**, and drag the Set Score icon into the **Actions:** area.

The Set Score icon

11. As can be seen in the next screenshot, set the new **score:** field to 50, check the box for **Relative**, and then click on **OK**. This will add 50 points to our score each time the object is collected. **Relative** makes the score add to the previous score.

Now we have something worth collecting. Only one issue remains and that is we get the points and sound just for touching the object. We can't let that go on forever!

[30]

Chapter 1

12. Navigate to **Actions | Main1**, and drag the Destroy Instance icon into the **Actions:** area. This action will remove the instance from the world. Leave the values as they are, and click on **OK**.

The Destroy Instance icon

13. We are done with this object, and if built correctly, it should look like the following screenshot. Click on **OK**.

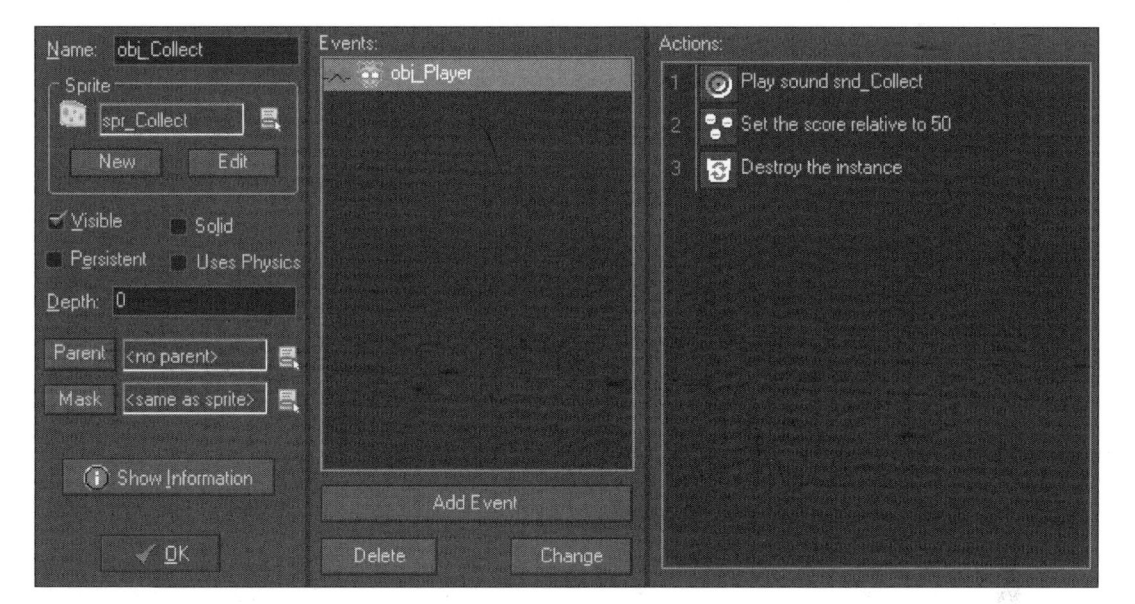

Let's place a couple of these collectibles into the room and run the game. We should be able to move the player around the world and collide with the collectibles. We should hear a sound play and the object disappears. But where is our score? Well, in order to display it, we need to bring in some text.

[31]

Getting to Know the Studio with Your First Game

Writing text and the Font Properties editor

You can import fonts to use them as text in your games. These fonts need to be installed on your machine in order to use them during development. Each font resource is set to a specific font type, size, and whether it is bold/italicized or not. If you want a slight variation, such as a font that is two points larger, than a separate font resource must be created. This is due to the fact that on export, GameMaker will convert the font into an image that will allow it to be used without the font being pre-installed on the user's machine.

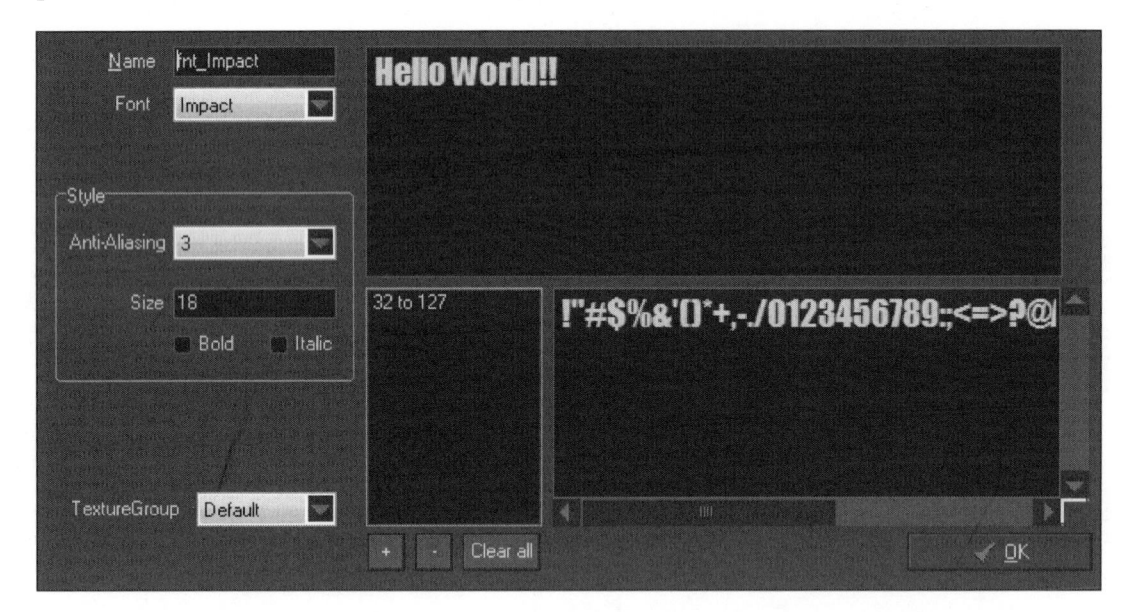

We are going to create a font that will be used to display the score of the game.

1. Create a new Font by navigating to **Resources | Create Font**. This will create a new Font in the Resource tree and open up the **Font Properties** editor.
2. Name this `fnt_Impact`.
3. From the **Font** drop-down menu, select **Impact**. This is a default Windows font.
4. Set the **Size** to 16. Then click on **OK**.

   We now have a font that we can use in our game. For this, we are going to have the Overlord object draw the game score at the top of the screen. We will also make the text white and align it to the center.

5. Reopen `obj_Overlord`.
6. Add a Draw GUI event by navigating to **Draw | Draw GUI**.

> Draw events occur at the very end of each step after everything has been calculated and need to be displayed on screen. The Draw GUI event is meant for the heads-up display and will always render on top of all other game graphics.

7. Navigate to **Actions** | **Draw**, and drag the Set Color icon into the **Actions:** area. This will open a dialog box where you can set a color.

The Set Color icon

8. We want to set the **color** to teal. In the color palette that pops up, select the teal color found on the bottom row, fifth column from the left. Click on **OK**.

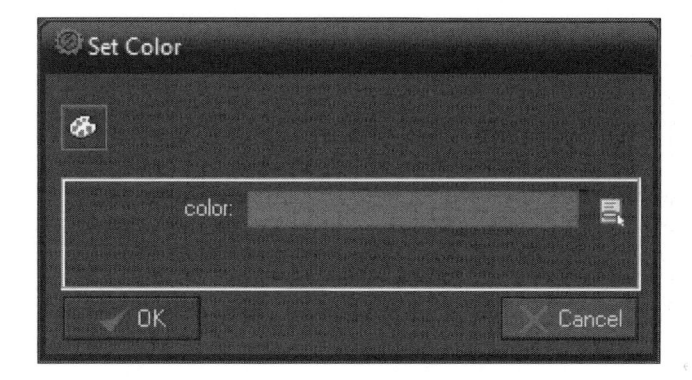

9. Navigate to **Actions** | **Draw**, and drag the Set Font icon into the **Actions:** area. This will open up a dialog box with two parameters: the font to use and how it should be aligned.

The Set Font icon

Getting to Know the Studio with Your First Game

10. Set the **Font:** field to `fnt_Impact` and align it to `center`. Click on **OK**.

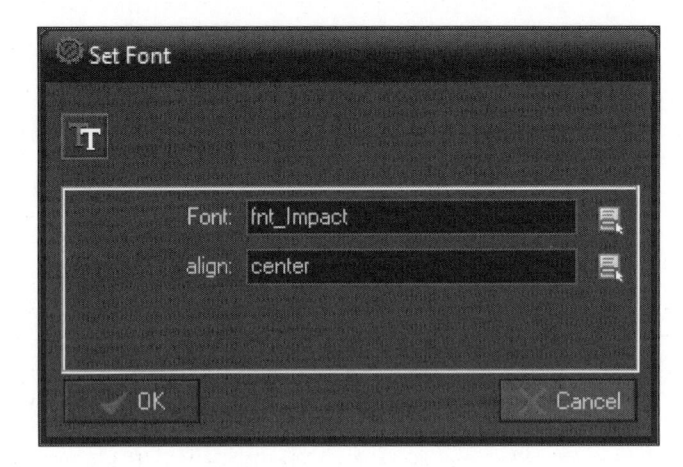

11. Finally, navigate to **Actions** | **Score**, and drag the Draw Score icon into the **Actions:** area. This will open up a dialog box with three parameters: the x and y coordinates, and an optional caption that can be placed in front of the actual score.

12. Set the **x:** field to `320`, the **y:** field can remain at `0`, and remove `Score:` from the **caption:** field, leaving it blank as can be seen in the following screenshot. Click on **OK**.

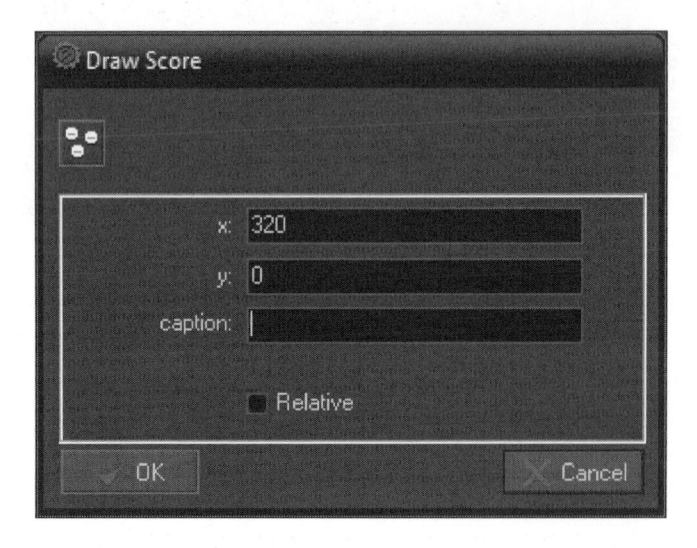

We can now run the game and the score will now be displayed at the top of the screen in the center. When you collide with the collectibles now, you should see the score increase.

[34]

Creating complex movements with the Path Properties editor

Paths are the best way to create complex movement patterns for objects. A path is made up of a series of points in which an object can move along. The transition between points can be straight, meaning the object will hit each point precisely, or curved, an interpolation between three points. The path can either be an open line or a closed loop. The following screenshot will be used as the reference image throughout this section.

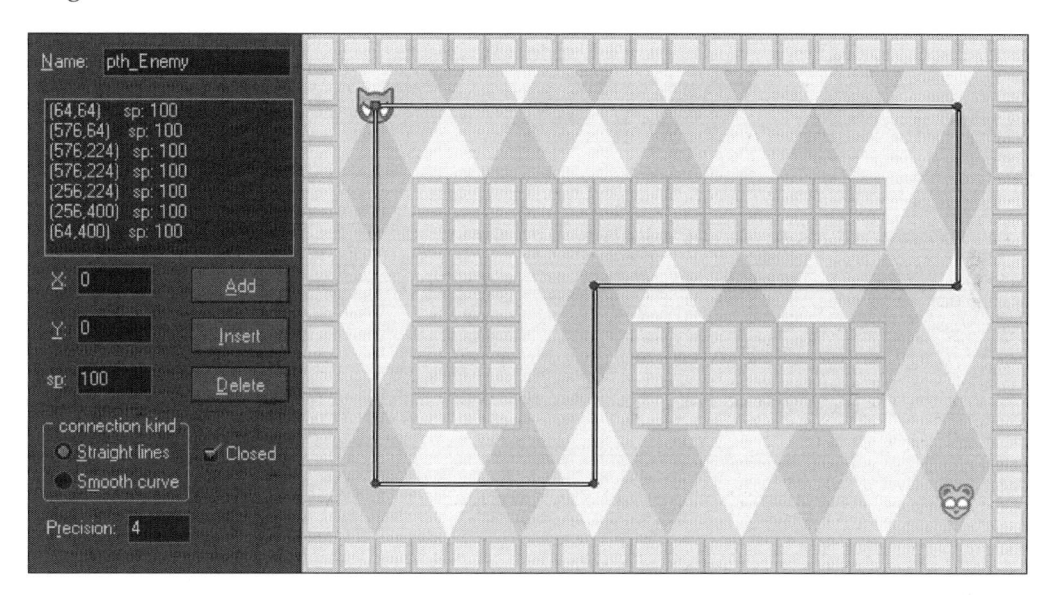

We are going to create a simple enemy that will follow a path around the room. If the player collides with the enemy, the player will be destroyed. Let's start by creating the path.

1. Create a new Path by navigating to **Resources | Create Path**. This will create a new Path in the Resource tree and open up the **Path Properties** editor.
2. Name this as `pth_Enemy`.
3. At the end of the editor toolbar we can set what room is displayed. This is very useful for creating accurate paths on a per room basis. Set this to `rm_GameArea`.

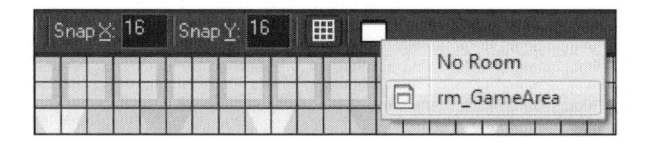

Getting to Know the Studio with Your First Game

To add a point for the path you can just left-click anywhere on the map. The very first point will be represented by a green square and all the points following will be circles.

4. Place the first point at `64, 64` of the map. If you make a mistake you can always drag the point to the proper position, or you can manually set the X and Y values.
5. To this path we are going to add five more points as seen in the reference image.
6. We will leave all the other settings at their defaults, so click on **OK**.

   The path is ready for use, now we just need to create an enemy to attach the path to. This enemy is going to simply move along the path and if it collides with the player, it will restart the game.

7. Create a new Sprite and name it `spr_Enemy`.
8. With **Remove Background** and **Smooth Edges** selected, load `Chapter 1/Sprites/Enemy.png` and center the origin.
9. Create a new Object and name it `obj_Enemy`.
10. Add a **Create** Event, navigate to **Actions | Move**, and drag the Set Path icon into the **Actions:** area. This will open the Set Path options dialog box.

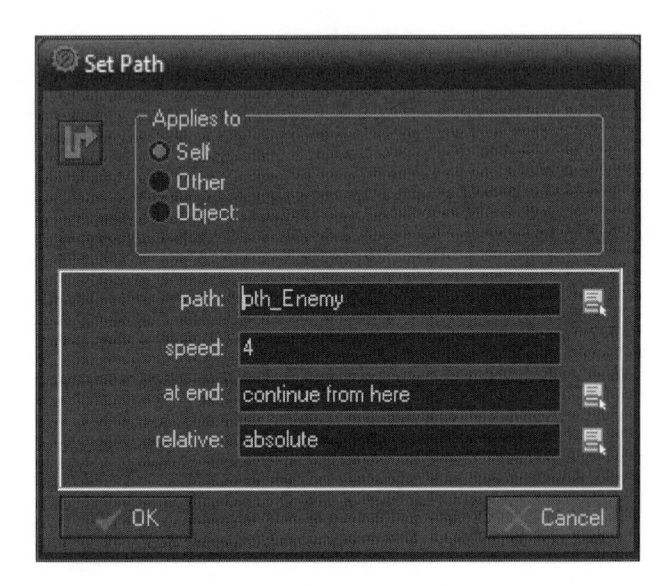

The Set Path icon

[36]

Chapter 1

11. Set **path:** to `pth_Enemy`.
12. Set the **speed:** field to 4.
13. The next option determines what should happen when the instance reaches the end of the path. There are options to **stop**, **continue on from the start** (for open paths), **continue from here** (for closed paths), and **reverse** directions. Set **at end:** to **continue from here**.
14. The **relative:** option here determines whether the path starts where the instance is (relative), or whether the instance starts at the path's first point (absolute). As we built it to fit the room, set **relative:** to **absolute**. Then click on **OK**.

    We now have an enemy ready to follow a path, but it isn't really a threat to the player. Let's put a collision event on the enemy and make it restart the game on contact.

15. Add a **Collision** Event with `obj_Player`, navigate to **Actions | Main2**, and drag the Restart Game icon into the **Actions:** area.

The Restart Game icon

16. The enemy is now complete, so click on **OK** to close it.
17. Place a single instance of the enemy anywhere in the room. It doesn't matter exactly where, as it will relocate itself to the proper location when the game runs.
18. Save the game and run it. We should see the enemy moving along the path around the room. If the player object collides with it, the game will restart.

We've now got some risk in the game, but not enough reward. Let's fix that, shall we?

Getting to Know the Studio with Your First Game

Using the Time Line Properties editor to spawn collectibles

Time Line is an advanced time tracking system that allows finite control of things that happen during gameplay. A Time Line is comprised of a list of moments. Each moment represents a number of steps from when the Time Line started.

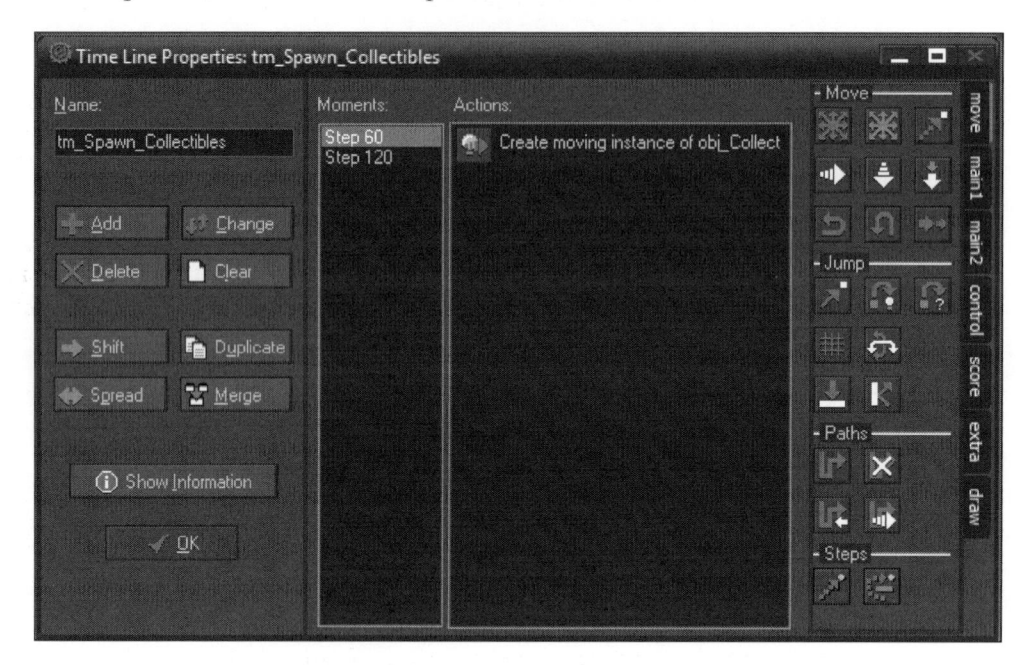

While a Time Line can be used for almost anything, one of the most common uses for one is to spawn instances. In this game, we are going to use it to spawn our Collectible objects, so that the player has something to chase after.

1. Create a new Time Line by navigating to **Resources | Create Time Line**. This will create a new Time Line in the Resource tree and open up the **Time Line Properties** editor.
2. Name this as `tm_Spawn_Collectibles`.
3. Click on the **Add** button and set **Steps** to 60.

4. We are going to make these collectibles move by applying a velocity to them. Navigate to **Actions | Main1**, and drag the Create Moving icon into the **Actions:** area.

The Create Moving icon

5. Set the object to `obj_Collect`.
6. We want the spawning to occur offscreen, so that the player doesn't see it blink into existence. We will make this Collectible move horizontally, so we will start from the left of the game area. Set the **x:** field to -64.
7. We don't want the collectibles always spawning in the exact same location, so we are going to add a random element to it. We will create the instance at a random vertical position between 48 pixels from the top and 48 pixels from the bottom of the screen. Set the **y:** field to `random(394) + 48`.
8. Give it a **speed** of 4, and set the **direction:** field to 0. It should look like the following screenshot. Click on **OK**.

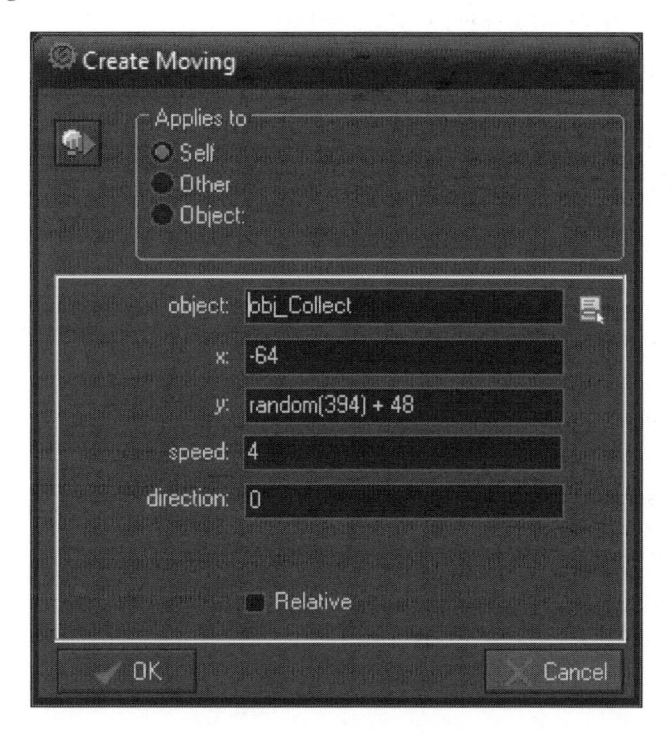

Getting to Know the Studio with Your First Game

9. Add another **Moment** at 120 and repeat the previous steps except this time make it vertical. To do this, the **x:** field should be set to random(546) + 48, the **y:** field should be -64, the **speed:** field should be 4, and the **direction:** field should be 270.

   We now have a Time Line that will spawn a new moving Collectible every two seconds. However, we need to attach this to an object so let's apply this to the obj_Overlord.

10. Reopen obj_Overlord.
11. In the **Game Start** Event that already exists, drag the Set Time Line icon into the **Actions:** area by navigating to **Actions | Main2**.

The Set Time Line icon

12. Set the **time line:** field to tm_Spawn_Collectibles.
13. Leave **position:** at 0; this will start it from the beginning.
14. Set **start:** to **Start Immediately**.
15. We want it to repeat itself infinitely, so set **loop:** to Loop.

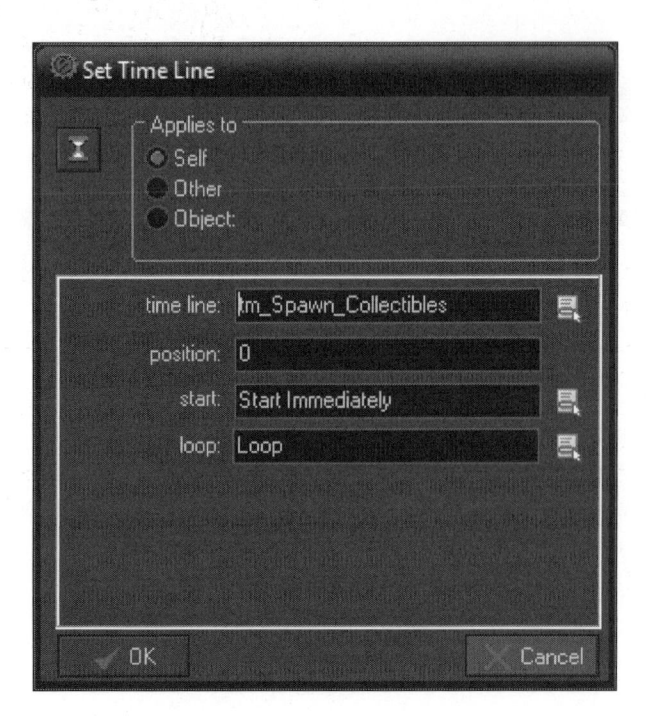

[40]

Chapter 1

There you have it! Run the game and you should see the collectibles start to spawn after two seconds and continue to be created forever. As you can see from the following screenshot, our game is complete, but there is still one component we need to take a look at.

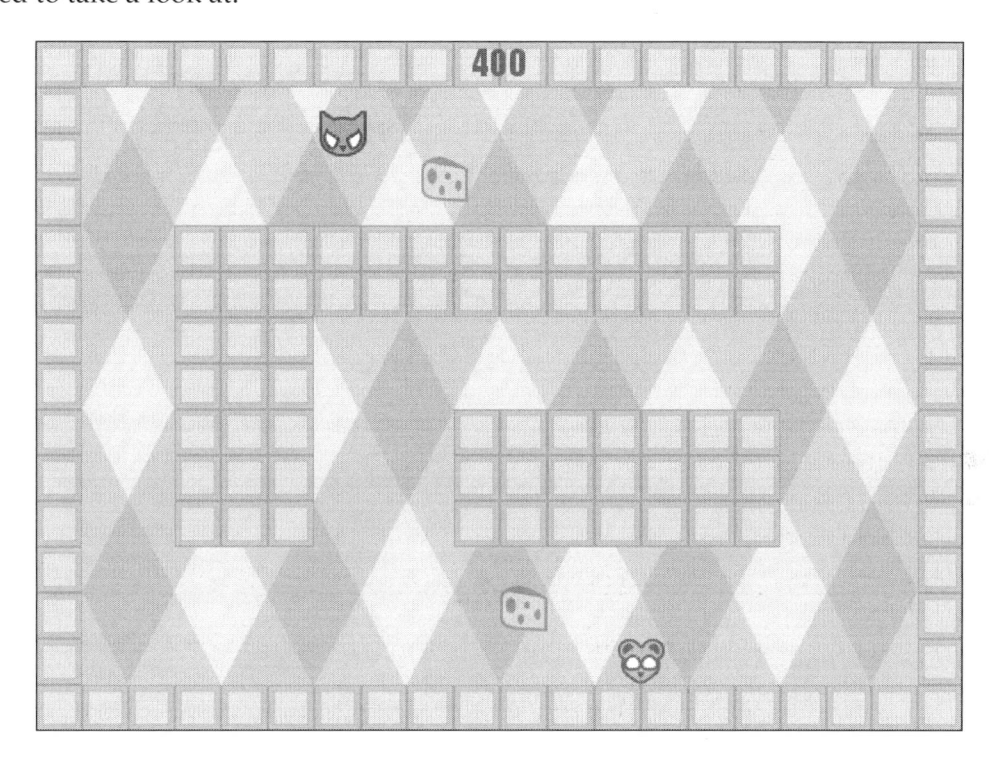

Tools for debugging your games

No matter how experienced you are at scripting and making games, mistakes will always be made. Sometimes it may be a typo or a missing variable, and in this case GameMaker: Studio will catch this and display a code error dialog. Other times, the game may not do what you are expecting it to do, such as passing through a wall when you should not. In this case, there is nothing technically wrong with the code, it is just constructed improperly. Tracking down these bugs can be very tedious and possibly impossible if it were not for debugging tools. In order to use these tools, the game must be run in the debug mode, which you can access by clicking on the **Run Debug Mode** button in the toolbar, or by going into the Menu and navigating to **Run | Run Debug Mode**.

Getting to Know the Studio with Your First Game

During the debug Mode, we can utilize **Debug Messages** to help us understand what is occurring in the game. These messages can only be implemented through the `show_debug_message()` function when scripting (there is no drag-and-drop option) and will appear in a Console window whenever the function is executed. You can use this to pass a string or display a variable, so you can compare the result with what you expect the result should be. This is your first line of defense when trying to solve a problem.

Using the HTML5 DEBUG console

The first console we should use is GameMaker: Studio's DEBUG console for HTML5. When the game is targeting HTML5 and run in the debug mode, a pop-up window will be created along with the game and contains the debug output where all the debug messages will appear, along with a list of the instance and their basic data information. Let's test this console out!

1. We will start by adding the traditional `Hello World` debug message on the creation of the player. Reopen `scr_Player_Create` and add the following code at the end of the script:

   ```
   myText = "Hello World";
   show_debug_message(myText);
   ```

   > **Downloading the example code**
   > You can download the example code files for all Packt books you have purchased from your account at http://www.packtpub.com. If you purchased this book elsewhere, you can visit http://www.packtpub.com/support and register to have the files e-mailed directly to you.

   We start by creating a variable to hold the string. While we can directly pass a string through the `show_debug_message` function without the variable, we will be using this variable in a later debug test.

2. As this script is already attached to our Player's Create event, we can just go ahead and run the game. Click on the Run Debug Mode icon.

3. When the game starts in the browser, a second window will pop up with the **DEBUG console** as seen in the next screenshot. If you do not see this window, check to ensure the browser allows pop ups. Scroll down to the bottom of the **Debug Output** column. Here you should see the debug message `Hello World`. This indicates that our code was successfully executed. If we didn't see it as expected, then we would have an idea of where the game is having issues.

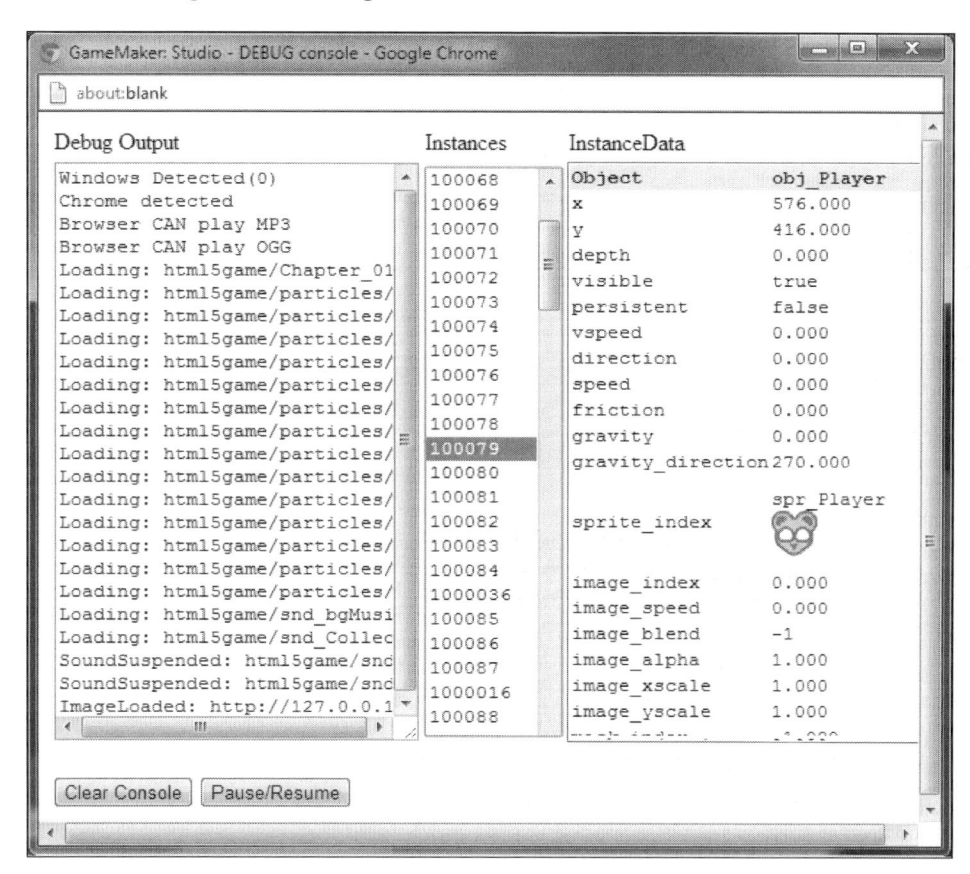

4. We can also see all the properties of each individual instance, represented by their instance number, in the game including the current position in the room, the sprite it is displaying and more. Click on any one of the numbers seen in the **Instances** column, and take a look at its properties in the **InstanceData** column.

5. Click on the **Pause/Resume** button. This allows us to pause the game, which is useful if you have lots of debug messages flooding the console, and you want to take time to see what is happening.

Getting to Know the Studio with Your First Game

6. Finally, we can click on the **Clear Console** button to remove everything from the **Debug Output** column.

Congratulations! You can now start debugging your scripts. While you will be using `show_debug_message` a fair amount of time during a game's development, it is important to keep the amount of active messages to a minimum. It doesn't make sense to have so many debug messages occurring that you can't see what is happening!

Using the Windows version debugger

While you can solve a large portion of your issues with debug messages, there are times when you will need more finite detail into what is happening in the game. GameMaker: Studio has a more advanced debugger that only runs if the game is being targeted for a Windows build. We would be remiss if we didn't at least have a cursory glance at this wonderful tool.

1. Change the **Target** to `Windows` and run the game in the debug mode. When the game opens up, the **GameMaker Debugger** will be displayed in a separate window, as shown in the following screenshot:

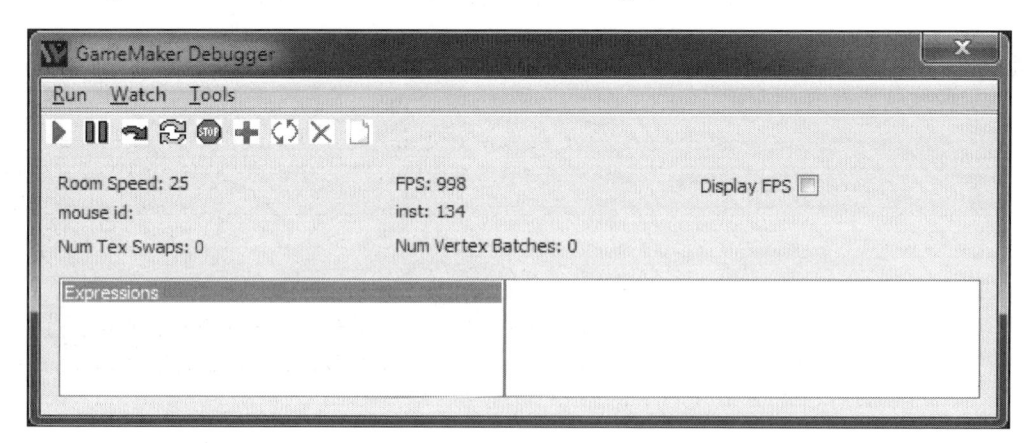

Some basic information is displayed immediately, such as how it is performing, by looking at **Room Speed:** (steps per second) and frames per second (**FPS:**). If you move your mouse cursor over the instances in your game, you will notice that the **mouse id:** will change. This ID is the unique identifier for that specific instance and will come in very handy.

The **GameMaker Debugger** window has many more options available for debugging the game. The **Run** menu not only allows us to pause the game, but we can also step forward one step at a time. The **Watch** menu allows you to track specific expressions, such as function calls or properties. The **Tools** menu gives access to debug messaging as we would expect, but can also display all the global variables, the per-instance variables, and a list of all the instances currently in existence. Let's take a look at what information the instance has in this Console.

2. Navigate to **Tools** | **Show Instances**. This will open a window that displays all the instances in the game.

3. Scroll down the list until you find `obj_Player`. Double-click on it so we can see all of its properties. Much like the HTML5 DEBUG console, we can see where it is in the world and what Sprite it has (by Sprite index number). However, if you scroll down the list there are many more properties. In fact, if we look at the bottom of the list we can see the `myText` variable. That's awesome!

Taking a look at the JavaScript code

The last thing we will take a look at is the compiled JavaScript code. All modern browsers, such as Mozilla Firefox, Microsoft Internet Explorer 9.0, and Google Chrome come with built-in debug consoles that allow anyone to look at the source code of any website, and even affect what is being displayed on your local screen. That's right. Everyone can see the code for the game. While that might scare you, fear not! When GameMaker: Studio exports a game or it is run normally, it obfuscates the code making it very difficult to decipher. When run in the debug mode on the other hand, it does not do any obfuscation other than the engine itself.

Let's take a quick look at what this code looks like. We will start with the debug version so we can see what it would look like without obfuscation. For this example, we will use Chrome as it has the most robust debug console.

1. With the **Target** platform set to `HTML5`, run the game in the debug mode.

2. In the browser window in the area below the game, right-click and select **Inspect Element**. This will open **Developer Tools** for Chrome.

3. Select the **Sources** tab, and in the upper-left corner click on the little icon called **Show Navigator**.

Getting to Know the Studio with Your First Game

4. In the Navigator there is a directory tree. Open the folders until you find the `html5` folder. Inside this folder is the game. Click on the game and we should see all the code as can be seen in the next screenshot. If we scroll through the code we can clearly see the scripts we have created, properties of objects, and so on.

```
Elements  Resources  Network  Sources  Timeline  Profiles  Audits  Console
Chapter_01.js?UPEZB=1289640712 ×
458 function gml_Object_obj_Player_Create_0( _inst, _other )
459 {
460 {
461 gml_Script_scr_Player_Create( _inst , _other , 0, 0, 0, 0, 0 );
462 }
463 ;
464 }
465
466 // ################################################################
467 // {
468 // action_move( "010000000", 8 );
469 // }
470 //
471 function gml_Object_obj_Player_Keyboard_40( _inst, _other )
472 {
473 {
```

5. Let's now take a look at the obfuscated version. Close down the browser tab and then run the game in normal mode. Repeat the same process and take a look at the code. It should look like the next screenshot. We can still read some bits and pieces, but none of it makes any sense. You can feel fairly secure that few people will want to mess with this.

```
Elements  Resources  Network  Sources  Timeline  Profiles  Audits  Console
Chapter_01.js?MSQAC=1746968676 ×
458 var _Nv=0;function _Ov(){this._W1=0;this._X1=0;this._pv=0;this._mv=0;this._ov=0;this.
459 return }}}}this._W1=_Rv;this._X1=_Sv};function log(_9w){setTimeout(function(){throw n
460 break;case "touchend":_dw=_aw(_hw["identifier"]);_Kv[_dw]=-1;break;case "touchmove":_
461 break;case "touchend":_ew[_dw]._pv=0;_qw[_dw]._rw=0;break;case "touchmove":default :br
462 _Nw){var _Ow=_Pw._2w(_Mw);if(!_Ow){_Lm("Error: invalid ds_grid ID (ds_grid_set)");ret
463 _Lm("Error: grid out of bounds(get) - GridID: "+_Mw+"  size["+_Ow._Hw+","+_Ow._Iw+"]
464 return 0}function _0x(_Mw,_Nw){var _Zw=_Xw._2w(_Mw);if(_Zw){return _Zw._gh(_Nw)}_Lm("
465 return 0}_Lm("Error: invalid ds_list ID (ds_list_find_value)");return -1}var _4x=1,_5
466 _Lm("Error: Key("+_e9+") NOT present in ds_map["+_Mw+"], you must add a key before re
467 return _bx[_e9]}var _qx=_bx[_e9];return _qx.Object}}_Lm("Error: Key ("+_e9+") not fou
468 for(var key in _bx){if(_bx[key]!=undefined){if((_vx-key)>0){_vx=key;_Qh=key}}}}if((_Q
469 if(_d2==',' || _d2==':'){_zx--;break}if(_d2>='A'){_a9=((_d2.charCodeAt()-65)+10)<<4}els
470 if(_d2>='A'){_a9|=(_d2.charCodeAt()-65)+10}else {_a9|=(_d2.charCodeAt()-48)}_Dx+=Stri
471 return 0}_Gx[_Gx.length]=_Nw}var _Lx=!1;var _Mx='Trying to stop non-existing sound.',
472 for(_N9=0;_N9<9;_N9++){b=((!0==b)||(_Yx[_N9]=='1'))?!0:!1}if(!0!=b){return }if(!0==_L
473 debug("Creating instance for non-existent object: "+_5y);return }var _8y=null;if(!0==
```

[46]

Summary

Well, there you have it. In the very first chapter of this book you have already made your very first HTML5 game. In doing so, you had the opportunity to explore the GameMaker: Studio interface and get comfortable with it. You also created and implemented every type of resource available while utilizing all the various resource editors. Hopefully, you have realized how incredibly easily the software allows you to make games for the web. With the knowledge you have already gained, you could start making more advanced games. For example, why not add shooting as you know how to use key press events, make objects move, and do stuff on collision?

In the next chapter, we are going to delve into asset creation. A game is only as good as it looks and sounds. We will learn how to create an animated character, build a tileset to decorate a room, and use audio to add atmosphere. Let's move on as things are about to get a lot more exciting!

2
Triple 'A' Games: Art and Audio

Now that we are comfortable navigating around the interface and have built a simple game, we can start to create more complex projects. In this chapter we are going to focus on creating art, adding animation, and implementing an audio soundscape. All three of these elements are incredibly important for the creation of a game as each of them helps the player to understand what is happening and makes the experience more immersive. How we go about building a game can be drastically affected by the types of assets we use and how they are implemented. We will start by looking at importing external images and move onto some practical examples of how to create a tileset and make an animated character. We will then move onto audio files and how to add ambience to a game. We will wrap up the chapter with a brief talk on how to make a game look more professional. Let's get started!

Manufacturing art assets

More often than not, when creating a game, the majority of the art assets will be created in an external program and it will need to be imported. It is true that GameMaker: Studio does have an in-built image editor that we will investigate later, but its capabilities are fairly limited. It's perfect for creating simple art, but there are many other tools that provide us with much more advanced techniques for creating complex art.

There are many popular software options you might want to consider. The most full featured option and the most expensive is **Adobe Photoshop**, which is the preferred option for most professional artists and can be purchased at `http://www.photoshop.com/`. A free alternative with many similar capabilities is **GIMP**, downloadable at `http://www.gimp.org/`. Both these packages offer a full suite of advanced tools for creating images. There are also many other simpler tools available, such as **Pickle** `http://www.pickleeditor.com/`, **Spriter** `http://www.brashmonkey.com/`, and **PyxelEdit** `http://pyxeledit.com/`, all of which are free and worth checking out.

If you just want to skip the art creation and prefer some premade pieces, there are plenty of places to download sprites. One of the most popular sites for sprites is the **Spriters Resource** `http://spriters-resource.com/`. They have assets for every type of game you can imagine. You can also check out the GameMaker forums `http://gmc.yoyogames.com/`. Here you will find many active people who are willing to make or share their art assets.

Understanding the image file formats

GameMaker: Studio is capable of importing four image types: BMP, GIF, JPG, and PNG. Each format has its own unique capability and drawback that will dictate how they should be used. The **BMP** format is the least used format these days because the data is not compressed. Uncompressed images are generally considered inefficient due to their large file size. **GIF** is the only format that can be animated, but is limited to 256 colors and a single level of transparency. This is perfect for classic 8-bit styled art where everything has a hard edge. **JPG** images have the smallest file size due to the lack of any transparency and their lossy compression format. This is a good choice for backgrounds and opaque sprites only. **PNG** image formats are the most useful because they are more efficient than BMPs, have 16 million colors and full transparency, and it is the format that GameMaker: Studio outputs as a texture page when the game is compiled.

Throughout this book we will be utilizing only two of the image formats, GIF and PNG. We will be using GIF images for everything that is animated as it is the simplest way to import animation. As in the previous chapter, if we load an animated GIF image, each frame of animation will be separated in the **Sprite Properties Editor**. Unfortunately this means that we are limited to an 8-bit art style with our characters having hard edges due to the single level of transparency. If we want to have a smoother, cleaner look we will want to have our edges anti-aliased and that requires the use of a PNG image. Attempting to have smooth edges in a GIF image is one of the most common mistakes an artist can make. As we will see in the following screenshot, on the left-hand side we have a GIF image in the 8-bit art style with crisp hard edges and on the right-hand side a PNG image with smooth, anti-aliased edges.

In the center we have the same smooth sprite used in the PNG but saved as a GIF. Notice the edge pixels that were once slightly transparent are now a solid white outline.

Importing sprite sheets

While all the animations in this book will be using GIF images for the sake of expediency, it would be remiss if we did not cover how to import a **sprite sheet**. A sprite sheet is generally a PNG file with all the frames of animation of an object, such as a character, placed evenly in a grid. We can then quickly cut out each frame of animation in GameMaker to build the individual sprites we need. Let's try this out!

1. Let's start by opening a **New Project** called `Chapter_02`.
2. Create a new Sprite and name it `spr_PlayerSpriteSheet`.
3. Click on the **Edit Sprite** button to open the **Sprite Editor**.
4. Under **File**, select **Create from Strip**, and then open `Chapter 2/Sprites/PlayerSpriteSheet.png` with nothing selected in the **Image Information** section. This will open the **Loading a strip image** editor.
5. The sprite sheet we just loaded consists of a six frame run cycle. Since we want all the frames, we need to set **number of images** to `6`.
6. The layout of the sprite sheet has two rows of three images. Set **images per row** to `3`.

Triple 'A' Games: Art and Audio

7. Since each image is 64 x 64 pixels in size we need to set **image width** and **image height** to 64. The other options for offsets and separation are not necessary for such a small sprite sheet, but they would come in handy if we had a complete set of animations for this character. The setting should look like the following image:

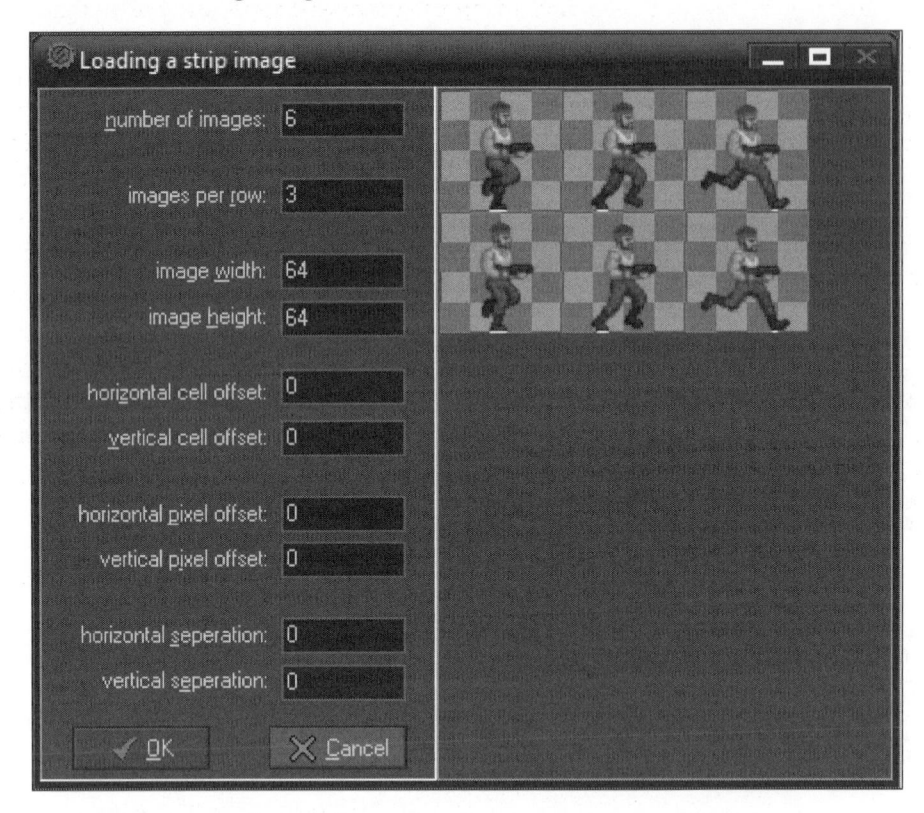

8. Click on **OK**. We now have an animated sprite with smooth edges!
9. We are finished with this sprite. Now click the check mark of the **Sprite Editor** and the **Sprite Properties** editor and click on the **OK** button to close it down.

Introducing the image editor

One of the big benefits of developing with GameMaker: Studio is that it has an in-built **Image Editor** for creating sprites and backgrounds. This editor may appear to be very basic but there are a lot of excellent tools available to use. There are a variety of different drawing tools including the standard tools such as pencil, eraser, and fill. One very useful and unique feature in the editor is the ability to paint with both mouse buttons. The **Colors | Left** and **Colors | Right** color options, as seen in the following image, indicate the color that will be used depending on whether the left or right mouse button is being used. We can also adjust a wide range of things through the **Transform** and **Image** menus. The **Transform** menu contains the ability to affect the size and placement of the pixels in the image. The **Image** menu contains the image alteration tools such as the ability to change the color, blur the image, and add glows.

Rather than talking about the image editor, let's build some art assets in it. We will start by creating a tileset and then move onto an animated character, both of which can be used later in *Chapter 4, The Adventure Begins*. If you would rather work in an external editor, feel free to still follow along as the general theory of creating these assets is somewhat universal.

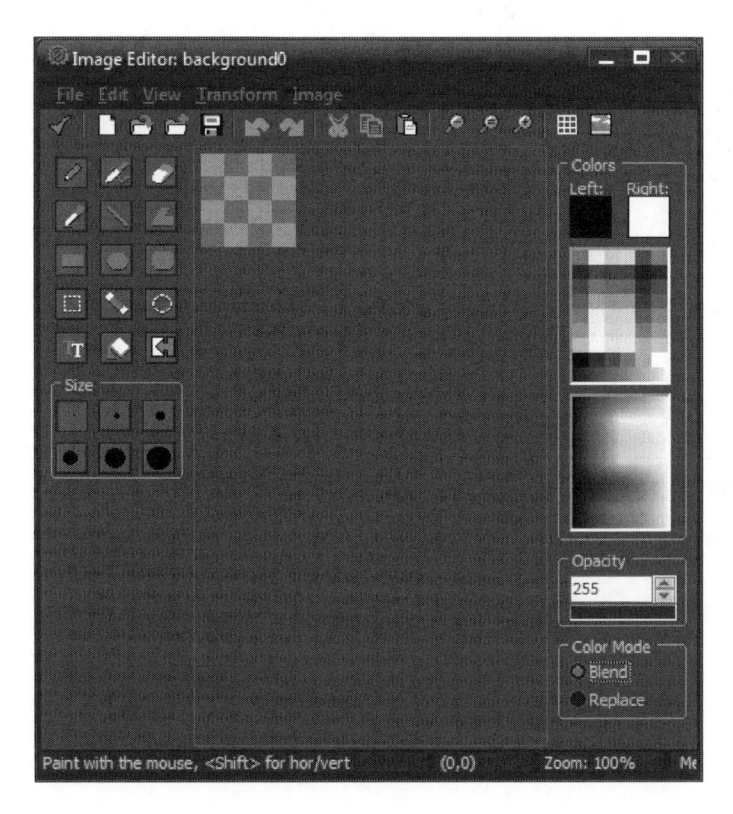

Triple 'A' Games: Art and Audio

Creating backgrounds with tilesets

A **tileset** is a special type of background asset that allows games to have an immense amount of variation in the environment without using a lot of computer memory. It is important to keep the file size and memory usage small, especially for HTML5 games. The browser needs to download all these assets because we have no idea how powerful a computer the user has.

Creating natural looking tilesets is all about tricking the eye. Our eyes are very good at spotting patterns; they recognize differences in shape, contrast, and color, when there is repetition. Knowing that our brains are hardwired this way allows us to use this to our advantage. We can break up patterns by using odd shapes, minimizing contrast, and using similar colors in our artwork.

We are going to create a tileset for one of the most common surfaces seen in games: a stone floor. Now this may seem easy, but it is amazing how often this is done incorrectly.

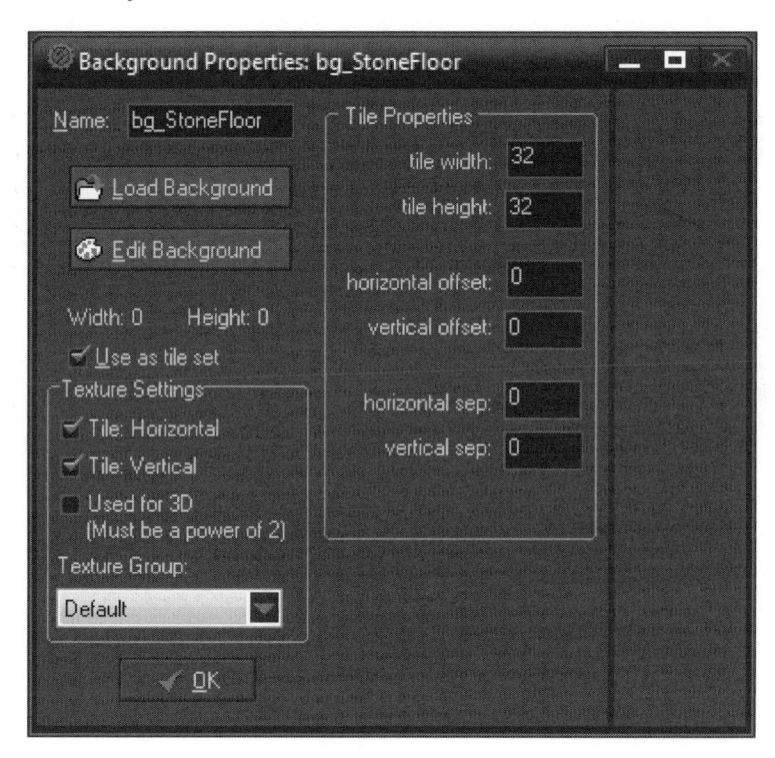

1. Create a new background resource and name it `bg_StoneFloor`.
2. Since we want this to be a tileset, make sure you check the box for **Use as tile set**. This will display the **Tile Properties** which allows you to set the tile width and height, offsets, and separation.
3. Set the **tile width** and **tile height** to 32 as seen in the preceding image. We are now ready to start building tiles.
4. Click the **Edit Background** button. This will open up the **Image Editor**.
5. We are going to start by creating the master tile from which all other tiles will be based. In the **Image Editor**, Select **File | New** and set the **Width** and **Height** to 32.

6. Select the **Fill an Area** tool and apply a light gray color to the entire sprite. This is the base and we will change the colors later.

   Before starting to paint in a bunch of stones, we need to first think about the potential issues and the best solution for solving them. The most common problem people have creating a tileset is that they start by trying to create the final product instead of building up to it. This includes choosing the colors and adding details before ensuring that it can, in fact, tile properly.

   When looking at tiling textures, we need to ensure that we try our best to break the grid. The entire world is going to be based on small, 32 x 32 pixel tiles, but we don't want the viewer to notice this. Our goal then, is to use irregular shapes and attempt to avoid horizontal and vertical alignment.

7. Select the **Draw on the Image** tool and a dark gray color.

8. To make life a bit easier we can zoom in on the image. This can be done with the magnifying glass or with the middle mouse scroll button.

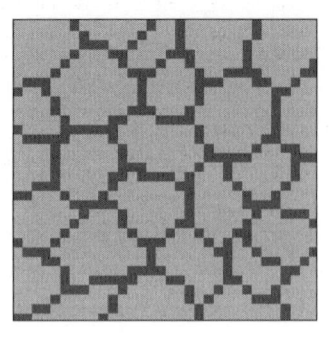

9. Draw the outlines of small rocks, but do remember to keep a bit of variety in the size and shape. Also, don't forget to keep the diagonal lines to a width of just one pixel! Once you have done this, it should look similar to the preceding example screenshot.

10. From the **Image Editor** menu, select **Transform | Shift**. This will open the **Shift the Image** dialog box that allows you to move pixels horizontally or vertically.

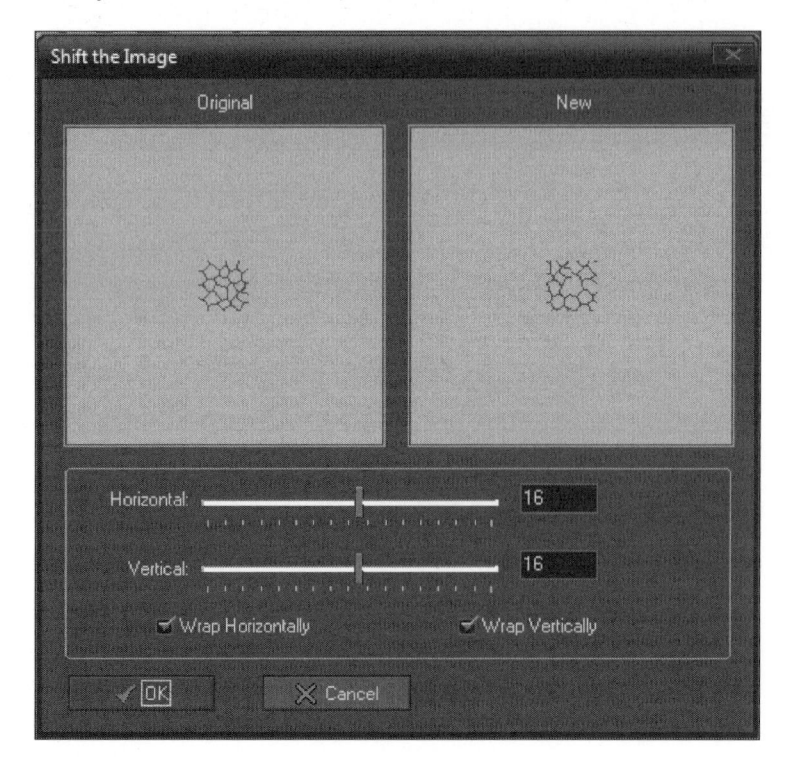

[56]

11. Set the **Horizontal** and **Vertical** values to `16` and check the **Wrap Horizontally** and **Wrap Vertically** boxes. This will move the image 16 pixels down and to the right (half the tile size), and wrap the remaining pixels as can be seen in the preceding screenshot.

12. Click on **OK**.

    By shifting the pixels we can now see how the edges would have tiled. You probably notice that it doesn't work perfectly. In the following example screenshot, you can see that there are several lines that just end without creating whole stones. You may also not like the size of certain stones or see lines that are too thick. The goal here is to fix this up and repeat the process until everything lines up as you like.

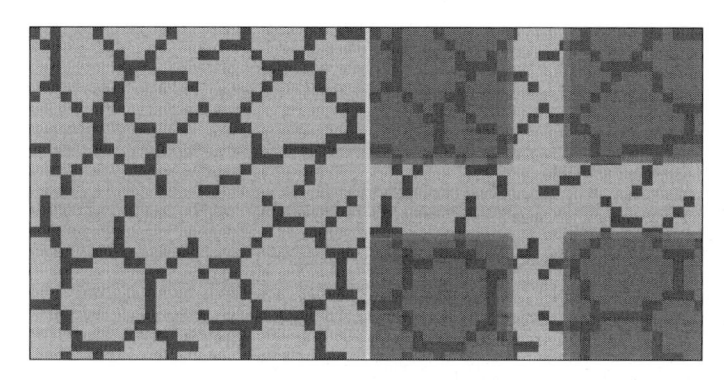

13. Draw the lines and cover over the old ones where necessary to fix any stones that appeared to be incorrect.

14. Re-apply the **Transform | Shift** tool with the same settings. If you see errors, fix them and repeat until you are happy.

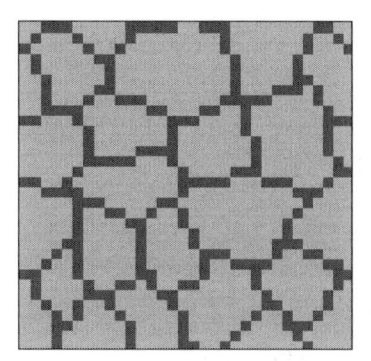

Once we are satisfied with the tile pattern and that it repeats correctly along the edges, we are ready to add color. In general, it is best not to use a fully desaturated gray color scheme to represent stone, as most stones have some color. When selecting colors, the goal is to avoid using just a single color with light/dark variations, but rather choose a range of similar colors. To do this, start by selecting a neutral base color like beige. From there, each additional color should have a slight change in **hue, saturation,** and **luminance.** For example, the second color could be slightly redder, a bit less vibrant, and darker than the first beige.

15. Select a light brown color and use the **Fill an Area** tool to fill in a few of the stones.
16. Repeat this process with the other brown variants until there are no gray colored stones remaining.

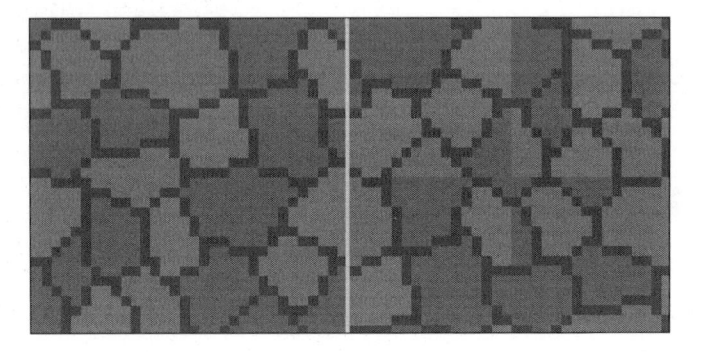

17. Once all the stones have been filled, we need to make sure it still tiles. Use **Transform | Shift** to see if the colors line up correctly. If there are any issues (as seen in the preceding screenshot) just adjust the colors until you are happy again.

    The final step for our base tile is to change the dark gray lines into a dark brown. Now you are probably thinking that this is going to be incredibly tedious, but luckily, the image editor has a tool to make this easy.

18. Select a dark brown color with the left mouse button. This color should appear under **Color | Left.**

19. Select the **Change all Pixels with the Same Color** tool, as seen previously, and left click on one of the dark gray pixels. The stone outline should all be the dark brown color now, as we will see in the following screenshot:

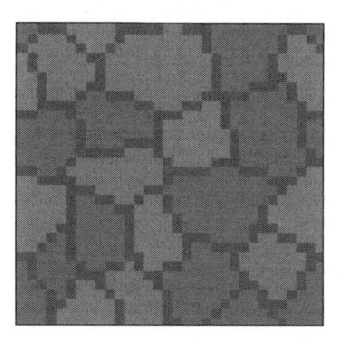

Excellent work! We now have a base tile to build all our other tiles from. The next step is to add border tiles so that there is an edge for separating different materials. If we are going to have a square room, we will need a total of nine tiles: the base tile and the eight tiles representing border edges and corners. Let's add some more space to our canvas and fill it up with our tiles.

20. Select **Transform | Resize Canvas**.
21. Increase the **New Size | Width** and **New Size | Height** by 300 percent or 96 pixels. Then under **Position** click on the center square so that the canvas expands all around the tile we created. The settings can be seen in the following screenshot.

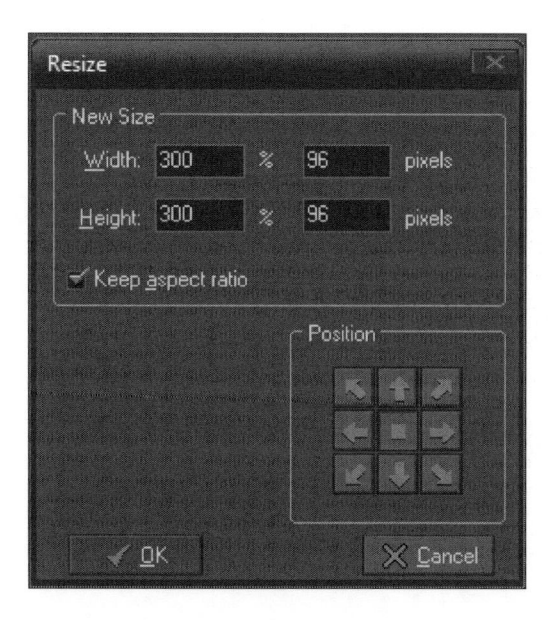

22. You will want to make sure that you line everything up correctly, so turn on the grid. Select **View | Toggle Grid** or click on the **Toggle Grid** icon.

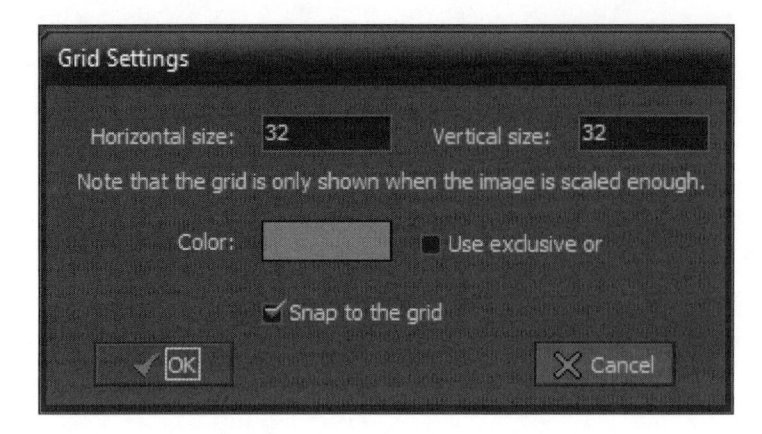

23. At this point you probably can't see any grid. This is because the default grid is set to 1 x 1 pixel. Select **View | Grid Options** to open the **Grid Settings**. Change the **Horizontal size** and **Vertical size** to 32 and check **Snap to the grid**. Feel free to change the **Color**, as we did in the previous screenshot, if you want. Then click on **OK**.

24. Using the **Selecting a Region** tool, drag to select the entire base tile.
25. **Copy** (*Ctrl + C*) and **Paste** (*Ctrl + V*) the tile and then drag it into one of the available spaces. Repeat this step until all nine spots have a base tile in them as seen in the following screenshot:

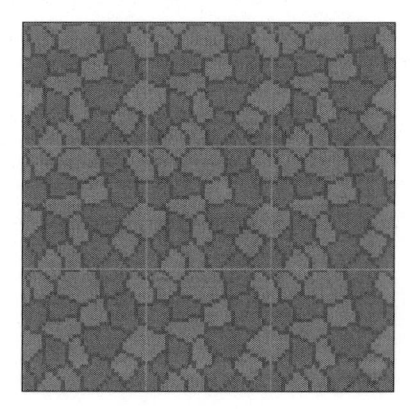

Chapter 2

26. Go back to the **View | Grid Options** and turn off **Snap to the grid**. Otherwise you will get very frustrated trying to draw the borders!

27. We want a border of eight pixels in thickness. Using the same colors as the stones, use the **Draw a Line** tool to create a border around the outer perimeter of the tileset as seen previously.

    Fantastic work! We now have a basic tileset, so let's test it out.

28. If you don't already have one, create a new room.

29. In the **Room Properties** editor, select the **tiles** tab.

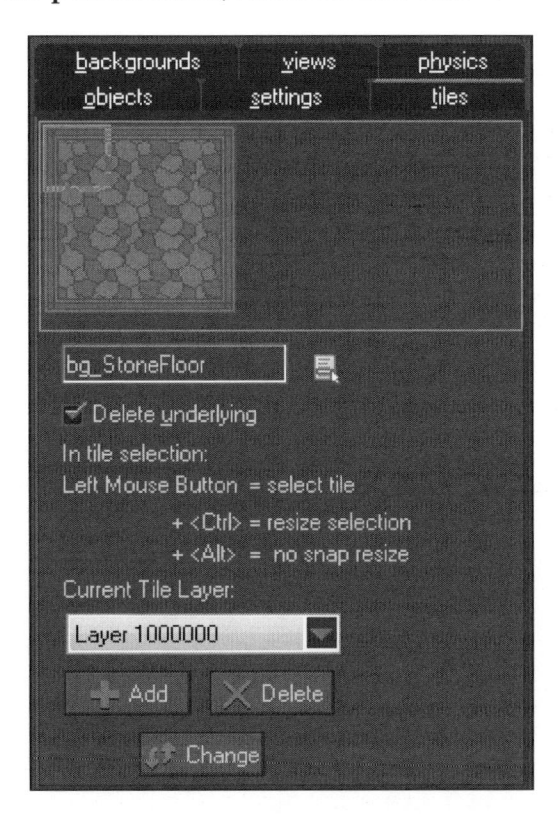

30. If it isn't already selected, set the background image to `bg_StoneFloor`.

Triple 'A' Games: Art and Audio

31. To select a tile, just left click on the one you want to use in the preview area as seen in the preceding screenshot.

    It is possible to have multiple layers of tiles which can be very useful when you want to place odd shaped tiles (a tree, a signpost) without having to create new ones for each surface type (stone floor, grass). It is also useful for compiling several tiles to create a more natural surface, such as the stone floor with a dirt tiles set on top.

32. We are going to keep this simple so let's leave the **Current Tile Layer** at `1000000`.

33. In the room, use left click to place an individual tile or hold *Shift* to paint tiles in the room. Try to layout the tiles as if there were multiple rooms with hallways, much like the following screenshot.

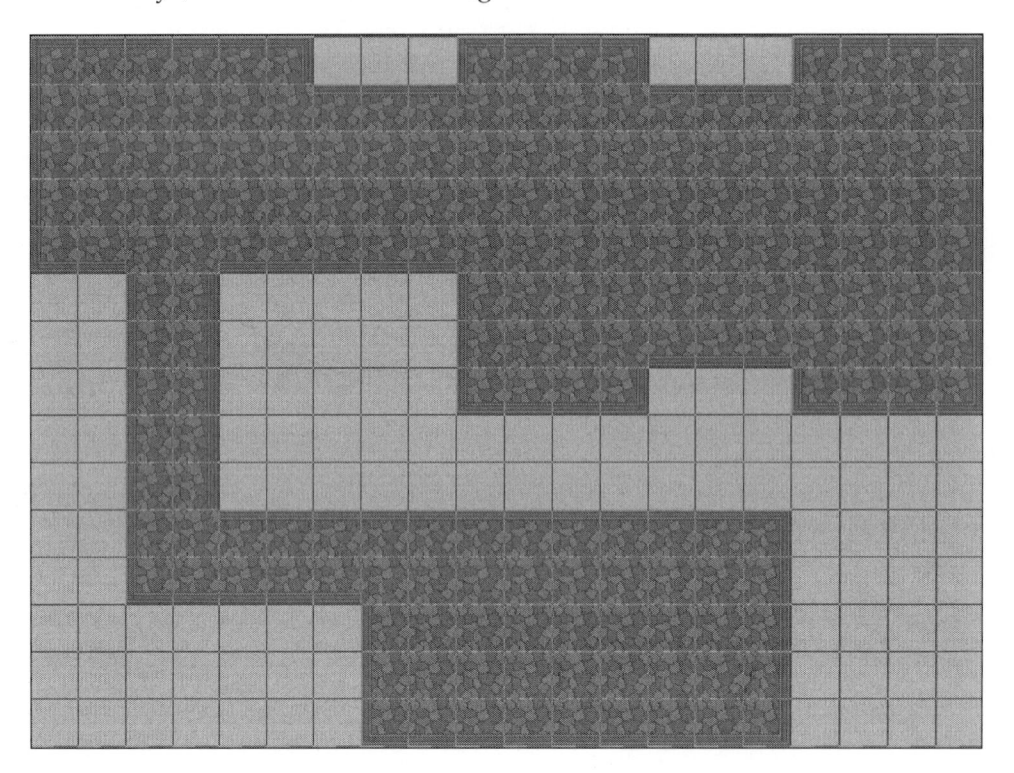

It looks fairly decent, but there are some noticeable issues, specifically that the inner corners do not have the borders on them. You may also feel that the tiles repeat a little too much with an area this large. Since we are going to create more tiles for the first problem, we might as well add a few for the second!

34. Reopen the `bg_StoneFloor` if it isn't still open and select **Transform | Resize Canvas**.
35. Increase the size by `133` percent or to `128` pixels. Under **Position** click on the upper left arrow, then click on **OK**. It should now look like the following screenshot.

36. Select **View | Toggle Grid** so that we can see the grid. We need to copy the original base tile, which we can find in row two and column two.
37. Using the **Selecting a Region** tool, select the pixels from the original base tile.
38. Copy and paste this tile into each empty cell on the outer edge of the image.
39. We need to create four corner pieces to fix our room layout. For this we will use the four tiles along the right-hand side edge that we just placed. Use the **Draw on the Image** tool to draw the corner trim and repeat this for all four corner tiles.

    We have three remaining tiles along the bottom which we will use as alternates to the base tile. As long as we don't affect a one pixel border around the outer edge, we can change the inside as much as we want and it will still tile properly.

40. Change the shape and alternate the colors of a few of the stones in the inner area of each of the three remaining tiles. The tileset, as seen in the following screenshot, is now complete!

41. Finally, go back to the room and place down the corner tiles where necessary and lay down a random variation of the alternate tiles.

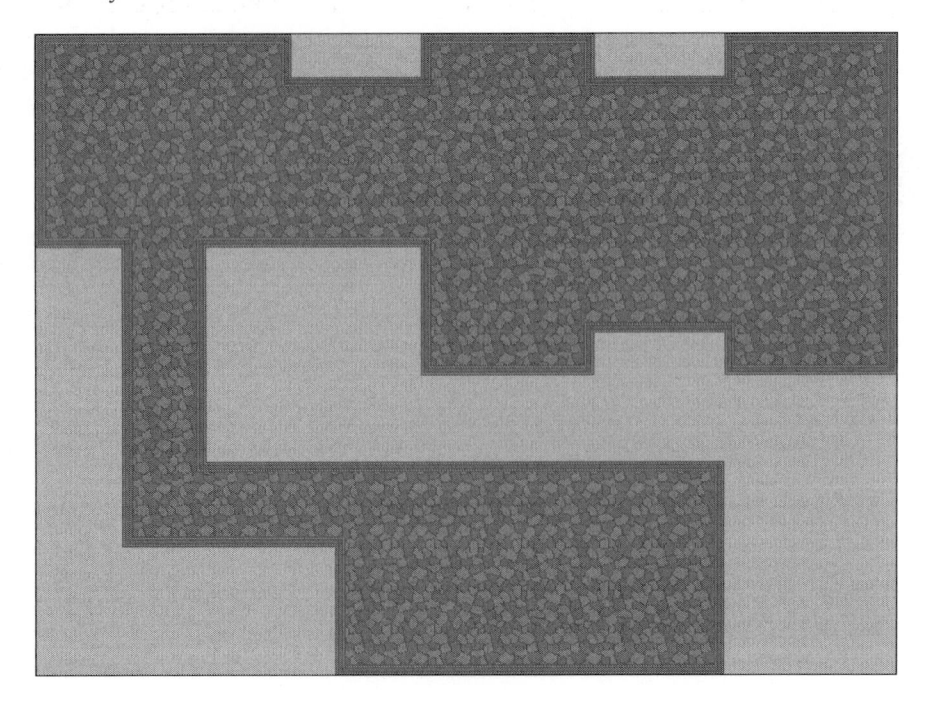

As you can see, with a small 128 x 128 texture we can easily fill a large area while providing the illusion of randomness. To add more variation, we could easily create palette swap versions, where we can adjust the hue and saturation. So we could have, for example, a blue-gray tileset. With more practice we can start adding details such as shadows to add more perspective to the world. For all your future tilesets, just remember to use non-uniform shapes, minimize the contrast, and vary the colors only slightly. More importantly, always ensure that the base tile repeats correctly before building the edges and alternates!

Animating and creating sprites

Animated sprites are a sequence of static images which, when played, appear to have a movement. It lets the player know that they are running, when they are attacking with a sword, and that a button is clickable. Good games have animation on everything interactive and often on many of the background elements, so much so that you may not even notice it. It is the tiny details such as animation that really breathe life into a game.

The illusion of action

Creating animation takes time and a sharp eye, but basic animation, even of characters, can be done by everyone. There are a few important rules to follow to make animating easier. First, it is about the appearance of an action, rather than the accuracy of an action. As can be seen in the following screenshot, the first sword set swinging animation is technically accurate; the sword would be in each of these positions. However, the second set will appear more natural as it includes a blur effect that one would expect to see in a sword swing.

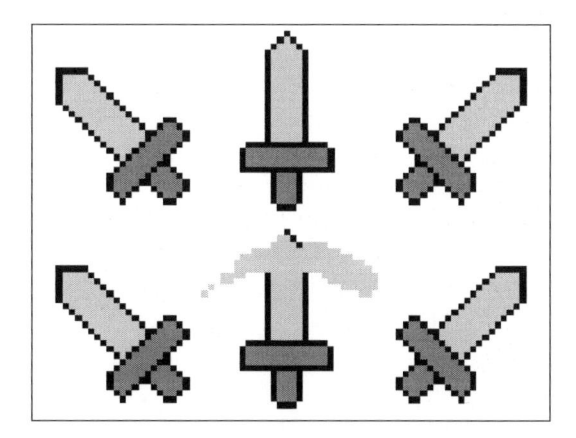

Triple 'A' Games: Art and Audio

Maximize the sprite space

The second rule is maximizing the sprite space. Most games use box-based collision rather than pixel perfect collision. Therefore you want to use as much of the sprite as available for the animation you need. Often developers waste a lot of space because they are thinking in terms of the real world instead of a game world. For example, one common issue can be seen in a jump animation. In the following screenshot, the first jump animation has the character starting from the ground, jumping up into the air, falling down, and landing. The second jump animation is the same, but all the empty space has been removed. Not only is this more efficient, but it can also help to prevent collision bugs since we always know where the collision box is.

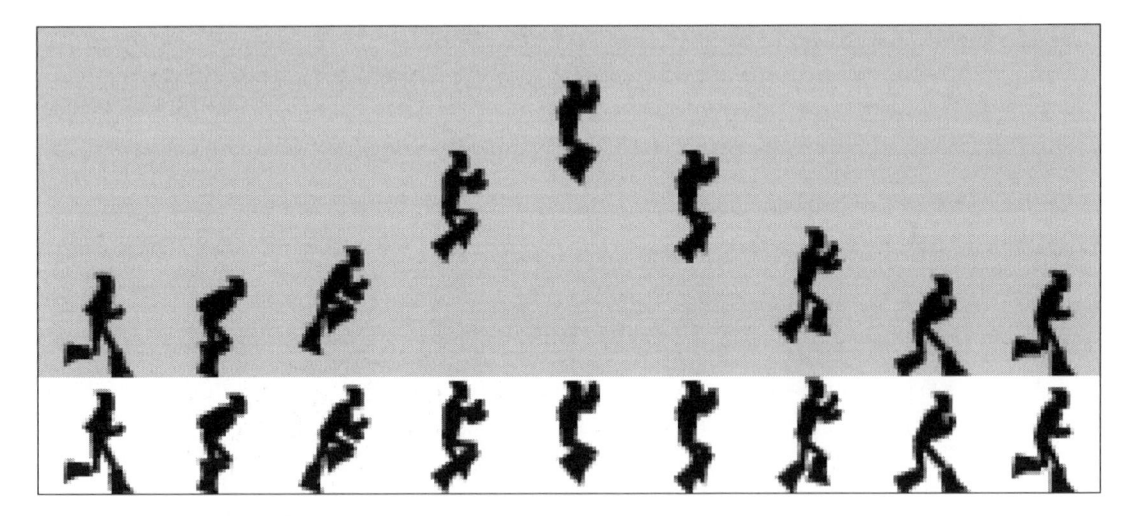

Looping an animation

The last major rule and probably the most important is repeatability. Most of the game animation is at some point going to loop, and having a noticeable repeating sequence is going to be very jarring to the player. One common cause of these repeatability issues is having too much animation. The more frames of animation you have, the more likely that something will pop out. The key here is simplicity and removing the frames you do not need. In the following screenshot you can see two running animations, the first with five frames and the second with only three. The top one will appear a bit smoother but also a bit less repeatable due to the slight differences in the stride. The second one in the end will look better as it has fewer frames and less difference in the stride as a result.

With those three rules in mind, let's build a simple character run cycle:

1. Create a new sprite and name it `spr_WalkCycle`.
2. Click on **Edit Sprite**; this will open the **Sprite Editor**. This editor is for dealing with the all the individual images that make up an animated sprite.
3. In the **Sprite Editor**, select **File | New** which will open a dialog box for the new image dimensions. Keep it at 32 x 32 and click on **OK**.

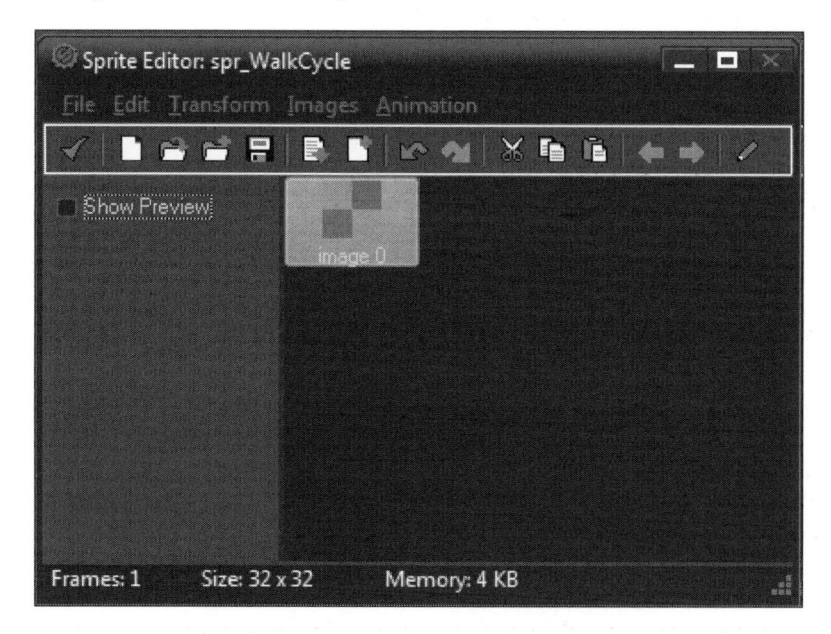

4. You should now see, as in the previous screenshot, an empty image titled **image 0** in the **Sprite Editor**. Double click on the image to open the **Image Editor**.

   Now we need a character design. When designing your character you need to think about what the character is going to do, the world they exist in, and the collision area. In our case, the character will only walk, the world will be an outdoor adventure game, and will have a large square collision box.

[67]

Triple 'A' Games: Art and Audio

> If you don't want to come up with your own character we have supplied a sprite, `Chapter_02/Sprites/WalkCycle.gif`, with the first frame of animation.

5. The first frame of animation that we will create should be the character at their full extension of their walk cycle, the legs far apart, and touching the bottom of the sprite. The character will be at the lowest point of the stride on this frame, so make sure that the head is at least one pixel, preferably two, away from the top of the sprite.

The character designed here in the preceding screenshot is an ape type creature wearing a jacket. The reason for the jacket is to make the arms more readable when they swing. We can see that this character is quite thick which makes the large collision area more believable. Finally, the back leg is a little darker as if there were a shadow. Once again, this is to help with readability.

Once we are happy with the first frame, we need to move onto the next keyframe. A **keyframe** is the point in an animation where the biggest amount of change happens. In this case it will be when the character is at their highest point and the arms and legs are crossing each other.

6. In the **Sprite Editor**, select **Animation | Set Length** and set the **Number of frames** to 3, as seen in the previous screenshot. This will duplicate the first frame twice, giving us two more frames of animation.

7. Open **image 1** and use the **Selecting a Region** tool to raise the upper half of the body to the top of the sprite as seen in the following screenshot. This frame will represent the highest point of the stride, where the character is on one foot with the other foot crossing over. We can also select and shift the hands and feet to quickly get them into position.

8. Using the pencil and eraser tools, paint the arms and legs into the appropriate position with the leg on the ground in the front of the leg being lifted and only one arm showing. Once you are happy with what it looks like, close the image.

9. Open **image 2**. This is the opposite motion of the first frame which makes things quite easy to change. The hands and feet are already in position, so we just need to repaint the arms and legs accordingly, as seen in the following screenshot on the left-hand side. Once this is done, close the image.

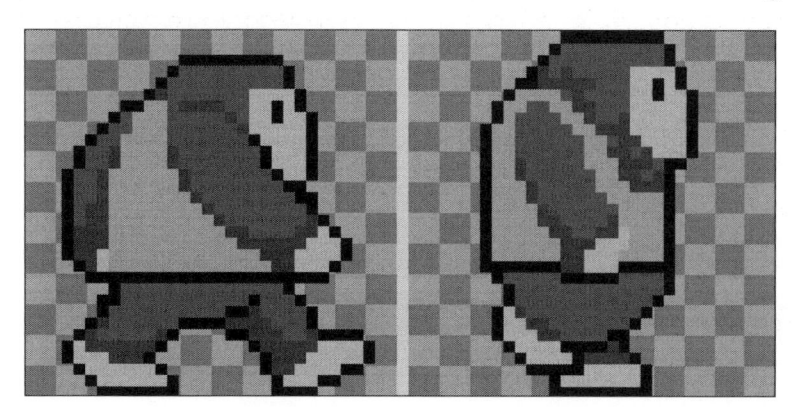

Triple 'A' Games: Art and Audio

10. Now we need to duplicate **image 1** and place it at the end so that the walk cycle can loop. Select **image 1** and copy and paste the frame. This will duplicate the frame and is labeled **image 2**.

11. Select **image 2** and click on the right facing arrow in the **Sprite Editor** toolbar. This will move the frame to the end of the animation. Select and open **image 3** so we can repaint the legs so that the back leg is on the ground and the front leg is in the air, crossing over. Once this is done, close the editor.

12. To see how the animation plays, check the **Show Preview** checkbox in the **Sprite Editor** and set the **Speed** to 5. See the following screenshot.

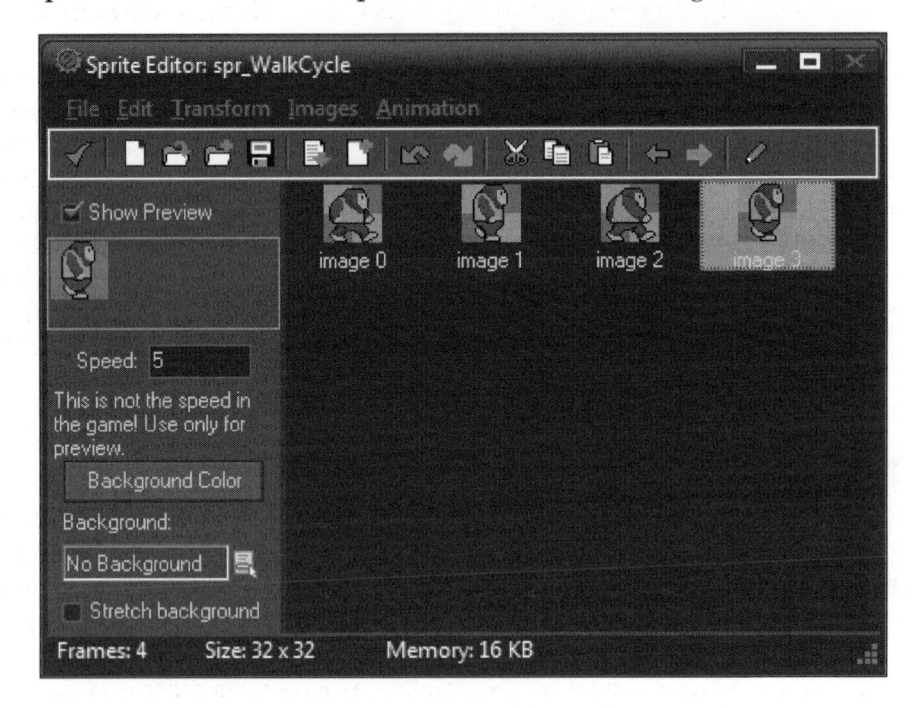

There we have it! A decent walk cycle that loops properly, if a little choppy. If we want to smoothen this animation a bit, just add a frame of animation in between the keyframes and follow the same procedure we just went through. It should end up looking something similar to the following screenshot:

Manufacturing audio

Audio is incredibly important for creating a professional quality game. Unfortunately, it is often the most neglected element and the last to be implemented. One reason for this is the fact that we can play a game without the audio and still enjoy the experience. However, a good soundscape in a game will make it much more immersive and help improve user feedback.

In order to create audio we will need to use external software, as GameMaker: Studio does not come with any built-in audio creation tools. There are a range of software choices to choose from. For creating sound effects and music there are popular programs such as the very full featured **Reason**, http://www.propellerheads.se/, which emulates a rack of synthesizers, mixers, and other components. On the free side, there is **BFXR**, http://www.bfxr.net/, that allows you to create game sounds online and then there is also **Sonant**, http://sonantlive.bitsnbites.eu/, for making music. All these packages are fun and easy to use. One thing to keep in mind is that audio is very challenging to create. Sometimes it is better to just download some free music or sounds and there are plenty of sites out there with both free and purchasable audio. **Freesound**, http://www.freesound.org, have thousands of audio clips that you can download and use. For a more classic chiptune style of music and sounds there is the **8-bit Collective**, http://8bc.org/, a site dedicated to game audio.

Understanding the audio file formats

If adding audio wasn't challenging enough already, HTML5 makes it just a little bit harder. The first difficulty we will encounter is the fact that the HTML5 audio tag has not been standardized as of yet. There are two file formats competing to be the official HTML5 standard: MP3 and OGG. The **MP3** file format is one of the most commonly used formats, but has the drawback of being licensed and patented, which could result in large fees being paid out. The **OGG** file format is both open source and patent free making it a viable alternative. On top of this issue is the fact that the various browsers have their own preference for file types. For example, Internet Explorer accepts MP3s but not OGG, while Opera accepts OGG but not MP3. Google Chrome and Mozilla Firefox are hedging their bets and support both. GameMaker: Studio deals with this issue by converting all audio to both MP3 and OGG file formats when the game is exported.

Using the GM:S Audio engine

GameMaker: Studio comes with two different sound engines for controlling the various audio in games: **GM:S Audio** and **Legacy Sound**. These systems are completely independent from each other and you can have one system or the other active in a game.

The GM:S Audio engine is the new, more robust sound system that was designed to allow a full 3D soundscape through the use of emitters and listeners. **Emitters** allow for the positioning in game space where sounds are going to occur. There are functions for adding falloff of the sounds, velocity to emulate movement, and more. **Listeners** give even more control by dictating how the sound is played based on where the player is in the game, including their orientation and velocity. If you do not declare a listener, then the sounds become universal. This will eventually become the primary audio engine in GameMaker: Studio, but because of the HTML5 audio issues, it doesn't work properly in all browsers.

The Legacy Sound engine is the original sound system that GameMaker used and as the name indicates, this engine is no longer being actively developed and many of the functions have already been made obsolete. It is a much simpler system with no 3D capabilities, though for most games this will be more than enough. The one big benefit this engine has is that the audio should work in all browsers.

We will be using the Legacy Sound engine throughout this book to ensure maximum capability, but we need to know how to use the GM:S Audio engine for the future. Let's test these features by creating a very simple demonstration of positional sound. We are going to create an object in our room and make it play a sound that can only be heard as the mouse approaches the location.

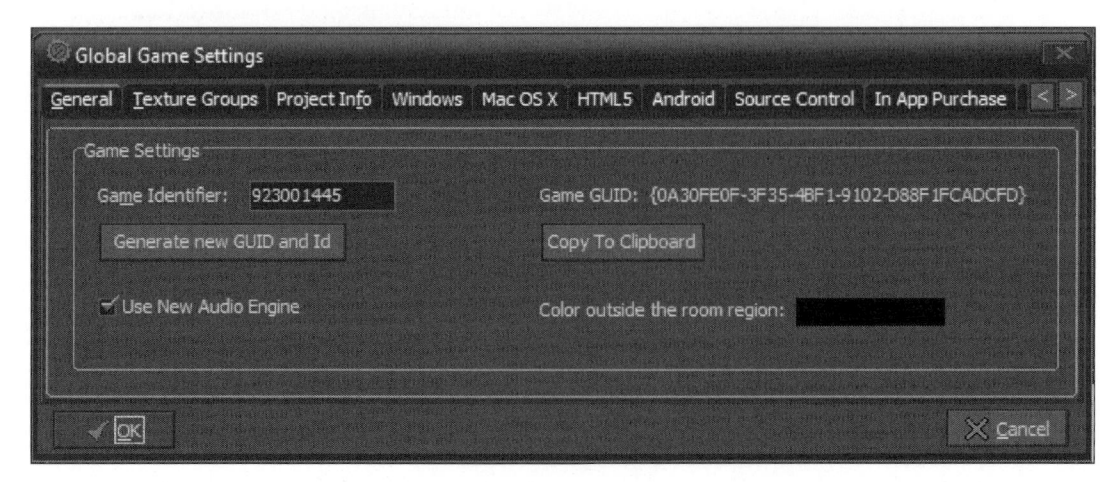

1. In order to select which system you are using, click on **Resources | Change Global Game Settings**. In the **General Tab**, there is a **Use New Audio Engine** checkbox; make sure you check this. If it is checked, it is using the GM:S Audio engine; if it is not, then it is using Legacy Sound.
2. Create a new Sound and name it `snd_Effect`.
3. Load `Chapter 2/Sounds/Effect.wav`. Make sure the **Kind** is set to **Normal Sound**.
4. Create a new Object and name it `obj_Sound`.
5. Create a new Script and name it `scr_Sound_Create`. First, we need to create an emitter and capture it in a variable:

   ```
   sem = audio_emitter_create();
   ```

6. Next we will position the emitter to where our object is. The parameters for this function are: the emitter to apply this to and the X/Y/Z coordinates. We will use the object's X and Y, but since this is a 2D example, we will set the Z to 0:

   ```
   audio_emitter_position(sem, x, y, 0);
   ```

7. We also want to have a **falloff** on the emitter so that the sound becomes louder as the listener approaches. The parameters we have are: the emitter, the distance for how far the sound should be at half volume, the total falloff distance, and the falloff factor:

   ```
   audio_emitter_falloff(sem, 96, 320, 1);
   ```

8. The emitter is all set up; now let's play the sound on the emitter. The parameters for this function are: the emitter, the sound to play, whether it should loop, and its priority. We will want this to **loop** so that we can hear the sound:

   ```
   audio_play_sound_on(sem, snd_Effect, true, 1);
   ```

9. This code is finished and should look like the following when all put together:

   ```
   sem = audio_emitter_create();
   audio_emitter_position(sem, x, y, 0);
   audio_emitter_falloff(sem, 96, 320, 1);
   audio_play_sound_on(sem, snd_Effect, true, 1);
   ```

10. Add a **Create** event and drag a **Control | Execute Script** icon into the Actions with this script attached.
11. The sound will play now, but it will not have a direction until we have a **listener**. We will move the listener position based on the location of the mouse on every step. Create a new Script and name it `scr_Sound_Step`.

12. We only need one line of code for positioning the listener's X/Y/Z coordinates. The X and Y will be set to the mouse X and Y and once again Z is set to 0.
    ```
    audio_listener_position(mouse_x, mouse_y, 0);
    ```
13. On the `obj_Sound` object, add a **Step | Step** event and drag an **Execute Script** icon into the Actions with the step script attached.
14. Open up the room and place the instance of `obj_Sound` object into the center of the room.
15. Run the game.

You should be able to hear the sound quietly and as you move the mouse around closer to the center of the screen the louder it should become. If you have surround sound or headphones, you will also notice that the sound moves from the left to the right channels. This is just a sample of what can be done with the GM:S Audio engine and it will be exciting to use once it works in all browsers.

Raising the quality bar

When looking at the hundreds of thousands of games out there, it is quite easy to recognize the top-tier games from the bottom-tier. However, when we look across the spectrum at all the best games, there is a stark difference between them. Some games are very minimalist, some are photo-realistic, while others are fantastical. These games might be made by a few people, or a large team of specialists. What is it that makes games that are fundamentally so different still able to achieve the same definition of quality? The answer is quite simple and can be summed up by three general principles: Consistency, Readability, and Polish. While creating high caliber art and audio, it does require plenty of acquired skills learned through years of study and practice. Following these few rules will help make any game appear more professional.

Consistency

Consistency sounds obvious but it is actually a lot more challenging than one might expect. Each sprite, background, or other art asset needs to be built with the same rule set. In the following screenshot you can see three variations of a plane flying with a city background. The first image is completely inconsistent as it has a flat shade with a pixel block styled plane and a photo-realistic background. The next image is more consistent than the first image as the city is flat shaded, but it lacks the crispness of the pixel block style. This is where most people might stop as it is close enough but there is still room for improvement. The final image is the most consistent as everything has the flat shading and the pixel block styling.

Chapter 2

This process works just as easily in the opposite direction by having the plane become more photo-realistic. All that is needed is to choose one set of options and apply it equally across everything.

Readability

Readability is all about ensuring that the correct information is being conveyed to the user. This can mean a wide range of things such as making sure the background is separated from the foreground, or making sure that collectible items don't look like hazards. In the following image, there are two sets of potions; one is poison and the other gives health. Just having a different color is not as readable to the player as indicating poison with a skull and the health with a heart. It is important to allow the player to easily understand what is going on so that they can react to it rather than contemplate it.

Polish

Finally, the biggest factor, though often the least visible, is polish. Polish is all about the small details. It is a wide ranging element that covers everything from having particle effects when you collect an item to ensuring that the scoreboard is properly centered. In the following image, we have two avatar icons with statistic bars. The one on the left is functionally correct and looks decent. The one on the right, however, appears to be much more polished. The statistic bars are moved to the left so that there is no gap between them and the avatar icon, which was also centered properly. Hopefully you can see how a few slight adjustments can add a lot to the quality of polish.

Summary

Creating art and audio for games is an enormous task, both in terms of the time it takes and the assets to be produced. As a game developer, it is your responsibility to ensure that everything is cohesive and aesthetically pleasing, whether you are creating the assets or working with artists and sound designers. In this chapter you have started to understand how art and audio works in GameMaker: Studio and what the difference is between good and good enough. You learned about the acceptable image formats and how to import a sprite sheet. You created a tileset that will make better use of computer memory and allow for large unique worlds. You animated a sprite and made it loop properly. You also learned how to control sounds and the direction they are heard from. You are now ready to start making real games!

In the next chapter we are going to build our second game, a side scrolling shooter. We will create a player that moves around the screen, build several enemies that shoot weapons, create moving backgrounds, and implement a win/lose condition. Most exciting of all is that we will do all of this while learning the **GameMaker Language (GML)**.

3
Shoot 'em Up: Creating a Side-scrolling Shooter

In this chapter, we will create a very simple side-scrolling shooter that will introduce us to the basics of making a complete game utilizing GML code. We will have a player character that can move around the play area and fire weapons. If they collide into an enemy or enemy bullet, they will be destroyed and can respawn if they have any remaining lives.

We will create three different types of enemies that fly across the screen:

- **FloatBot**: It has no weapons but is hard to hit, because it floats up and down as it moves.
- **SpaceMine**: It is the slowest enemy and will fire a ring of bullets if the player gets too close.
- **Strafer**: It is the fastest enemy that flies in a straight line and fires bullets directly at the player's location.

Shoot 'em Up: Creating a Side-scrolling Shooter

We will polish the game by displaying the score and player lives, scroll the background to create the illusion of movement, play music, and add explosions. Finally, we will restart the game by implementing a win/lose condition. The game will look as shown in the following screenshot:

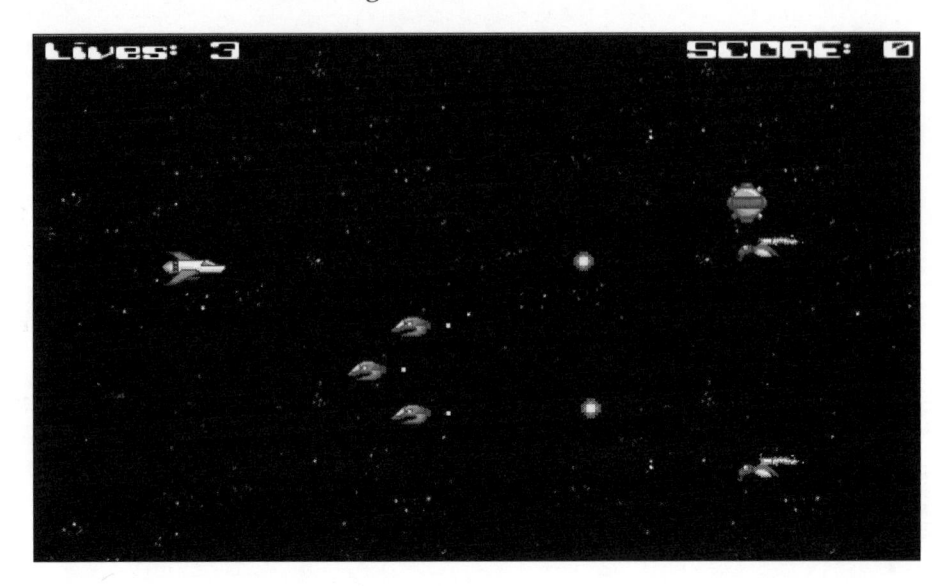

Coding conventions

In order to write effective code, regardless of programming language, it is important to follow the recommended coding conventions. This will help ensure that other people can read and understand what the code is attempting to do and debug it. There is no universal standard for programming practices, though many languages follow similar guidelines. The **GameMaker Language (GML)** does not have an official recommended set of conventions, partially due to the fact that it was developed to be a learning tool and is very forgiving as a result.

For this book, we will define our own conventions based on common practices and ease of learning.

- All assets, except Rooms, will start with a simple type signifier and an underscore. For example:
    - **Sprites**: `spr_`
    - **Objects**: `obj_`
    - **Scripts**: `scr_`

- Even though it is possible to use the Execute Code DnD to write code directly on an event, all code will be placed into Scripts and the naming convention will indicate the Object it is attached to and the Event it is applied to. This will make it easier to find later for debugging purposes. For example, code placed onto the player object's **Create** event would have a Script named `scr_Player_Create`.

- If a Script is intended to be used by multiple objects, the name should use a clear description of what it is doing. For example: for removing an object after it goes offscreen, the Script would be named `scr_OffScreenRemoval`.

- Variables will be written using CamelCase wherever multiple words are used; the first word starts with a lowercase letter, and each following word starts with an uppercase letter, for example: `variableWithManyWords`.

- Boolean variables should be posed as a question, for example: `canShoot`, `isPlaying`.

- Constants are written using all uppercase letters and underscores to separate words, for example: `LEFT`, `MAX_GRAVITY`.

- Expressions in `if` statements are always enclosed in parentheses. GameMaker does not require this, but it does make it easier to read the code; for example: `if (x > 320)`.

Building the player

We are going to start by building our player object. We have briefly described the design already, but we have not broken the design down into something that we can start creating. First, we should bullet point each feature and what it entails to ensure we have all the **Variables** and **Events** we will need.

- Arrow keys will move the player around the play area
    - Must remain in play area

- Spacebar will fire weapon
    - A single bullet fired with each button press

- Colliding with bullets or enemies causes damage
    - Should be different values based on type

Shoot 'em Up: Creating a Side-scrolling Shooter

Setting up the player sprite

Let's create the player sprite and prepare it for the game:

1. Create a new project and call it `Chapter_03`.
2. Create a new Sprite and name it `spr_Player`.
3. Click on **Load Sprite** and load `Chapter 3/Sprites/Player.gif`, with **Remove Background** checked. This `.art` file has a spaceship with transparency and several frames of animation.

   Next, we want to adjust the collision area of the spaceship. The default collision is a rectangle covering the entire area of the Sprite that has pixel data. This means that the ship will take damage even though it has not visually come into contact with anything. What we want is to have a really small collision area.

4. Click on **Modify Mask**. This will open the **Mask Properties** editor as shown in the following screenshot:

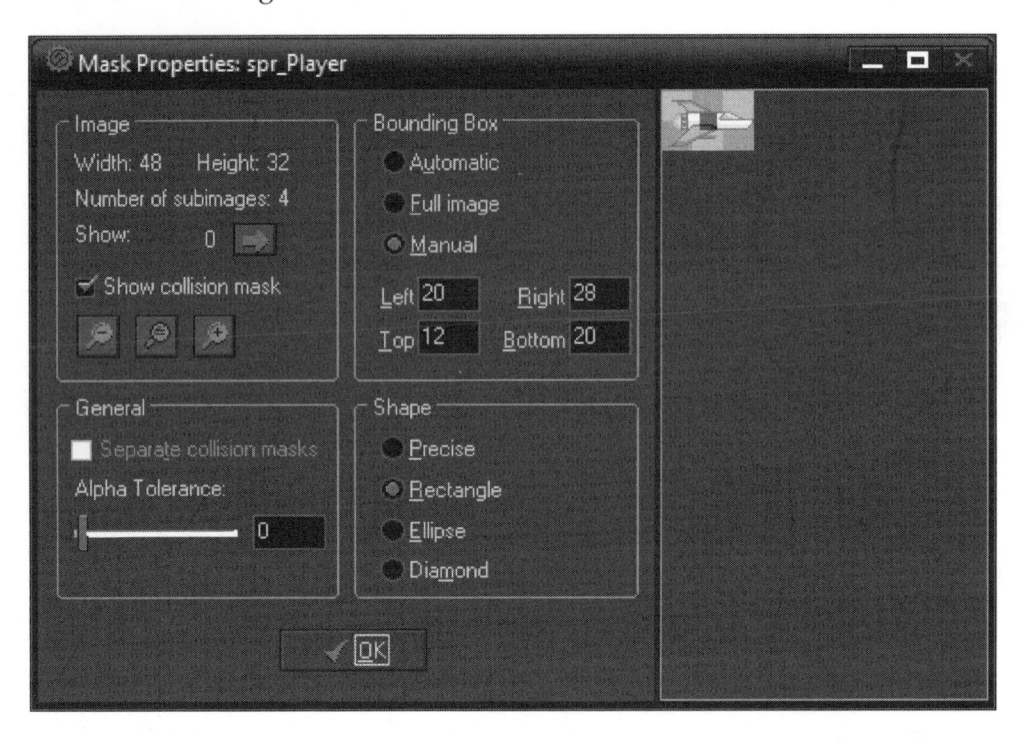

[80]

Chapter 3

In the **Mask Properties** editor, we are able to control the size, shape, and placement of the collision mask, the area of a sprite where collision detection will occur. Some games require pixel perfect collision, where collision is determined on an individual pixel basis. This is the most precise collision possible, but it is also computationally expensive. The majority of games, however, can get away with a much simpler shape, such as a rectangle. This method is much more efficient, but limits the visual accuracy of the collision. The choice of which one to choose is dependent on the game's design and how much control is necessary to achieve the desired results.

5. We want full control of the collision area, so set the **Bounding Box** to **Manual** and leave **Shape** as **Rectangle**.

6. There are two ways to adjust the parameters of the **Bounding Box**. We can either enter exact positions for the corners of the box, or we can draw the box directly on the image of the Sprite. Left mouse drag a small box roughly in the center of the spaceship as shown in the previous screenshot.

7. Click on **OK**.

    We are now back in the **Sprite Properties** editor and we can see that **Collision Checking** now states that it has been **Modified**. The last thing we will do to this Sprite is to move the origin to the tip of the spaceship's gun. By doing this we won't have to worry about offsetting the bullets upon creation through code.

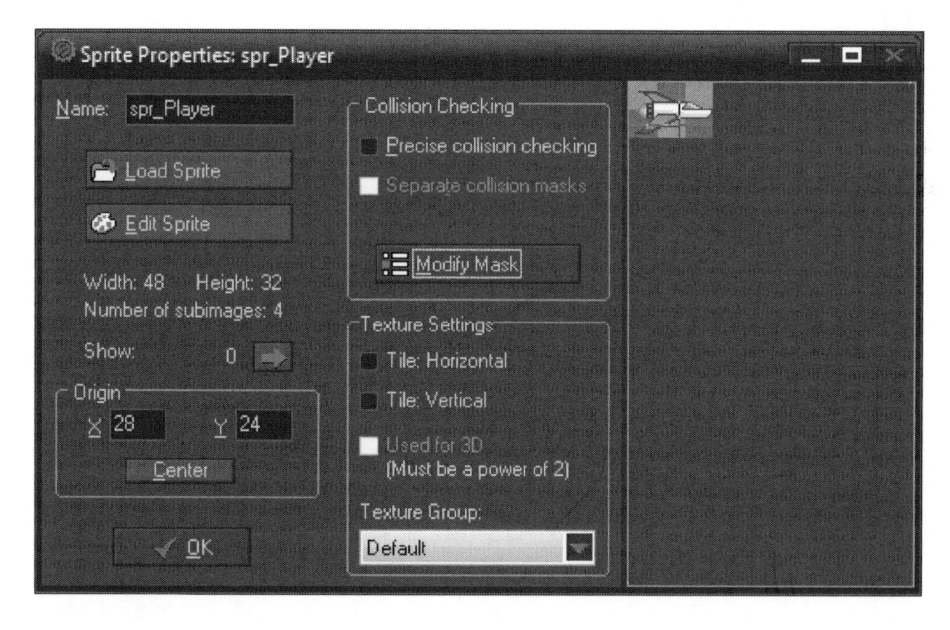

8. Set **Origin** to **X**: 28, **Y**: 24, and then click on **OK**.

[81]

Controlling the player object

Let's create the player object and get it moving around the world.

1. Create a new Object and name it `obj_Player`.
2. Assign `spr_Player` as its Sprite.
3. We need to initialize a variable for the speed we want the player to move at. This will make it easier to change the value later and have all scripts in `obj_Player` refer to it. Create a new Script and name it `scr_Player_Create`.

   ```
   mySpeed = 8;
   ```
4. In `obj_Player`, add a **Create** event.
5. Drag an Execute Script icon from **Control** into the **Actions:** area, and apply the `scr_Player_Create` to the script option. Click on **OK**.
6. Create a new Script and name it `scr_Player_Key_Left`. This script will have the code for the left arrow key.
7. While we want the player to be able to move left, we also want to prevent the player from going offscreen. Write the following code into the script:

   ```
   if ( x >= sprite_width )
   {
       x -= mySpeed;
   }
   ```

   We start with a conditional `if` statement that queries whether the player's current x position is greater than or equal to the width of the sprite. In this case, it would mean that the origin of the player is greater than the image's width of 48 pixels. If it is greater, we place the object eight pixels to the left of the current position.

   The method of movement we are using here is not movement in the traditional sense. There is no velocity being applied to the object, but rather we are teleporting the object from one position to the next. The benefit of using this method is that if the key isn't being pressed, the Object won't move. This is necessary in this game, because we cannot use a **No Key** event due to having to shoot weapons.
8. In `obj_Player`, add a **Left** event under **Keyboard**.
9. Drag an Execute Script icon from **Control** into the **Actions:** area, and apply the `scr_Player_Key_Left` to the **Script** option. Click on **OK**.

   Before we move on to all the other keys and their scripts, it is always good to check to see if the Object works as intended.

10. Create a new Room.

11. In the **settings** tab, change the name to `TheGame` and **Width** to `800`. Making the Room wider will give the player more area to maneuver around and recognize enemies easier.

12. In the **objects** tab, select `obj_Player` and place a single instance near the center of the room as seen in the following screenshot:

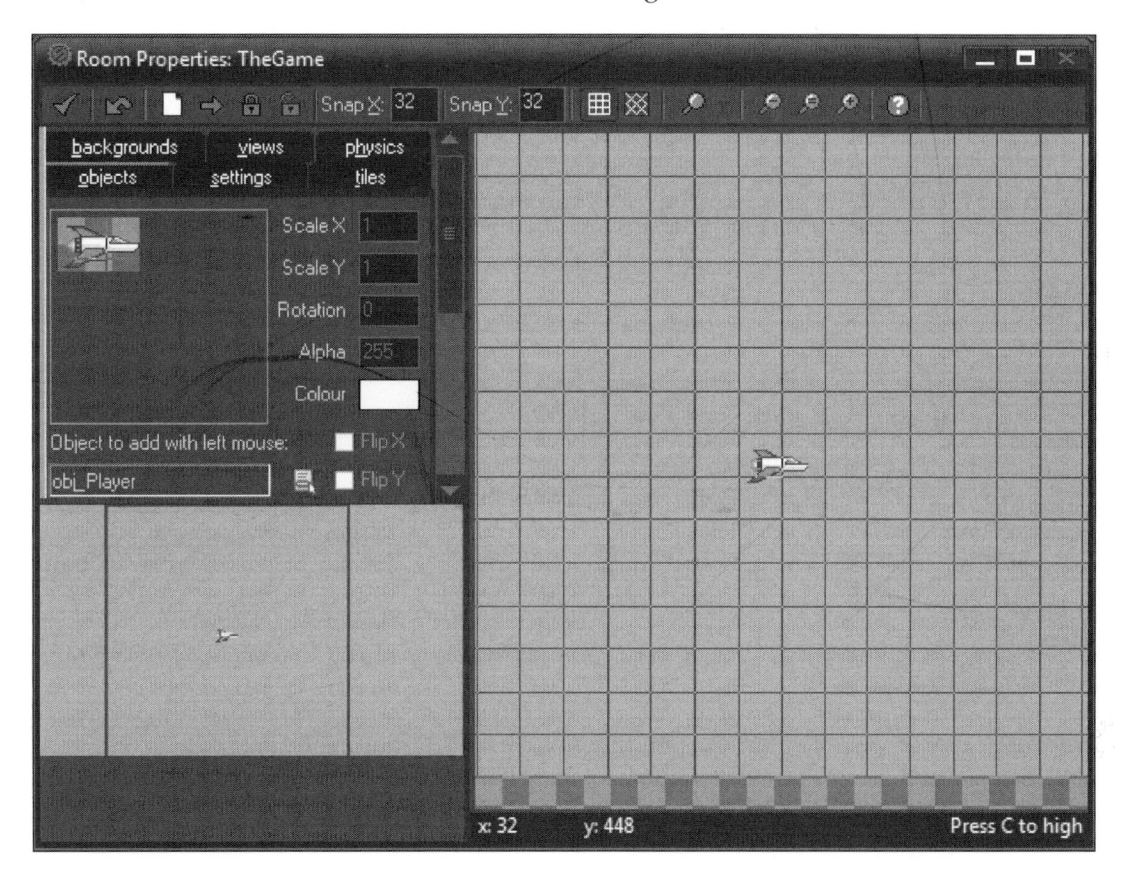

13. Run the game.

    If everything is set up properly, the player should move to the left only when the left arrow is pressed down and should remain in the play area. We can now move onto the other controls.

14. Create a new Script and name it `scr_Player_Key_Right`. This will be for the right arrow key.

15. The script will be similar to the left, except we need to also take into consideration the width of the room. Write the following code:

    ```
    if (x <= room_width - sprite_width)
    {
        x += mySpeed;
    }
    ```

    Here we are testing whether the player's current x position is less than the width of the room minus the width of the sprite. If it is less than that, we add `mySpeed` to the current location. This will ensure the player stays on-screen when moving to the right.

16. In `obj_Player`, add a **Right** event under **Keyboard**.

17. Drag an Execute Script icon from **Control** into the **Actions:** area, and apply `scr_Player_Key_Right`. Click on **OK**.

    We now have our horizontal controls and need to add the vertical movement. We will go over the code for the up key and down key scripts, but by now you should be able to implement them into the object.

18. For the up arrow key, create a new Script and name it `scr_Player_Key_Up`, and write the following code:

    ```
    if (y >= sprite_height)
    {
        y -= mySpeed;
    }
    ```

    It is similar to the horizontal code except now we are looking at the y position and the height of the Sprite.

19. For the down arrow key, create a new Script and name it `scr_Player_Key_Down`, and write the following code:

    ```
    if (y <= room_height - sprite_height)
    {
        y += mySpeed;
    }
    ```

Again, here we are looking at the height of the room minus the height of the sprite as being the furthest point we can move downwards. The movement controls are now complete and the Object properties should look like the following screenshot:

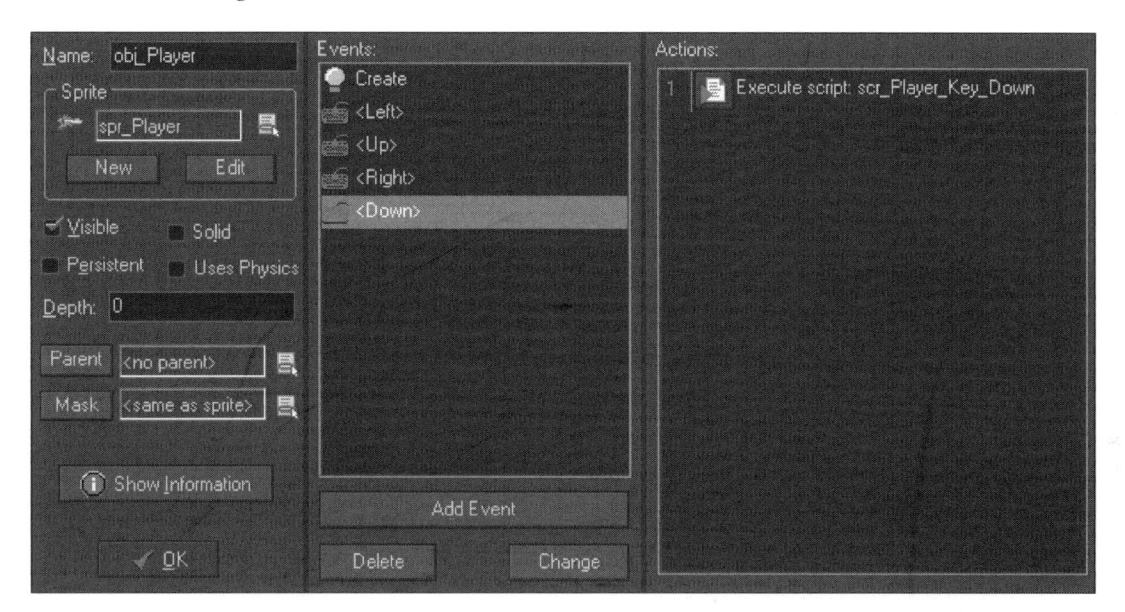

20. Run the game.

The player should be able to move around the entire screen, but never off of it. The only remaining control we have left is the button for firing the gun. However, before we can implement that we need a bullet!

Building the bullet

Bullets are easy to make, as they generally just move along in a straight line once they have been fired.

1. Create a new Sprite and name it `spr_Bullet_Player`.
2. Click on **Load Sprite** and load `Chapter 3/Sprites /Bullet_Player.gif`.
3. As we currently have the origin of the player object set to the tip of the gun, we will want **Origin** of the bullet to be at the front. This will help make the bullet appear to come out of the gun without having to code it directly. Set the values to **X**: `17`, **Y**: `4`.
4. We can leave everything else as it is, so click on **OK**.

[85]

Shoot 'em Up: Creating a Side-scrolling Shooter

5. Bullets should also make a sound when they are fired so let's bring in a sound. The first thing we need to do is to switch back to the Legacy Sound engine, so that we ensure the audio is heard in all browsers. Navigate to **Resources | Change Global Game Settings** and under the **General** tab, uncheck the box for **Use New Audio Engine**.
6. Create a new Sound and name it `snd_Bullet_Player`.
7. Click on **Load Sound** and load `Chapter 3/Sounds/Bullet_Player.wav`.
8. Make sure **Kind** is set to **Normal Sound**. Then click on **OK**.
9. Now it is time to make the bullet move on its own. Create a new Script and name it `scr_Bullet_Player_Create`.
10. We want the bullet to move horizontally to the right. This is easy to do with the following code:

    ```
    hspeed = 16;
    sound_play(snd_Bullet_01);
    ```

    Hspeed is a property representing the horizontal velocity of an object in GameMaker: Studio. We need to apply this code the moment the bullet is instantiated in the world. We also play the sound of the bullet a single time.

11. Create a new Object and name it `obj_Bullet_Player`, and set the Sprite to `spr_Bullet_Player`.
12. Add a **Create** event. The **Create** event is only ever executed once, upon creation.
13. Apply the `scr_Bullet_Player_Create` and click on **OK**.

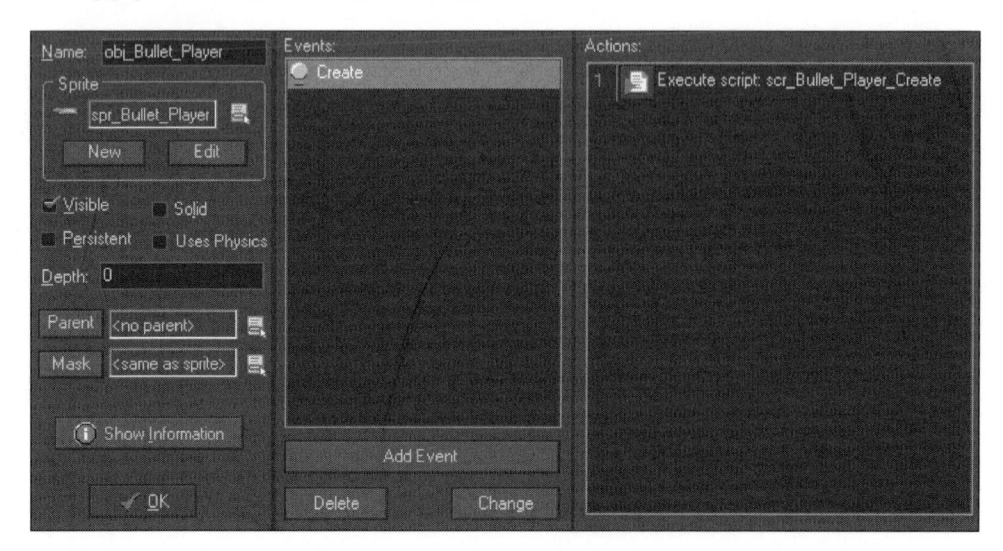

As shown in the preceding screenshot, the bullet is now complete and ready to be fired. Let's go back to the spaceship!

Firing the bullet

A bullet is only dangerous to enemies if it has been fired. The player ship will handle this code.

1. Create a new Script and name it `scr_Player_KeyPress_Space`.
2. Write the following code:

   ```
   instance_create(x, y, obj_Bullet_Player);
   ```

   With this code, we are simply creating an instance of a bullet where the current position of the player ship is, or more specifically, where the origin of the player ship Sprite is. This will make the bullet appear to be shot from the ship's gun.

3. In `obj_Player`, add a **Space** event from **Key Press** and apply `scr_Player_KeyPress_Space`. The **Key Press** event checks if the indicated key has been pushed down. This will run once and requires the key to be released before being able to run again.

4. Run the game.

If everything is working properly, we should be able to move around the screen and fire bullets as fast as we can hit the spacebar, as shown in the following screenshot. We are almost ready to start adding in gameplay, but before we do, we have a little bit of cleanup to do.

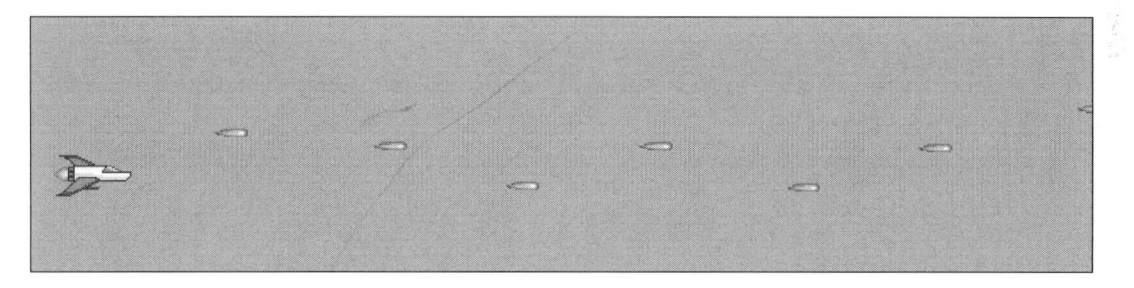

> If everything appears to be correct, but you are still unable to see the intended result, try refreshing your browser. Occasionally, browsers will keep the game in memory and won't load the updated version immediately.

Removing bullets from the world

Every time we create an instance of an object, it needs to be placed into the memory and the computer will need to keep a track of it. We have all these bullets that are going offscreen never to be seen again, but the computer sees them. This means that over time the computer could be trying to watch millions of wasted bullets, which in turn means that the game will start to slow down. As we don't want that to happen, we need to get rid of all these offscreen bullets.

1. Create a new Script and name it `scr_OffScreenRemoval`. This Script can be applied to any object in the game that goes offscreen and that we want to get rid of.

2. To remove an instance from the world, write the following code:
   `instance_destroy();`

3. In `obj_Bullet_Player`, add an **Outside Room** event from **Other** and apply the script. The **Outside Room** event is a special event that checks if the entire sprite of an instanced object is completely outside the room.

There we go! We now have a spaceship that moves around the screen, shoots bullets, and we keep the memory usage low. Let's make some enemies!

Constructing three little enemies

In this game we are going to have three unique types of enemies for the player to fight against: the FloatBot, the SpaceMine, and the Strafer. Each of these enemies will move differently and have a distinct attack. However, there are some common elements that they share, such as they will all have collision with bullets and the player, but not with each other.

It is always useful to think about the commonalities of the various objects as there may be ways to simplify and reduce the amount of work needed. In this case, as we are dealing with collision, we can use a **parent** object.

Making the enemy parent

Parenting object is an incredibly useful ability in GameMaker: Studio. It allows for one object, the **parent**, to pass its attributes down to other objects called **child** objects in what is generally known as **inheritance**. The best way to think of this relationship is that parents are a group and children are individuals. This means we can tell a group to do something and every individual will do it.

Chapter 3

We will create a parent object and use it for all the common collision events. This way we don't have to apply a new collision event for each different enemy.

1. Create a new Object and name it `obj_Enemy_Parent`. We do not need a Sprite for this Object, as it will never be seen in the game.
2. Create a new Script and name it `scr_Enemy_Collision_Player`.
3. Write the following code:

   ```
   with (other)
   {
           instance_destroy();
   }
   instance_destroy();
   ```

   Here we are using a `with` statement which allows us to apply code to another object. In this case, we are also able to use a special variable called `other` which is only available in collision events. This is because there are always two instances involved and only one collision between the two. Whoever has the code is identified as `self` and then there is the other. When there is a collision between `obj_Enemy_Parent` or any child of it with `obj_Player`, we will remove the player, and then remove the instance it collided with.

4. In `obj_Enemy_Parent`, add an `obj_Player` event from **Collision** and apply this collision script.

   Player collision now works, but currently nothing happens when bullets collide. We could use the same script if all the instances were going to be removed. In this case, we want to do something different if an enemy is hit by the player bullet. We want to award points.

5. Rather than creating a new script, let's just duplicate the collision Script we just created. In the Resource tree, hold right-click on `scr_Enemy_Collision_Player` and select **Duplicate**.

6. Name this script `scr_Enemy_Collision_Bullet`, and add the following line of code at the top of the script:

   ```
   score += 20;
   ```

   This will add 20 points to the total score of the game. Just to make sure everything is set up correctly, the entire code for this script should look like the following:

   ```
   score += 20;
   with (other)
   {
           instance_destroy();
   }
   instance_destroy();
   ```

Shoot 'em Up: Creating a Side-scrolling Shooter

7. Back in `obj_Enemy_Parent`, add an `obj_Bullet` event from **Collision** and apply `scr_Enemy_Collision_Bullet`. Enemies will now be destroyed and points will be awarded when they collide with bullets!

   The final event we need the parent object to watch over is to remove enemies if they go offscreen. We can't use the same script as our bullet cleanup script, because we will be spawning enemies offscreen to the right. Therefore, we need to make sure they are only removed when they go off the left-hand side.

8. Create a new Script and name it `scr_Enemy_Removal`.

9. Write the following code:

   ```
   if (x < 0)
   {
       instance_destroy();
   }
   ```

   First, we check to see if the x position of the instance is less than 0, or offscreen to the left. If it is, we remove it from the game.

10. In `obj_Enemy_Parent`, add an **Outside Room** event from **Other** and apply this script. We are done with the parent object and it should look like the following screenshot:

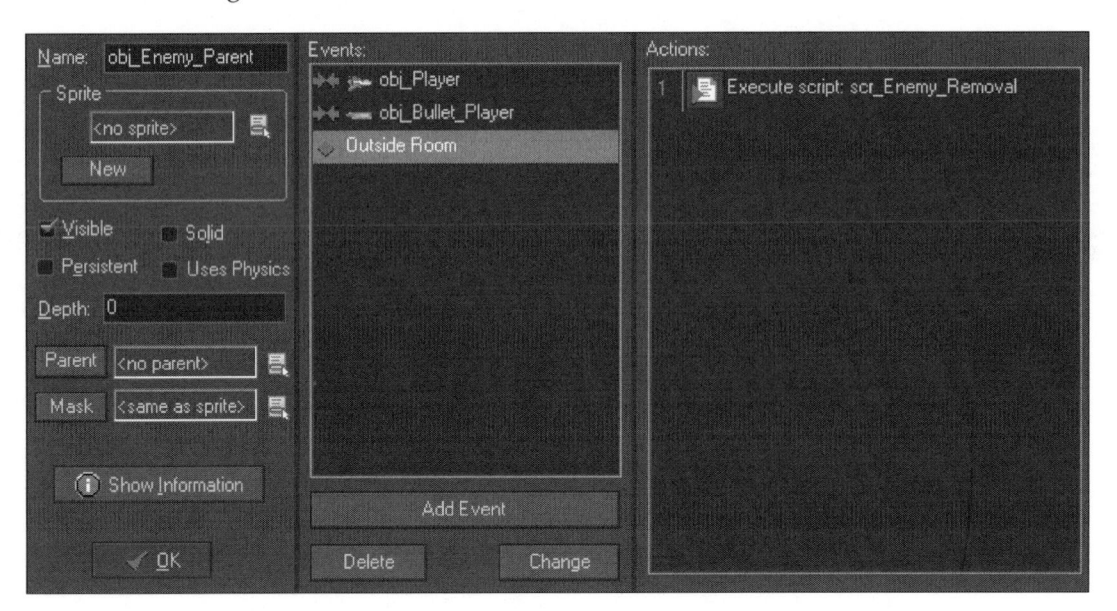

We now have a parent object that will deal with the bullet collision and remove the enemies when they go offscreen. Let's test it out by making some children.

Building the FloatBot

The FloatBot is the most basic enemy in the game. It will not fire a weapon, which makes it more of an obstacle to be avoided. The FloatBot will move across the screen to the left, bobbing up and down as it goes.

1. Create a new Sprite and name it `spr_FloatBot`.
2. Load the Sprite `Chapter 3/Sprites/FloatBot.gif` with **Remove Background** checked.
3. This is an animated Sprite whose shape changes on each frame. Therefore, we want to make sure the collision changes accordingly. In **Collision Checking**, check the box for **Precise Collision Checking**.
4. We want the origin to be in the center of this Sprite, so that it moves correctly when we add the bobbing motion. Set **Origin** to **X**: 16, **Y**: 16. Click on **OK**.

   We need two scripts to make the FloatBot fly the way we intend. On creation we will apply the horizontal movement, and then at every step after that we will adjust the vertical bobbing motion.

5. Create a new Script and name it `scr_FloatBot_Create`.
6. Write the following code:

   ```
   hspeed = -4;
   angle = 0;
   ```

   The negative value of the horizontal speed means that it will move to the left. `angle` is a variable we will be using in the next script for the bobbing motion.

7. Create a new Script and name it `scr_FloatBot_Step`.
8. To get the vertical motion we desire, we are going to use some simple trigonometry. Write the following code:

   ```
   vspeed = sin(angle) * 8;
   angle += 0.1
   ```

   Here we are changing the vertical speed based on the sine value of the variable angle in radians, multiplied by a base speed of 8. We also increase the value of `angle` every step, which is necessary to have it follow the sine wave.

9. Create a new Object, name it `obj_FloatBot`, and set `spr_FloatBot` as the Sprite.
10. We want to make this object a child, so in the **Parent** drop-down box, select `obj_Enemy` Parent.

Shoot 'em Up: Creating a Side-scrolling Shooter

11. Add a **Create** event and apply the `scr_FloatBot_Create` script.
12. Add a **Step** event and apply the `scr_FloatBot_Step` script. The FloatBot is now ready for testing and should look like the following screenshot:

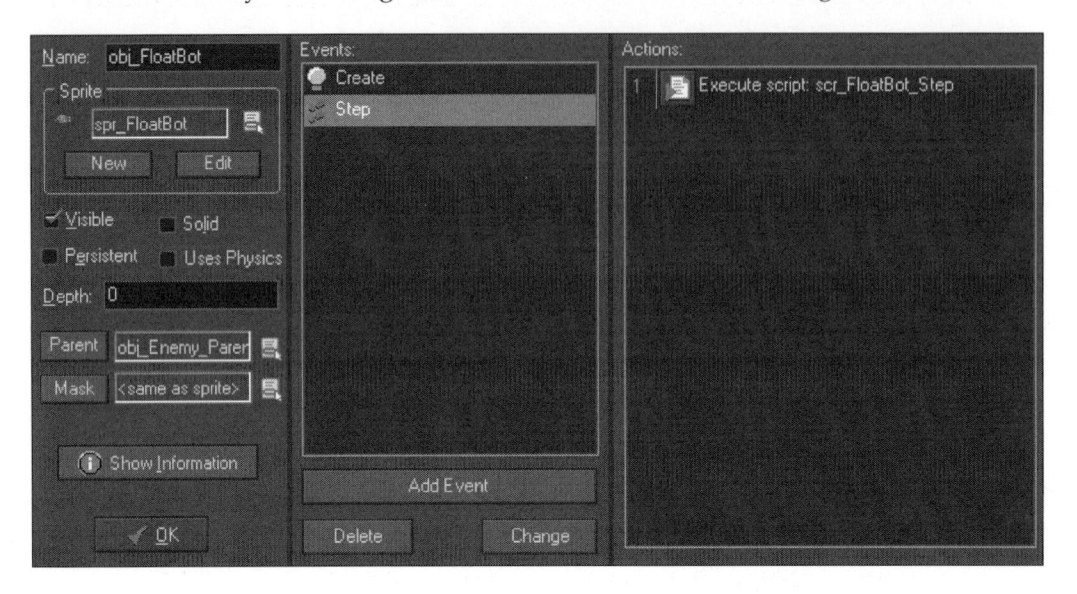

13. Reopen the room `TheGame` and place an instance of `obj_FloatBot` somewhere on the right-hand side of the screen.
14. Run the game.

If everything is working correctly the FloatBot should move across the screen to the left and have a bob up and down around 240 pixels in height in a similar pattern as shown in the next screenshot. If we hit the FloatBot with a bullet, both the bullet and the FloatBot will disappear. We have also successfully created a parent-child relationship. Let's create another!

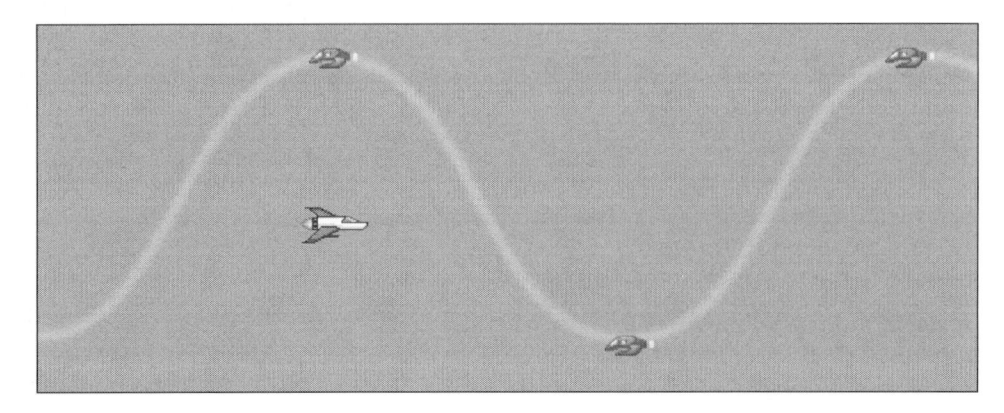

Creating the SpaceMine

The SpaceMine is going to be a slow moving object that will shoot a ring of bullets if the player gets too close. As this is going to require two objects, we should always start with the simplest one, the bullet.

1. Create a new Sprite and name it `spr_Bullet_SpaceMine`. Load `Chapter 3/Sprites/Bullet_SpaceMine.gif` with **Remove Background** checked.

2. Center the origin. We don't need to change **Collision Checking**, as a square will work fine for this object.

3. Create a new Object, name it `obj_Bullet_SpaceMine`, and set the Sprite to `spr_Bullet_SpaceMine`.

4. Create a new Script and name it `scr_Bullet_SpaceMine_Create`.

5. This time we want to use the instance properties of `speed` and `direction`, as we will require the direction to be set later. Write the following code:

   ```
   speed = 16;
   direction = 180;
   ```

6. In `obj_Bullet_SpaceMine`, add a **Create** event and apply this script.

7. We need to add collision to the bullet and to do this quickly, we can reuse the `scr_Enemy_Collision_Player` script. Add an `obj_Player` event from **Collision** and apply the script. We are done with the bullet for now, as can be seen in the following screenshot:

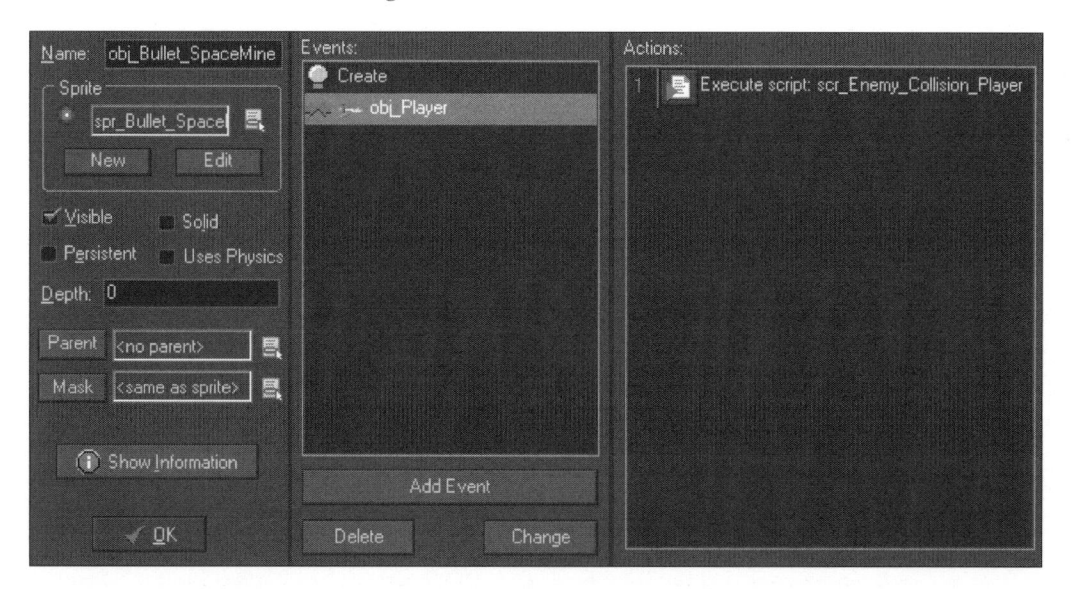

[93]

Shoot 'em Up: Creating a Side-scrolling Shooter

8. Time to build the SpaceMine itself. Create a new Sprite, name it `spr_SpaceMine`, and load `Chapter 3/Sprites/SpaceMine.gif` with **Remove Background** checked. As you can see, the SpaceMine has animated blinking lights.

9. Center the origin and check **Precise Collision Checking**.

10. We want a shooting sound when the SpaceMine fires, so create a new Sound, `snd_Bullet_SpaceMine` and load `Chapter 3/Sounds/Bullet_SpaceMine.wav`. We won't be attaching this to the bullets themselves as we will be creating eight bullets, but we only need the sound to be played once.

11. Set **Kind** to **Normal Sound** if it isn't already, and click on **OK**. Create a new Object and name it `obj_SpaceMine`.

12. Set **Sprite** to `spr_SpaceMine` and **Parent** to `obj_Enemy_Parent`.

13. Create a new Script and name it `scr_SpaceMine_Create`.

    We need the SpaceMine to do a few things. It is going to fire bullets, so we will need a variable to control when it shoots. It needs to move across the screen, so we need to apply velocity. Finally, we will want to slow down the animation so that it doesn't blink too fast.

14. Write the following code:

    ```
    hspeed = -2;
    canFire = false;
    image_speed = 0.2;
    ```

    First, we are setting the horizontal speed to move slowly to the left. `canFire` is a Boolean variable that will determine if it is to shoot or not. Finally, `image_speed` sets the speed of the animation. At a speed of `0.2`, it animates at 20 percent of normal, or in other words, each frame of animation will be held for five steps.

15. In `obj_SpaceMine`, add a **Create** event and apply this script.

16. Create another new script and name it `scr_SpaceMine_Step`.

    Each step we will want to see whether the player is within proximity of the SpaceMine. If the player is too close, the SpaceMine will start firing rings of bullets. We don't want a stream of bullets, so we are going to need to add a delay between each firing.

17. Write the following code:
    ```
    if ( distance_to_object( obj_Player ) <= 200 && canFire == false )
    {
        alarm[0] = 60;
        sound_play(snd_Bullet_SpaceMine)
        for (i = 0; i < 8; i += 1)
        {
            bullet = instance_create(x,y,obj_Bullet_SpaceMine);
            bullet.direction = 45 * i;
                bullet.hspeed -= 2;
        }
        canFire = true;
    }
    ```

    We start by checking two statements; the distance between the SpaceMine and `obj_Player`, and whether we are able to shoot. The distance we have chosen is `200` pixels, which should be enough space for the player to avoid triggering it occasionally. If the player is in range and we can shoot, we set `alarm` for `60` steps (2 seconds) and play the bullet sound once.

    > An alarm is an event that, when triggered, will execute code a single time.

    To create the ring of bullets we will use a `for` loop. When we create an instance of an object it returns the unique ID of that instance. We need to capture this in a variable, so that we can talk to the object and affect it. Here we are using a variable called `bullet` which is an instance of `obj_Bullet_SpaceMine`. We can then change the properties of the bullet such as direction. In this case, each bullet will be offset by 45 degrees. We also apply some additional `hspeed` to the bullets, so that they move along with the SpaceMine. Finally, we set the `canFire` variable to `true` to indicate that we have fired our bullets.

18. In `obj_SpaceMine`, add a **Step** event and apply this script.
19. We are almost done with the SpaceMine, we just need to add some code to an alarm that we can trigger, so that it can shoot more than once. Create a new Script and name it `scr_SpaceMine_Alarm0`.

Shoot 'em Up: Creating a Side-scrolling Shooter

20. Set the `canFire` variable back to `false`:

    ```
    canFire = false;
    ```

21. In `obj_SpaceMine`, add an **Alarm 0** event and apply this script. We are now done with the SpaceMine and it should look like the following screenshot:

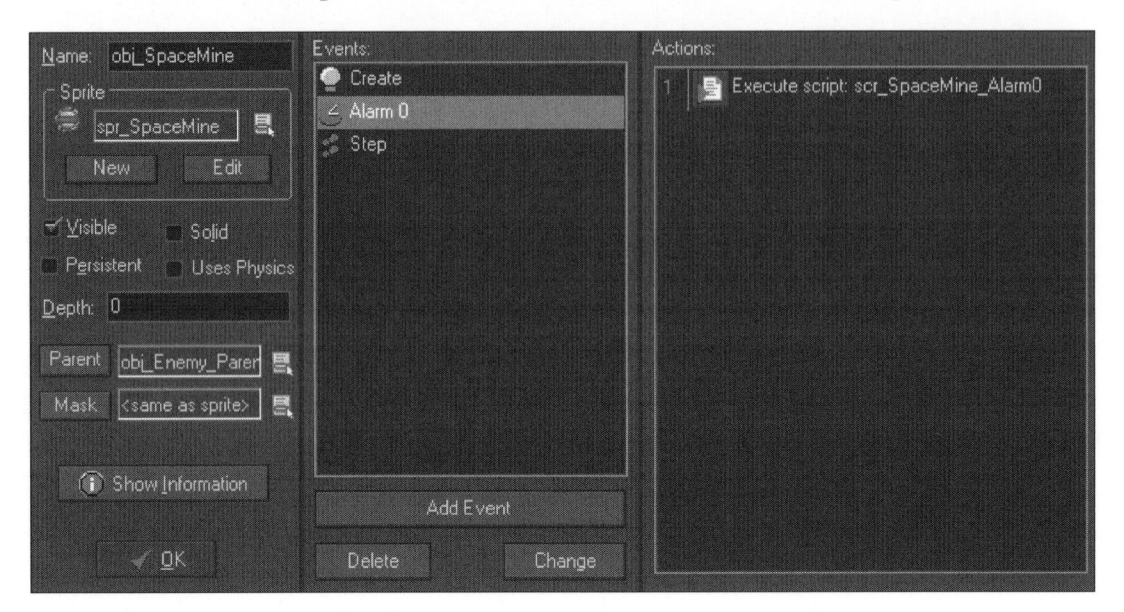

22. Open `TheGame`, add an instance of `obj_SpaceMine` on the right-hand side of the screen, and then run the game.

If everything is set up properly, the SpaceMine will slowly move across the screen to the left and blink. When the player approaches the SpaceMine, eight bullets should blast out from it as seen in the next screenshot. Every two seconds, another ring will be fired from this instance, so long as the player is still within range. If the SpaceMine is hit by one of the player bullets, it will be destroyed. Finally, if the player collides with the enemy's bullet the player disappears. Let's move on to our final enemy!

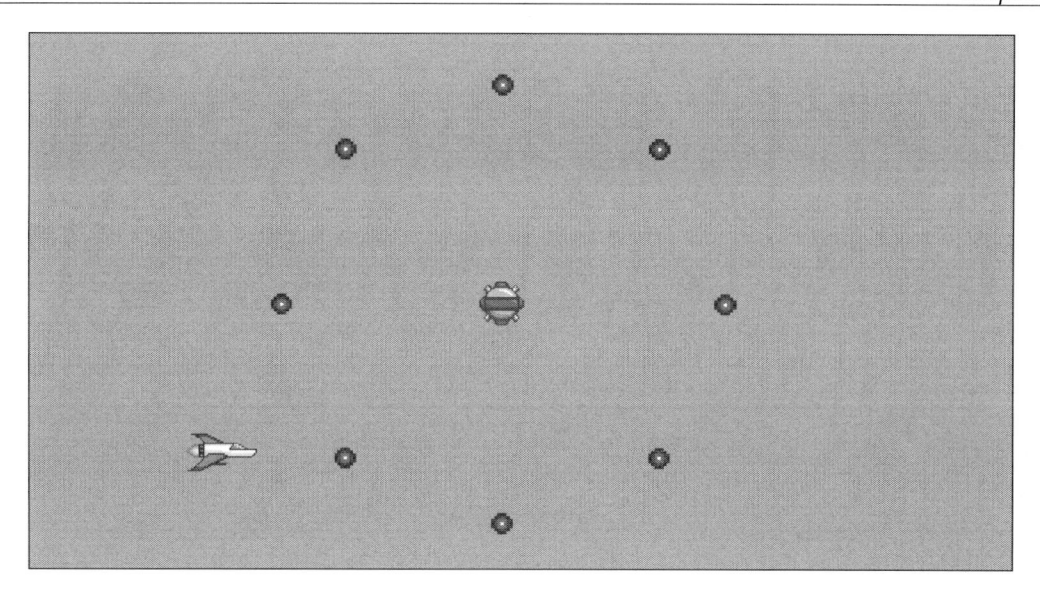

Making the Strafer

The Strafer is the most dangerous enemy in the game. It moves very quickly in a straight line and will target the player no matter where they are. Once again, there are two objects needed, so let's start with the bullet.

1. Create a new Sprite and name it `spr_Bullet_Strafer`. Load `Chapter 3/Sprites/Bullet_Strafer.gif` with **Remove Background** checked.
2. Center the origin.
3. Create a new Object and name it `obj_Bullet_Strafer` and set the Sprite to `spr_Bullet_Strafer`.
4. We want a unique shooting sound, so create a new Sound, `snd_Bullet_Strafer`, and load `Chapter 3/Sounds/Bullet_Strafer.wav`.
5. Set **Kind** to **Normal Sound** if it isn't already, and click on **OK**.
6. Create a new Script and name it `scr_Bullet_Strafer_Create`.
7. This script will be similar to `scr_Bullet_SpaceMine_Create`, except that this bullet is faster and playing the bullet sound. Write the following code:
   ```
   speed = 20;
   direction = 180;
   sound_play(snd_Bullet_Strafer);
   ```

8. In `obj_Bullet_Strafer`, add a **Create** event and apply this script.
9. As with the other enemy bullet, let's add collision to the bullet by reusing the `scr_Enemy_Collision_Player` script. Add an `obj_Player` event from **Collision** and apply the script. We are done with this bullet, so let's build the enemy.
10. Create a new Sprite and name it `spr_Strafer`, and load `Chapter 3/Sprites/Strafer.gif` with **Remove Background** checked.
11. We want the bullet to come from the front of the ship, so we need to manually move the origin to the proper location. Set **Origin** to **X**: 0, **Y**: 19.
12. Create a new Object and name it `obj_Strafer`.
13. Set **Sprite** to `spr_Strafer` and **Parent** to `obj_Enemy_Parent`.
14. Create a new Script and name it `scr_Strafer_Create`.
15. The Strafer is going to move quickly across the screen and fire bullets at the player constantly. Write the following code:

```
hspeed = -10;
alarm[0] = 10;
```

Much like the SpaceMine, we have set `hspeed` to move left, and are also setting an alarm so that the Strafer will start shooting immediately.

16. In `obj_Strafer`, add a **Create** event and apply this script.
17. We only need one more script and that is for the alarm. Create a new Script and name it `scr_Strafer_Alarm0`.
18. When the alarm goes off, we need to create a bullet, launch it at the player, and then reset the alarm so that it can fire again. To do this write the following code:

```
bullet = instance_create(x, y, obj_Bullet_Strafer);
if (instance_exists(obj_Player))
{
    bullet.direction = point_direction(x,y, obj_Player.x,obj_Player.x, obj_Player.y);
}
alarm[0] = irandom(30) + 15;
```

We start here by creating an instance of `obj_Bullet_Strafer`. When an instance is created, the function returns the unique ID of that instance; we then capture it in a variable, such as `bullet`. Next, we query whether the player exists or not. This is a very important step, as without this check if the player is dead and the Strafer tries to target it, the game will error out and crash.

[98]

If the player does exist, we set the bullet direction at the player. This is done through the `point_direction` function that takes any two points in space (x1, y1) and (x2, y2) and returns the angle in degrees.

Finally, we reset the alarm. In this case, to make things more interesting we have added a bit of randomness to it. The `irandom` function will return a whole number between zero and the number you pass to it. The code we have here will give us a random value between `0` and `30` and we will add `15` to it. This means a new bullet will be created between every half second to a second and a half.

19. In `obj_Strafer`, add an **Alarm 0** event and apply this script.

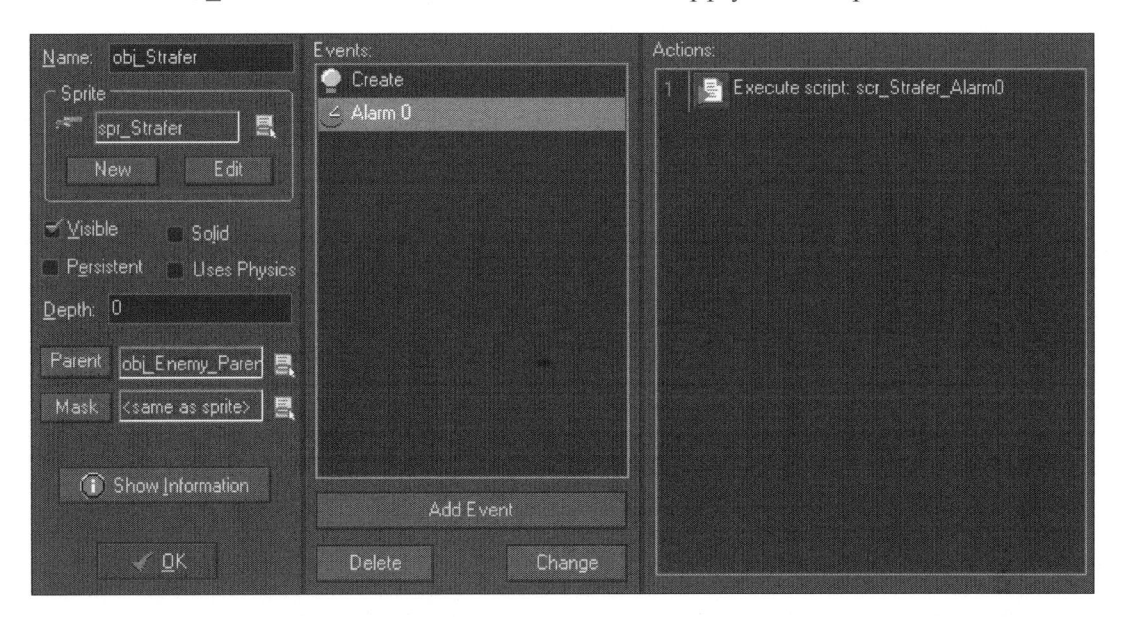

20. The Strafer is now complete, so let's test it out and place one in `TheGame` on the left-hand side.

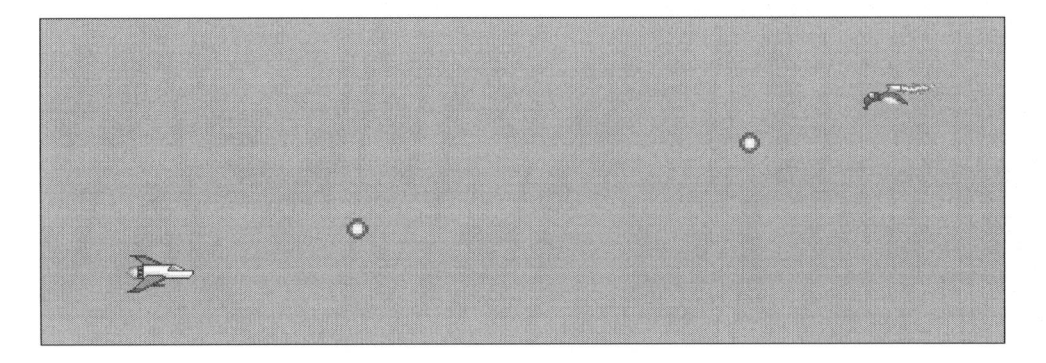

Shoot 'em Up: Creating a Side-scrolling Shooter

If everything is working correctly, the Strafer will quickly move across the screen and fire bullets directly at the position of the player. Make sure you move the player around the room to make sure it fires in all directions! The player should be able to shoot and destroy the Strafer. If hit by the Strafer's bullet, the player should disappear.

The enemies for the game are all complete; now we just need a way to populate the game world. Let's bring in an Overlord!

Controlling the game with the Overlord

In this game, we will be using the Overlord, the master controller of the game, to control the spawning of enemies, monitor the player's lives, and deal with the win/lose condition. The win condition will simply be to survive for two minutes against waves of enemies. The lose condition will be that the player runs out of lives.

Spawning waves of enemies

We need to start by creating the wave of enemies, so that the game is playable. For this, we will utilize a looping timeline to spawn the various enemies. We are going to have three different waves, each one spawning a different enemy every two seconds.

1. Create three new scripts, and name them: `scr_Wave_Strafer`, `scr_Wave_SpaceMine`, and `scr_Wave_FloatBot`.

2. We will start with the wave of Strafer, as it will be the simplest wave. Write the following code in `scr_Wave_Strafer`:

   ```
   instance_create(room_width - 64, room_height/2 - 64, obj_Strafer);
   instance_create(room_width - 64, room_height/2 + 64, obj_Strafer);
   ```

   Here we spawn two instances of the Strafer located `64` pixels off the right-hand side of the screen. This will ensure that we don't see them pop into existence. We have also offset them by `64` pixels from the vertical center of the room.

3. For the SpaceMine, we will want them vertically placed in random positions to keep things interesting. Write the following code in `scr_Wave_SpaceMine`:

   ```
   placeY = irandom_range(64, room_height - 64);
   instance_create(room_width - 64, placeY, obj_SpaceMine);
   ```

   We are creating a variable called `placeY` to hold a value for the vertical position. GameMaker: Studio has a special function, `irandom_range`, which will return a whole number between any two numbers passed to it. The numbers we used will ensure that the SpaceMine will remain at least 64 pixels away from the top and bottom of the screen. We then use the `placeY` variable when we create the instance.

4. The FloatBot is going to use a similar setup for placement on the vertical axis, but we will want three instances flying in a "V" formation. Write the following code in `scr_Wave_FloatBot`:

   ```
   placeY = irandom_range(80, room_height - 80);
   instance_create(room_width - 32, placeY, obj_FloatBot);
   instance_create(room_width - 64, placeY - 32, obj_FloatBot);
   instance_create(room_width - 64, placeY + 32, obj_FloatBot);
   ```

   Here we are using the `placeY` variable again, but the range of numbers is narrower. We need some extra padding, so that all three planes stay onscreen. The first instance created is the front unit of the formation. The next two instances spawn 32 pixels behind and offset 32 pixels above and below the first.

5. All the waves are scripted, so we can now implement them in a Time Line. When first implementing a Time Line, it is useful to keep the numbers simple, such as two seconds apart. Properly balancing the timing comes during the polish phase of a game's development, and spending too much time trying to get this right before all content is in is most likely wasted time. Create a new Time Line and name it `tm_Wave_Spawning`.

6. Click on **Add**, set **Indicate the Moment** as 60, and apply the `scr_Wave_FloatBot` script. This will spawn the first enemy into the game for two seconds.

7. We will want to add the SpaceMines two seconds later. Click on **Add**, set **Indicate the Moment** as 120, and apply the `scr_Wave_SpaceMine` script.

Shoot 'em Up: Creating a Side-scrolling Shooter

8. Finally we bring in the Strafer after six seconds. Click on **Add**, set **Indicate the Moment** as 180, and apply the scr_Wave_Strafer script. The Time Line is now ready to be used and should look like the following screenshot:

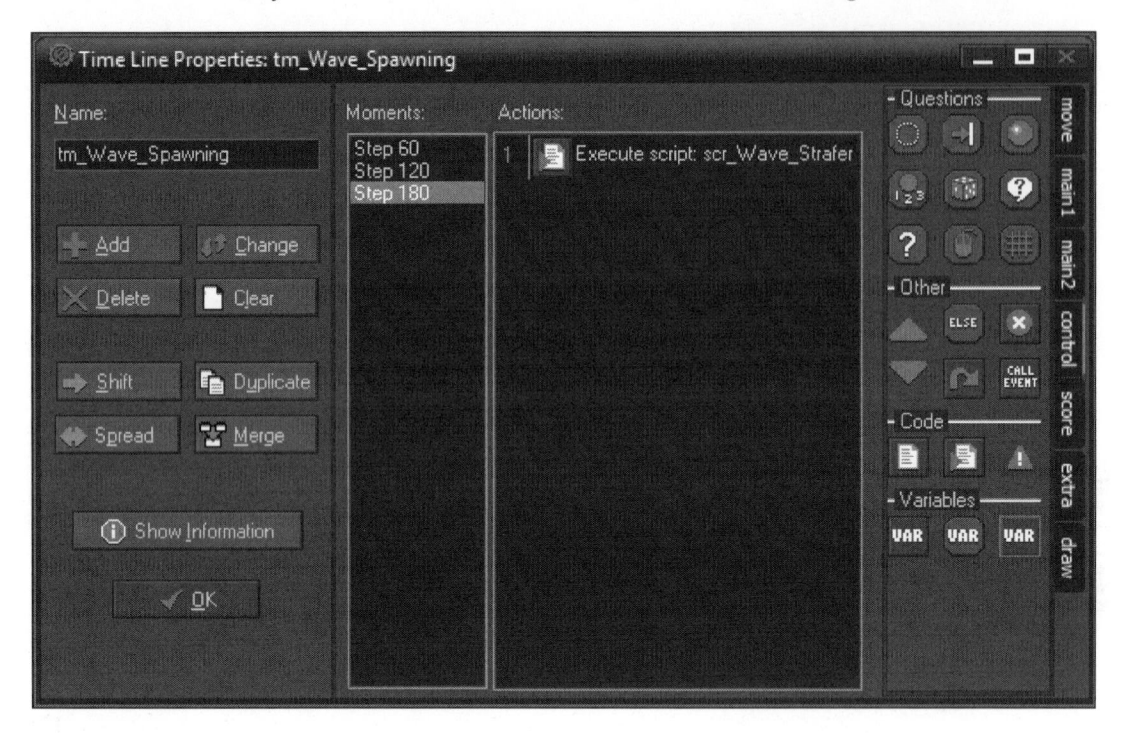

Building the Overlord

We are now ready to start building the Overlord and apply our spawning system.

1. Create a new Object and name it obj_Overlord.
2. There is no Sprite needed, so set **Sprite** to **no sprite**.
3. We will start the Time Line immediately upon creation of the Overlord. Create a new Script, name it scr_Overlord_Create, and write the following code:

   ```
   timeline_index = tm_Wave_Spawning;
   timeline_running = true;
   timeline_loop = true;
   ```

The first line of code defines what Time Line we want to run, in our case we only have one: `tm_Wave_Spawning`. Next, we start the Time Line and then tell it to loop. These last two are Boolean variables, which means that they can only be turned on and off.

4. In the Overlord, add a **Create** event and apply this script.
5. Open **TheGame** and place a single instance of the Overlord anywhere in the room. The location does not matter, but the upper-left corner is a common place to put it.
6. Remove any instances of the enemies that remain in the room. There should be only one instance of the Player and one of the Overlord as can be seen in the following screenshot:

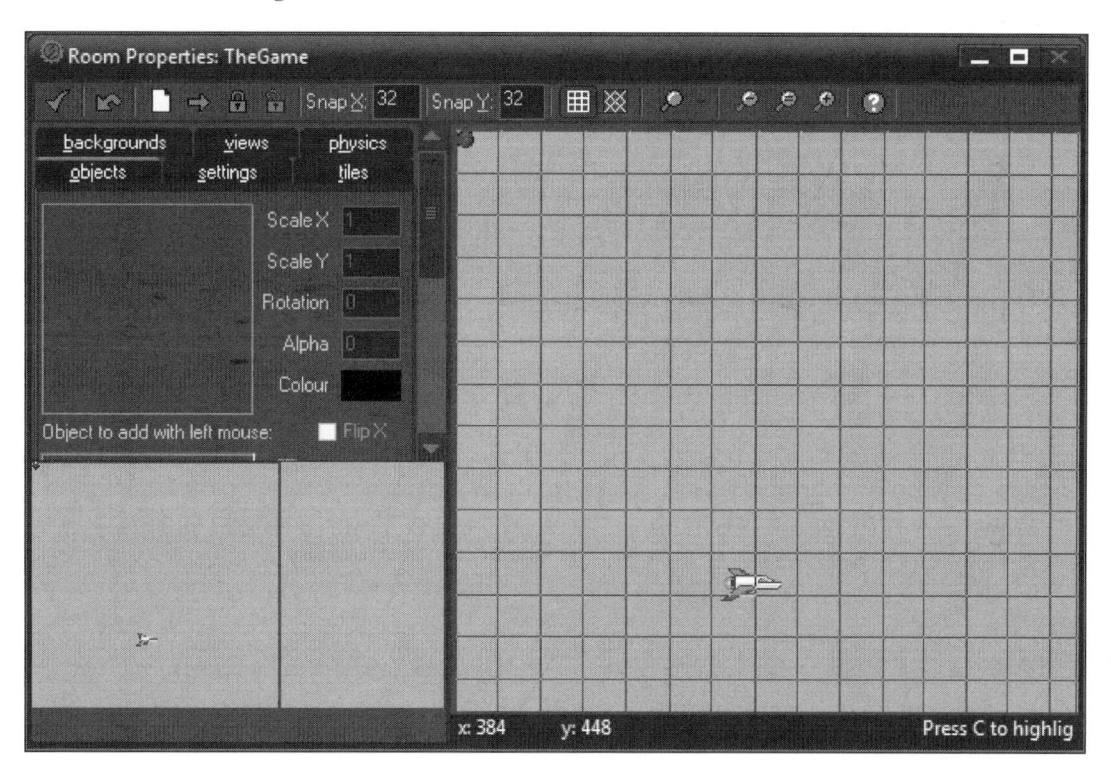

7. Run the game.

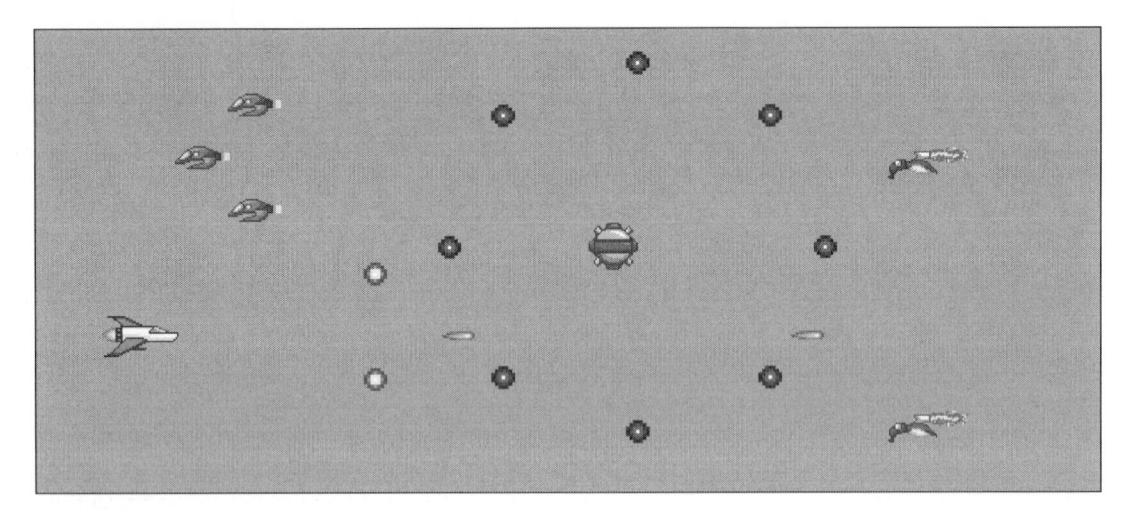

The game now has enemies! It will take a couple of seconds for the first enemy, the FloatBots, to appear, but after that the enemies will continue to spawn forever. At this point we have most of the core gameplay implemented as follows:

- We can move the player around the screen, but not out of it
- We can shoot and destroy enemies
- Enemies can shoot and destroy the player
- Enemies will spawn continuously

The only element remaining is very obvious when playing the game at this stage; the player can die, but the game doesn't stop. We need to implement the win/lose condition.

Dealing with the life and death of the player

As this is a game about survival, we will want the win/lose condition to be fairly simple. For the win condition, we will make the player survive for a set amount of time. The lose condition will be the player dying, but we don't want to come across as too hard to play, so we will give the player three lives. This means that we are going to need to respawn the player. Finally, to get this to work properly, we will need to give the Overlord some more duties.

Setting up the win condition

The win condition for this game is to survive for a set amount of time. We can achieve this through the use of an alarm and a variable to signal to the Overlord that the player has survived.

1. We will need to set up some variables for the lives, win, and lose conditions. Reopen scr_Overlord_Create and add the following code at the bottom:

    ```
    lives = 3;
    isVictory = false;
    isDefeat = false;
    ```

    GameMaker: Studio has a few built-in global variables including `lives`. This variable is accessible by every instance in the game and never goes away. Here we have set it to 3 and will use that as our starting point. We also create two other variables, `isVictory` and `isDefeat`, which we have set to `false`. The reason we are using two variables to represent winning and losing the game instead of one is that we will want to check these during gameplay when they have neither won nor lost.

2. We can also set our win condition in this script by setting an alarm for 90 seconds. To do this add the following line of code after the code in step 1:

    ```
    alarm[0] = 2700;
    ```

    The scr_Overlord_Create script should now look like the following in total:

    ```
    timeline_index = tm_Wave_Spawning;
    timeline_running = true;
    timeline_loop = true;

    lives = 3;
    isVictory = false;
    isDefeat = false;

    alarm[0] = 2700;
    ```

3. Next, we have to set up a script for the alarm event for the victory condition. Create a new Script, name it scr_Overlord_Victory, and write the following code:

    ```
    timeline_running = false;
    with ( obj_Enemy_Parent )
    {
        instance_destroy();
    }
    alarm[1] = 90;
    isVictory = true;
    ```

Shoot 'em Up: Creating a Side-scrolling Shooter

The very first thing we do is stop the Time Line, as we don't want any more enemies to spawn. The next step is to remove all enemies still alive in the game. We do this by using a `with` statement that is going to execute code to all instances of `obj_Enemy_Parent`. As all the enemies are children of this object, they too will be destroyed. We will eventually want to restart the game, so we set another alarm for three seconds. Finally, we set the `isVictory` variable to true.

4. In `obj_Overlord`, add an **Alarm 0** event and apply the victory script.
5. Let's wrap this up by creating the restart script. Create a new Script, name it `scr_Overlord_GameRestart` and write this code:

   ```
   game_restart();
   ```

6. Add an **Alarm 1** event and apply this restart script. The win condition is now working, so feel free to try it out.

Respawning with a Ghost object

We can now move on to the losing condition and respawning. When the player dies, we don't want to have the player respawn immediately, but instead have a smaller buffer of invulnerability. To do this, we will want to create a Ghost object that will temporarily stand in for the player.

1. Create a new Sprite, name it `spr_Ghost`, and load `Chapter 3/Sprites/Ghost.gif` with **Remove Background** checked. It looks just like the plane, but is slightly transparent and flickers when animated.
2. We need to set the origin to be exactly the same as the origin of `spr_Player`. Set **Origin** to **X**: 43, **Y**: 22, and then click on **OK**.
3. Create a new Object, name it `obj_Ghost`, and apply `spr_Ghost` as the Sprite.
4. When the player dies, we are going to have the Ghost appear offscreen to the left and then move into the gameplay area. Create a new Script, name it `scr_Ghost_Create`, and write the following code:

   ```
   x = -64;
   y = room_height * 0.5;
   hspeed = 4;
   ```

   We start by setting the x coordinate to be offscreen by 64 pixels. We then center the Ghost vertically by setting the y coordinate to half of the room height. Finally, we are applying a positive velocity to the Ghost, so that it starts moving on its own.

5. Add a **Create** event to `obj_Ghost` and apply this script.

6. The Ghost is going to move on the screen, and we will need to change it into the player at some point. In our case, we will make the switch once the Ghost has passed quarter way into the gameplay area. Create a new script, name it scr_Ghost_Step, and write the following code:

```
if ( x >= 200 )
{
    hspeed = 0;
    instance_change(obj_Player, true);
}
```

Here we check to see if the Ghost's x coordinate has crossed 200 pixels or not. If it has, we stop the forward velocity and then we transform into the player. The instance_change function asks for two arguments: what object to transform into and whether we want to run the **Create** event of this new object.

7. Add a **Step** event to obj_Ghost and apply this script.

8. One issue we will encounter with this setup is that the player has no control of the Ghost, and could end up in a dangerous position near an enemy when they transform. We don't want that, so let's give the player some limited controls. We can reuse the existing scr_Player_Key_Up and scr_Player_Key_Down scripts, so that the player has vertical movement. Add the appropriate Keyboard events and attach these scripts.

The Ghost Object's properties should look like the following screenshot and is now ready to become a part of the game. We just need to change what happens when the player is hit.

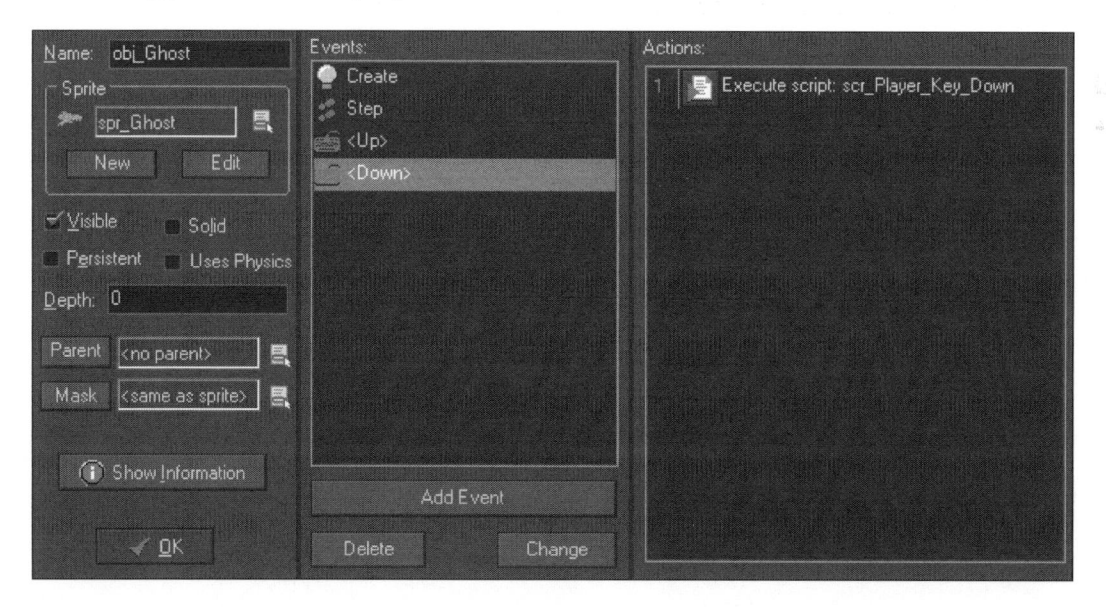

9. Reopen `scr_Enemy_Collision_Player`.
10. Currently, we are destroying both the bullet and the player. We need to change the `with` statement to allow for respawning. Remove line **3**:

```
instance_destroy();
```

And replace it with:

```
if ( lives > 0 )
{
    instance_change(obj_Ghost, true);
}
else
{
    instance_destroy();
}
lives -= 1;
```

We only want to become a Ghost if we have lives available, so we start by checking that. If we do have at least one life, we transform the Player into a Ghost. Otherwise, we just destroy the Player and the Player will be permanently dead. Finally, we subtract a life every time, whether we have lives or not. The final code should look like the following:

```
with ( other )
{
    if ( lives > 0 )
    {
        instance_change(obj_Ghost, true);
    }
    else
    {
        instance_destroy();
    }
    lives -= 1;
}
instance_destroy();
```

At this point we can play the game. Notice that when the player dies:

- The player disappears
- A Ghost is created and moves into the play area
- The Ghost can move up and down
- The Ghost turns back into the Player

This of course happens three times and then the player disappears forever. The rest of the game, however, is continuing on as if nothing happened. We need to add in the defeat condition.

11. Create a new Script, `scr_Overlord_Step`, and write the following code:
    ```
    if ( lives < 0 && isDefeat == false ) {
        alarm[1] = 90;
        isDefeat = true;
    }
    ```

    Every step in this code will check to see if the player has any lives left. If the player has no lives left and the variable `isDefeat` is still `false`, it will set the *Restart Game* alarm for three seconds. Lastly, we set the `isDefeat` variable to `true`, so that we don't run this code again.

12. In `obj_Overlord`, add a **Step** event and apply this script. The game will now restart after the player dies three times.

The core mechanics of the game are now complete, but it's not very clear to the player as to what is going on. The player can die and respawn a few times, but there is no indication of how many lives are left. Nor is there any information being displayed on whether the player has won or lost the game. Let's fix this!

Drawing the user interface

One of the most important elements in creating a great game is ensuring that the player has all the information they need to play the game. Much of this is usually presented in the **heads-up display**, otherwise known as the **HUD**. Every game has different components that can be a part of the HUD including things we need such as scoreboards and life counters.

1. To start with, we are going to need a font for the text we intend to display. We have supplied a font called **Retroheavyfuture** for use in this game that will need to be installed on your computer. To install this font on a Windows 7 computer, right-click on `Chapter 3/Fonts/RETRRG__.ttf` and click on **Install**. Then follow the directions when prompted.

2. Back into GameMaker: Studio, create a new font and name it `fnt_Scoreboard`.

3. Select **Retroheavyfuture** as **Font**.

4. Set **Size** under **Style** to `16`.

[109]

Shoot 'em Up: Creating a Side-scrolling Shooter

5. We want a decent sized font to display the score and lives during the game. It should look like the following screenshot, so click on **OK**:

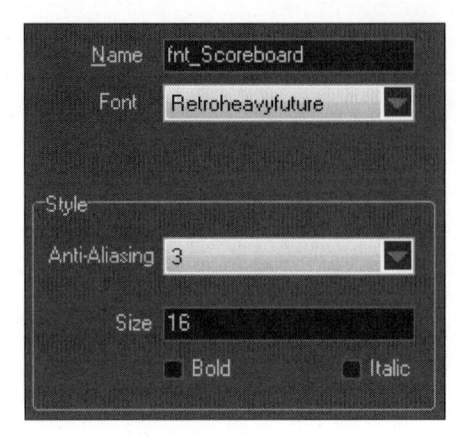

6. We will need a second version of the font when we display the win/lose condition. Create a new font and name it `fnt_WinLose`.

7. Once again, select **Retroheavyfuture** as **Font**, but this time set **Size** to 32. We now have all the in-game fonts we need, so click on **OK**.

8. Let's move on to the new Script, `scr_Overlord_Draw`. We will start by setting the color and the font for the scoreboard text with this code:

```
draw_set_color(c_white);
draw_set_font(fnt_Scoreboard);
```

The first line of code sets the color with one of GameMaker: Studio's premade colors, `c_white`. The next line then sets the scoreboard as the font.

> Setting colors are globally applied to the `draw` events. That means if you don't set a color, it will use the color last set, regardless of the object.

9. With the font set we can start applying the HUD. We will start with the player lives. Add this code to the script:

```
draw_set_halign(fa_left);
if ( lives >= 0 )
{
    draw_text(8, 0, "Lives: " + string(lives));
} else {
    draw_text(8, 0, "Lives: " );
}
```

To ensure the text is properly formatted, we set the horizontal alignment of the text to be aligned left. The text itself needs to be a string, which can be done in two ways. First, anything in quotation marks is considered a string, such as `"Lives: "`. If we want to pass a number, such as the amount of lives we have, we need to convert it by passing through the string function. As seen here, if we have lives remaining we can concatenate the two things to create a single sentence *Lives: 3* and draw it in the upper-left corner of the screen. If we are out of life, we draw the text without the concatenated value.

10. The other HUD element we want is the score, which we will place on the opposite side of the screen in the upper-right corner. Add the following code:

    ```
    draw_set_halign(fa_right);
    draw_text(room_width-8, 0, "SCORE: " + string(score));
    ```

    As we did with the previous text, we are setting the horizontal alignment, this time to the right. We then place the text in the proper position using the same concatenation method for the score.

11. Let's test this out now by adding a **Draw GUI** event to `obj_Overlord` and apply this script.

12. Run the game. As seen in the next screenshot, the game should now display the lives in the upper-left corner and update each time the player dies. It should also display the score in the upper right-hand corner and increase with every enemy killed.

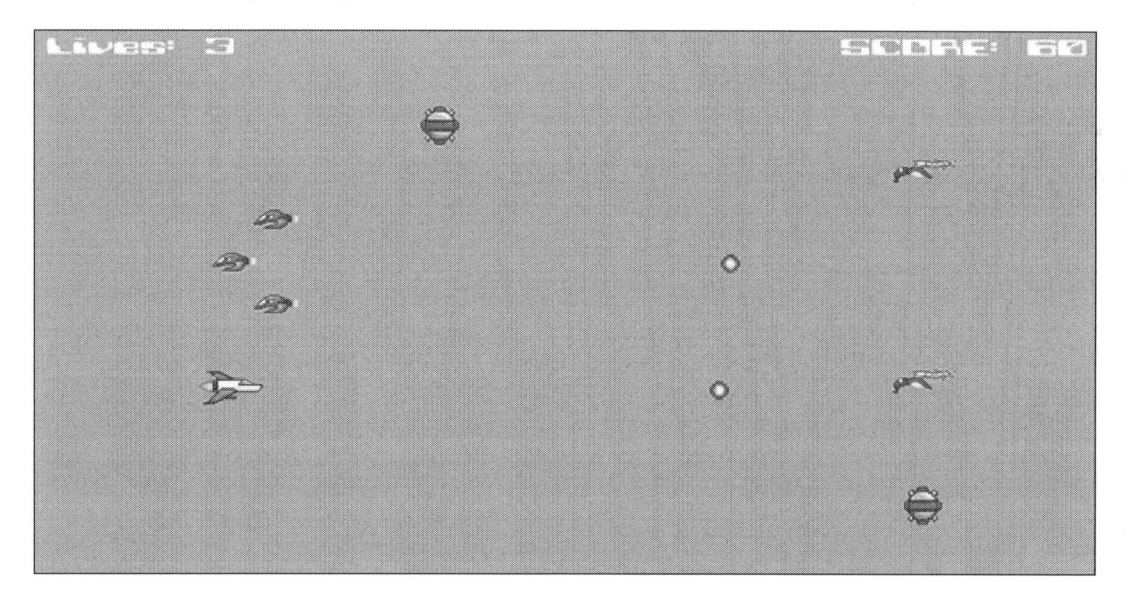

Shoot 'em Up: Creating a Side-scrolling Shooter

13. We now need to add the display for when the player wins or loses. Add the following code at the end of `scr_Overlord_Draw`:

    ```
    draw_set_font(fnt_WinLose);
    draw_set_halign(fa_center);
    if ( isVictory == true )
    {
        draw_text(room_width / 2, room_height/2, "VICTORY");
    }
    if ( isDefeat == true )
    {
        draw_text(room_width / 2, room_height/2, "DEFEAT");
    }
    ```

    We change the font to `fnt_WinLose` and set the horizontal alignment to be in the center. We don't want the text to be displayed all the time, instead we should only show either **VICTORY** or **DEFEAT** when it is appropriate. We have already implemented the code in the Overlord for the game condition, so we just check every step whether `isVictory` is `true` or `isDefeat` is `true`. As soon as the game is either won or lost, we draw the appropriate text in the center of the room.

    The complete `scr_Overlord_Draw` script should look like the following code:

    ```
    draw_set_color(c_white);
    draw_set_font(fnt_Scoreboard);

    draw_set_halign(fa_left);
    draw_text(8, 0, "LIVES: " + string(lives));

    draw_set_halign(fa_right);
    draw_text(room_width-8, 0, "SCORE: " + string(score));

    draw_set_font(fnt_WinLose);
    draw_set_halign(fa_center);
    if ( isVictory == true )
    {
        draw_text(room_width / 2, room_height/2, "VICTORY");
    }
    if ( isDefeat == true )
    {
        draw_text(room_width / 2, room_height/2, "DEFEAT");
    }
    ```

Adding the finishing details to the game

The game is now functionally complete, but it doesn't have any polish or the finishing details we would expect of a full game. There is no music, no background art, and no explosions! Let's fix that right now.

Adding the game music

We want the music to start at the beginning and play for the duration of the game. When the win/lose condition occurs, we want the music to fade out to let the player know that the game is over.

1. Create a new Sound and name it `snd_Music`.
2. Load `Chapter 3/Sounds/Music.mp3`. **Kind** should be set to **Background Music**.
3. Reopen `scr_Overlord_Create`. Since the Overlord controls the overall game, we will use it to control the music as well. After the last line of code, add the following:

    ```
    sound_play(snd_Music);
    sound_loop(snd_Music);
    volume = 1;
    sound_global_volume(volume);
    ```

    We start by playing the music and set it to loop. We then create a variable, `volume`, that we will use for controlling the sound level and the fade out. We have set the sound level to `1`, which is full volume. Finally, we set the global sound level, or master gain level, to the variable `volume`.

4. Reopen `scr_Overlord_Step`. To fade the music out we will need to lower the global volume over several steps, but only if the game has ended. After the last line of code, add the following:

    ```
    if ( isDefeat == true || isVictory == true )
    {
        volume -= 0.02;
        sound_global_volume(volume);
    }
    ```

    Here we check to see if either the win or lose condition has been set to `true`. If it has been, we decrease the volume variable by `0.02` and apply it to the master gain level. It will take 50 steps for the sound level to go from full volume to silent, which is about half the duration before the game restart kicks in.

Shoot 'em Up: Creating a Side-scrolling Shooter

5. Run the game. You should now hear the background music playing. If the player dies quickly three times and the defeat condition is triggered, you should hear the sound fade out.

Making the background move

This game takes place in outer space, so we will need to add in a space backdrop. In order for the game universe to feel as though the player is moving, we need to make the background shift constantly to the left.

1. Create a new Background and name it `bg_Starscape`.
2. Load `Chapter 3/Backgrounds/Starscape.gif` with **Remove Background** unchecked. This is all we need to do for this, so click on **OK**.
3. Open `TheGame` and select the **backgrounds** tab.
4. Set `bg_Starscape` as **background image**. It should happen automatically, but ensure that **Background 0** is highlighted and that **Visible when room starts** is checked.
5. The starscape is only going to move horizontally, therefore we only need **Tile Hor.** checked so that the image wraps around.
6. To move the background, set **Hor. Speed:** to -2. This will make it move to the left, which will make the player appear to move to the right. The settings should look like the following screenshot:

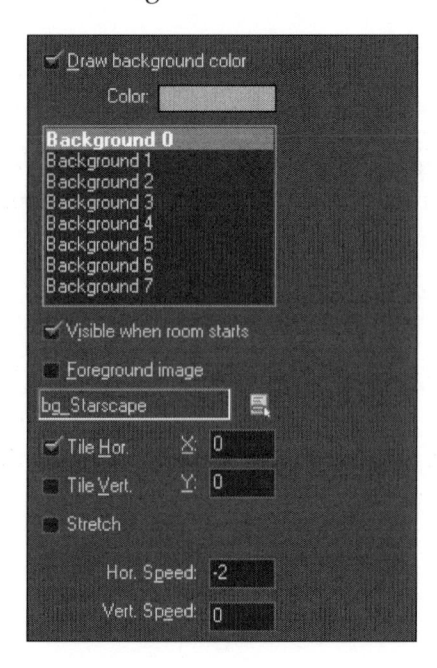

[114]

Chapter 3

7. Run the game. You should now see a moving starscape! Check out the following screenshot:

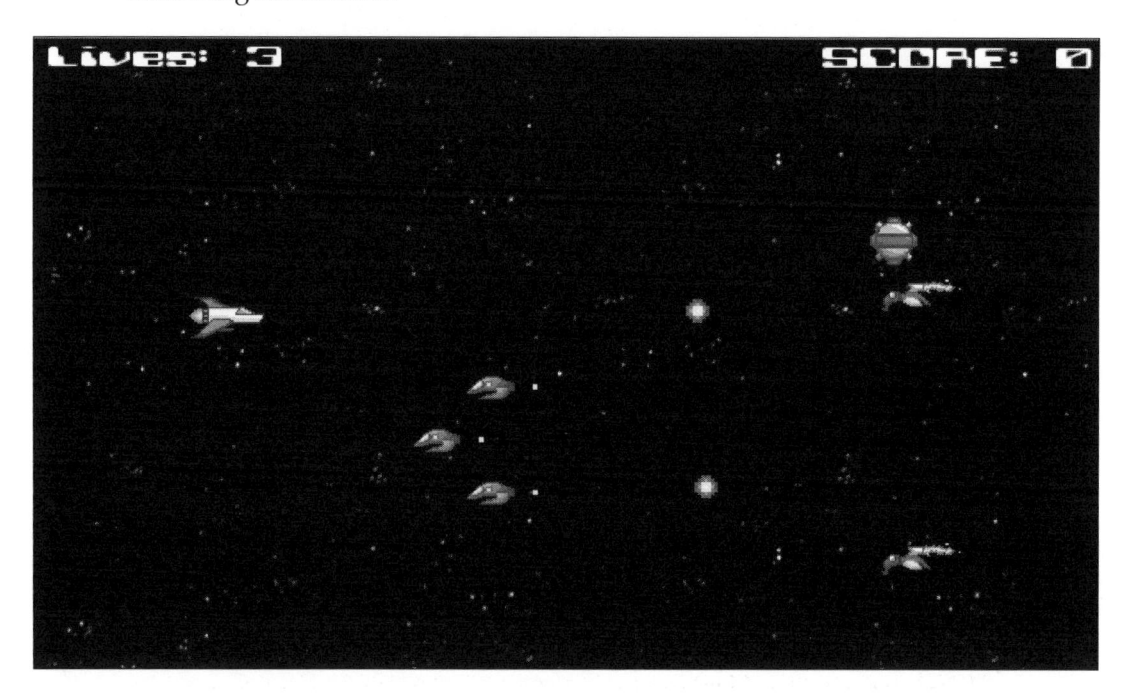

Creating the explosions

Having enemies just blink out of existence not only looks bad, it is not very rewarding to the player. Let's make this more exciting by adding in some explosions!

1. Create a new Sprite, spr_Explosion, and load Chapter 3/Sprites/Explosion.gif with **Remove Background** checked.
2. Set the origin to the center and click on **OK**.
3. Create a new Sound, snd_Explosion, and load Chapter 3/Sounds/Explosion.wav.
4. Set **Kind** to **Normal Sound** if it isn't already, and click on **OK**.
5. Create a new Object, obj_Explosion, and set the sprite to spr_Explosion.

   We want the explosion to make a sound, play its animation, and then remove itself from the game.

6. Create a new Script, scr_Explosion_Create, and write the following code to play the explosion sound a single time:

   ```
   sound_play(snd_Explosion);
   ```

[115]

7. Add a **Create** event and apply this script.
8. To get the explosion to remove itself is best done when the animation is finished. Luckily for us, GameMaker: Studio has an event for that. Add an **Animation End** event from **Other**, and then create a new Script to apply to it named `scr_Explosion_AnimEnd` with the following code to remove the instance:

```
instance_destroy();
```

9. The explosion is now prepared and all we have to do is spawn it when we destroy an enemy. Open `scr_Enemy_Collision_Bullet` and add the following line of code at the very top of the script on line **1**:

```
instance_create(x,y, obj_Explosion);
```

This will create an explosion right where the enemy is located. This needs to happen before we remove the enemy from the game.

10. Repeat this code addition with `scr_Enemy_Collision_Player`.
11. Run the game. You should now see explosions whenever something is destroyed as shown in the following screenshot:

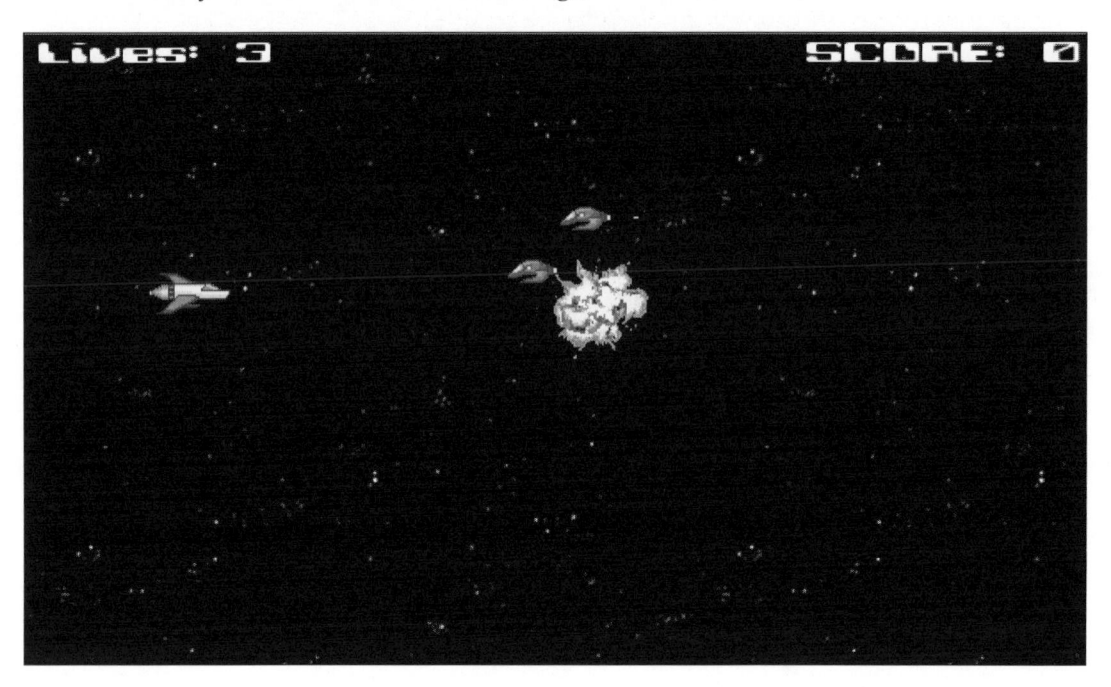

Summary

Congratulations! You have just finished creating your first side-scrolling shooter. We covered quite a lot in this chapter. We have applied all three methods of movement: manually adjusting the X and Y coordinates, using `hspeed` and `vspeed`, and setting the `speed` and `direction` variables. We are now able to add and remove instances from the game world dynamically. With the bullets, we learned to transfer information from one instance to another, such as the direction to move, by capturing the ID of the instance and accessing it through the dot operator.

We discovered the wonderful `with` statement that gave us the ability to affect a single instance, all instances of an object, or even the `other` instance involved in a collision. We took a look at global variables, such as `lives` and `score`, and used the **Draw** event to display it. Waves of enemies were spawned using Time Lines. The illusion of movement was created by scrolling the background image. Sound was applied and the volume adjusted to create a fade out effect. We even used a bit of trigonometry!

With the skills and knowledge developed in this chapter it is now your turn to take this game and extend it even further. Try adding your own enemies, collectible items, and weapon power-ups. Have some fun with it!

In the next chapter, we are going to learn more about collision and player controls by making a spooky adventure game. We will also take a look at artificial intelligence and using paths to make the enemies appear to think and act on their own.

4
The Adventure Begins

In this chapter, we will create a fun little action adventure game that will build upon our foundational knowledge. We will start with an animated player character that can navigate the world and has a short range melee attack. The game world will consist of multiple rooms, and the player will be able to move from one room to another while keeping all their stats. We will place all the code for the player controls and deal with wall collision in a single script to create a more efficient project.

As can be seen in the next screenshot, the theme of this game is the horrors of high school, and there will be three enemies in the world with basic artificial intelligence: a Ghost Librarian, a Brawl, and a Coach. The Ghost Librarian will appear if the player approaches its resting place and will chase the player until it gets too far away, and then return to where it came from. The Brawl will wander through the room on a path, and if it spots the player, it will increase in size and velocity. The Coach is the protector of trophies and will navigate the world on its own. If it sees the player it will pursue while avoiding walls and other Coaches, and if it is close enough it will melee attack the player.

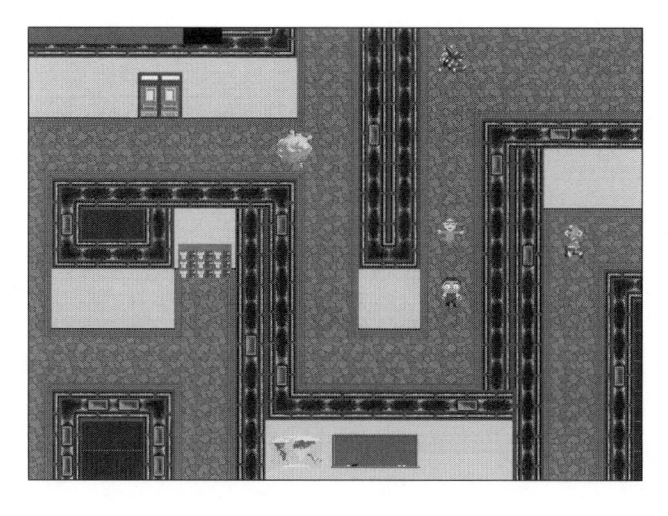

The Adventure Begins

Creating animated characters

So far, the player objects we have created have been very basic. In *Chapter 1, Getting to Know the Studio with Your First Game*, the player had no animation. In *Chapter 3, Shoot 'em Up: Creating a Side-scrolling Shooter*, the ship had animation, but always faced to the right. In this chapter, we are going to have a character that can move in four directions and have an animated sprite for each direction. We will also implement a melee attack that can be used in the direction the character is facing.

Simplifying the character movement

There are four separate sprites necessary for the player character's walk cycle. We will walk through the first one and then you can create the other three.

1. Let's start by creating a new project called `Chapter_04`.
2. Create a Sprite and name it `spr_Player_WalkRight`.
3. Load `Chapter 4/Sprites/ Player_WalkRight.gif` with **Remove Background** checked.
4. Set **Origin** to **Center**.
5. Click on **Modify Mask** to open the **Mask Properties** editor, and select the radio button of **Full image** under **Bounding Box**. The will set the collision box to be the entire sprite as shown in the following screenshot:

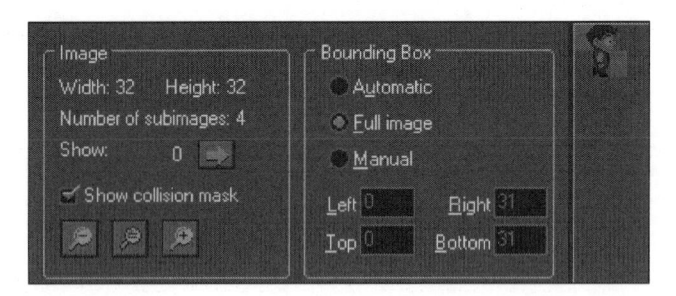

6. Click on **OK**. Repeat this process to load `spr_Player_WalkLeft`, `spr_Player_WalkUp`, and `spr_Player_WalkDown`.
7. Create an Object, `obj_Player`, and assign `spr_Player_WalkRight` as the Sprite. It actually doesn't matter which of the player sprites we set here, as we will be using code to change what sprite is being displayed.
8. We need to set up some initial variables, so create a new Script, `scr_Player_Create`, and write the following code:
   ```
   mySpeed = 4;
   myDirection = 0;
   ```

```
isAttacking = false;
isWalking = false;
health = 100;
image_speed = 0.5;
```

The first two variables are placeholders for the speed and direction of the player. This will be useful as we can affect these values without affecting the object's local `mySpeed` and `myDirection` variables for things, such as a knockback effect in which the object would be facing one direction while moving in the other. The variable `isAttacking` will be used to indicate when we have initiated combat, and `isWalking` will indicate when the player is moving. Next, we have the global variable `health`, which is set to 100 percent. Finally, we set the animation speed at 50 percent, so that the walk cycle plays properly.

> To know more about GameMaker: Studio's built-in variables and functions, check out the GameMaker User Manual by clicking on **Help** | **Contents**.

9. Now we can go onto the player movement. Instead of having multiple scripts for each key, we are going to simplify the code by placing all the controls into a single script. Create a new Script, `scr_Player_Step`, and we will start with the following code:

```
isWalking = false;
if (keyboard_check(vk_right) && place_free(x + mySpeed, y))
{
    x += mySpeed;
    myDirection = 0;
    sprite_index = spr_Player_WalkRight;
    isWalking = true;
}
```

We start by setting `isWalking` to `false`, so that it becomes the default state of what the player is doing. After that we are checking whether the keyboard has the right arrow key (`vk_right`), currently pressed down, and we check whether there is a solid object to the right of the current position. The `place_free` function will return whether the specified point is collision free. If the player is able to move and the key is pressed, we then move to the right and set the direction to zero to indicate right. We change the sprite to the right facing walk cycle, and then we change `isWalking` to `true`, which will overwrite the first line of code where we set it to `false`.

The Adventure Begins

10. Repeat this code for each of the remaining three directions and adjust accordingly. Each one should look at what key is being held, and see if there is any collision ahead from that position.

11. We have one more thing to do before the movement controls are complete. If the player is not moving, we want the animation to stop and start playing again once it starts moving. At the end of the script, add the following code:

```
if (isWalking == true)
{
    image_speed = 0.5;
} else {
    image_speed = 0;
}
```

We created the variable `isWalking` to switch between a walking and stopped state. If the player is moving, the sprite will animate. If the player isn't moving, we stop the animation as well.

The code should look like the following when it is complete:

```
isWalking = false;
if (keyboard_check(vk_right) && place_free(x + mySpeed, y))
{
    x += mySpeed;
    myDirection = 0;
    sprite_index = spr_Player_WalkRight;
    isWalking = true;
}
if (keyboard_check(vk_up) && place_free(x, y - mySpeed))
{
    y -= mySpeed;
    myDirection = 90;
    sprite_index = spr_Player_WalkUp;
    isWalking = true;
}
if (keyboard_check(vk_left) && place_free(x - mySpeed, y))
{
    x -= mySpeed;
    myDirection = 180;
    sprite_index = spr_Player_WalkLeft;
    isWalking = true;
}
if (keyboard_check(vk_down) && place_free(x, y + mySpeed))
{
    y += mySpeed;
    myDirection = 270;
```

```
            sprite_index = spr_Player_WalkDown;
            isWalking = true;
    }
    if (isWalking == true)
    {
        image_speed = 0.5;
    } else {
        image_speed = 0;
    }
```

12. Apply these scripts to the appropriate events, a **Create** event for `scr_Player_Create`, and a **Step** event for `scr_Player_Step`.

    The player is ready to move and animate properly, but we won't be able to fully test out the code without adding in some solid obstacles. Let's make a wall.

13. Create a new Sprite, `spr_Wall`, load `Chapter 4/Sprites/Wall.png`, and uncheck **Remove Background**. We are using a PNG file, as this wall is slightly transparent which will be useful later when we decorate the room.

14. Create a new Object, `obj_Wall`, and set the sprite to `spr_Wall`.

15. Check the box for **Solid**. The wall is now identified as being a collidable object.

16. Create a new Room and name it `Sandbox`. We will use this room for testing out features.

17. Place a single instance of `obj_Player` somewhere in the center of the room.

18. Place instances of `obj_Wall` around the perimeter of the room, and add a few extra sections as can be seen in the following screenshot:

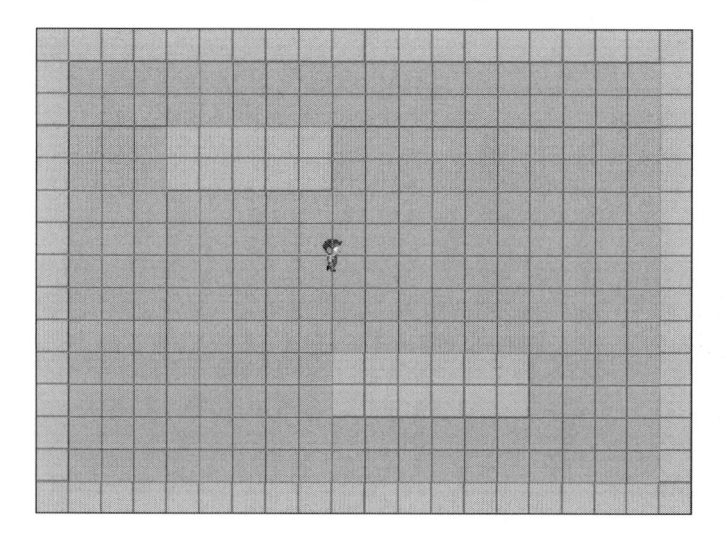

The Adventure Begins

19. Run the game. The player at this point should be able to move around the room freely in the open areas, and stop when they collide with a wall.

Implementing a melee attack

Now that we have the player movement functioning we can move onto the attack. The attack we are creating needs to only affect objects in front of the player character. To achieve this we will create a melee attack object that will spawn on command and remove itself from the game on its own.

1. Create a Sprite, `spr_Player_Attack`, and load `Chapter 4/Sprites/Player_Attack.gif` with **Remove Background** checked. This is an animated Sprite that will represent a swinging melee attack.

2. We want the collision area to affect the entire height of the sprite, but not the entire width. Click on **Modify Mask** and in the **Mask Properties** editor, select the radio button for **Manual** under **Bounding Box**.

3. Adjust the **Bounding Box** values for **Left**: 0, **Right**: 24, **Top**: 0 and **Bottom**: 4. The end result should look like the following screenshot. Click on **OK**.

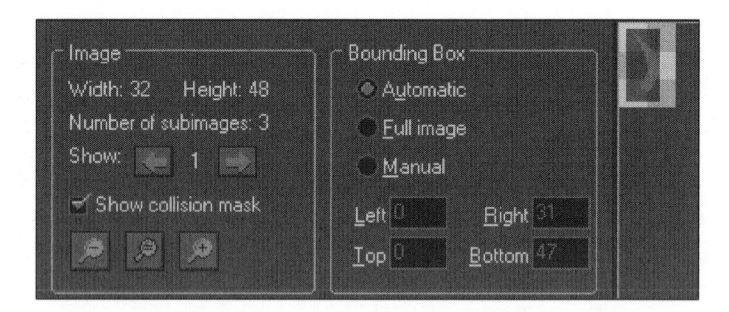

4. We want this object to always spawn in front of the player. One of the easiest ways to ensure this is to have this object rotate along with the player. To achieve this, set **Origin** to **X**: -16 **Y**: 24. Setting the X coordinate off to the left means that this object will have a 16 pixel offset when spawned. We can then rotate the attack to match the player's direction.

5. Create an Object, `obj_Player_Attack`, and assign `spr_Player_Attack` as its Sprite.

6. Set **Depth** to -100. **Depth** determines whether an instance of an object is drawn on-screen behind or above another object. Setting it to a negative value means that it will draw on top of any object with a higher depth value. Setting the value to -100 allows us to have other objects with depths between the default 0 and -99 without needing to worry about readjusting things later.

7. Create a new Script, `scr_Player_Attack_Create` with the following code:

```
image_angle = obj_Player.myDirection;
image_speed = 0.3;
alarm[0] = 6;
obj_Player.isAttacking = true;
```

Here is where we rotate the image to face the same direction as the player, which with the offset origin we set means it will be in front of the player. We also slow the animation speed down and set an alarm for six frames. This alarm will remove the attack object when it goes off. Finally we tell the player that it is attacking.

8. Add a **Create** event in `obj_Player_Attack` and attach this script.

9. Let's move onto the alarm script, `scr_Player_Attack_Alarm`. It will not only need to remove the attack, but it also needs to let the player know that it is gone and that they can attack once again. We only need two lines of code to do all this:

```
obj_Player.isAttacking = false;
instance_destroy();
```

We can talk directly to the player's `isAttacking` variable and set it back to `false`. Then we destroy the instance of the melee attack. Attach this script to an **Alarm 0** event.

10. All we need to do now is to get the player to spawn an instance of the attack. Reopen `scr_Player_Step` and at the bottom, add the following code:

```
if (keyboard_check_pressed(ord('Z')) && isAttacking == false)
{
    instance_create(x, y, obj_Player_Attack);
}
```

The `keyboard_check_pressed` function only activates on the actual pressing down action of a key, as opposed to being in the down position, and in this case, we are checking for the Z key. There are no special commands for the various letters on the keyboard, so we need to use the `ord` function that returns the corresponding ASCII code for the character it has been passed. We also check to see if the player is currently not attacking already. If that is all true, we spawn the attack, and that attack will change the `isAttacking` variable to true, so that this only happens once.

> When using the `ord` function, always use capital letters, or it may give the wrong number!

The Adventure Begins

11. Run the game. You should be able to tap the Z key and see the distinctive swinging motion in front of the player no matter which way the character is facing as shown in the following screenshot. The player is now ready for battle!

Navigating between rooms

An adventure game would be quite boring if everything took place in one incredibly large room. Not only is it not very efficient, but the world will also lack the feeling of exploration. Switching from one room to another is easy to do, but it does pose a problem.

The first issue is retaining the player stats, such as health, from one room to the next. One solution to this is to activate **persistence** on the player. Persistence means that we only need to place a single instance of an object in a room, and from that point onwards it will remain in the game world.

The second issue is where to place the player in a room with multiple entry points. If the player isn't persistent, we can place the player in the room, but it would always start in the same spot. If the player is persistent, then when they change rooms they will remain at the exact same coordinates they were at in the previous room. This means we are going to need to relocate the player to a position of our choice in each room.

This could end up being a lot of work if your game is going to have a lot of rooms. There is a simple way to solve this by creating self-aware teleporters and the use of room creation code.

Setting up the rooms

Let's start by building a few rooms, starting with a title screen.

1. Create a new Room and in the **Settings**, name it `TitleScreen`.
2. Create a new Background, `bg_Title`, and load `Chapter 4/Backgrounds/Title.png` with **Remove Background** left unchecked.

3. In the **Backgrounds** tab of `TitleScreen`, apply `bg_Title` as **Background 0** and check **Visible at Start**.
4. Create another Room and name it `C04_R01`. The names here represent the chapter and the room, as in Chapter 4, Room 1.
5. Set **Width** and **Height** to `1024`. This will allow us to have lots of space to explore.
6. We don't want to see everything in the room all at once, therefore we need to constrain the view. Click on the **Views** tab and check the box for **Enable the Use of Views**. Select **View 0** and check the box for **Visible when room starts**. This will activate the camera system for the room.
7. We will also want the view to focus on the player and move with it. Still in the **Views** tab, select `obj_Player` under **Object following** and set **Vbor:** and **Hbor:** to `200`. This will make the camera follow the player and leave a buffer of 200 pixels around the edges of the view. Look at the following screenshot to ensure you have everything set up correctly:

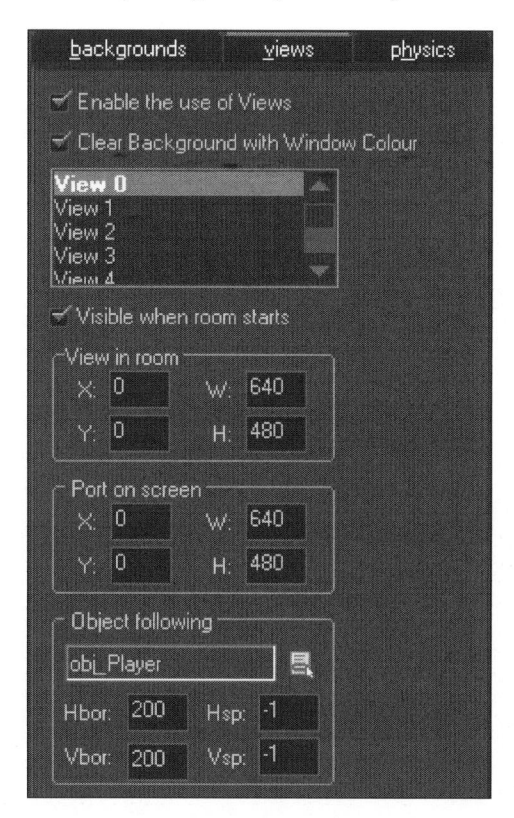

The Adventure Begins

8. Create two more rooms `C04_R02`, and `C04_R03` with the same settings we just used with `C04_R01`.

9. In the Resource tree, reorder the room by dragging `Sandbox` down to the bottom and `TitleScreen` to the very top. It should look like the following screenshot:

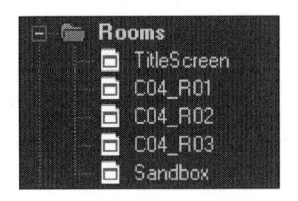

```
Rooms
    TitleScreen
    C04_R01
    C04_R02
    C04_R03
    Sandbox
```

10. Finally with all three rooms, create a labyrinth using the wall objects. The design isn't important at the moment; just make sure that the player would be able to get from one side to the other. An example of what it could look like can be seen in the following screenshot:

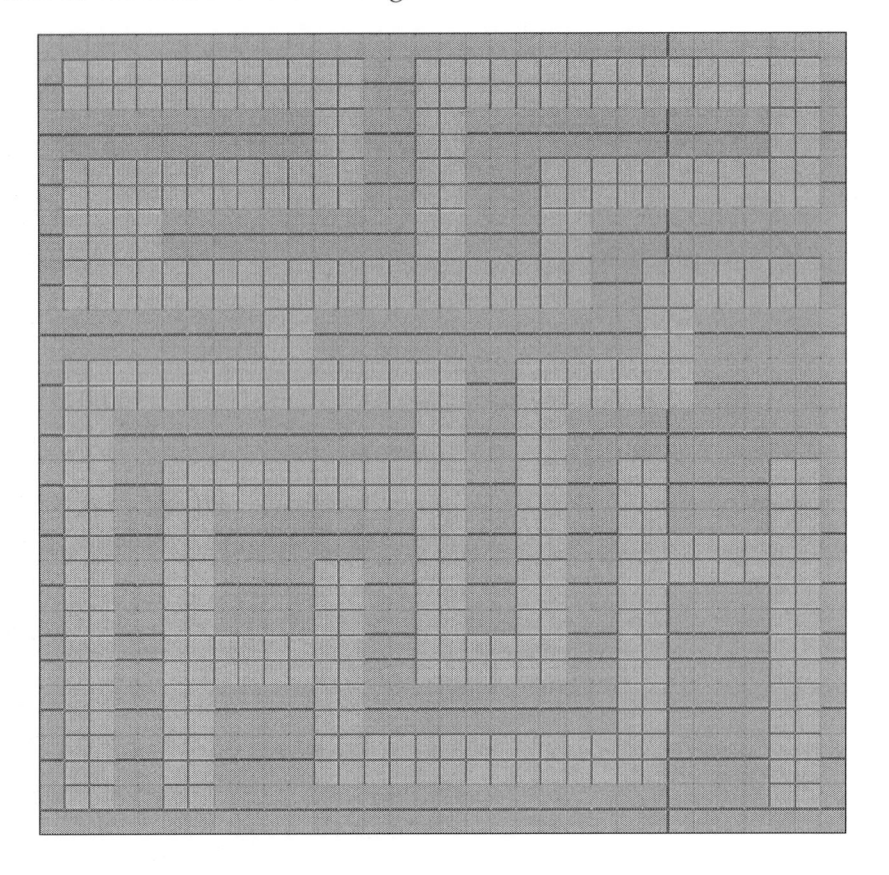

Creating Room Portals

In order to change rooms we are going to create reusable Portals. Each portal actually consists of two separate objects, a **Start** object and an **Exit** object. The Start object will represent the landing pad for where the player should be placed when they enter a room. The Exit object is the teleporter that changes what room the player is in. We will utilize four unique portals which will allow us to have one door on each side of the map if we want.

1. For the room teleportation system to work we are going to need to use some global variables, which need to be initialized at the start of the game. Create a new Script, scr_Globals_StartGame, with the following code:

   ```
   global.portalA = 0;
   global.portalB = 0;
   global.portalC = 0;
   global.portalD = 0;
   global.lastRoom = C04_R01;
   ```

   We create global variables for the four portals and give them a zero value to start. We also keep track of the last room we were in, so that we know what portal we need to go to in the new room.

2. Create a new Object, obj_Globals, add a **Game Start** event, and attach this script. This object does not need a sprite, as it is a data object only.

3. Place a single instance of obj_Globals into TitleScreen.

4. We need to be able to enter the game from the title screen, so let's create a quick fix by adding a **Draw** event and creating a new Script, scr_Globals_Draw, and with this code add the following:

   ```
   draw_set_color(c_white);
   draw_set_halign(fa_center);
   draw_text(room_width/2, 360, "Press ANY key");
   if (keyboard_check_pressed(vk_anykey))
   {
       room_goto_next();
   }
   ```

   Here we are just writing some white, centered text letting the player know how they can start the game. We use the special variable vk_anykey to see if the keyboard has been pressed, and if it has, we go to the next room as ordered in the Resource tree.

The Adventure Begins

> You don't always have to close your scripts, as the game will run even if multiple script windows are open.

5. Let's make some portals! Create a new Sprite, `spr_Portal_A_Start`, load `Chapter 4/Sprites/Portal_A_Start.png`, and uncheck **Remove Background**. Center the origin and then click on **OK**.

6. Create a new Object, `obj_Portal_A_Start`, set the Sprite to `spr_Portal_A_Start`. This is the landing pad that we will move the player to when they enter into a room. It does not need any code, so click on **OK**.

7. Create a new Sprite, `spr_Portal_A_Exit`, and load `Chapter 4/Sprites/Portal_A_Exit.png`, with **Remove Background** unchecked and the origin centered.

8. Create a new Object, `obj_Portal_A_Exit`, and set the Sprite accordingly. This is the actual teleporter and we will change rooms upon collision with the player.

9. For an `obj_Player` event, create a new Script, `scr_Portal_A_Exit_Collision`, and write the following code:

   ```
   global.lastRoom = room;
   room_goto(global.portalA);
   ```

   Before we can teleport we need to set the last room to the room the player is currently in. To do this we use the built-in variable `room`, which stores the index number of the room the game is currently displaying. After that we go to the room that this portal's global variable indicates we should go to.

10. Repeat steps 5 to 9 for portals B, C, and D making sure to change all the appropriate values to reflect the proper portal name.

The portals are complete and we can add them into the rooms. It is not necessary to utilize all four portals in every room; you just need a minimum of one Start and one Exit. When placing these objects in the room, it is important that there be only one of the same type of portal used. The Start portal should always be placed in the playable area and ensure that the Exit can only be accessed from one direction. You should also make sure that if one room has **PORTAL A** at the bottom, the room it is to enter should have the **PORTAL A** on top, as can be seen in the following screenshot. This will help the player understand where they are in the world.

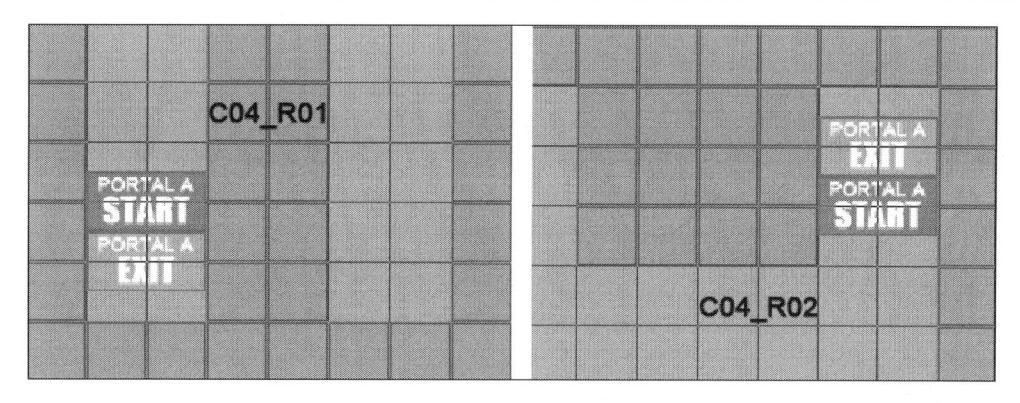

Now comes the interesting part. We need to change the global portal values in each room and we don't want to have a massive script that checks all rooms to see what is happening. Instead, we can use **Creation Code** in the rooms themselves to change these values upon the player entering. Let's try this out by making Portal A in C04_R01 go to C04_R02 and vice-versa.

1. In the C04_R01 **Settings** tab, click on **Creation Code** to open a code editor and write the following code:

   ```
   global.portalA = C04_R02;
   global.portalB = 0;
   global.portalC = 0;
   global.portalD = 0;
   ```

   We set **PORTAL A** to be the second room. All the other portals are not being used, so we set the variables to zero. Every room needs to have all of these variables set to some value, either a specific room or zero, otherwise it can cause errors.

2. In the C04_R02 **Settings** tab, click on **Creation Code** to open a code editor and write the following code:

   ```
   global.portalA = C04_R01;
   global.portalB = 0;
   global.portalC = 0;
   global.portalD = 0;
   ```

Now we have set PORTAL A to the first room, which makes sense. If we go through that portal, we should be able to go back through it. Feel free to change these settings to apply to all the portals you want.

The Adventure Begins

Teleporting a persistent player

The rooms have all been built and are ready to go. All that is left for us to do is to have the player move from room to room. Let's start by making the player persistent, so that we only need one in the game.

1. Open `obj_Player` and check **Persistent**.
2. Next, we need to relocate the player to the proper portal. We will create a new Script, `scr_Player_RoomStart`, with this code on a **Room Start** event for `obj_Player`.

```
if (global.lastRoom == global.portalA)
{
    obj_Player.x = obj_Portal_A_Start.x;
    obj_Player.y = obj_Portal_A_Start.y;
} else if (global.lastRoom == global.portalB) {
    obj_Player.x = obj_Portal_B_Start.x;
    obj_Player.y = obj_Portal_B_Start.y;
} else if (global.lastRoom == global.portalC) {
    obj_Player.x = obj_Portal_C_Start.x;
    obj_Player.y = obj_Portal_C_Start.y;
} else if (global.lastRoom == global.portalD) {
    obj_Player.x = obj_Portal_D_Start.x;
    obj_Player.y = obj_Portal_D_Start.y;
}
```

When the player enters a room we check to see which portal is associated with the room the player just exited from. We then move the player to the appropriate landing pad. To make sure the player is built correctly, its properties should look like the following screenshot:

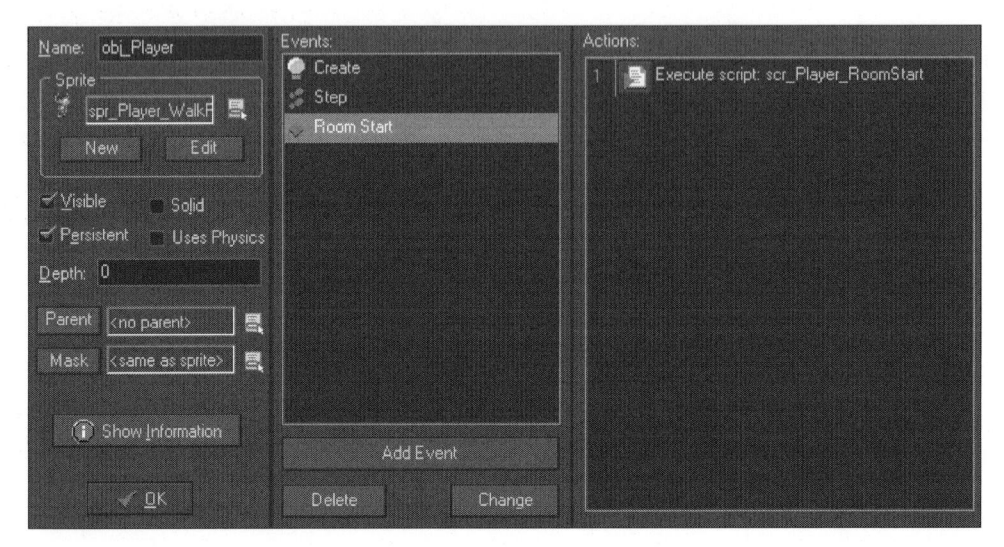

[132]

3. Place an instance of the player into C04_R01. Do not put the player into any other room or you will end up with multiple instances of the player in the game.

4. Run the game. We should be able to move around the first room and go through PORTAL A, which will take us to the PORTAL A landing pad in the second room. With this system, a game could have hundreds of rooms and there only ever needs to be four portals to manage.

Bringing enemies to life

Enemies are more than just obstacles to be avoided. Good enemies give the player a sense that there is some underlying **artificial intelligence** (**AI**). The enemies seem to know when you are near, can chase you around walls, and wander on their own. In this chapter we will create three creatures that will inhabit the world, each with their own unique AI.

Summoning the Ghost Librarian

The first creature will consist of two parts: the overdue BookPile and the Ghost Librarian that protects it. If the player approaches a BookPile, a Ghost will spawn and chase the player. If the player gets too far away from the Ghost, the Ghost will return to the BookPile that spawned it. If the player attacks the Ghost, it will disappear and respawn from the BookPile. If the player destroys the BookPile, the Ghost it spawned will be destroyed as well.

1. Let's start with the BookPile. Create a new Sprite, `spr_BookPile`, and load `Chapter 4/Sprites/BookPile.gif` with **Remove Background** checked.

2. Center the origin and click on **OK**.

3. We will also want a scary noise to alert the player of the danger. Create a new Sound, `snd_GhostMoan`, and load `Chapter 4/Sounds/GhostMoan.wav`. Click on **OK**.

4. Create a new Object, `obj_BookPile`, and assign `spr_BookPile` as the Sprite.

5. We don't want the player to be able to walk through the BookPile, so check the box for **Solid**.

6. We will need to initialize some variables, so create a new Script, `scr_BookPile_Create`, and write the following code:

    ```
    myRange = 100;
    hasSpawned = false;
    ```

The Adventure Begins

The first variable sets the value for how close the player needs to be to become active and the second variable is Boolean that will determine if this BookPile has spawned a Ghost or not.

7. Add a **Create** event and apply this script.
8. Next we need a new Script, `scr_BookPile_Step`, which will be applied to a **Step** event and contain the following code:

```
if (instance_exists(obj_Player))
{
    if (distance_to_object(obj_Player) < myRange && hasSpawned == false)
    {
        ghost = instance_create(x, y, obj_Ghost);
        ghost.myBooks = self.id;
        sound_play(snd_GhostMoan);
        hasSpawned = true;
    }
}
```

The first line of the code is incredibly important. Here we are checking to see if the player exists before we do anything else. If the player does exist, we check if the distance to the player object is within the range, and whether this BookPile has spawned a Ghost yet. If the player is within range and hasn't spawned anything, we spawn a Ghost. We will also send the unique ID of this BookPile, using the `self` variable, into the ghost so it knows where it came from. Next we play the Ghost moaning sound, making sure that it does not loop. Finally, we indicate that we have spawned a Ghost by changing the `hasSpawned` variable to `true`.

9. The only element remaining is to add an `obj_Player_Attack` event with a new Script, `scr_BookPile_Collision`, and write the following code:

```
if (instance_exists(ghost))
{
    with (ghost)
    {
        instance_destroy();
    }
}
instance_destroy();
```

Once again, we start by checking to see if a Ghost has spawned from this BookPile and is still in existence. If it is, we destroy that Ghost and then remove the BookPile itself. The BookPile is now complete and should look like the following screenshot:

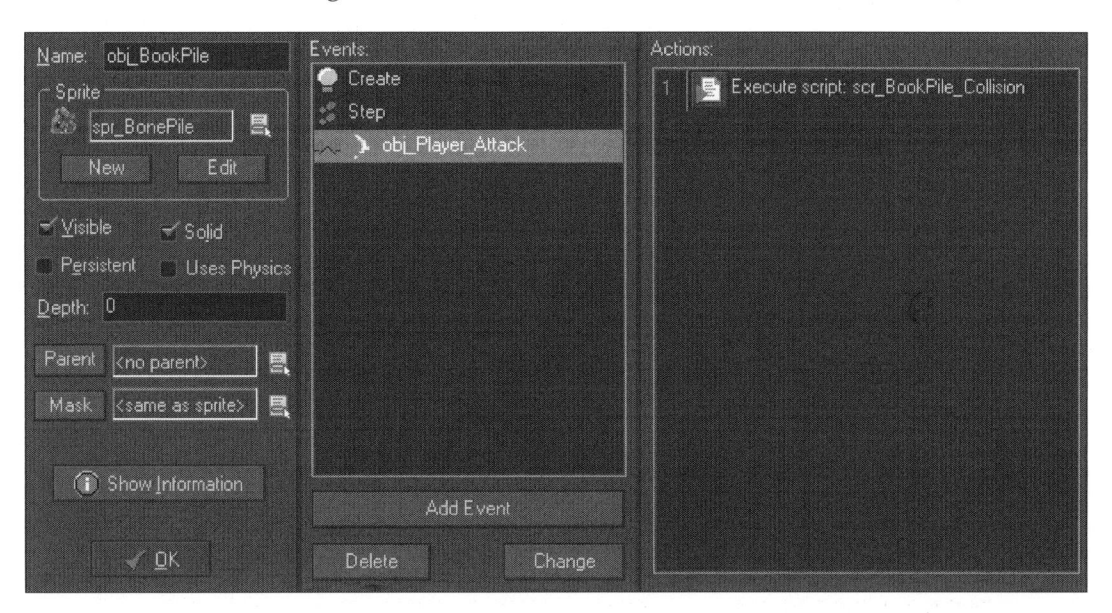

10. Now we need to build the Ghost. For this we will need to bring in two sprites, one for the spawning and one for the chase. Create sprites with **Remove Background** checked for spr_Ghost and spr_Ghost_Spawn, and load Chapter 4/Sprites/Ghost.gif and Chapter 4/Sprites/Ghost_spawn.gif, respectively.

11. In both the sprites, center the origin.

12. Set the **Depth:** field to -50 so that the ghost will appear over most objects, but below the player attack object. There is nothing else we need to do, so click on **OK**.

13. Create a new Object, obj_Ghost, and apply spr_Ghost_Spawn as the Sprite. This will make the spawn animation the initial sprite, and then we will change it to the regular Ghost through code.

The Adventure Begins

14. We have several variables that we need to initialize in a new Script, `scr_Ghost_Create`, as seen in the following code:

    ```
    mySpeed = 2;
    myRange = 150;
    myBooks = 0;
    isDissolving = false;
    image_speed = 0.3;
        alarm[0] = 6;
    ```

15. We set variables for the movement speed, the range the Ghost will track within, who spawned the Ghost, (which we will change through the BookPile),and one for whether the Ghost has returned to the BookPile. Notice that the range of the Ghost is larger than the range of the BookPile. This will ensure that the Ghost starts chasing the player immediately. We then set the animation speed and set an alarm for six steps which we will use to change sprites.

16. Add an **Alarm0** event and then apply a new script, `scr_Ghost_Alarm0`, that has the following line of code to change sprites:

    ```
    sprite_index = spr_Ghost;
    ```

We are now ready to start implementing some artificial intelligence. The Ghost is going to be the most basic enemy that will chase the player through the room, including passing through walls and other enemies, until the player gets out of range. At that point the Ghost will float back to the BookPile it came from.

1. We will start with chasing the player. Create a new script, `scr_Ghost_Step`, and write the following code:

   ```
   if (instance_exists(obj_Player))
   {
       targetDist = distance_to_object(obj_Player)
       if (targetDist < myRange)
       {
           move_towards_point(obj_Player.x, obj_Player.y, mySpeed);
       }
   }
   ```

   After checking to ensure that the player is alive, we create a variable that will hold the distance from the Ghost to the player. The reason we have created a `targetDist` variable is that we will be needing this information a few times and this will save us from having to recheck the distance each time we have an `if` statement. We then compare the distance to the chase range and if the player is within range, we move towards the player. The `move_towards_point` function calculates the direction and applies a velocity to the object in that direction.

2. Add a **Step** event and apply this script. We will be continuing to add code to this script, but it will function properly already.
3. Let's take a moment to test everything we have done so far. First, in the Resource tree, move Sandbox up to the near top, so that it is the room immediately after the title screen. Open the Sandbox room and place a couple of instances of obj_BookPile around the edges as shown in the following screenshot:

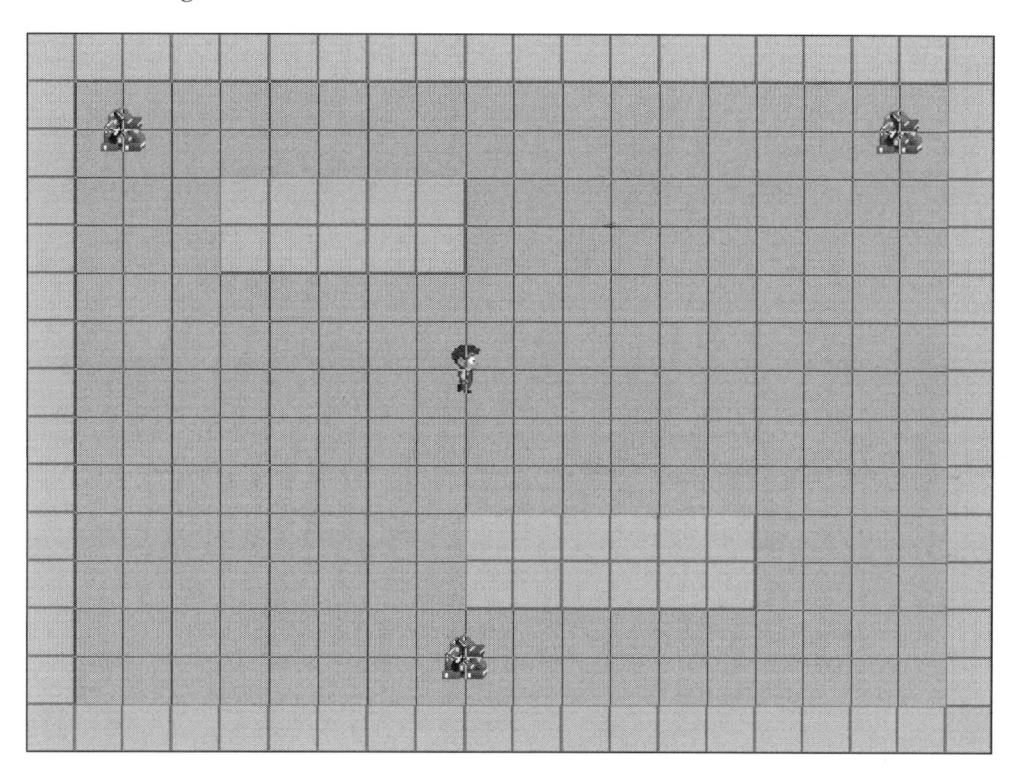

4. Run the game. If you get too close to a BookPile, a single Ghost will spawn from it and it will slowly chase the player. If the player gets too far away from the Ghost, the Ghost will continue moving in the direction it was last heading in and will eventually go offscreen.
5. Let's get the Ghost to return to its BookPile. In scr_Ghost_Step, within the braces for the player existence check, add the following code:

```
else if (targetDist > myRange && distance_to_point(myBooks.x, myBooks.y) > 4)
{
move_towards_point(myBooks.x, myBooks.y, mySpeed);
}
```

The Adventure Begins

First we check to see if the player is out of range and that the Ghost isn't near its own BookPile. Here we are using `distance_to_point`, so that we are checking the origin of the BookPile rather than the edges of the collision area that `distance_to_object` would look for. If this is all true, the Ghost will start moving back to its BookPile.

6. Let's run the game again. As before, the Ghost will chase the player, and if the player gets too far away, the Ghost will return to its BookPile.

7. There is an issue with the fact that the Ghost ends up ping-ponging over the top of the BookPile. This is due to the Ghost having velocity-based speed and not having any code telling it to stop. We can fix this by adding this code after the last `else if` statement:

```
else
{
speed = 0;
if (isDissolving == false)
{
      myBooks.hasSpawned = false;
sprite_index = spr_Ghost_Spawn;
image_speed = -1;
alarm[1] = 6;
isDissolving = true;
}
}
```

Here we have a final `else` statement that will execute if the player is out of range and the Ghost is near its BookPile. We start by stopping the speed of the Ghost. Then we check to see if it can dissolve. If so, we tell the BookPile that the Ghost can be spawned again, we change the sprite back to the spawn animation, and by setting the `image_speed` to `-1` it will play that animation in reverse. We also set another alarm, so that we can remove the Ghost from the world and deactivate the dissolve check.

Altogether the entire `scr_Ghost_Step` should look like the following code:

```
 if (instance_exists(obj_Player))
{
    targetDist = distance_to_object(obj_Player)
    if (targetDist < myRange)
    {
       move_towards_point(obj_Player.x, obj_Player.y, mySpeed);
    } else if (targetDist > myRange && distance_to_
point(myBooks.x, myBooks.y) > 4) {
       move_towards_point(myBooks.x, myBooks.y, mySpeed);
    } else {
```

```
            speed = 0;
            if (isDissolving == false)
            {
                myBooks.hasSpawned = false;
                sprite_index = spr_Ghost_Spawn;
                image_speed = -1;
                alarm[1] = 6;
                isDissolving = true;
            }
        }
    }
}
```

8. One last Script is needed, `scr_Ghost_Alarm1`, that is attached to an **Alarm 1** event and has one line of code to remove the instance:

   ```
   instance_destroy();
   ```

   The Ghost is almost complete. It spawns, chases the player, and returns to its BookPile, but what happens if it catches the player? With this Ghost we will want it to smash into the player, cause some damage, and then vanish in a puff of smoke. For this we will need to create a new asset for the dead Ghost.

9. Create a new Sprite, `spr_Ghost_Dead`, and load `Chapter 4/Sprites/Ghost_Dead.gif` with **Remove Background** checked.

10. Center the origin and click on **OK**.

11. Create a new Object, `obj_Ghost_Dead`, and apply the Sprite.

12. In a new Script, `scr_Ghost_Dead_AnimEnd`, write the following line of code and attach it to an **Animation End** event:

    ```
    instance_destroy();
    ```

    The **Animation End** event will execute code when the last image of the Sprite is played. In this case, we have a poof of smoke animation that at the end will remove the object from the game.

13. All we need now is to reopen `obj_Ghost` and add an **obj_Player** event with a new script, `scr_Ghost_Collision`, with the following code:

    ```
    health -= 5;
    myBooks.hasSpawned = false;
    instance_create(x, y, obj_Ghost_Dead);
    instance_destroy();
    ```

The Adventure Begins

We start by removing five points of health, and then telling the Ghost's BookPile that it can be respawned. Next we create the Ghost death object which will hide the real Ghost when we remove it from the game. If everything is built correctly, it should look like the following screenshot:

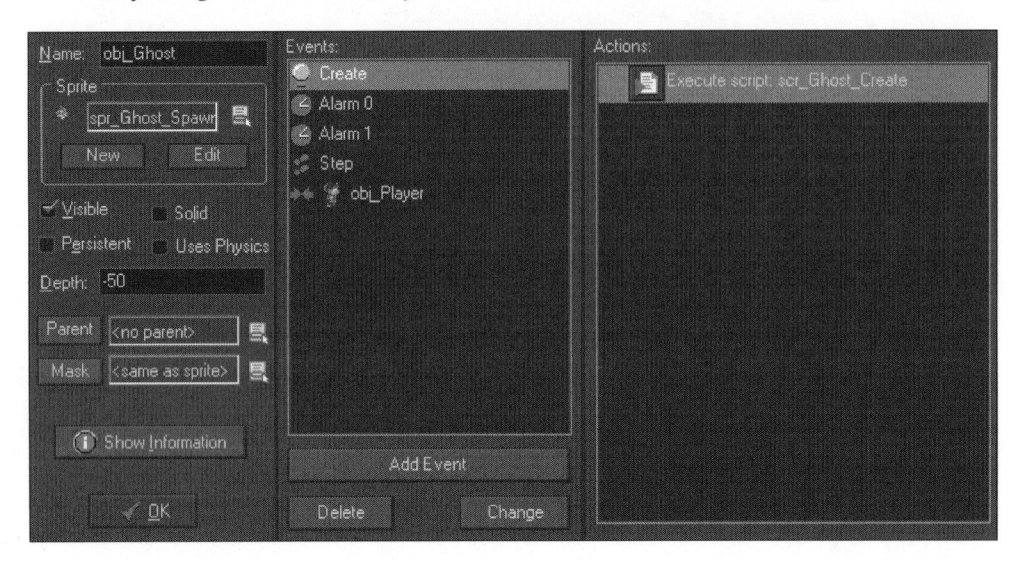

14. Run the game. The Ghost should now function exactly as designed. It will spawn and chase the player. If it catches the player it will cause damage and disappear. If the player gets away, the Ghost will return to its BookPile and dissolve out of existence. Great work!

    One last thing, as the room is meant to be a sandbox for experimenting in and not part of the actual game, we should clean up the room to prepare for the next enemy.

15. Open the `Sandbox` room and remove all instances of the BookPiles.

Building a wandering Brawl

The next enemy we will create is a Brawl that will wander around the room. If the player gets too close to this enemy, the Brawl will become enraged by growing larger and moving faster, though it won't leave its path. Once the player is out of range, it will calm back down and shrink to its original size and speed. The player won't be able to kill this enemy, but the Brawl will damage the player if there is contact.

For the Brawl, we will be utilizing a path and we will need three sprites: one for the normal state, one for the transition of states, and another for the enraged state.

1. Create a new Sprite, `spr_Brawl_Small`, and load `Chapter 4/Sprites/Brawl_Small.gif` with **Remove Background** checked. This is the Sprite for the normal state. Center the origin and click on **OK**.

2. Create another new Sprite, `spr_Brawl_Large`, and load `Chapter 4/Sprites/Brawl_Large.gif` with **Remove Background** checked. We need to center the origin, so that the Brawl will scale properly with this image. The enraged state is twice the size of the normal state.

3. We also need to undergo transition between these two states, so let's create a new Sprite, `spr_Brawl_Change` and load `Chapter 4/Sprites/Brawl_Change.gif`, still with **Remove Background** checked. Don't forget to center the origin.

4. Next we need a path for the Brawl to follow. Create a new Path and name it `pth_Brawl_01`.

5. We want the Brawl to move smoothly, so check **Smooth Curve** under **Connection Kind** and change the **Precision** to 8.

6. To see what we can do with paths, let's make the Path in the shape of a figure eight as can be seen in the following screenshot:

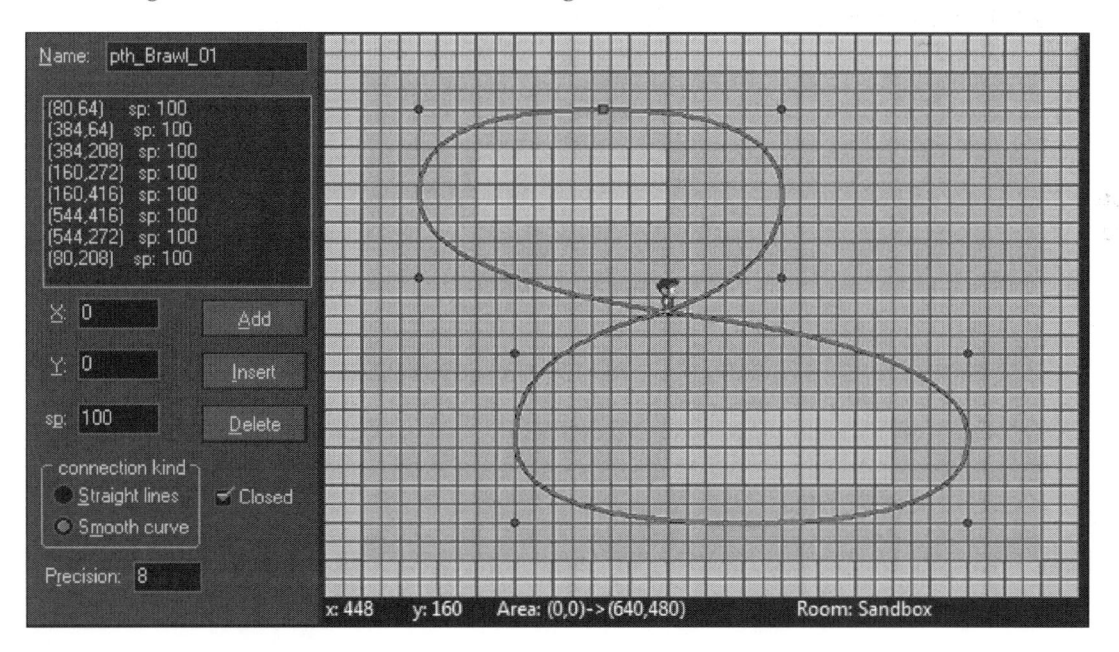

7. Let's also create a new Sound, `snd_Brawl`, and load `Chapter 4/Sounds/Brawl.wav`.

8. Create a new Object, `obj_Brawl`, and apply `spr_Brawl_S` as the default Sprite.

9. We'll start with initializing some variables in a Create event script, `scr_Brawl_Create`.

   ```
   mySpeed = 2;
   canGrow = false;
   isBig = false;
   isAttacking = false;
   image_speed = 0.5;
   sound_play(snd_Brawl);
   sound_loop(snd_Brawl);
   path_start(pth_Brawl_01, mySpeed, 1, true);
   ```

   The first variable sets the base speed of the Brawl. The next three variables are checks for the transformation and enraged states, and whether it has attacked. Next, we set the animation speed and then we play the Brawl sound, and in this case we want the sound to loop. Finally, we set the Brawl onto the path with a speed of two; when it hits the end of the path it will loop and most importantly, the path is set to absolute, which means it will run based as designed in the Path editor.

10. We can now start working on the AI of the Brawl. Create a new script for a **Step** event named `scr_Brawl_Step` and we will start by getting the movement working.

    ```
    image_angle = direction;
    if (isBig == true)
    {
        path_speed = mySpeed * 2;
    } else {
        path_speed = mySpeed;
    }
    ```

    Here we start by rotating the Sprite itself to face in the proper direction. This will work, because we have the Sprite images facing to the right, which is the same as zero degrees. Next, we check to see if the Brawl is big or not. If the Brawl is the enraged version, we set the path speed to be the base speed times two. Otherwise, we set the speed to the default base speed.

11. Place an instance of the Brawl anywhere in the room and run the game. The Brawl should move around the figure eight and properly face in the proper direction.

12. Next, we will add in the first transformation, becoming enraged. Right after the previous line of code, add:

    ```
    if (instance_exists(obj_Player))
    {
        if (distance_to_object(obj_Player) <= 200)
        {
            if (canGrow == false)
            {
                if (!collision_line(x, y, obj_Player.x, obj_Player.y, obj_Wall, false, true))
                {
                    sprite_index = spr_Brawl_Change;
                    alarm[0] = 12;
                    canGrow = true;
                }
            }
        }
    }
    ```

    We start by making sure the player exists, and then we check to see if the player is within range. If the player is in range, we check to see if we have become enraged or not. If the Brawl hasn't grown yet, we use the `collision_line` function to see if the Brawl can actually see the player or not. This function draws a line between two points, in this case the location of the Brawl and the player positions, and determines if an instance of an object, or a wall crosses that line. If the Brawl can see the player, we change the sprite to the transformation sprite, set an alarm so we can finalize the transformation, and indicate that the Brawl has grown.

13. Let's create a script `scr_Brawl_Alarm0` for an **Alarm 0** event with the code that will switch to the enraged sprite and indicate that the Brawl is now full size.

    ```
    sprite_index = spr_Brawl_Large;
    isBig = true;
    ```

14. Run the game to make sure that the code is working. The Brawl should remain small until it can clearly see the player, in which case it will then transform into the large, enraged Brawl.

The Adventure Begins

15. We have the Brawl growing larger, now we need to calm it down and have it shrink. Back in `scr_Brawl_Step`, add an `else` statement on the distance check, which would be before the final brace and add the following code:

```
else
{
if (canGrow == true)
{
sprite_index = spr_Brawl_Change;
alarm[1] = 12;
canGrow = false;
}
}
```

If the player is out of range, this `else` statement will become active. We check to see if the Brawl is still enraged. If it is, we change the Sprite to the transformation, set a second alarm, and indicate that the Brawl is back to normal.

Here is the full `scr_Brawl_Step` script:

```
image_angle = direction;
if (isBig == true)
{
    path_speed = mySpeed * 2;
} else {
    path_speed = mySpeed;
}

if (instance_exists(obj_Player))
{
    if (distance_to_object(obj_Player) <= 200)
    {
        if (canGrow == false)
        {
            if (!collision_line(x, y, obj_Player.x, obj_Player.y, obj_Wall, false, true))
            {
                sprite_index = spr_Brawl_Change;
                alarm[0] = 12;
                canGrow = true;
```

```
            }
          }
        }
        else
        {
            if (canGrow == true)
            {
                sprite_index = spr_Brawl_Change;
                alarm[1] = 12;
                canGrow = false;
            }
        }
    }
```

16. Duplicate the `scr_Brawl_Alarm0` script, name it `scr_Brawl_Alarm1`, and adjust the values as shown in the following code. Remember to add this as an **Alarm 1** event.

    ```
    sprite_index = spr_Brawl_Small;
    isBig = false;
    ```

17. Run the game and confirm that the Brawl grows larger and faster when the player is near and in sight, and returns to normal when out of range.

18. The only thing we have left is the attack. Create a new Script, `scr_Brawl_Collision`, for a **obj_Player** event with the following code:

    ```
    if (isAttacking == false)
    {
        health -= 10;
        alarm[2] = 60;
        isAttacking = true;
    }
    ```

    If the player collides with the Brawl for the first time, we remove 10 points of health and set an alarm for two seconds that will allow the Brawl to attack again.

19. To wrap up the Brawl, all we need is the final **Alarm 2** event with a new Script, `scr_Brawl_Alarm2`, that contains the following line of code:

    ```
    isAttacking = false;
    ```

The Adventure Begins

The Brawl is now complete and functions as designed. If everything is implemented correctly, the object properties should look like the following screenshot:

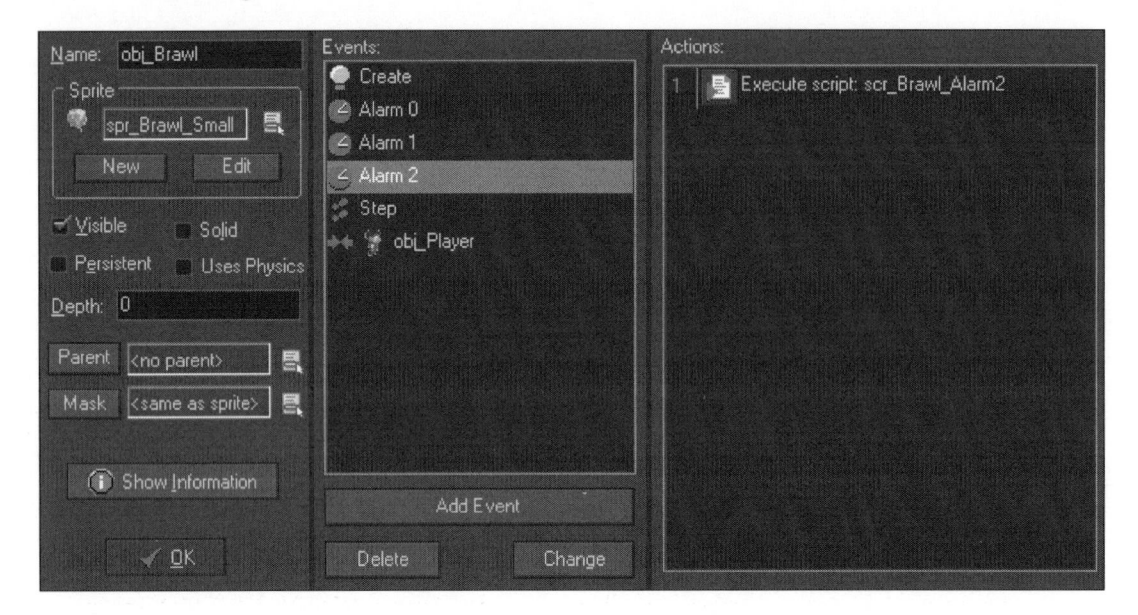

20. Remove any instances of `obj_Brawl` from the `Sandbox` room, so that we can start fresh for the final enemy.

Creating the Coach

The final enemy we will create, the Coach, is going to be the most challenging opponent yet. This enemy will move all around the room, randomly going from trophy to trophy to make sure it is still there. If it sees the player, it will chase them and if it gets close enough, it will have a melee attack. If the player escapes, it will wait for a moment before returning to duty. The Coach has a body, so it will need to go around obstacles and even avoid other coaches. This also means that it can die if the player is able to attack it.

1. As this enemy is guarding something, we will start by creating the trophy. Create a new Sprite, `spr_Trophy`, and load `Chapter 4/Sprites/Trophy.gif` with **Remove Background** checked.
2. Create a new Object, `obj_Trophy`, and apply `scr_Trophy` as its Sprite.

3. As this is an animated sprite, we will want to add a **Create** event and have it not animate by writing the following code in a new Script, `scr_Trophy_Create`:

   ```
   image_speed = 0;
   image_index = 0;
   ```

4. This is all we need for now for the trophy, so click on **OK**.

   Much like the player, we will need four sprites for the four directions this enemy will move in.

5. Create a new Sprite, `spr_Coach_WalkRight`, and load `Chapter 4/Sprites/Coach_WalkRight.gif` with **Remove Background** checked.

6. Center the origin, click on **Modify Mask**, and check **Full image** under **Bounding Box**.

7. Repeat this process for `spr_Coach_LWalkLeft`, `spr_Coach_WalkDown`, and `spr_Coach_WalkUp` sprites.

8. Create a new Object, `obj_Coach`, and apply `spr_Coach_WalkRight` as its Sprite.

   We are going to be dynamically creating paths for this enemy, so that it can navigate to the trophies on its own. We also want it to avoid obstacles and other enemies. This isn't too difficult to achieve, but it is going to require a lot of setup on initialization.

9. Create a new Script, `scr_Coach_Create`, apply it to a **Create** event, and then we will start with some basic variables:

   ```
   mySpeed = 4;
   isChasing = false;
   isWaiting = false;
   isAvoiding = false;
   isAttacking = false;
   image_speed = 0.3;
   ```

   Once again we start by setting the speed of the object. Then we have four variables representing the various states we will need to check, all set to `false`. We also set the animation speed for the sprite.

   Next we need to set up the pathing system which will utilize some of GameMaker's **motion planning** functions. The basic concept here is that we create a grid that covers the area we want to be able to move the enemy in. We then locate all the objects we want the enemy to avoid, such as walls, and mark those areas of the grid as forbidden. We can then assign a start and goal location in the free area and create a path between them while avoiding obstacles.

The Adventure Begins

10. Still in `scr_Coach_Create`, add the following code to the end of the script:
    ```
    myPath = path_add();
    myPathGrid = mp_grid_create(0, 0, room_width/32, room_height/32,
    32, 32);
    mp_grid_add_instances(myPathGrid, obj_Wall, false);
    ```

    The first thing needed is an empty path that we can use for all future paths. Next we create a grid that will set the dimensions of the pathing map. The `mp_grid_create` attribute has parameters for where it's located in the world, how many grids in width and height, and the size of each grid cell. In this case, we start in the grid in the upper-left corner and cover the entire room in 32 pixel increments. Dividing the room dimensions by 32 means that this will work in any size room without having to adjust the code. Finally, we take all instances of the wall found in the room and add it to the grid as areas where pathing is not allowed.

11. Now, we need to find a destination for the Coach to go. Continue adding the following code at the end of the script:
    ```
    nextLocation = irandom(instance_number(obj_Trophy)-1);
    target = instance_find(obj_Trophy, nextLocation);
    currentLocation = nextLocation;
    ```

    We start by getting a rounded random number that is based on the amount of trophies in the room. Notice that we subtracted one from the number of trophies. We need to do this because in the following line of code, we are searching for a specific instance using the `instance_find` function. This function is pulling from an array and the first item in an array always starts with a zero. Lastly, we have created a second variable for when we want to change destinations.

12. All we have to do now is make a path and use it. Add the following code at the end of the script:
    ```
    mp_grid_path(myPathGrid, myPath, x, y, target.x, target.y, false);
    path_start(myPath, mySpeed, 0, true);
    ```

    Here we select the grid we created and the empty path, and have a new path created that goes from the Coach's position to the targeted location and will not go on diagonals. Then we set the Coach into motion and this time, when it hits the end of the path, it will come to a stop. The final value in the `path_start` function sets the path to absolute, which we want in this case as the path is created dynamically.

Here is the entire `scr_Coach_Create` script:

```
mySpeed = 4;
isChasing = false;
isWaiting = false;
isAvoiding = false;
isAttacking = false;
image_speed = 0.3;

myPath = path_add();
myPathGrid = mp_grid_create(0, 0, room_width/32, room_height/32,
32, 32);
mp_grid_add_instances(myPathGrid, obj_Wall, false);

nextLocation = irandom(instance_number(obj_Trophy)-1);
target = instance_find(obj_Trophy, nextLocation);
currentLocation = nextLocation;

mp_grid_path(myPathGrid, myPath, x, y, target.x, target.y, false);
path_start(myPath, mySpeed, 0, true);
```

13. Open up Sandbox, and place two instances of `obj_Coach` in the corners and three instances of `obj_Trophy` as seen in the following screenshot:

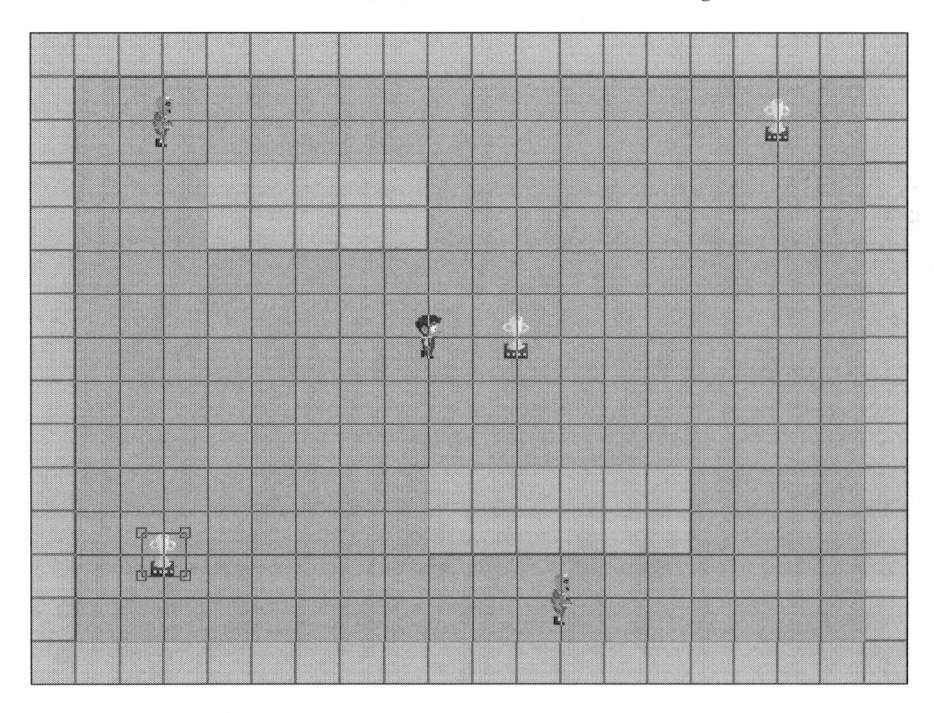

14. Run the game. You should see the coaches randomly select a trophy and move towards it. Try and restart it a few times to see the different paths each Coach takes.

15. With the basic setup complete, we can move on to the AI. We will start by switching the sprites based on the direction of movement. Create a new Script, `scr_Coach_Step`, apply it to a **Step** event and write the following code:

```
if (direction > 45 && direction <= 135) { sprite_index = spr_Coach_WalkUp; }
else if (direction > 135 && direction <= 225) { sprite_index = spr_Coach_WalkLeft; }
else if (direction > 225 && direction <= 315) { sprite_index = spr_Coach_WalkDown; }
else { sprite_index = spr_Coach_WalkRight; }
```

Here we are changing the Sprite based on the direction of the instance as it moves. We can do this here, because we are not allowing diagonal movement on the path.

16. Next, we will get the Coach to watch for the player, and if spotted, they will leave their path in pursuit. Add the following code after the Sprite change code:

```
targetDist = distance_to_object(obj_Player);
if (targetDist < 150  && targetDist > 16)
{
    canSee = collision_line(x, y, obj_Player.x, obj_Player.y, obj_Wall, false, false)
    if (canSee == noone)
    {
        path_end();
        mp_potential_step(obj_Player.x, obj_Player.y, 4, all);
        isChasing = true;
    }
}
```

Once again we are using a variable to hold the value of how far away the player is to save us some coding time and minimize function calls. If the player is within range and not within striking distance, we do a sightline check. The `collision_line` function returns the ID of any wall instance that the line crosses. If it does not intersect with any wall instances, it will return a special variable called `noone`. If the player is in sight, we end the path the Coach is following, and start moving towards the player. The `mp_potential_step` function will make an object move in the desired direction while avoiding obstacles, and in this case we are avoiding all instances. Finally we indicate that the Coach is chasing the player.

17. This works well for starting the chase, but what if the player escapes? Let's have the Coach wait for a moment and then go back to patrolling. Add an `else` statement to the sightline check with the following code:

    ```
    else if (canSee != noone && isChasing == true)
    {
        alarm[0] = 60;
        isWaiting = true;
        isChasing = false;
    }
    ```

    This `else` statement states that if the player cannot be seen and the Coach is chasing, it will set an alarm for finding a new destination, tell it to wait, and the chase is over.

18. We have set an alarm, so let's create a new Script, `scr_Coach_Alarm0`, and apply it to an **Alarm 0** event. Write the following code in the script:

    ```
    while (nextLocation == currentLocation)
    {
        nextLocation = irandom(instance_number(obj_Trophy)-1);
    }

    target = instance_find(obj_Trophy, nextLocation);
    currentLocation = nextLocation;

    mp_grid_path(myPathGrid, myPath, x, y, target.x, target.y, false);
    path_start(myPath, mySpeed, 1, false);

    isWaiting = false;
    ```

    We start with a `while` loop checking to see if the next location is the same as the old location. This will ensure that the Coach always moves to another trophy. Just as we did in the initial setup, we select a new target and set the current location variable. We also create a Path and start moving on it, which means the Coach is no longer waiting.

19. We have one last element we need to add to the chase sequence, the attack. If the Coach gets close enough to the player, it should melee attack the player. For this we need to first create a new Sprite, `spr_Coach_Attack`, with `Chapter 4/Sprites/Coach_Attack.gif` loaded and **Remove Background** checked.

20. Just like the player's attack, set **Origin** to **X**: -16, **Y**: 24 and adjust the **Bounding Box** values to **Left**: 0, **Right**: 24, **Top**: 0, and **Bottom**: 4.

The Adventure Begins

21. Create a new Object, `obj_Coach_Attack`, apply the Sprite to it, and set **Depth** to -100.

22. Add a **Create** event and apply a new Script, `scr_Coach_Attack_Create`, with code to control the animation speed, set an alarm to remove the instance, and a variable that we can turn on.

    ```
    image_speed = 0.3;
    alarm[0] = 6;
    isHit = false;
    ```

23. Add an **Alarm 0** event with a new Script, `scr_Coach_Attack_Alarm0`, that removes the instance.

    ```
    instance_destroy();
    ```

24. Finally, add an **obj_Player** event, and apply a new Script, `scr_Coach_Attack_Collision` with the following code:

    ```
    if (isHit == false)
    {
        health -= 15;
        isHit = true;
    }
    ```

    If this is the first collision, we remove a point of health and then deactivate this check.

25. We are done with the attack. Now to have it activated in the Coach, reopen `scr_Coach_Step` and add the attack code as an `else if` statement, after the last brace:

    ```
    else if (targetDist <= 16)
    {
        if (isAttacking == false)
        {
            swing = instance_create(x, y, obj_Coach_Attack);
            swing.image_angle = direction;
            alarm[1] = 90;
            isAttacking = true;
        }
    }
    ```

    If the Coach is near the player and has not attacked yet, we create an instance of the Coach Attack. We then rotate the attack Sprite to face the same direction as the Coach. An alarm is set for three seconds to allow for a breather before this code can be run again.

[152]

Chapter 4

26. We need an **Alarm 1** event to reset the attack, so create a new script, `scr_Coach_Alarm1` and turn off the attack.

    ```
    isAttacking = false;
    ```

27. Run the game. The Coach will now chase the player, and if it gets close enough to the player it will attack.

    The Coach is now only doing half of its job, chasing the player. We still need to add in the regular patrol duties. Currently, if the Coach doesn't see the player and it gets to the end of the path, it stops and does nothing again. It should only wait a few seconds and then move on to the next trophy.

28. Reopen `scr_Coach_Step` and add an `else` statement to the very end of the script with this code:

    ```
    else
    {
        if (isWaiting == false)
        {
            if (distance_to_object(target) <= 8)
            {
                alarm[0] = 60;
                path_end();
                isWaiting = true;
            }
        }
    }
    ```

    This `else` statement means that the player is out of range. We then check to see if the Coach is waiting or not. If it isn't waiting, but is within eight pixels of its targeted trophy, we set the alarm for choosing a new destination for two seconds, end the path to stop movement, and state that we are now waiting.

29. Run the game and you should see the coaches, when not chasing the player, stopping near a trophy, pausing for a moment, and then moving to another trophy.

30. There is an issue, however, if both coaches go to the same trophy. Sometimes they will both overlap each other. Let's fix that by adding the following code after the distance check for the trophy:

    ```
    if (isAvoiding == true)
    {
        mp_potential_step (target.x, target.y, 4, all);
    }
    ```

[153]

The Adventure Begins

The first thing we need to do is do a variable check to see if the Coach needs to avoid something. If it does, we use the `mp_potential_step` function which will move an instance towards a specified goal while attempting to avoid certain objects, or in this case, all instances.

31. Now, we need to set up the condition for when avoidance should occur. Immediately after the last code is inserted, write the following:

    ```
    if (distance_to_object(obj_Coach) <= 32 && isAvoiding == false)
    {
        path_end();
        isAvoiding = true;
    }
    else if (distance_to_object(obj_Coach) > 32 && isAvoiding == true)
    {
        mp_grid_path(myPathGrid, myPath, x, y, target.x, target.y, false);
        path_start(myPath, mySpeed, 1, true);
        isAvoiding = false;
    }
    ```

    First we check to see if an instance of the Coach is nearby and it hasn't tried to avoid it. If that is true then we take the Coach off of its path and start to avoid. We follow this with an `else if` statement checking to see if we are far enough away from another Coach that we were trying to avoid. If so, we set a new path to the destination, start moving on it, and end the avoidance.

32. There is still one little issue remaining, which you can see if you run the game for a while. Sometimes two coaches will get too close together and they both stop. This is because they are trying to avoid each other, but are actually touching and can't let go. At the very end of the `scr_Coach_Step` Script, write the following:

    ```
    if (place_meeting(x, y, obj_Coach))
    {
        x = xprevious;
        y = yprevious;
        mp_potential_step(target.x, target.y, 4, all);
    }
    ```

This will check to see if two instances of the Coach are colliding with each other. If they are, we set the x and y coordinates to the special variables xprevious and yprevious, which represent the position of the instance in the previous step. Once they have taken a step back, we can then attempt to move around them again.

The Coach is now complete. To check to see if you have all the code for scr_Coach_Step written correctly, here it is in its completed form:

```
if (direction > 45 && direction <= 135) { sprite_index = spr_Coach_WalkUp; }
else if (direction > 135 && direction <= 225) { sprite_index = spr_Coach_WalkLeft; }
else if (direction > 225 && direction <= 315) { sprite_index = spr_Coach_WalkDown; }
else { sprite_index = spr_Coach_WalkRight; }

targetDist = distance_to_object(obj_Player);
if (targetDist < 150  && targetDist > 16)
{
    canSee = collision_line(x, y, obj_Player.x, obj_Player.y, obj_Wall, false, false)
    if (canSee == noone)
    {
        path_end();
        mp_potential_step(obj_Player.x, obj_Player.y, 4, all);
        isChasing = true;
    }
    else if (canSee != noone && isChasing == true)
    {
        alarm[0] = 60;
        isWaiting = true;
        isChasing = false;
    }
}
else if (targetDist <= 16)
{
    if (isAttacking == false)
    {
        swing = instance_create(x, y, obj_Coach_Attack);
        swing.image_angle = direction;
        alarm[1] = 90;
```

```
            isAttacking = true;
        }
    }
    else
    {
        if (isWaiting == false)
        {
            if (distance_to_object(target) <= 8)
            {
                alarm[0] = 60;
                path_end();
                isWaiting = true;
            }
            if (isAvoiding == true)
            {
                mp_potential_step(target.x, target.y, 4, all);
            }
            if (distance_to_object(obj_Coach) <= 32 && isAvoiding == false)
            {
                path_end();
                isAvoiding = true;
            }
            else if (distance_to_object(obj_Coach) > 32 && isAvoiding == true)
            {
                mp_grid_path(myPathGrid, myPath, x, y, target.x, target.y, false);
                path_start(myPath, mySpeed, 1, true);
                isAvoiding = false;
            }
        }
    }
    if (place_meeting(x, y, obj_Coach))
    {
        x = xprevious;
        y = yprevious;
        mp_potential_step(target.x, target.y, 4, all);
    }
```

Adding finishing details to the game

The game is now functionally complete, but there are a few elements left to polish up. To start, the player takes damage but never dies, nor is there a **heads-up display (HUD)** to show this. Let's create a quick Overlord.

1. Create a new Object, `obj_Overlord`, with no sprite applied and persistence is checked.

2. Add a **Draw GUI** event and a new Script for it, `scr_Overlord_DrawGUI`, with the following code:

   ```
   draw_healthbar(0, 0, 200, 16, health, c_black, c_red, c_green, 0, true, true);

   if (health <= 0)
   {
       with (obj_Player) { instance_destroy(); }
       room_goto(TitleScreen);
       instance_destroy();
   }
   ```

   First, we use the function `draw_healthbar` which you can see has a lot of parameters. The first four are the size and placement of a rectangular bar. Next is the variable to be used for how full the bar is, in our case, the global health variable. The next three are the background color, and the min/max colors. Next is the direction the bar should fall, zero being to the left. The final two Booleans are for drawing the background and border that we want.

   After that we do a health check and if the player should be dead, we remove the player, return to the frontend, and then remove the Overlord itself. It is important to remove any persistent instances in the world or they won't go away!

3. Place a single instance of `obj_Overlord` into `C04_R01`.

4. Populate the rooms with a variety of enemies. If we use the Brawl we will either need to create a room that works with the path we created, or even better, redraw the path to fit our room layout.

The Adventure Begins

5. Make sure the `Sandbox` room is moved back to the bottom of the Resource tree and run the game. We should see the health bar at the top of the screen and if you take damage, the health bar should go down. If the player takes too much damage, the game will end and return to the frontend.

All that is left is to create levels, paint the world with a tile set, and add some background music. At this point you should know how to do that, so we will leave it up to you. We have supplied some additional assets for this purpose in the `Chapter 4` folder. You should have something that looks like the following screenshot when you are done:

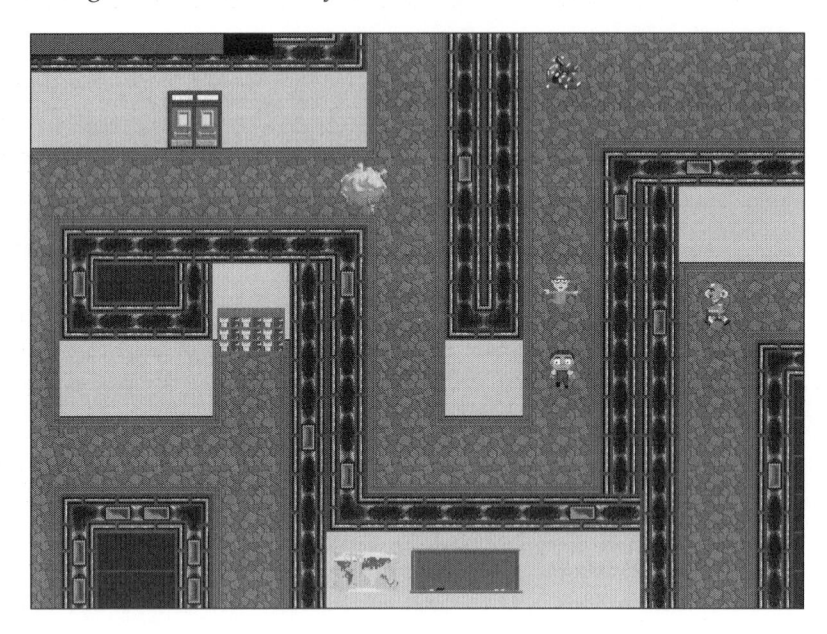

Summary

Congratulations on completing your second game! We learned how to simplify the player controls by placing the keyboard checks and collision forecasting into a single script. We covered several ways to deal with Sprite animation from rotating the image to setting what sprites should be displayed. We dealt with global variables and used them to implement a room transitioning system. We covered some new object properties in depth and persistence. Then we spent some time dealing with artificial intelligence through the use of proximity detection and path finding. We even discovered how to make an object navigate a room on its own while avoiding obstacles.

With the skills you have honed in this chapter, you will now be able to build games with multiple rooms with enemies that appear to think. It's your turn now to extend this game by adding more unique enemies, have the trophy open, and spawn loot. Have fun and explore your new found abilities!

In the next chapter we are going to build an epic boss fight for a platformer style game. There will be guns and lasers, and lots of fun. We will be starting to make our code more efficient by looking at creating reusable scripts, and learning how to structure our code systematically. All of this will help us to make our games faster and easier, so let's get going!

5
Platform Fun

Now that we have a good grounding in the basics of building a game, we are ready to create more complex and more efficient projects. In this chapter we are going to develop a classic platforming game with an epic boss battle. We will focus on building systems and utilizing reusable scripts to simplify our code and save time. This will also reduce the total size of the game, making it faster to download.

The gameplay itself will consist of a player character that can run around the world, jump onto platforms, and shoot in several directions. The player will need to defeat a giant machine Boss that will have three distinct stages. In the first stage the player will need to blow up three powerful Cannons that are exposed for a short period of time. The second stage requires the destruction of a large Laser Cannon that will move up and down firing its massive Laser Beam intermittently. The final stage will have Shields that protect the Boss Core, occasionally opening to allow the player to eradicate the heart of the boss. All of this will happen while the player tries to avoid being hit by an indestructible turret.

Structuring systems-based code

When making a game, it is common to build each component all on its own and not to think about how it will affect the game as a whole. The developer will build a basic framework and then add features as they come along, often resorting to special conditional statements to make the code work without breaking the game. This methodology eventually will start creating bugs in the software requiring more time and effort to fix each one. The bigger the game, the more likely problems will be to arise. It can be an incredibly frustrating experience.

Platform Fun

This is where breaking the code into individual systems can really save time and effort. Rather than rewriting elements of code over and over again for each object, we can write self-contained processes into scripts that can be shared. For this game we are going to separate out some of the more basic components, such as gravity and animation, into their own systems.

Creating gravity

The first system we are going to build is one for dealing with gravity. While GameMaker: Studio does have a gravity property, it adds a level of complexity not needed in a platformer game. Gravity is a force that is applied to an object's speed cumulatively, which means that the longer an object is falling, that faster it will move. The issue we have is that setting gravity to zero just means it will not move faster. We need the object to come to a full stop. Therefore, we we will create our own gravity system that not only makes objects fall, but will deal with landing on the ground as well. Instead we will create our own gravity system that not only makes objects fall, but will deal with landing on the ground as well.

We are going to start by introducing **constants**. Constants allow us to use names to represent values that will never change. This has the double benefit of making it easier for us to read the code and help improve performance as compared to variables:

1. Let's get started by creating a **New Project** called `Chapter_03`.
2. Open the **Resources** | **Define Constants** editor. In the **Name** column write MAXGRAVITY with a **Value** of 16. At this speed we can be sure that a falling object will not move so fast that it will miss the bounding box of another object in the game. From now on, whenever we see MAXGRAVITY the computer will see 16.

   > It is convention to write all constants in all capital letters, though it won't break if the convention isn't followed.

3. Next we can create a new Script , scr_Gravity, and write the following code to create gravity:

   ```
   if (place_free( x, y + vspeed + 1))
   {
       vspeed   += 1;
   } else {
       move_contact_solid(direction, MAXGRAVITY);
       vspeed = 0;
   }
   ```

First we check to see whether the area below the instance is clear of any collidable objects at the speed the instance is currently travelling. If it is clear, then we know that we are in the air and that gravity should be applied. We do this by increasing the vertical speed each step by a small amount. If there is a collidable object, then we are about to hit the ground, so we move the instance to the surface of the object in the direction the instance is travelling up to our MAXGRAVITY, 16 pixels. At that point, the instance is on the ground so we set the vertical speed to zero.

4. We now have gravity working, but it will pick up too much speed if we don't limit how fast an instance can fall. Add this code to the bottom of the script:

```
vspeed = min(vspeed, MAXGRAVITY);
```

Here we are setting the vspeed value to the lower value between the current vspeed and MAXGRAVITY. If the instance is moving too fast, this code will slow it down to the maximum allowed speed. We now have a simple gravity system that all objects in the game could utilize.

Building an animation system

The next system we will create is for animation and it will be implemented as a state machine. A state machine breaks down all the conditions of an object into distinct states. An object can only be in one stage at any one time, so the code related to it can be contained and managed more effectively.

To understand this concept better, think about a door. A door has several unique states of being. The two states that probably spring to mind are that the door can be open or it can be closed. There are also two other states, opening and closing, as can be seen in the following image. If the door is opening, it is neither open nor is it closed, but rather it is in a unique state of action. This makes state machines perfect for animation. Almost every interactive object in a game is likely to have some animation or utilize several different images.

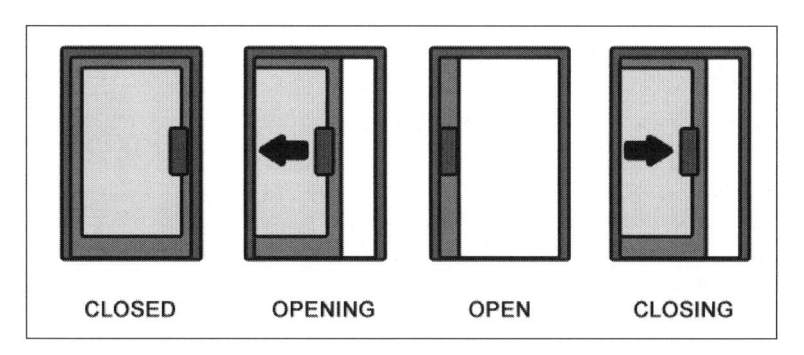

Platform Fun

Since the player character is generally the most robust object in terms of different animations, we will start by breaking down its unique states. Our player can be either in the air or on the ground, so we will want to make sure to separate those controls. We also want the player to be able to shoot in multiple directions and take damage. All together we will have a total of eight different states:

- Idle
    - Idle aiming up
    - Idle aiming down
- Run
    - Run aiming up
    - Run aiming down
- InAir
- Damage

Let's start by defining these states as constants:

1. Open the **Resources** | **Define Constants** editor and in the **Name** column write IDLE with a **Value** of 0.
2. Click on **Add** or just press *Enter* to add a new row and write IDLEUP with a value of 1. Repeat this process for all the states with increasing numbers as can be seen in the following screenshot. Then click on **OK**.

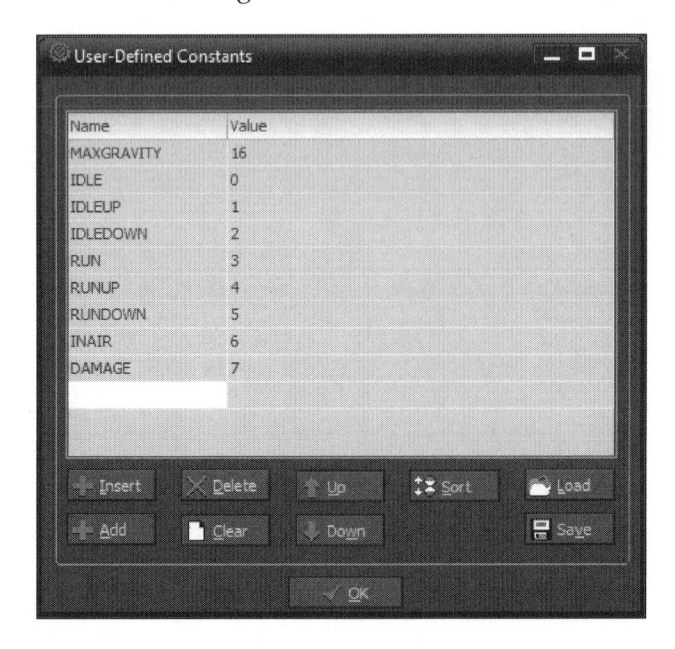

Name	Value
MAXGRAVITY	16
IDLE	0
IDLEUP	1
IDLEDOWN	2
RUN	3
RUNUP	4
RUNDOWN	5
INAIR	6
DAMAGE	7

Chapter 5

3. Create a new Script and name it `scr_Animation_Control`. We will start by using a `switch` statement to control the various states. We also want this script to be reusable, so we will want to use some generic variables to make the code more universal. Let's start by adding in the idle state with the following code:

```
switch (action)
{
    case IDLE :
        sprite_index = myIdle;
        image_speed = 0.1;
    break;
}
```

Here we are going to use a variable called `action` to switch states. If the action happens to be `IDLE`, we then change the sprite; in this case we are using another variable, `myIdle`, that we will define in each object which will allow us to reuse this script. We also set the animation rate which will allow us to have different playback speeds for different actions.

4. We will need to insert all the cases into this script with a similar setup of changing the sprite and setting the image playback speed. Here is the rest of the code for the states:

```
case IDLEUP :
    sprite_index = myIdleUp;
    image_speed = 0.1;
break;
case IDLEDOWN :
    sprite_index = myIdleDown;
    image_speed = 0.1;
break;
case RUN :
    sprite_index = myRun;
    image_speed = 0.5;
break;
case RUNUP :
    sprite_index = myRunUp;
    image_speed = 0.5;
break;
case RUNDOWN :
    sprite_index = myRunDown;
    image_speed = 0.5;
break;
case INAIR :
    sprite_index = myInAir;
```

[165]

Platform Fun

```
            image_speed = 0.5;
        break;
        case DAMAGE :
            sprite_index = myDamage;
            image_speed = 0.5;
        break;
```

5. We have all the states we need, but what about dealing with the direction that the player is facing. It's a platformer so they will need to go right and left. For this we will just flip the image by scaling it inversely with the following code after the switch statement closing brace:

    ```
    image_xscale = facing;
    ```

    Once again we are utilizing a variable, `facing`, to make the script more universal. We are now done with this script and the animation system is ready to be implemented.

Creating a collision forecasting system

The next system we are going to build is for dealing with world collision. We want to move away from using GameMaker: Studio's collision system as it requires two instances to intersect with each other. This works great for a bullet colliding with a player, but it is less effective if the player needs to sink into the ground in order to know when to stop. Instead, we want to forecast whether a collision will happen before an instance moves:

1. We will start with forecasting wall collision to the left and right of the instance. Create a new Script, `scr_Collision_Forecasting` and write the following code:

    ```
    if (place_free(x - mySpeed, y))
    {
        canGoLeft = true;
    } else {
        canGoLeft = false;
        hspeed = 0;
    }

    if (place_free(x + mySpeed, y))
    {
        canGoRight = true;
    } else {
        canGoRight = false;
        hspeed = 0;
    }
    ```

We start by checking to see if the area to the left of the instance is free of collidable objects. The distance away that we are looking is determined by a variable, mySpeed, which will allow this check to be adjustable to whatever speed the instance may be travelling at. If the area is clear we set the canGoLeft variable to true, otherwise the area is blocked and we stop the horizontal speed of the instance. We then repeat this check for collision to the right.

2. Next we need to check for the ground collision. After the previous code we need to add:

```
if (!place_free(x, y+1))
{
    isOnGround = true;
    vspeed = 0;
    action = IDLE;
} else {
    isOnGround = false;
}
```

Here we are checking if there is a collidable object directly beneath the instance. If there is collision, we set the variable isOnGround to true, to stop the vertical speed and then change the state of the instance to IDLE. Changing the state like this will guarantee that the instance escapes from an INAIR state.

At this point we have the majority of our collision detection built, but we haven't covered all the edge cases. We are currently only checking to the left, right, and below the instance, but not on diagonals. The issue here is that it is possible for all conditions to prove true, but when the instance is moved on an angle it can result in the instance becoming stuck within a collidable object.

3. Rather than building conditional checks for all angles, we will instead allow the collision to happen and then pop it back into the proper position. Add this next code at the end of the script:

```
if (!place_free(x, y))
{
    x = xprevious;
    y = yprevious;
    move_contact_solid(direction, MAXGRAVITY);
    vspeed = 0;
}
```

Platform Fun

Here we are checking to see if the instance is currently intersecting with a collidable object. If so we set the X and Y coordinates to their position on the previous step, then snap it to the surface in the direction of the movement and set the vertical speed to zero. This will clean up the edge case scenario in a realistic manner. The whole script should look like this:

```
if (place_free(x - mySpeed, y))
{
    canGoLeft = true;
} else {
    canGoLeft = false;
    hspeed = 0;
}

if place_free(x + mySpeed, y)
{
    canGoRight = true;
} else {
    canGoRight = false;
    hspeed = 0;
}

if (!place_free(x, y+1))
{
    isOnGround = true;
    vspeed = 0;
    action = IDLE;
} else {
    isOnGround = false;
}

if (!place_free(x, y))
{
    x = xprevious;
    y = yprevious;
    move_contact_solid(direction, MAXGRAVITY);
    vspeed = 0;
}
```

Checking the keyboard

As we are breaking systems down into more usable scripts we might as well put all the keyboard controls into a single script. This will simplify the code that we will be creating in the future and also allow us to easily change the controls or offer alternative controls.

Create a new Script, scr_Keyboard_Input and write the following code:

```
keyLeft  = keyboard_check(vk_left);
keyRight = keyboard_check(vk_right);
keyDown  = keyboard_check(vk_down);
keyUp    = keyboard_check(vk_up);
keyJump  = keyboard_check(ord('X'));
keyShoot = keyboard_check(ord('Z'));
```

Our code will be much easier to read with variables such as keyJump and keyShoot to represent the controls than actual key names. In order to use the letter keys on a keyboard we need the associated ASCII number. Rather than having to look up each key number we can use the ord function, which will convert a letter into the proper number.

> When using the ord function, always use capital letters or it may give the wrong number!

We now have all our universal systems that we will need for this game. Next we will implement them.

Building the player

The player character we are building is the most complex object we have created yet. Not only will the player run and jump, the controls themselves will be slightly different depending on whether the player is on the ground or in the air. The player will need to know what direction they are facing, what animation to be playing, whether they can shoot their weapon, and at what angle. Let's construct this, starting with importing all the sprites:

1. Create a new Sprite, spr_Player_Idle, and load Chapter 5/Sprites/Player_Idle.gif with **Remove Background** checked.

2. Set the **Origin** to **X**: 32 **Y**: 63 so that it rests in the center horizontally and rests on the bottom of the sprite vertically.

Platform Fun

3. Click on **Modify Mask** to open the **Mask Properties** editor and select **Bounding Box | Manual**. Set the values to **Left**: 16, **Right**: 48, **Top**: 8, and **Bottom**: 63.

4. Repeat this process, including the same **Origin** and **Mask Properties** for the following sprites:
    - spr_Player_IdleUp
    - spr_Player_IdleDown
    - spr_Player_Run
    - spr_Player_RunUp
    - spr_Player_RunDown
    - spr_Player_InAir
    - spr_Player_Damage

5. Create an Object, obj_Player, and assign spr_Player_Idle as the **Sprite**.

6. First we need to initialize all the variables the player character will need, starting with the ones necessary for animation. Create a new Script, scr_Player_Create, with the following code:

```
myIdle = spr_Player_Idle;
myIdleUp = spr_Player_IdleUp;
myIdleDown = spr_Player_IdleDown;
myRun = spr_Player_Run;
myRunUp = spr_Player_RunUp;
myRunDown = spr_Player_RunDown;
myInAir = spr_Player_InAir;
myDamage = spr_Player_Damage;
```

Here we are establishing what sprites are to be used for the various states of animation. The variables we are using here must be the same as the ones we declared in scr_Animation_Control in order to use the animation system we created.

7. Next we will add the variables for the collision system, but before we do that, we should add two more constants for the facing direction. Open the **Resources | Define Constants** and add RIGHT with a value of 1 and LEFT with a value of -1. These numbers will represent the scale of the drawn image, with the negative value inverting the sprite.

8. At the end of scr_Player_Create add the rest of the variables we need:

```
mySpeed = 8;
myAim = 0;
facing = RIGHT;
```

```
action = IDLE;
isDamaged = false;
canFire = true;
```

Here we have variables for the speed of the player, the direction the player is aiming, the direction they are facing, and the state they are in. We have also added variables for whether the player can take damage or is invulnerable, and whether they are able to shoot or not. We now have all our variables initialized.

9. In `obj_Player`, add a **Create** event and apply the `scr_Player_Create` script.

10. We have a collision forecasting system ready to go, we just need to use it appropriately. Create a new Script, `scr_Player_BeginStep`, and use it to call the forecasting script and the keyboard checks:

    ```
    scr_Collision_Forecasting();
    scr_Keyboard_Input();
    ```

    Every script you create is actually an executable function. As seen here you just need to write the name of the script and place parentheses at the end to have that code run. We will be using this method often.

11. In `obj_Player` add a **Step | Begin Step** event and apply `scr_Player_BeginStep`. The **Begin Step** event is the very first event in every step to be executed. The **Step** event follows it and **End Step** is the last event before the instance is drawn on screen. This allows us more control over when the code is run.

12. Next we need to create the controls. As we mentioned earlier, there are actually two separate control systems, one for on the ground and one for in the air. We will start with the latter as it is the simplest. Create a new Script, name it `scr_Player_AirControls` with the following code:

    ```
    scr_Gravity();

    if (keyLeft && canGoLeft)
    {
        if (hspeed > -mySpeed) { hspeed -= 1; }
        facing = LEFT;
        myAim = 180;
    }
    if (keyRight && canGoRight)
    {
        if (hspeed < mySpeed) { hspeed += 1; }
        facing = RIGHT;
        myAim = 0;
    }
    ```

Platform Fun

The first thing you should notice is that we are no longer using operators such as == in our code. These variables are all Booleans, so they can only be true or false. Writing `keyLeft` is the same as writing `keyLeft == true`, but is more efficient.

Now, since the player is in the air, the first thing we do is apply gravity. Next we have the controls for horizontal movement. We check to see if the appropriate key is pressed and if the player is able to move in said direction. If these are true, we check the horizontal speed against the maximum speed. If the player is able to increase speed, we increment it slightly. This prevents the player from changing directions too quickly while in the air. We follow this up by setting the facing and aiming directions.

13. We can now move on to the much more complicated ground controls. Create a new Script and name it `scr_Player_GroundControls`. We will start by writing the idle state:

    ```
    if (!keyLeft && !keyRight)
    {
        if (hspeed >= 1) { hspeed -= 1; }
        if (hspeed <= -1) { hspeed += 1; }
    }
    ```

    We start by checking whether neither the left nor right keys are being pressed. If the keys aren't pressed and the player is moving, we check to see which way they are moving and then reduce the speed accordingly. What this really means is that the player will slide to a halt.

14. The player has come to a stop, but it is not yet idling. To do this we need to determine if the player is using the up or down keys as that will affect which direction the player is aiming. Insert this next code immediately after the last line of code, but inside the last brace:

    ```
    if (keyUp)
    {
        action = IDLEUP;
        myAim = 45;
    } else if (keyDown) {
        action = IDLEDOWN;
        myAim = 315;
    } else {
        action = IDLE;
        if (facing == LEFT) { myAim = 180; }
        if (facing == RIGHT) { myAim = 0; }
    }
    ```

We start by checking if the up key is pressed, and if it is, we change the action to IDLEUP and set the aim to 45 degrees so that the player will shoot upwards. If that isn't true, we check the down key and change the action and aim if appropriate. Finally, if neither of those keys is pressed, we go into the standard IDLE. For the aim, however, we need to see which way the player is facing first. The player will properly idle from now on.

15. Next we can add the left and right controls. After the very last brace, write the following code:

```
if (keyLeft && canGoLeft)
{
    hspeed = -mySpeed;
    facing = LEFT;
    if (keyUp)
    {
        action = RUNUP;
        myAim = 150;
    } else if (keyDown) {
        action = RUNDOWN;
        myAim = 205;
    } else {
        action = RUN;
        myAim = 180;
    }
}
```

We check to see if the left key has been pressed and that the player is able to move left. If so, we set the horizontal speed and set the facing direction to go left. Once again, we check to see if the up or down keys are currently pressed or not and then set the action and aim to their proper values.

16. Repeat the last step for the right key with the values accordingly. The player will now be able to move left and right.

17. All we need now is to add in the jump. Immediately after the previous code add:

```
if (keyJump && isOnGround)
{
    vspeed = -MAXGRAVITY;
    action = INAIR;
}
```

We check to see if the jump key has been pressed and if the player is on the ground or not. If this is true, we set the vertical speed upwards to the maximum gravity and set the action to INAIR.

Platform Fun

18. The ground controls are now complete; here is what `scr_Player_GroundControls` should look like:

```
if (!keyLeft && !keyRight)
{
    if (hspeed >= 1) { hspeed -= 1; }
    if (hspeed <= -1) { hspeed += 1; }

    if (keyUp)
    {
        action = IDLEUP;
        myAim = 45;
    } else if (keyDown) {
        action = IDLEDOWN;
        myAim = 315;
    } else {
        action = IDLE;
        if (facing == LEFT) { myAim = 180; }
        if (facing == RIGHT) { myAim = 0; }
    }
}
if (keyLeft && canGoLeft)
{
    hspeed = -mySpeed;
    facing = LEFT;
    if (keyUp)
    {
        action = RUNUP;
        myAim = 150;
    } else if (keyDown) {
        action = RUNDOWN;
        myAim = 205;
    } else {
        action = RUN;
        myAim = 180;
    }
}
if (keyRight && canGoRight)
{
    hspeed = mySpeed;
    facing = RIGHT;
    if (keyUp)
    {
        action = RUNUP;
        myAim = 30;
```

[174]

```
        } else if (keyDown) {
            action = RUNDOWN;
            myAim = 335;
        } else {
            action = RUN;
            myAim = 0;
        }
    }
    if (keyJump && isOnGround)
    {
        vspeed = -MAXGRAVITY;
        action = INAIR;
    }
```

19. Let's move onto the player attack. First we need to build the Bullet, so create a new Sprite, `spr_Bullet`, and load `Chapter 5/Sprites/Bullet.gif` with **Remove Background** checked. Center the **Origin** and then click on **OK**.

20. Create a new Object, `obj_Bullet`, and apply `spr_Bullet` as the **Sprite**.

21. We will want the Bullet to always be in front of everything, so set the **Depth** to `-2000`.

22. We are now done with the Bullet and can now write the attack code. Create a new Script, `scr_Player_Attack`, and write the following:

```
if (keyShoot && canFire)
{
    bullet = instance_create(x + (8 * facing), y-32, obj_Bullet)
    bullet.speed = 16;
    bullet.direction = myAim;
    bullet.image_angle = myAim;
    alarm[0] = 10;
    canFire = false;
}
```

We start by checking to see if the attack key is pressed and whether the player is allowed to shoot. If so, we create an instance of the Bullet from the tip of the gun and capture the unique ID into a variable. The horizontal position of this Bullet uses the facing variable to offset it to the left or right. We set the speed of the Bullet and then set the direction and image rotation to where the player is aiming. We then set an alarm which will be used to reset the `canFire` variable, which we are changing to `false`.

Platform Fun

23. At this point we have several scripts for movement, attacking, and animation, but none of them have been applied. To do this we need one more script, `scr_Player_Step`, calling the other scripts as follows:

    ```
    if (isOnGround)
    {
        scr_Player_GroundControls();
    } else {
        scr_Player_AirControls();
    }
    scr_Player_Attack();
    scr_Animation_Control();
    ```

    First we determine what controls we need to use by seeing if the player is on the ground or not. We then run the appropriate control script, followed by the attack script and finally the animation controls.

24. In `obj_Player`, add a **Step | Step** event and apply `scr_Player_Step`.

25. Before we test this out, we still need to reset that alarm. Create a new Script, `scr_Player_Alarm0`, and set `canFire` to `true`.

    ```
    canFire = true;
    ```

26. Add an **Alarm | Alarm 0** event and apply this script.

    The player is ready to be tested. To ensure that you have the player set up properly, it should look like the following screenshot:

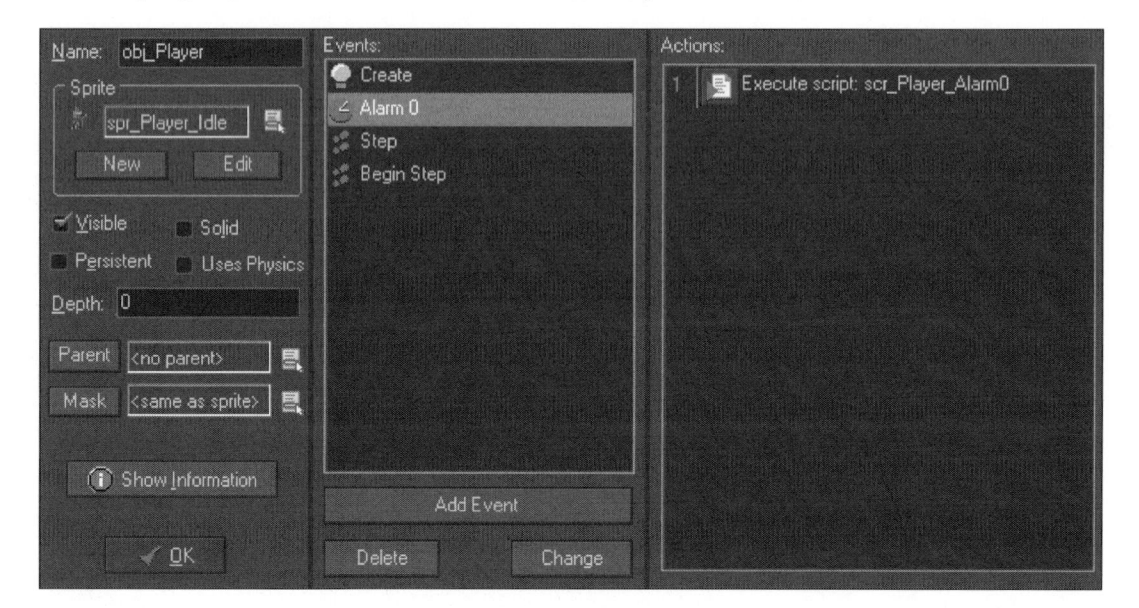

Setting up the room

We have the player, now we need a world to place it in. Since we are making a platformer, we are going to use two types of building block: a ground object and a platform object. The ground will be impassable to the player and will be used for the outer perimeter. The platform object will allow the player to jump through and then land upon it:

1. Create a new Sprite, spr_Ground, and load Chapter 5/Sprites/Ground.gif with **Remove Background** not checked. Click **OK**.
2. Create a new Object, obj_Ground, and assign spr_Ground as the **Sprite**.
3. Check the box for **Solid**. This is necessary as our collision code is looking for solid objects.
4. Let's test this out. Create a new Room, and under the **Settings** tab, change the name to BossArena and change the **Width** to 800. We will want a good size room to fight in.
5. Add instances of obj_Ground around the border of the room. Also add a single instance of obj_Player near the floor of the room.
6. Run the game. At this point the player should be able to run and jump around the room, but not be able to pass through the walls or floor. You should also be able to shoot your weapon in a variety of directions. Also notice that the animation system is working as intended, with sprites changing based on the player's actions.
7. Now to build the platforms. Create a new Sprite, spr_Platform, and load Chapter 5/Sprites/Platform.gif with **Remove Background** not checked. Click on **OK**.
8. Create a new Object, obj_Platform, and assign spr_Platform as the **Sprite**.
9. We want the platform to be solid only when the player is above it. For this we will need to create a new Script, scr_Platform_EndStep, with the following code:

```
if (obj_Player.y < y)
{
    solid = true;
} else {
    solid = false;
}
```

Here we compare the player's Y coordinate with the Y coordinate of the instance. If the player is above it, then the platform should be solid. Otherwise it is not solid and the player can jump through it.

Platform Fun

10. In `obj_Platform`, add a **Step | End Step** event and apply this script. We run this code at the end of the step because we want to change only after the player has actually moved, but before it does another forecast.

11. Go back into the `BossArena` and add some platforms for the player to jump onto. The player can only jump around 128 pixels, so make sure the platforms are placed appropriately, such as can be seen below.

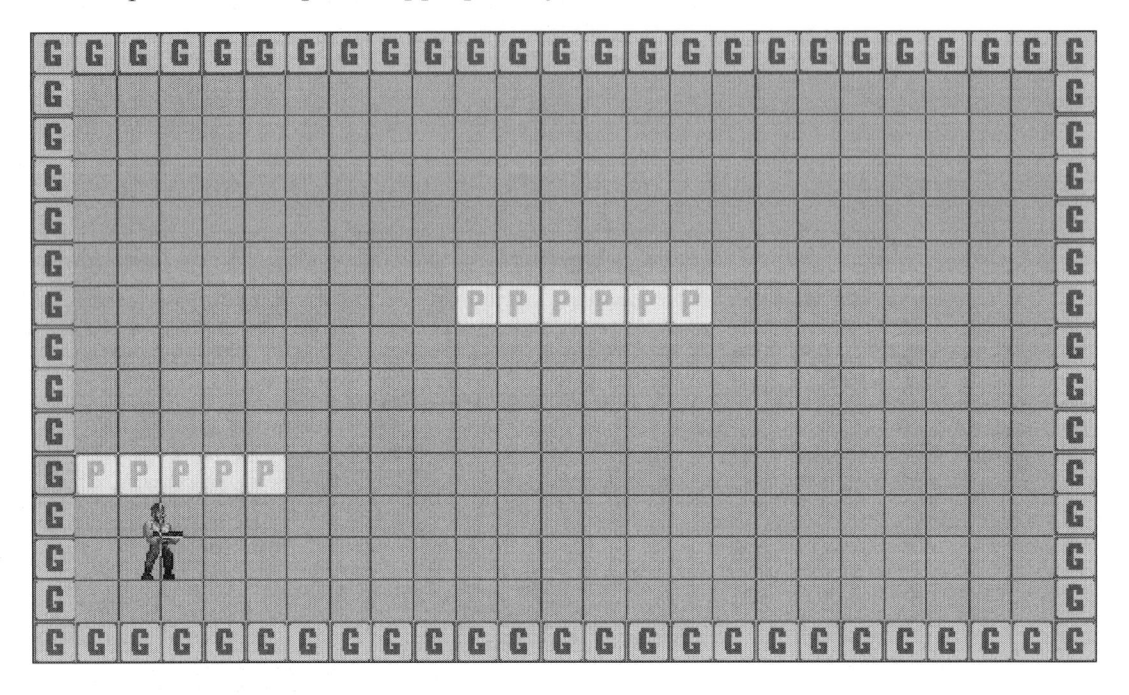

12. Run the game. The player should be able to jump through the platforms and land on top.

We have successfully developed a series of systems for a platforming game. It required us to separate common elements such as the animation system and controls into unique scripts. If we were to stop here, it may feel like we did a lot of extra work for nothing. However, as we start building our boss battle, we will start reaping the rewards for this effort.

Building a boss battle

Boss battles are one of the most enjoyable experiences in games. Building a good boss battle is always a challenge, but the theory behind it is quite simple. The first rule to follow is that a boss should consist of three unique stages of increasing difficulty. The second rule is that the boss should emphasize the latest skills that the user has acquired. The third and final rule is that the player should always have something to do.

Our boss battle will not be against another character, but against a fortress. The first stage will consist of three retractable Cannons that will shoot Cannonballs across the room. All three Cannons must be destroyed to move onto the second stage. Stage two will have a powerful LaserCannon that will move up and down and shoot a room wide Laser Beam that the player will need to avoid. The final stage will be to destroy the Boss Core that is protected by two Shields. The Shields will only be open for a short period of time. During the entire boss fight, there will be an indestructible Gun that will shoot bullets at the player wherever they are in the room. Each progressing stage, this Gun will fire more rapidly, making the game more challenging. Let's start building the boss!

Creating the indestructible Gun

We will start with the indestructible Gun since it will be the primary boss attack through the battle. The Gun will need to rotate so that it always points towards the player. When it shoots a Gun Bullet, the instance of the Gun Bullet will come from the tip of the Gun and move in the direction that the Gun is pointing:

1. Let's start by building the Gun Bullet. Create a new Sprite, spr_Gun_Bullet, and load Chapter 5/Sprites/Gun_Bullet.gif with **Remove Background** checked. Center the **Origin** and click on **OK**.

2. Create a new Object, obj_Gun_Bullet, and assign spr_Gun_Bullet as the **Sprite**.

3. We want the bullets to always appear on top of the ground and platforms. Set the **Depth** to -2000.

4. The Gun Bullet is going to damage the player on contact, as will all the other projectiles. Once again, let's build a single system that all weapons can use. Create a new Script, scr_Damage, with the following code:

```
if (obj_Player.action != DAMAGE)
{
    health -= myDamage;
    with (obj_Player)
    {
        y -= 1;
```

Platform Fun

```
        vspeed = -MAXGRAVITY;
        hspeed = 8 * -facing;
        action = DAMAGE;
        isDamaged = true;
    }
}
```

This script is specifically for the enemy weapons. We start by checking to see if the player is not already damaged so that the player isn't punished repetitively. Then we reduce the global health by the value indicated by the variable `myDamage`. By using a variable like this, we can have different weapons apply differing amounts of damage. We then affect the player directly through a `with` statement. We want to launch the player into the air, but first we need to raise the player off the ground by one pixel first to ensure the ground collision code doesn't snap it back down. Next we apply a vertical velocity and a horizontal velocity in the opposite direction that they are facing for a push back effect. We set the player's action to the `DAMAGE` state and indicate that damage has happened.

5. Create another new Script, `scr_Gun_Bullet_Create`, and initialize the `myDamage` variable. Then apply it to a **Create** event in `obj_Gun_Bullet`.

   ```
   myDamage = 5;
   ```

6. Next let's create a collision script, `scr_Gun_Bullet_Collision`, which calls the damage script and removes the Bullet. We did not put the destruction of the instance into `scr_Damage` so that we have the option for weapons that can't be destroyed, use this script:

   ```
   scr_Damage();
   instance_destroy();
   ```

7. We can now add a **Collision | obj_Player** event to `obj_Gun_Bullet` with this script attached. The Gun Bullet is now complete.

8. We can now move onto the Gun itself. Start by creating two new Sprites, `spr_Gun_Idle` and `spr_Gun_Run`. Load `Chapter 5/Sprites/Gun_Idle.gif` and `Chapter 5/Sprites/Gun_Run.gif` to their associated sprite with **Remove Background** checked.

9. The Gun sprite has the barrel facing to the right so we need to set the origin on the left side so that it pivots properly. Set the **Origin** to **X**: 0 and **Y**: 16 on both sprites and click on **OK**.

10. Create a new Object, `obj_Gun`, and assign `spr_Gun_Idle` as the **Sprite**.

11. We will want to make sure that the Gun remains visually on top of the Boss at all times so set the **Depth** to -1000.

Chapter 5

12. We need to initialize some variables in a new Script, `scr_Gun_Create`, which will be added to `obj_Gun` as a **Create** event:

    ```
    action = IDLE;
    facing = RIGHT;
    tipOfGun = sprite_width;
    canFire = false;
    delay = 90;
    alarm[0] = delay;

    myIdle = spr_Gun_Idle;
    myRun = spr_Gun_Run;
    ```

    We will be using the animation system here, so we need to set values for the action and facing variables which are required. The following four variables relate to the shooting of the Gun. First is `tipOfGun` for where the end of the barrel is located, `canFire` is the trigger, `delay` is how long to pause between shots, and the alarm will shoot the Gun Bullet. Finally, we have two states of animation that we need to apply. We do not need to add all the other variables such as `myDamage` unless the object utilizes that state.

13. Next we will have the Gun track the player and determine when to shoot. Create a new Script, `scr_Gun_Step`, which will be placed in a **Step | Step** event. Here's the code we need:

    ```
    scr_Animation_Control();

    if (image_index > image_number-1)
    {
        action = IDLE;
    }

    if (canFire)
    {
        action = RUN;
        alarm[1] = 5;
        canFire = false;
    }

    image_angle = point_direction(x, y, obj_Player.x, obj_Player.y);
    ```

Platform Fun

We start by running the animation script. We want the Gun to play the firing animation only once, so we check the currently displayed image against the last image of the sprite. Using `image_number` gives us the number of frames, but we need to subtract by one as frames of animation start at zero. If it is the last frame, then the Gun goes into the `IDLE` state. Next we check to see if the Gun is to shoot. If it is, we change states to play the shooting animation, set a second alarm for 5 frames, and then turn off `canFire`. Finally we track the player by rotating the sprite based on the angle between the Gun and the player.

14. We are using two alarms on this object. The first alarm starts the firing animation and the second creates the Gun Bullet. Let's start with the first alarm by creating a new Script, `scr_Gun_Alarm0`, for an **Alarm | Alarm 0** event:

    ```
    canFire = true;
    ```

15. The second alarm has the code for firing the Gun Bullet. Create a new Script, `scr_Gun_Alarm1`, that will be added as an **Alarm | Alarm 1** event:

    ```
    myX = x + lengthdir_x(tipOfGun, image_angle);
    myY = y + lengthdir_y(tipOfGun, image_angle);
    bullet = instance_create(myX, myY, obj_Gun_Bullet);
    bullet.speed = 16;
    bullet.direction = image_angle;
    alarm[0] = delay;
    ```

    Since we need the bullet to leave the end of the barrel of the gun we are going to need some trigonometry. We could use sine and cosine to calculate the X and Y values from the origin of the circle and radial distance, but there is a much easier way. Here we are using `lengthdir_x` and `lengthdir_y` to do the math for us. All that it needs is the radial distance and the angle which we can then add to the local coordinates of the Gun. Once we have those variables, we can create the bullet in the proper position, set its speed, and direction. Finally we reset the first alarm so that the Gun will fire again.

16. We are ready to test the Gun. Open BossArena and place an instance of the Gun on the far right side of the room. Once we are done testing we will be removing the gun from the room, so exact placement doesn't matter at this time.

17. Run the Game. The Gun should follow the player wherever they are in the room and fire Gun Bullets every three seconds. If the player is hit by a Gun Bullet, they will be launched into the air and pushed back with the damage animation playing as seen in the previous screenshot.

18. There is one issue, however, with the player's damage state; the player can still move and shoot. This isn't much of a deterrent to being shot, so let's fix this. Create a new Script, scr_Player_Damage, with the following code:

```
if (isOnGround)
{
    isDamaged = false;
} else {
    scr_Gravity();
}
```

We check to see if the player is on the ground or not as that will deactivate the damage state. If the player is in the air, we apply gravity and that is it.

19. Now we need to call this script. Reopen scr_Player_Step and add a conditional statement for whether the player is damaged or not. Here is the entire script with the new code in bold:

```
if (isDamaged)
{
    scr_Player_Damage();
```

```
} else {
    if (isOnGround)
    {
        scr_Player_GroundControls();
    } else {
        scr_Player_AirControls();
    }
    scr_Player_Attack();
}
scr_Animation_Control();
```

We check to see if the player is in damage mode, and if it is, we run the damage script. Otherwise, we function as normal with all the control systems in the `else` statement. The animation script is always called regardless of damage.

20. Run the game. Now when the player is hit, the impact is really noticeable.

Constructing the first phase: The Cannons

The first stage weapon is a Cannon that hides itself for protection and only exposes itself to shoot. We will have three Cannons stacked on top of each other to make the player have to jump onto platforms. To destroy the Cannons the player will need to shoot each Cannon while it is exposed:

1. Starting with the Cannonball, create a new Sprite, `spr_Cannonball`, and load Chapter 5/Sprites/Cannonball.gif with **Remove Background** checked.
2. Set the **Origin** to **X**: 12, **Y**: 32 and click on **OK**.
3. Create a new Object, `obj_Cannonball`, and assign `spr_Cannonball` as the **Sprite**.
4. Set the **Depth** to -900 so that it will appear in front of most objects.
5. To use the damage system, we need to set the proper variables in the **Create** event with a new script, `scr_Cannonball_Create`:

   ```
   myDamage = 10;
   hspeed = -24;
   ```

   This weapon is powerful and will cause 10 points of damage. We also set the horizontal velocity so that it quickly moves across the room.

6. We are not going to destroy the Cannonball if it contacts the player, so all we need to do is apply `scr_Damage` to a **Collision | obj_Player** event. The Cannonball is now ready to be shot.

7. The Cannon is going to need five sprites, `spr_Cannon_IdleDown`, `spr_Cannon_IdleUp`, `spr_Cannon_RunDown`, `spr_Cannon_RunUp`, and `spr_Cannon_Damage`. Load the associated files from the `Chapter 5/Sprites/` folder without checking **Remove Background**.

8. Create a new Object, `obj_Cannon`, and assign `spr_Cannon_IdleDown` as the **Sprite**.

9. Set the **Depth** to `-1000` so that the Cannon will be in front of the rest of the Boss parts.

10. As always, let's create a new Script, `scr_Cannon_Create`, to initialize all the variables in the **Create** event:

```
myHealth = 20;
action = IDLEDOWN;
facing = RIGHT;
canFire = false;

myIdleUp = spr_Cannon_IdleUp;
myIdleDown = spr_Cannon_IdleDown;
myRunUp = spr_Cannon_RunUp;
myRunDown = spr_Cannon_RunDown;
myDamage = spr_Cannon_Damage;
```

The Cannon will take several hits before it is destroyed, so we have a `myHealth` variable to track the damage. We then set the action state by facing to the right, as we are not flipping the sprite, and establish a shooting variable. We then have all the animation states we need for the Cannon to work.

11. Next we can create a new Script, `scr_Cannon_Step`, for a **Step | Step** event with the functionality for switching states and firing the Cannonballs:

```
scr_Animation_Control();

if (image_index > image_number-1)
{
    if (action == RUNUP) { action = IDLEUP;}
    else if (action == RUNDOWN) { action = IDLEDOWN;}
}

if (canFire)
{
    action = RUNUP;
    alarm[0] = 60;
```

```
        canFire = false;
}

if (myHealth <= 0)
{
    instance_destroy();
}
```

Similar to the Gun, we start with calling the animation system script. We then check if the Cannon is on the last frame of the animation. Here we have two different idle states depending on whether the Cannon is exposed or not. We check to see which state we are in and set the appropriate idle state. Next we check if the Cannon should shoot, and if it should, we expose the Cannon and set an alarm to create the Cannonball in two seconds. Finally, we do a health check and if the Cannon is out of life, it removes itself from the game.

12. Create a new Script, scr_Cannon_Alarm0, and add it to an **Alarm | Alarm 0** event with the following code:

```
instance_create(x, y, obj_Cannonball);
action = RUNDOWN;
```

Here we just create a Cannonball and then set the animation to retract the Cannon.

13. The last thing we need to do with the Cannon is have it take damage. Create a new Script, scr_Cannon_Collision, and apply it to a **Collision | obj_Bullet** event with the following code:

```
if (action == IDLEUP)
{
    myHealth -= 10;
    action = DAMAGE;
    with (other) {instance_destroy();}
}
```

We start by making sure that damage will only be applied if the Cannon is exposed. If it is, then we take 10 points of its health, change to the damage animation, and remove the bullet. The Cannon is now complete.

14. Before we try to test the Cannon out, we are going to start constructing the Boss. The Cannon doesn't run on its own, but is controlled by the Boss. Create a new Object called `obj_Boss`. There is no sprite to assign as the Boss is comprised of other objects.

15. Create a new Script, `scr_Boss_Create`, to initialize variables in the **Create** event:

    ```
    isPhase_01 = true;
    isPhase_02 = false;
    isPhase_03 = false;
    isBossDefeated = false;

    boss_X = 672;
    gun = instance_create(32, 32, obj_Gun);
    cannonA = instance_create(boss_X, 64, obj_Cannon);
    cannonB = instance_create(boss_X, 192, obj_Cannon);
    cannonC = instance_create(boss_X, 320, obj_Cannon);
    ```

    We start by establishing variables for the three phases and whether the boss has been defeated. We then create a variable for the X location of the boss with the indestructible Gun located in the upper left corner of the room and a tower of Cannons right where the Boss is. We establish variables for each weapon so that the Boss can control them.

16. We want the Cannons to shoot in a sequence rather than all together. To do this we are going to use a Time Line. Create a new Time Line and name it `tm_Boss_Phase01`.

17. Add a **Moment** and set **Indicate the moment** to `180`. This will start six seconds into the battle.

18. Create a new Script, `scr_Phase01_180`, and fire the middle Cannon. Apply this script to the Time Line:

    ```
    if (instance_exists(cannonB)) { cannonB.canFire = true;}
    ```

    Since the player can destroy the Cannons, we need to check to see if the Cannon is still in existence. If it is, we set the Cannon's `canFire` variable to true and the Cannon code will handle the rest.

19. Add another **Moment** at `360`.

Platform Fun

20. Create a Script, `scr_Phase01_360`, and activate the other two Cannons:
    ```
    if (instance_exists(cannonA)) { cannonA.canFire = true; }
    if (instance_exists(cannonC)) { cannonC.canFire = true; }
    ```
    We need to check both Cannons individually so that if one is destroyed, the other will still shoot.

21. Reopen `scr_Boss_Create` and start a looping Time Line after the last line of code:
    ```
    timeline_index = tm_Boss_Phase01;
    timeline_running = true;
    timeline_loop = true;
    ```

22. Reopen `BossArena` and make sure you remove the instance of the Gun if it is still in the room.

23. Place an instance of `obj_Boss` on the right side of the map, though the actual location does not matter.

24. None of the parts of the Boss have the **Solid** attribute, which means the player can run through them. To fix that, create a barrier wall in front of the Boss with instances of `obj_Ground` as seen in the following screenshot:

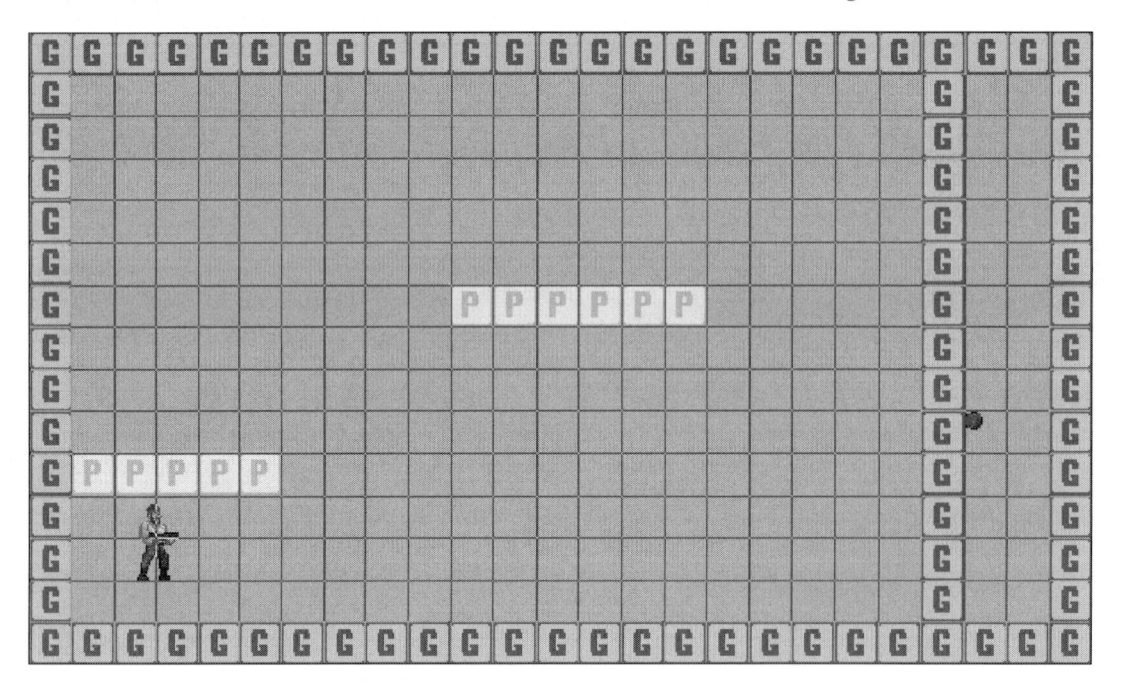

25. Run the game. At the start we should see three Cannons stacked on top of each other and the indestructible Gun. The Gun should aim at the player and shoot a Gun Bullet every few seconds. Six seconds into the game we should see the middle Cannon power up and shortly afterwards shoot a Cannonball. Six seconds after that, the upper and lower Cannons should do the same. If the player is hit by an enemy projectile they will be knocked back. The player's bullets will pass by the Cannons unless they have been exposed, in which case the Cannon will go into its damage state and the bullet disappears. If any Cannon is hit two separate times it will blink out of existence. The first phase is now complete and should look like the following screenshot:

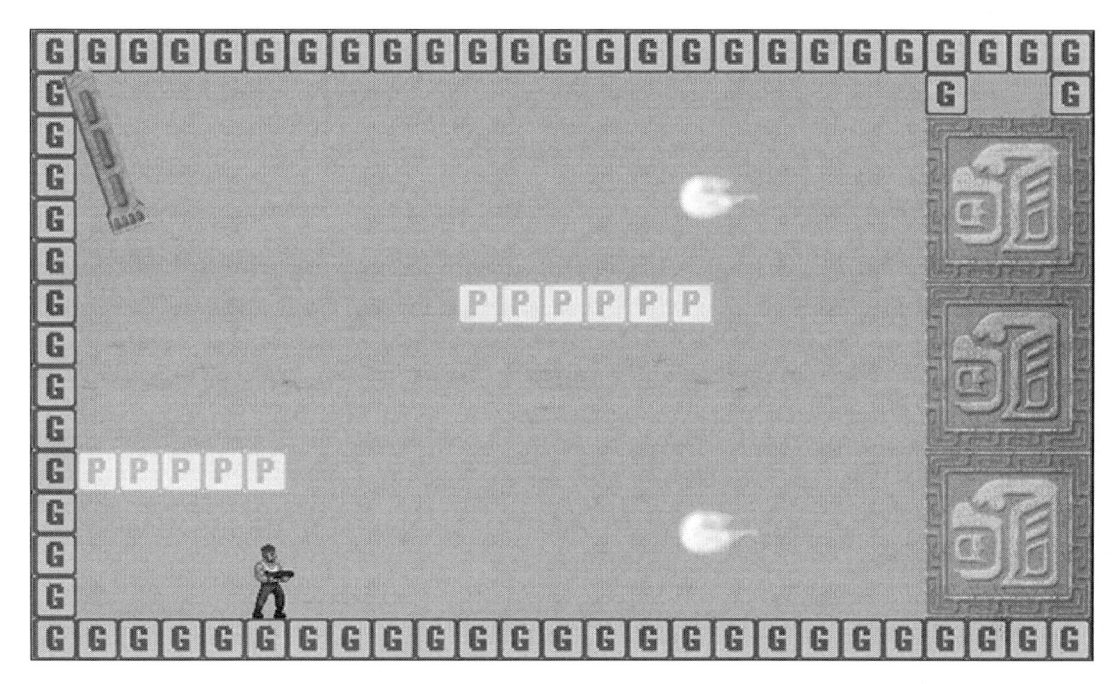

Platform Fun

Building the second phase: The giant LaserCannon

Once the player destroys all the Cannons, the second phase will begin. Here we will have a giant LaserCannon that moves constantly up and down. Every few seconds it will fire a large Laser Beam that will stretch across the entire room. The player can damage the LaserCannon at all times, though it will have much more health:

1. First we will create the Laser Beam. Create a new Sprite, `spr_LaserBeam`, and load `Chapter 5/Sprites/LaserBeam.gif` without checking **Remove Background**. The sprite may appear small, being only eight pixels wide, but we will stretch this sprite across the screen so it could work in any room.

2. We need the origin to be on the right side so that it lines up with the LaserCannon barrel properly. Set the **Origin** to **X**: 8 and **Y**: 32.

3. Create a new Object, `obj_LaserBeam`, apply `spr_LaserBeam` as the **Sprite** and set the **Depth** to -600.

4. Create a new Script, `scr_LaserBeam_Create`, to initialize variables in a **Create** event:

   ```
   myDamage = 20;
   myLaserCannon = 0;
   image_xscale = room_width / 8;
   ```

   The amount of damage from this weapon is much higher than the other weapons, which is fitting for the second phase. We also have a `myLaserCannon` variable that will be used to keep the Laser Beam aligned with the LaserCannon as it moves. The value has been set to zero, though this will become the ID of the LaserCannon that spawns it, which we will get to in a moment. Finally, we stretch the sprite across the room. The variable `image_xscale` is a multiplier, which is why we are dividing the room width by eight, the width of the sprite.

5. Next we will use a **Step | End Step** event with a new Script, `scr_LaserBeam_EndStep`, to make the beam move with the LaserCannon.

   ```
   x = myLaserCannon.x;
   y = myLaserCannon.y;
   ```

   We move the X and Y coordinates with the LaserCannon that creates the Laser Beam. We are placing this into the **End Step** event because the LaserCannon will move on a **Step** event and this will ensure that it is always in the correct position.

6. All that is left is for `scr_Damage` to be added to a **Collision | obj_Player** event. The Laser Beam is now complete.

7. Moving onto the LaserCannon, we will need to create three sprites: `spr_LaserCannon_Idle`, `spr_LaserCannon_Run`, and `spr_LaserCannon_Damage`. Load the associated files from the `Chapter 5/Sprites/` folder all of which need to have **Remove Background** checked.

8. Set the **Origin** of all three sprites to **X**: 16 and **Y**: 56. This will help place the Laser Beam where we want it to be.

9. Create a new Object, `obj_LaserCannon`, and assign `spr_LaserCannon_Idle` as the **Sprite**.

10. Set the **Depth** to -700 so that the LaserCannon is behind the Cannons and Gun, but in front of the Laser Beam.

11. For initializing variables in the **Create** event, create a new Script, `scr_Laser_Create`, with the following code:

    ```
    myHealth = 50;
    mySpeed = 2;
    myBuffer = 64;
    action = IDLE;
    facing = RIGHT;
    canFire = false;

    myIdle = spr_LaserCannon _Idle;
    myRun = spr_LaserCannon _Run;
    myDamage = spr_LaserCannon _Damage;
    ```

    We first set all the standard variables for the LaserCannon's health, current state, facing direction, and that it isn't shooting. We then set all the animation system variables for the three states that the LaserCannon has.

12. Next is building the functionality of the laser. Create a new Script, `scr_LaserCannon_Step`, and add it to a **Step | Step** event with the following code:

    ```
    scr_Animation_Control();

    if (image_index > image_number-1)
    {
        action = IDLE;
    }

    if (canFire)
    {
        action = RUN;
    ```

```
        alarm[0] = 5;
        canFire = false;
}

if (myHealth <= 0)
{
    instance_destroy();
}
```

This should be starting to look quite familiar. We start by running the animation system script. We then check to see if the last frame of animation has played, and if so, set the LaserCannon to its idle state. Next, if the LaserCannon is to shoot, we change states and set a short alarm so that the Laser Beam is created after the shooting animation has played. Finally, we do a health check and remove the LaserCannon if it is out of health.

We aren't done with this script yet. We still need to add in the movement. When the LaserCannon is first created, it will not be moving. We don't want it to start moving until the second phase has started. After that point we want the LaserCannon to take care of the vertical motion.

13. To make the LaserCannon move up and down, all we need to do is send it in the opposite direction when it passes an end point. Add this code immediately after the last line of code in scr_LaserCannon_Step:

    ```
    if (y < myBuffer)
    {
        vspeed = mySpeed;
    }
    if (y > room_height - myBuffer)
    {
        vspeed = -mySpeed;
    }
    ```

14. We are going to have the LaserCannon move the entire height of the room. If the Y coordinate is less than 64 pixels from the top, we send it downwards. If it is greater than 64 pixels from the bottom of the room, we send it upwards. We will start the movement in the Boss script in a while.

15. Let's get the LaserCannon shooting a Laser Beam! The Laser Beam will be created in an **Alarm** | **Alarm 0** event with a new Script, scr_LaserCannon_Alarm0, attached with the Laser Beam creation code:

    ```
    beam = instance_create(x, y, obj_LaserBeam);
    beam.myLaserCannon = self.id;
    ```

We create an instance of the beam right at the tip of the LaserCannon and then we set the Laser Beam's `myLaserCannon` variable to be the unique ID of the LaserCannon that created it. The benefit of doing this means that we could have more than one LaserCannon in the room if we wanted.

16. The last element we need to construct is the damage state. Create a new Script, `scr_LaserCannon_Collision`, and place it into a **Collision | obj_Bullet** event:

```
if (obj_Boss.isPhase_02)
{
    myHealth -= 5;
    action = DAMAGE;
    with (other) { instance_destroy(); }
}
```

Since we don't want the player to be able to destroy the LaserCannon before the second phase, we check what phase the Boss is currently in, to determine if damage should be applied or not. If the Boss is in the second phase, we reduce the LaserCannon's health, change it to the damage state and remove the Bullet. The LaserCannon is now complete and ready to be implemented into the Boss.

17. The first thing we need to do is add an instance of the LaserCannon. Reopen `scr_Boss_Create` and insert this code before the Time Line is run:

    `laser = instance_create(boss_X, 352, obj_LaserCannon);`

18. Next we will build the functionality of the LaserCannon by creating a new Time Line and naming it `tm_Boss_Phase02`.

19. To shoot the Laser Beam, add a **Moment** and set **Indicate the moment** to `210`.

20. Create a new Script, `scr_Phase02_210`, and assign it with the code to activate the LaserCannon:

    `laser.canFire = true;`

21. We want to have full control over the duration of the LaserCannon, so we will use the Time Line to remove the Laser Beam. Add a **Moment** at `270`. This will give us a Laser Beam that lasts two seconds.

22. Create a new Script, `scr_Phase02_270`, and remove the Laser Beam.

    `with (laser.beam) { instance_destroy(); }`

    When the LaserCannon shoots, it creates the `beam` variable which we can now use to remove it.

23. All that is left is to have the Boss change from the first phase to the second phase. For this we will need to add a **Step | Step** event to `obj_Boss` with a new Script, `scr_Boss_Step`, assigned with the following code:

```
if (!instance_exists(obj_Cannon) && !isPhase_02)
{
    laser.vspeed = laser.mySpeed;
    timeline_index = tm_Boss_Phase02;
    timeline_position = 0;
    gun.delay = 45;
    isPhase_02 = true;
}
```

We start by checking if there are any instances of the Cannon remaining in the world and if they have all been destroyed, we check to see if the second phase has started. Upon the second phase starting, we set the LaserCannon into motion downwards and switch the Time Line to the new phase and reset the Time Line to the beginning. We are also going to make the challenge a bit more difficult by decreasing the delay between shots from the Gun. We end this code by changing `isPhase_02` to true so that this is only executed once.

24. Run the game. The gameplay starts out the same as before, but after the three Cannons have been destroyed, we should see the LaserCannon starts to move up and down and fire a Laser Beam every seven seconds. The LaserCannon can be hit at any time and will take several hits before being destroyed. The indestructible Gun should still function as before, but shoot twice as often. The second phase is now complete and should look like the following screenshot:

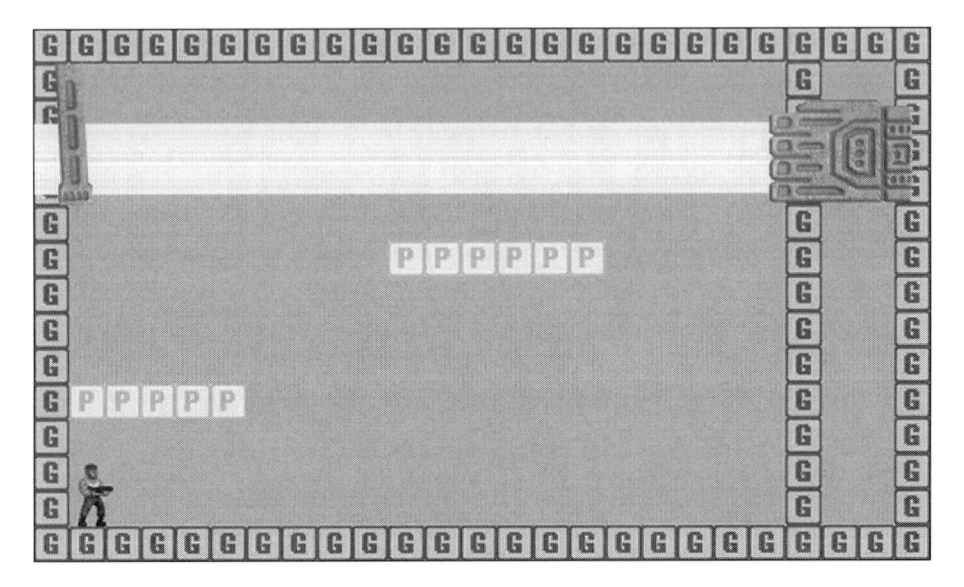

Setting the final stage: The shielded Boss Core

For the final stage we are not going to add another weapon, but instead we will create a destructible Boss Core that is protected by two Shields. The Shields will open every few seconds to expose the Boss Core. We will also change the Gun to shoot in quick bursts:

1. We will start with the Boss Core. We need to create two new Sprites, `spr_BossCore_Idle` and `spr_BossCore_Damage`. With **Remove Background** checked, load `Chapter 5/Sprites/BossCore_Idle.gif` and `Chapter 5/Sprites/BossCore_Damage.gif` to the appropriate sprite.

2. Set the **Origin** of both sprites to **X**: -32 and **Y**: 64 so that it will be properly located behind the Shields.

3. Create a new Object, `obj_BossCore`, and assign `spr_BossCore_Idle` as the **Sprite**.

4. The Boss Core is a simple object that only requires some animation states and health. Create a new Script, `scr_BossCore_Create`, and initialize the required variables as follows. Remember to assign this to a **Create** event:

   ```
   myHealth = 100;
   action = IDLE;
   facing = RIGHT;

   myIdle = spr_BossCore_Idle;
   myDamage = spr_BossCore_Damage;
   ```

5. We need a **Step | Step** event to control the animation states and deal with the health, so create another new Script, `scr_BossCore_Step` with the following code:

   ```
   scr_Animation_Control();

   if (action == DAMAGE)
   {
       if (image_index > image_number-1)
       {
           action = IDLE;
       }
   }

   if (myHealth <= 0)
   {
       instance_destroy();
   }
   ```

Platform Fun

6. All the Boss Core now needs is a **Collision | obj_Bullet** event to deal with damage. Create a new Script, `scr_BossCore_Collision`, and write the following code:

```
if (obj_Boss.isPhase_03 && action == IDLE)
{
    myHealth -= 2;
    action = DAMAGE;
    with (other) { instance_destroy(); }
}
```

We first check to see if the Boss is in the final phase and that the Boss Core is in its idle state. If it is, we reduce the health and switch over to the damage animation. We also make sure that the Bullet is removed. The Boss Core is now complete and we can move onto the Shields.

7. We will have two Shields, one that lifts up and the other that will drop down. Let's bring in the two sprites that we will need. Create two new Sprites, `spr_Shield_Upper` and `spr_Shield_Lower`. Load Chapter 5/Sprites/Shield_Upper.gif and Chapter 5/Sprites/Shield_Lower.gif to the associated sprite. Remember to check **Remove Background**.

8. Set the **Origin** of `spr_Shield_Upper` to **X**: 0 and **Y**: 269 so that the origin is on the bottom of the image. We don't need to change the **Origin** of `spr_Shield_Lower`.

9. Create two new Objects, `obj_Shield_Upper` and `obj_Shield_Lower`, and assign the appropriate sprites.

10. On both the Shields, set the **Depth** to -500 so that they are in front of the Boss Core but behind all the other parts of the Boss.

11. We will build the upper Shield first and we need to initialize some variables in a new Script, `scr_ShieldUpper_Create`, applied to a **Create** event in `obj_Shield_Upper`:

```
isShielding = true;
openPosition = y-64;
mySpeed = 2;
```

The first variable will activate whether the Shield is up or down. The second variable sets the value for how high to lift the Shield; in this case it will move up 64 pixels. Finally we set a variable for the movement speed.

Chapter 5

12. The lower Shield is almost exactly the same except that it moves in the opposite direction. Once again, create a new Script, `scr_ShieldLower_Create`, and apply it to the **Create** event of `obj_Shield_Lower`:

    ```
    isShielding = true;
    openPosition = y+64;
    mySpeed = 2;
    ```

13. Next we will add a **Step | Step** event to `obj_Shield_Upper`, with a new Script, `scr_ShieldUpper_Step`, attached with the following code to control the shield's movement:

    ```
    if (isShielding && y < ystart) { y += mySpeed; }
    if (!isShielding && y > openPosition) { y -= mySpeed; }
    ```

    We start by checking if the Shield is supposed to be down and whether it is all the way down or not. If it isn't all the way down, we move the Shield a bit down. The second `if` statement does the opposite, checking to see if the Shield is supposed to be up and whether it is all the way up. If not, we lift the Shield up a bit.

14. Once again, the lower Shield is almost exactly the same. Create a new Script, `scr_ShieldLower_Step`, attached to a **Step | Step** event in `obj_Shield_Lower`:

    ```
    if (isShielding && y > ystart) { y -= 2; }
    if (!isShielding && y < openPosition) { y += 2; }
    ```

15. The last element we need to deal with is a **Collision | obj_Bullet** event, which both the Shields can use. Create a new Script, `scr_Shield_Collision`, with the following code:

    ```
    if (obj_Boss.isPhase_03)
    {
        with (other) { instance_destroy(); }
    }
    ```

    The Shields will never take damage, but they should only detect collision during the final phase.

16. Now that all the objects have been prepared, it is time to implement them into the Boss. Reopen `scr_Boss_Create` and insert the following code after the last weapon:

    ```
    core = instance_create(boss_X, 272, obj_BossCore);
    shieldUpper = instance_create(boss_X, 272, obj_Shield_Upper);
    shieldLower = instance_create(boss_X, 272, obj_Shield_Lower);
    ```

    We create the Boss Core and the Shields all at the same location.

17. Next we will create a Timeline, tm_Boss_Phase03, to deal with the Shields and Gun functionality.

18. Add a **Moment** at 120, and then create a new Script, scr_Phase03_120, with the following code:
    ```
    shieldUpper.isShielding = false;
    shieldLower.isShielding = false;
    gun.delay = 10;
    ```
    Here we are setting the Shields to open and increasing the shooting rate of the Gun.

19. Add a **Moment** at 180 and create a new Script, scr_Phase03_180. All we are going to do here is turn off the Gun's alarm so that there is a brief respite in the shooting. This is achieved by setting the delay to -1.
    ```
    gun.delay = -1;
    ```

20. Add another **Moment** at 300, and create a new Script, scr_Phase03_300. Now we reactivate the Gun's alarm.
    ```
    gun.delay = 10;
    ```

21. Finally we add a **Moment** at 360 with another new Script, scr_Phase03_360, where we lower the Shields and return the Gun to a regular shooting rate:
    ```
    shieldUpper.isShielding = true;
    shieldLower.isShielding = true;
    gun.delay = 45;
    ```

22. Now we need to add in the switch from the second phase to the final phase. Reopen scr_Boss_Step and add the following code at the end:
    ```
    if (!instance_exists(obj_LaserCannon) && !isPhase_03)
    {
        timeline_index = tm_Boss_Phase03;
        timeline_position = 0;
        isPhase_03 = true;
    }
    ```
    We check whether the LaserCannon has been destroyed and if we are supposed to be in the final phase or not. If we are, all we need to do is switch the timeline, set it to the beginning, and set it to the final phase.

23. All we need now is a win condition which we will add to the same script. At the end of `scr_Boss_Step` write the last conditional statement:

    ```
    if (!instance_exists(obj_BossCore) && !isBossDefeated)
    {
        timeline_running = false;
        with (gun) { instance_destroy(); }
        isBossDefeated = true;
    }
    ```

    We check to see if the Boss Core has been destroyed and if the win condition has been called. If the Boss has been defeated, we stop the Timeline and declare the defeat.

24. Run the game. It will take some time, but the first two phases should be the same as before and once the LaserCannon has been destroyed, the final phase activates. The Shields should open and the Gun shoots a burst of bullets. There then should be a quiet moment where the player can attack the Boss Core. A few seconds later the Gun should start firing and the Shields will close. This will repeat until the player defeats the Boss. This phase should look like the following screenshot:

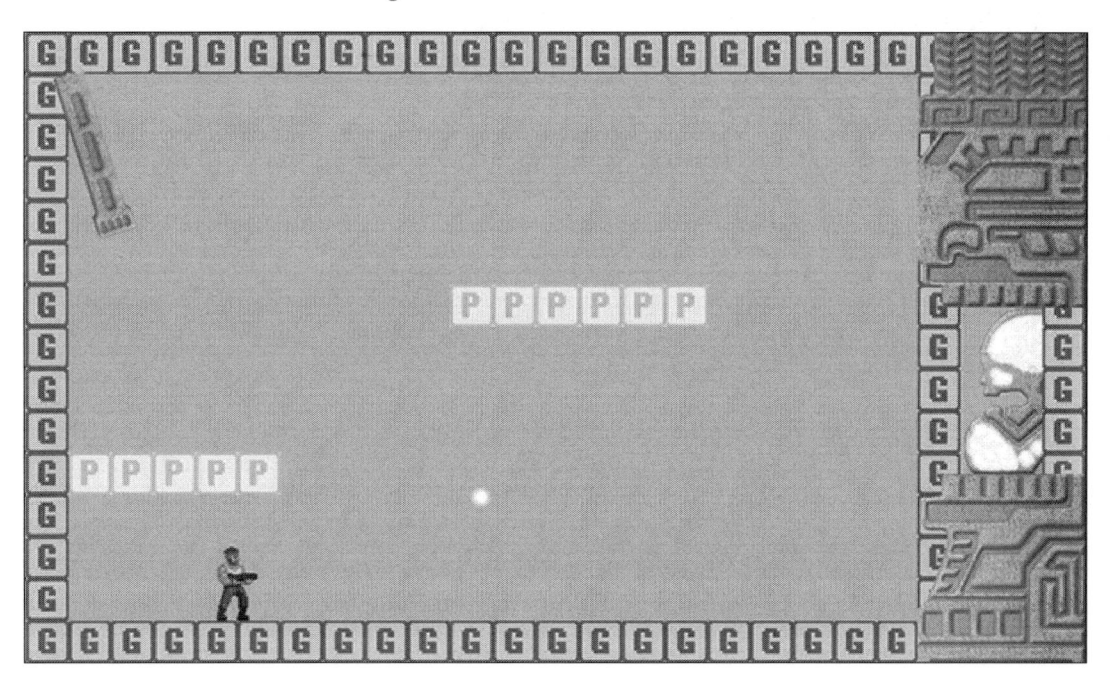

Platform Fun

Winding it up

We are wrapping up this chapter with some elements still left undone, but you already have the ability to do this on your own. There are still all the sounds, background art, and front end to build. Not only that, but you may have noticed that the player cannot be killed. Making the player invincible made it easier for us to test out the boss battle, so try the fight again after you have added it in. The boss battle is pretty difficult, but also easily altered. Why not try changing up the timing in each phase or try adjusting the values of the damage. To take this even further you can build levels and enemies that lead up to the battle. Have fun with it and it could look something like the following screenshot below!

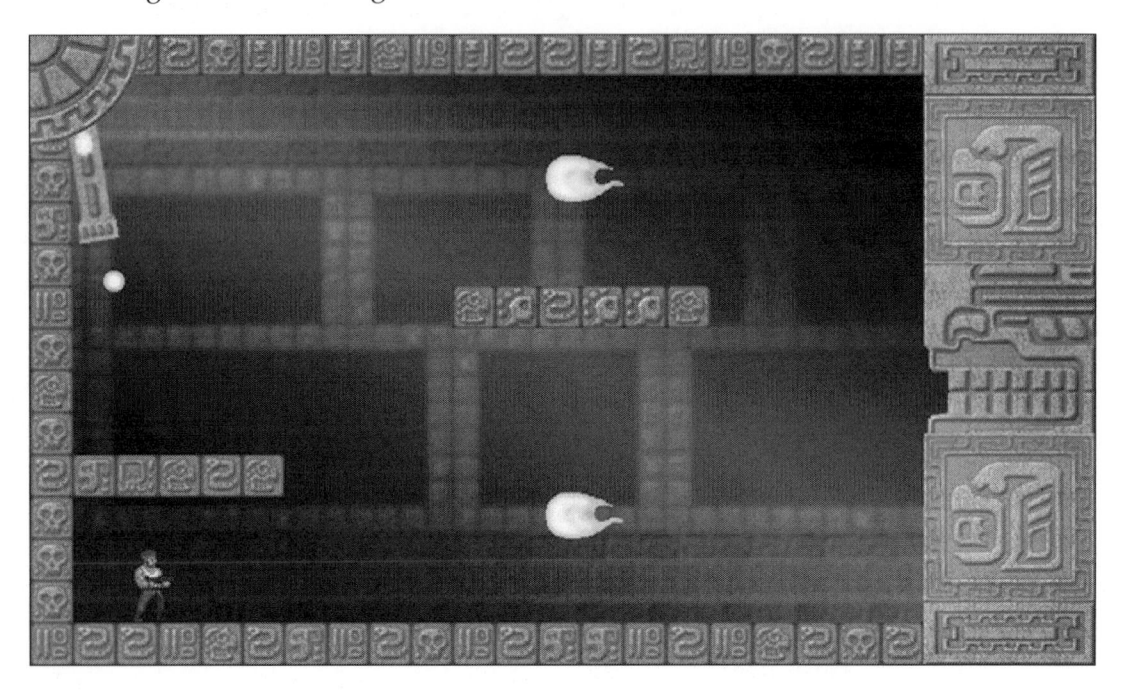

Summary

Congratulations, you have just built an epic boss battle! We started this chapter by delving into systems design and creating some very useful scripts. We built an animation system that most objects in the game utilized. We learned how to forecast for collision and apply our own custom gravity on the player. We even created platforms that the player could jump through and land on. We were introduced to constants, which has the benefit of making the code easier to read for us and more efficient to the computer. We then went on to build a three-phase boss fight utilizing all our previous knowledge along with our new systems.

In the next chapter we are going to move onto creating a physics-based game utilizing GameMaker: Studio's Box2D implementation. This will use a completely different method of collision detection and physics systems. It will also allow us to have objects that react to the world with little or no code!

6
Toppling Towers

For the rest of the book we are going to focus on creating a single game from concept to a completed, released product. We will be utilizing everything we have learned so far and will be introduced to a variety of additional features, such as GameMaker: Studio's physics and particle systems. We will build some more systems to allow character dialog and an inventory. Finally, we will look at the different ways to release the game, including onto Facebook.

In this chapter we are going to build a physics-based tower toppling game that will demonstrate GameMaker: Studio's implementation of the Box2D open source physics engine. It will feature towers made out of a variety of different materials, such as glass, wood, and steel. The goal of the game will be to clear a restricted zone by destroying these towers utilizing a variety of tools. We will create TNT that will blast outwards, a Wrecking Ball that will swing down, and a Magnet that will attract loose parts. Best of all, all the collision and movement will be done by the engine itself!

Understanding the physics engine

When building a physics-based game, it requires a different way of thinking about how you go about creating things. So far, we have focused on applying movement to an instance by either teleporting it via the X/Y coordinates, or by changing the `speed`, `vspeed`, and `hspeed` variables. When we use the physics engine, these properties are ignored. Instead, the system itself deals with movement by applying a force onto the instance. That instance will react to the force based on its own properties and will act accordingly.

Additionally, the direction of the world coordinates is not the same in physics world. Zero degrees in the GameMaker standard physics world indicates a direction of right, whereas in the Box2D physics world, zero degrees indicates up, as can be seen in the following diagram:

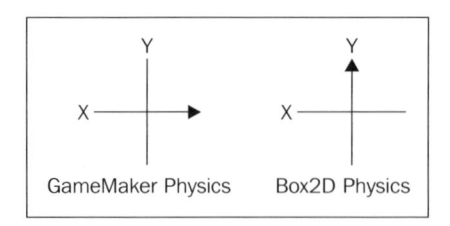

```
        Y                    Y
        |                    ▲
  X ────┼──▶          X ─────┼─────
        |                    |
  GameMaker Physics      Box2D Physics
```

To fully understand how the Box2D physics engine works, we need to take a look at the following four components that it is comprised of:

- The physics world
- Fixtures
- Joints
- Forces

Activating the world

Much like the real world, the physics world starts with the application of gravity. The amount of gravity will determine how fast the objects will fall and how much force is necessary to counteract it. Before we can use any of the physics functions in a game, we need to activate the world physics.

1. Let's start a new project called `Chapter_06`.
2. Create a new Room, and name it `Sandbox`. We will use this Room for testing purposes only.
3. Click on the **physics** tab and check **Room is Physics World**.
4. In the **Physics World Properties:**, set **Gravity:** to **X:** `0.0` and **Y:** `20.0`. This will set the direction and strength of the gravity in the world. If you wanted to have gravity as it is on Earth, we would set the value to **Y:** `9.8`. We are setting it to `20.0`, so objects appear to fall faster.
5. Finally, there is an option to set **Pixels To Meters:**. The entire physics system is based on real-world measurements, so we need to determine how many real-world meters are represented by a single pixel so that the calculations are accurate. We will leave this at the default value of 0.1 meters per pixel, or about 10 centimeters.

The world is now ready to use the physics engine! The physics settings of the room should look like the following screenshot:

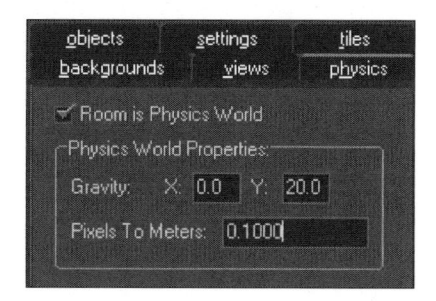

Defining properties with fixtures

In order for something to be affected by gravity and other such forces, an object requires a **Fixture**. A Fixture is what defines the shape and properties of a physics object. We will need to build two Objects: a Ground object that will never move, and a Steel Pillar which will react to gravity.

1. We will start by creating the Ground object. Create a new Sprite, `spr_Ground`, and load `Chapter 6/Sprites/Ground.png` with **Remove Background** unchecked. Leave **Origin** at **X**: 0, **Y**: 0, and click on **OK**.
2. Create a new Object, `obj_Ground`, and assign `spr_Ground` as the Sprite.
3. In order to make this object responsive in the physics engine, we need to check **Uses Physics**. This will display **Physics Properties** as shown in the following screenshot:

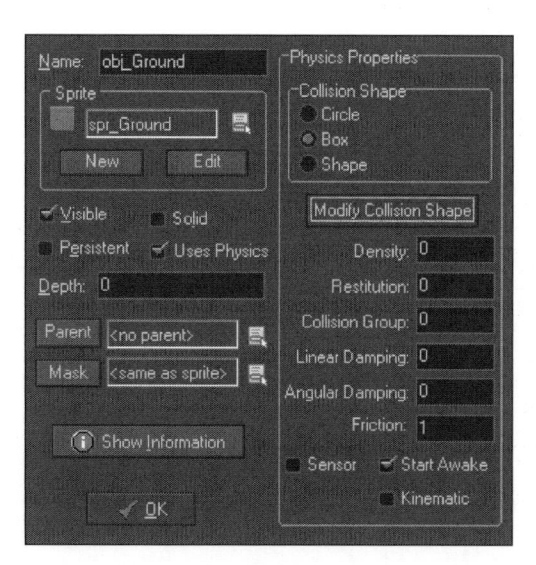

[205]

The first element we need to set up is **Collision Shape**. There are three options to choose from: **Circle**, **Box**, and **Shape**. The most common shape is **Box**, which just has four points and is always in a rectangular form. The **Circle** shape is useful for perfectly round objects as it is determined by a radius, thus not useful for round shapes like an egg. **Shape** is the most useful option in that you can have up to eight points of collision. One drawback for this is that all shapes must be convex, or it will not work. See the following screenshot to better understand what is acceptable:

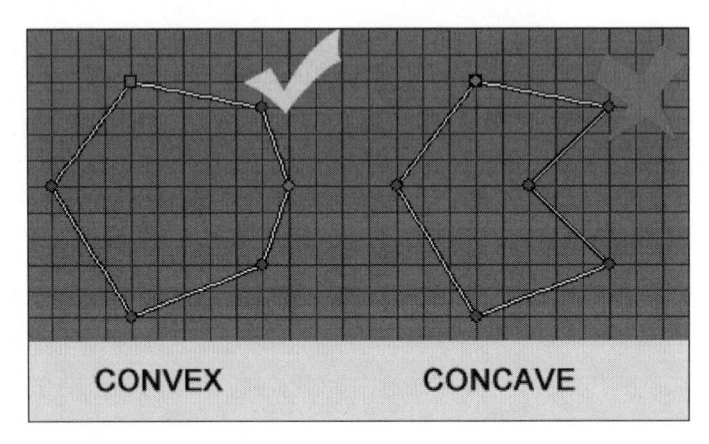

4. The Ground is a rectangular object, so in **Collision Shape** under **Physics Properties**, select **Box**.
5. The default shape will be created with its starting point based on the origin of the Sprite, which in this case is in the upper-left corner. That means we will need to either adjust the **Origin**, or the **Physics Shape** to make it fit properly. For this object we will do the latter. Click on **Modify Collision Shape** to open the **Physics Shape** editor. Place the points so that they are correctly positioned on the sprite, as seen in the following screenshot, and then click on **OK**.

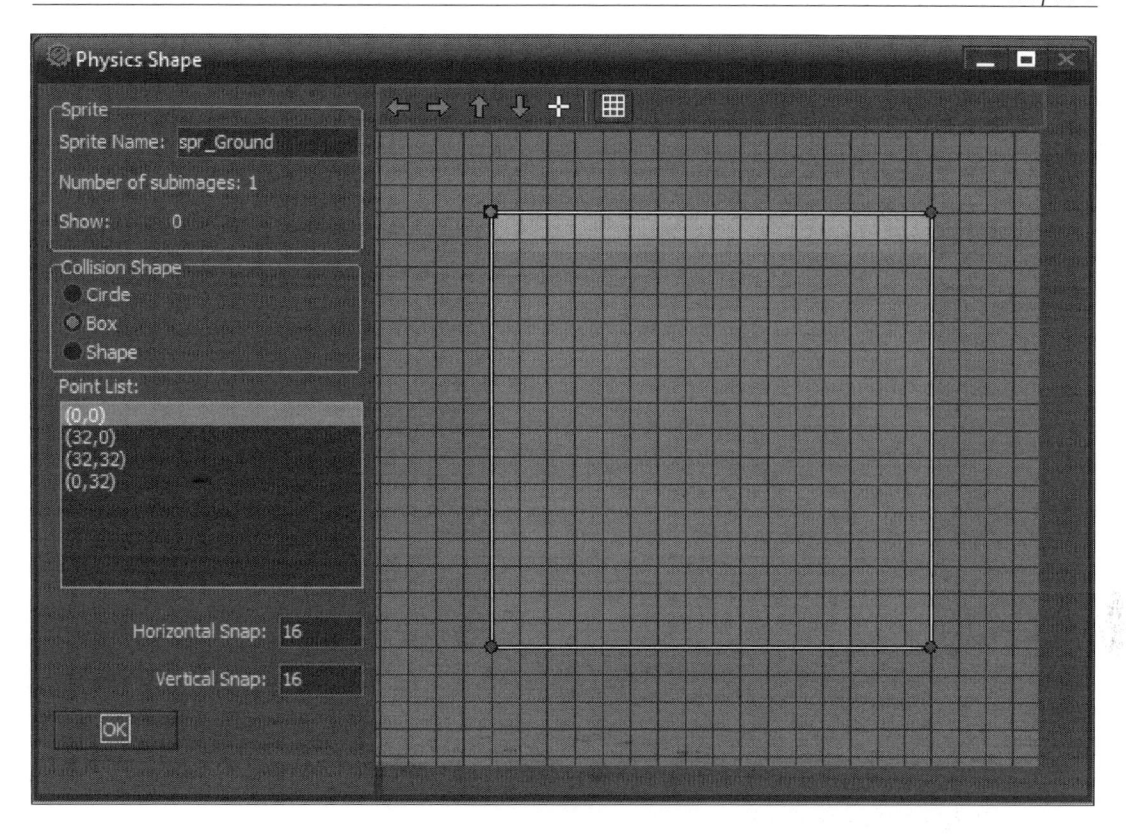

Now that the shape is complete, we can set the other physics properties. There are six adjustable properties available to us here:

- **Density**: This represents the mass of the Object per unit of volume. You can think of this as how heavy an object is compared to its overall size.
- **Restitution**: This represents how bouncy an object is. Higher the number, more bounce the object will have on collision. This does not mean that the shape of the object will deform. It won't as this is a rigid body physics simulation.
- **Collision Group**: These groups help simplify what objects can collide with each other. A positive number here will mean that all objects within that group number will always collide. A negative number means that the objects in that group number never collide with each other. If set to zero, a collision event will need to be placed into each object in order for it to collide. Using groups should be kept to a minimum, as it will dramatically increase processing time.

- **Linear Damping**: This represents the reduction of velocity of an object in motion. You can think of it as air friction as the object does not need to be in contact with any other object to slow down.
- **Angular Damping**: Much like **Linear Damping**, this is the reduction of rotational movement of an object.
- **Friction**: Friction is the force that acts opposite to a moving object during collision. This works in a similar fashion to **Linear Damping** in that it slows down objects. The difference is that it requires a collision to occur.

Different materials in the real world will have different values for each of these properties. There are many charts available that will show values for many types of materials, such as steel that has a density of 7,820 kilograms per cubic meter, and has a friction coefficient of 0.78 when touching other steel. Trying to think of all these values as they correspond to objects in a game can quickly become overwhelming. Luckily, games don't need to use real-world values, but instead we can use general concepts for the materials, such as steel has a high density while ice has a low density. Below is a chart with some basic concepts for how we need to treat the values for **Density**, **Restitution**, and **Friction**. For **Linear Damping** and **Angular Damping** it is a bit trickier, as they relate more to the shape of an object. For example, a round steel pin would have less **Angular Damping** than a square steel pin. All of these materials, whatever we set the values to, should always be tweaked until they feel correct for the game they are in. It is completely valid for a metal bar to have a density of three in one game and 300 in another, so long as it acts as the developer intends.

Material	Density	Restitution	Friction
Steel	High	Low	Medium
Glass	Low	Medium	Low
Wood	Medium	Medium	Medium
Rubber	Medium	High	Medium
Stone	High	Low	High

6. As this Ground is intended to never move or feel the effects of gravity, we need to set **Density** to 0. When an object has no density it is considered to be a static object.

7. We don't want the Ground to be bouncy, so set **Restitution** to 0.
8. We will leave **Collision Group** at the default 0.
9. As the object isn't moving, we might as well set **Linear Damping** and **Angular Damping** to 0.
10. Finally, we do want objects to come quickly to a stop on the ground, so let's set **Friction** to 1. We are done with obj_Ground, so click on **OK**.
11. Next, we will make the Steel Pillar. Create a new Sprite, spr_Pillar_Steel, and load Chapter 6/Sprites/Pillar_Steel.png with **Remove Background** checked. Center the origin and click on **OK**.
12. Create a new Object, obj_Pillar_Steel, and set spr_Pillar_Steel as its **Sprite**.
13. Check the box for **Uses Physics**.
14. In **Collision Shape** under **Physics Properties**, select **Box**. As we placed the origin into the center of the Sprite, the shape should be correctly conformed to the Sprite so that we do not have to modify it. However, we should always open the **Physics Shape** editor to ensure that it is properly located to prevent any major issues.
15. We want this object to be fairly heavy, so set **Density** to 20.
16. The Steel Pillar shouldn't be very slick either, so set **Friction** to 2.
17. Set all the other properties to 0, as we do not want to slow this object or have it bounce. We have now finished setting the properties of this object.
18. The only thing we have left to do is to add an obj_Ground event. As can be seen in the next screenshot, we don't need any code, we just need a comment. Drag a **Comment** from the **Controls** tab under **Actions:** and write Collide with Ground. With this little trick the Pillar will now have active collision with the Ground.

Toppling Towers

19. Reopen the `Sandbox` room and place an instance of `obj_Pillar_Steel` somewhere near the top in the center horizontally. Also, place instances of `obj_Ground` along the bottom with one additional instance located right above the floor and just slightly under where the Steel Pillar will fall, as seen in the following screenshot. To move an instance freely in the **Room Properties** editor, hold down the *Alt* key while holding down the left mouse button.

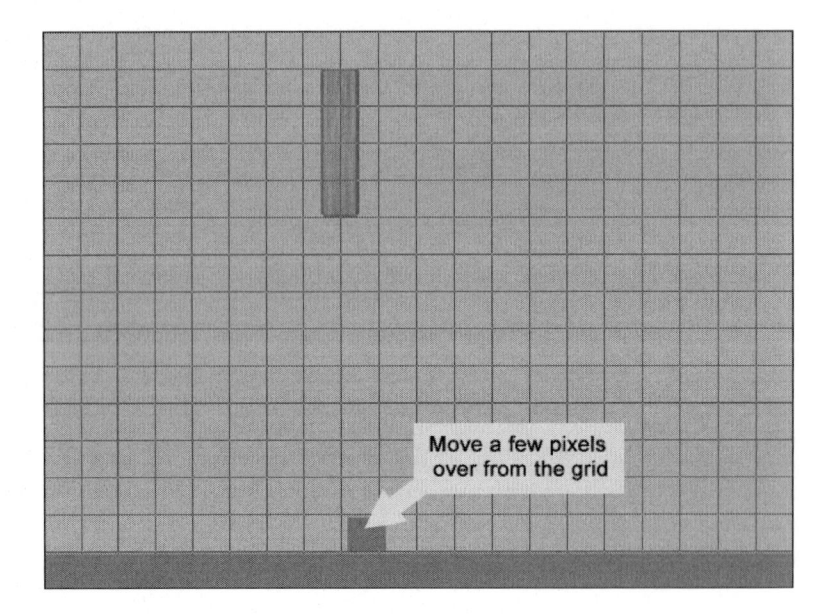

Move a few pixels over from the grid

20. Run the game. The Steel Pillar should fall down and collide with the little stump on the ground. It should then fall over onto its side and come to a rest.

We have just completed our first physics simulation! Let's now take a look at Joints.

Connecting objects with Joints

There are times when we will want two or more objects to be constrained to each other, such as a chain, or a ragdoll body. In the physics engine it is achieved through the use of **Joints**. There are five different types of Joints that we can use:

- **Distance Joints**: These will keep two instances connected at a set distance apart from each other. For example, a wheelbarrow would have a Distance Joint to keep the front wheel a set distance away from the handles, no matter how it is pushed.

- **Revolute Joints**: These will rotate one instance around another. For example, a door hinge is a Revolute Joint that rotates a door around the door frame.

- **Prismatic Joints**: These will allow one instance to move in a single direction relative to another. For example, a pinball plunger would have a Prismatic Joint, as it can only pull back or push forward into the machine.
- **Pulley Joints**: These will allow one instance to influence another in relation to its movement. For example, a set of scales uses a Pulley Joint to weigh things. If it is heavier on one side it will go down, while the other side would go up.
- **Gear Joints**: These will affect the movement of one instance based on the rotation of another. For example, the spinning reel of a fishing rod is a Gear Joint; when it is rotated it will pull in the fish.

Let's take a look at how Joints work by creating a simple chain that is attached to an Anchor.

1. We will start by building the anchor, which will be a stationary static object in the world. Create a new Sprite, spr_Anchor, and load Chapter 6/Sprites/Anchor.png with **Remove Background** checked. Center the origin and click on **OK**.
2. Create a new Object, obj_Anchor, and set spr_Anchor as the Sprite.
3. Check the box for **Uses Physics** and change the **Collision Shape** to **Box**.
4. Set **Density** and **Restitution** to 0. We can leave the other properties at the default values and it should look like the following screenshot:

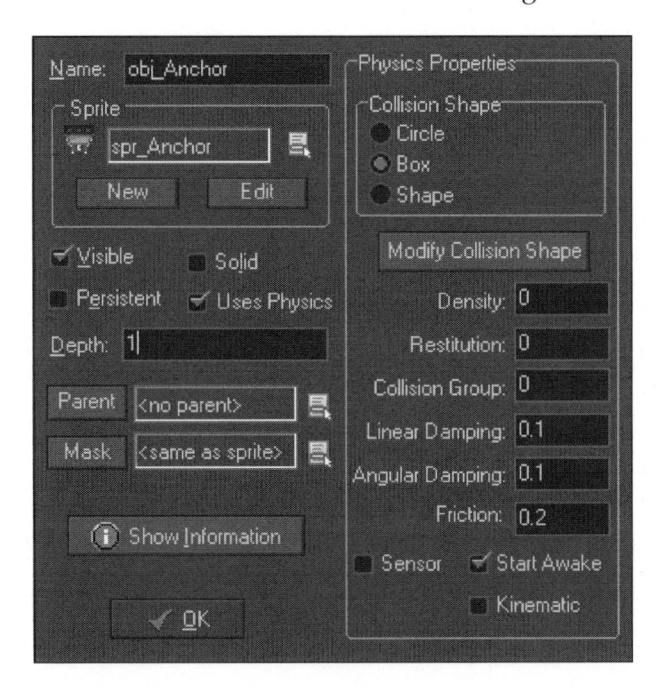

Toppling Towers

5. Next, we need to create the Chain Links. Create a new Sprite, `spr_ChainLink`, and load `Chapter 6/Sprites/ChainLink.png` with **Remove Background** checked. Center the origin and click on **OK**.
6. Create a new Object, `obj_ChainLink`, and set `spr_ChainLink` as the **Sprite**.
7. Check the box for **Uses Physics** and change the **Collision Shape** to **Box**.
8. We want the Chain to be quite strong and heavy, so set **Density** to 50.
9. The Chain should not stretch and swings freely, therefore we need to set the **Restitution**, **Linear Damping**, **Angular Damping**, and **Friction** to 0. The final settings should look like the following screenshot:

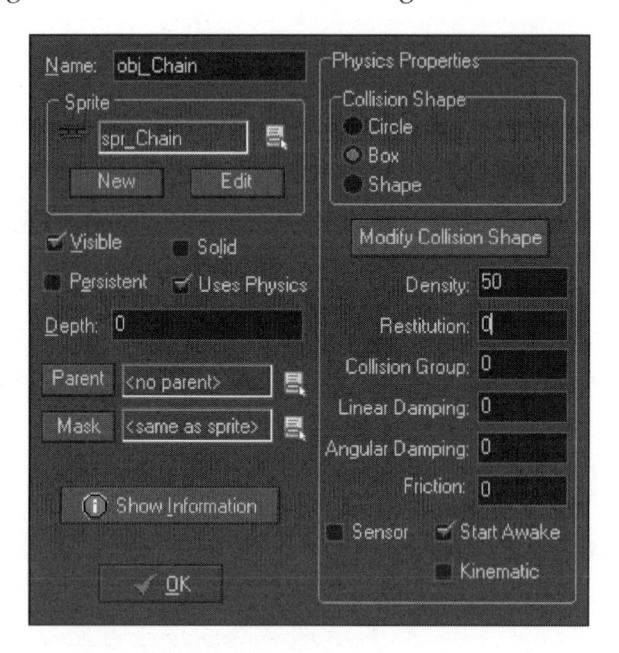

10. The component parts are now complete; we will just need to build the entire Chain and attach it to the Anchor. Create a new Script, `scr_Anchor_Create`, write the following code, and add this to a **Create** event in `obj_Anchor`:

    ```
    for (i = 1; i < 10; i++)
    {
        chain[i] = instance_create(x+ (i * 16), y, obj_ChainLink);
    }
    ```

[212]

Chapter 6

To build the Chain we run a loop starting to create nine links of the Chain. We start the loop at 1 so that the Chain is offset correctly. We use a basic one-dimensional array to store the ID of each Chain Link, as we will need this when we add the joints. The x offset we have in the creation will create each link an equal distance apart horizontally.

11. Next, we need to apply a Revolute Joint to the first link of the Chain. After the previous code, add:

    ```
    physics_joint_revolute_create(self, chain[1], self.x, self.y, 0, 0, false, 0, 0, false, false);
    ```

    We start by creating a Revolute Joint from the anchor to the very first Chain Link. The rotation will occur around the Anchor's X and Y axes. The next three parameters relate to the limitations of the rotation: the minimum and maximum angles of rotation, and whether these limits are active. In this case we don't care, so we have turned off any angle limitation. The following three parameters are for whether the joint will rotate on its own or not, with values for the maximum speed, the set speed, and whether it is active. Again, we have turned it off so the Chain will just hang in the air. The last parameter is for whether the Anchor can collide with the Chain, and we do not want that to occur here.

12. Now that we have the first link attached, let's join the rest of the Chain together. Still in the same script, at the end add:

    ```
    for (i = 1; i < 9; i++)
    {
        physics_joint_revolute_create(chain[i], chain[i+1], chain[i].x, chain[i].y, -20, 20, true, 0, 0, false, false);
    }
    ```

    Here we are using a loop again, so that we can go through each link and attach the one that follows. Notice that the loop stops at 9, as we have already connected one piece of Chain. In the case of the Chain, we don't want each Link to have full freedom of rotation. We have activated the rotational limit and set it to 20 degrees in either direction.

13. We now have a small Chain attached to an anchor. Let's add it to the world. Reopen the Sandbox and add a single instance of obj_Anchor near the top of the room.

Toppling Towers

14. Run the game. The Anchor should remain at the top of the room with the Chain Links extending out to the right of it. The Chain will fall due to the gravity in the room, though each link will remain attached to the one above it, with the top link still attached to the Anchor. It should look something like the following screenshot:

Applying forces to objects

In order to move an object in the physics world, excluding movement due to gravity, it requires that a **Force** be applied to it. These forces can be applied from a point in the world or locally to the instance. How the object reacts to the force depends on the properties it has. Just like the real world, the heavier the object, the more force is required to move it.

In order to take a look at Forces we are going to create TNT, which will explode, shooting out eight fragments. These fragments will be very dense and will require a lot of force to make them move.

1. Let's start with the fragments first. Create a new Sprite, `spr_TNT_Fragment`, and load `Chapter 6/Sprites/TNT_Fragment.png` with **Remove Background** unchecked. Center the origin and click on **OK**.

2. Create a new Object, `obj_TNT_Fragment`, and assign `spr_TNT_Fragment` as the **Sprite**.

3. Check the box for **Uses Physics** and change **Collision Shape** to **Box**.
4. Set the **Density** to 10. We are making this value very high, so that when it collides with objects, such as the Steel Pillar, it will be able to move it.
5. Set all remaining properties to 0.
6. As we need several fragments to shoot out from the TNT, we need to be able to control the direction in which it is going to move. Therefore, we need to establish some variables. Create a new Script, scr_TNT_Fragment_Create, with the following variables:

```
mySpeedX = 0;
mySpeedY = 0;
```

The strength and direction of a force is determined by a vector, which is why we need X and Y variables. We have set it to zero, so that it is not moving by default. Don't forget to apply this to a **Create** event in obj_TNT_Fragment.

7. As these fragments are meant to represent an explosion, we will want to constantly apply force to them, so that they aren't overly affected by gravity. Create a new Script, scr_TNT_Fragment_Step, and apply some force. Add this script to a **Step** event.

```
physics_apply_force(x, y, mySpeedX, mySpeedY);
```

The function physics_apply_force is a world based force, with the first two parameters representing where in the world the force is coming from, and the second two parameters being the vector of force to be applied.

8. Currently, these fragments will never stop moving, which is a problem. We are going to want to limit how far they can move outwards. Add the following code at the end of the script:

```
if (point_distance(x, y, xstart, ystart) > 128)
{
    instance_destroy();
}
```

All we are doing here is checking to see if the Fragment has moved more than 128 pixels from where it was created. If it has, we remove it from the world.

9. We want these fragments to collide with some of the other elements in the game. At the same time, we don't want them to go through anything, so we will destroy them. Create a new Script, scr_TNT_Fragment_Collision and remove the instances.

```
instance_destroy();
```

Toppling Towers

10. Add an `obj_Ground` event and add this script. This will remove the Fragment if it hits the Ground.

11. We want it to affect the Steel Pillar, but since we are planning on creating many more types of Pillars, let's build a parent object for the Pillars for collision detection. Create a new Object, `obj_Pillar_Parent`. This is all that it needs for now, so click on **OK**.

12. Reopen `obj_Steel_Pillar` and set **Parent** to `obj_Pillar_Parent`.

13. While we are in `obj_Steel_Pillar`, we might as well have it react to other Pillars as well. Add an `obj_Pillar_Parent` and drag a **Comment** from **Controls** into the **Actions:** area, and enter `Collides with Pillars` as the comment.

14. Go back into obj_TNT_Fragment and add an `obj_Pillar_Parent` and apply `scr_TNT_Fragment_Collision`. We will now have collision with all Pillars!

15. All we need to do now is to create the TNT and have it explode. Create a new Sprite, `spr_TNT`, and load `Chapter 6/Sprites/TNT.png` with **Remove Background** checked. Center the origin and click on **OK**.

16. Create a new Object, `obj_TNT`, and apply `spr_TNT` as the Sprite. We will be manually placing the TNT in the game, and we don't need it to react to the world physics, so we do *not* need to turn on **Use Physics**.

17. Let's create a new Script, `scr_TNT_Activate`, and for testing purposes, add it to a **Space** event under **Key Press**. We are going to create only a single Fragment and have it launch outwards to the right, so we can see how forces work in the world.

    ```
    frag_01 = instance_create(x, y, obj_TNT_Fragment);
    frag_01.mySpeedX = 100;
    ```

    We first create a Fragment and capture its ID in a variable. We are then setting the horizontal force to be 100 units. This value seems like it should be enough force to push this object to the right.

18. Let's test it out. Reopen `Sandbox` and place a single instance slightly to the left of where the Steel Pillar will fall and three grid spaces above the Ground. Also, let's remove the extra instance of Ground and the Chain. The Room should look like the following screenshot:

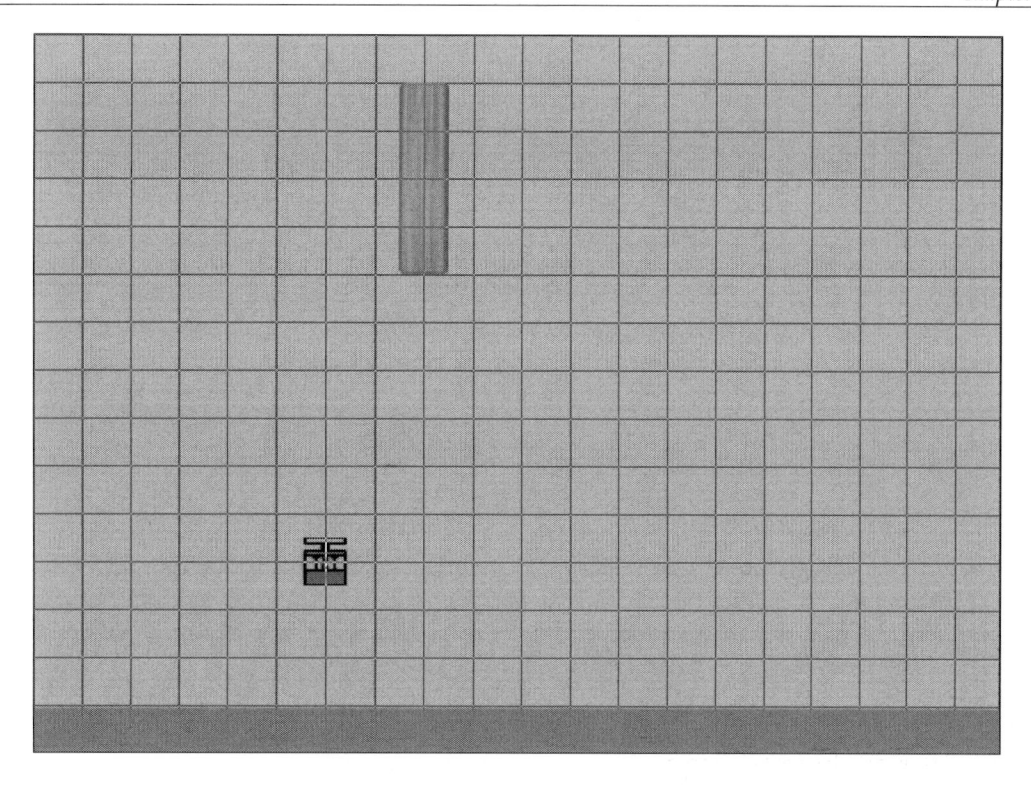

19. Run the game and press the space key to spawn a Fragment. You should see the Fragment come out moving to the right, but it is falling downwards as well. When the Fragment collides with the Steel Pillar, the Fragment disappears and nothing happens to the Steel Pillar. All of this is a result of the Fragment not having enough force.

20. Let's increase the force. Reopen `scr_TNT_Activate` and change the second line to:

    `frag_01.mySpeedX = 1000;`

21. Run the game and press space to see how this changes things. The Fragment now appears to move only to the right, and on contact with the Steel Pillar, it makes it rock a little bit. However, no matter how many times we hit the Steel Pillar, it will never fall over. This is due to the fact that the Steel Pillar has double the density of the Fragment, and it needs significantly more force to knock it down.

22. Once again, let's adjust the number by adding a zero to the end. Change the force to:

    `frag_01.mySpeedX = 10000;`

Toppling Towers

23. Run the game again and try to knock the Steel Pillar over. It should take three quick taps and it will fall over. As we can see, a small object like the Fragment is going to require a very large amount of force in order to move a large object such as the Steel Pillar.

24. Now that we have one Fragment working, let's get the rest in. We need seven more fragments moving in 45 degree increments. We will also want to remove the TNT so it can only be triggered once.

```
frag_01 = instance_create(x, y, obj_TNT_Fragment);
frag_01.mySpeedX = 10000;
frag_02 = instance_create(x, y, obj_TNT_Fragment);
frag_02.mySpeedX = -10000;
frag_03 = instance_create(x, y, obj_TNT_Fragment);
frag_03.mySpeedY = 10000;
frag_04 = instance_create(x, y, obj_TNT_Fragment);
frag_04.mySpeedY = -10000;
frag_05 = instance_create(x, y, obj_TNT_Fragment);
frag_05.mySpeedX = 5000;
frag_05.mySpeedY = 5000;
frag_06 = instance_create(x, y, obj_TNT_Fragment);
frag_06.mySpeedX = 5000;
frag_06.mySpeedY = -5000;
frag_07 = instance_create(x, y, obj_TNT_Fragment);
frag_07.mySpeedX = -5000;
frag_07.mySpeedY = -5000;
frag_08 = instance_create(x, y, obj_TNT_Fragment);
frag_08.mySpeedX = -5000;
frag_08.mySpeedY = 5000;
instance_destroy();
```

As we can see, for each Fragment we apply an appropriate value for the forces in the X and Y directions. There is no need for us to pull out a calculator and some fancy equations to figure out exactly how much force is needed, especially on the angled pieces. Remember, this is a video game and we should only worry about the overall effect and experience the player has to see if the results are correct. When you run the game it should look something like the following screenshot:

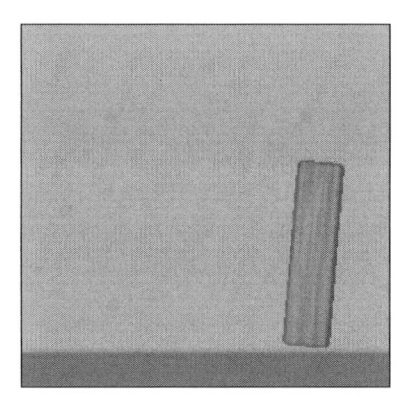

At this point we have a good foundational knowledge of how the Box2D physics engine works. We have built a room with physics activated and created several objects with fixtures and physics properties. We have used joints to connect a series of instances together and we have applied forces to an object to make it move. We are now ready to start building the tower toppling game!

Building a tower toppling game

In order to build a tower toppling game, the first elements we need to create are the support structures. We already have a Steel Pillar, which will be the strongest piece, but we will need several more. There will be three material types that will each have unique physics properties: Steel, Wood, and Glass. There will also need to be two different sizes, large and small, for variation. Finally, we want the large structures to be able to break apart into small chunks of Debris.

Constructing the Pillars and Debris

We will start by building all the additional Steel Pillars and Debris.

1. Create a new Sprite, spr_Pillar_Steel_Small, and load Chapter 6/Sprites/Pillar_Steel_Small.png with **Remove Background** checked. Center the origin and click on **OK**.

2. Rather than making a new object, right click on obj_Pillar_Steel and **Duplicate** the object. This will keep the properties the same so we don't have to repeat most of that work. Rename this to obj_Pillar_Steel_Small.

3. Change the Sprite to spr_Pillar_Steel_Small.

Toppling Towers

4. As this is a duplicate of a larger object, we need to adjust the fixture. Click on **Modify Collision Shape** to open the **Physics Shape** editor, and move the points to properly fit the smaller sprite. We are done with this Pillar and the **Object Properties** should look like the following screenshot:

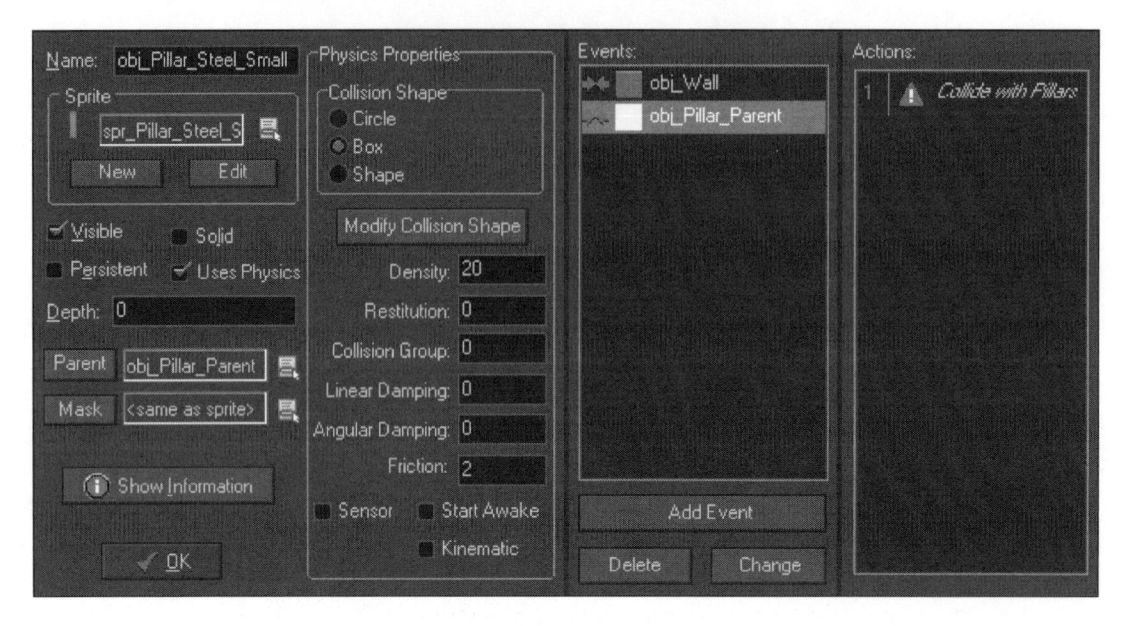

5. Create a new Sprite, `spr_Debris_Steel_01`, and load `Chapter 6/Sprites/Debris_Steel_01.png` with **Remove Background** checked.

6. When a Pillar becomes Debris, we will want to make sure each piece is placed and rotated correctly. In order to do this, we will need to place the origin as it would correspond to the Pillar's origin. This debris comes from the upper-left corner, so set the origin to **X**: 16, **Y**: 64 and click on **OK**.

7. Let's duplicate the `obj_Pillar_Steel` again, name it `obj_Debris_Steel_01` and change the sprite to `spr_Debris_Steel_01`.

8. All Debris comes in odd shapes and we will want the collision to reflect that. In the **Physics Properties** editor, change **Collision Shape** to **Shape**.

9. Click on **Modify Collision Shape** to open the **Physics Shape** editor and move the points to properly fit the Debris. You will notice that it likely has given you a triangle to start. To add additional points, just click away from the existing points. One other important note is that a Shape fixture must always be built in a clockwise manner in order for the physics to work properly. The collision shape should look like the following screenshot:

[220]

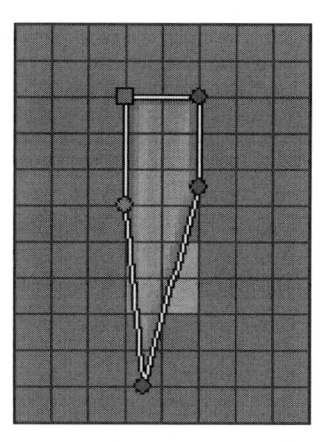

10. Create a new Sprite, spr_Debris_Steel_02, and load Chapter 6/Sprites/Debris_Steel_02.png with **Remove Background** checked.
11. Set the origin to **X**: 0, **Y**: 64 and click on **OK**.
12. Duplicate obj_Debris_Steel_01, rename it obj_Debris_Steel_02, and set the **Sprite** to spr_Debris_Steel_02.
13. Once again, click on **Modify Collision Shape** and adjust the points appropriately as seen in the following screenshot:

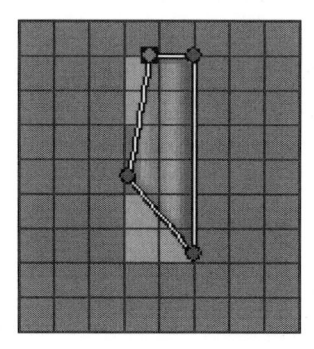

14. We have one more piece of Debris to make, create a new Sprite, spr_Debris_Steel_03, and load Chapter 6/Sprites/Debris_Steel_03.png with **Remove Background** checked.
15. Set the origin to **X**: 16, **Y**: 0 and click on **OK**.
16. Duplicate obj_Debris_Steel_01, rename it obj_Debris_Steel_03, and change the **Sprite** to spr_Debris_Steel_03.

17. We will need five total points on this object, so click on Modify **Collision Shape** and adjust the points appropriately as seen in the following screenshot. We are done with the Steel Debris:

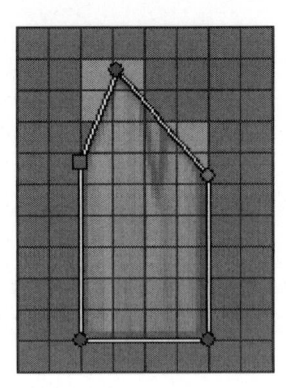

18. Next, we will build the Wood Pillar and associated parts. We won't go through every step, as it is just going to be repeating the process we just went through with the Steel Pillar. We will, however, build the first Pillar of the other material types. Create a new Sprite, spr_Pillar_Wood and load Chapter 6/Sprites/Pillar_Wood.png with **Remove Background** checked. Center the origin and click on **OK**.

19. Create a new Object, obj_Pillar_Wood, and assign spr_Pillar_Wood as the **Sprite**.

20. Set the **Parent** to obj_Pillar_Parent.

21. Check **Uses Physics**.

22. Change the **Collision Shape** to **Box**. The collision shape should automatically fit the Sprite as it is a new object, so we don't need to modify the shape.

23. Wood is much lighter than Steel, so we want to make it move with just a little force. Set the **Density** to 8.

24. Wood also bounces a lot more as it can easily flex, therefore we should set **Restitution** to 0.2.

25. We will say that this Wood is less coarse than the Steel and set **Friction** to 0.5.

26. Set the values for **Collision Group**, **Linear Damping**, and **AngularDamping** to 0, as we will not want the Pillar affected by them.

27. We need to add events for obj_Ground and obj_Pillar_Parent with comments attached for the collision detection to work. If you are wondering why we don't just put it in the obj_Pillar_Parent, it's because we will be adding scripts for Debris to these events later.

28. We are done with the Wood Pillar, which means we can now create the Small Wood Pillar and the Wood Debris. Go ahead and build all these parts with the files provided in Chapter 6/Sprites/. Make sure the object properties are all the same as can be seen in the following screenshot:

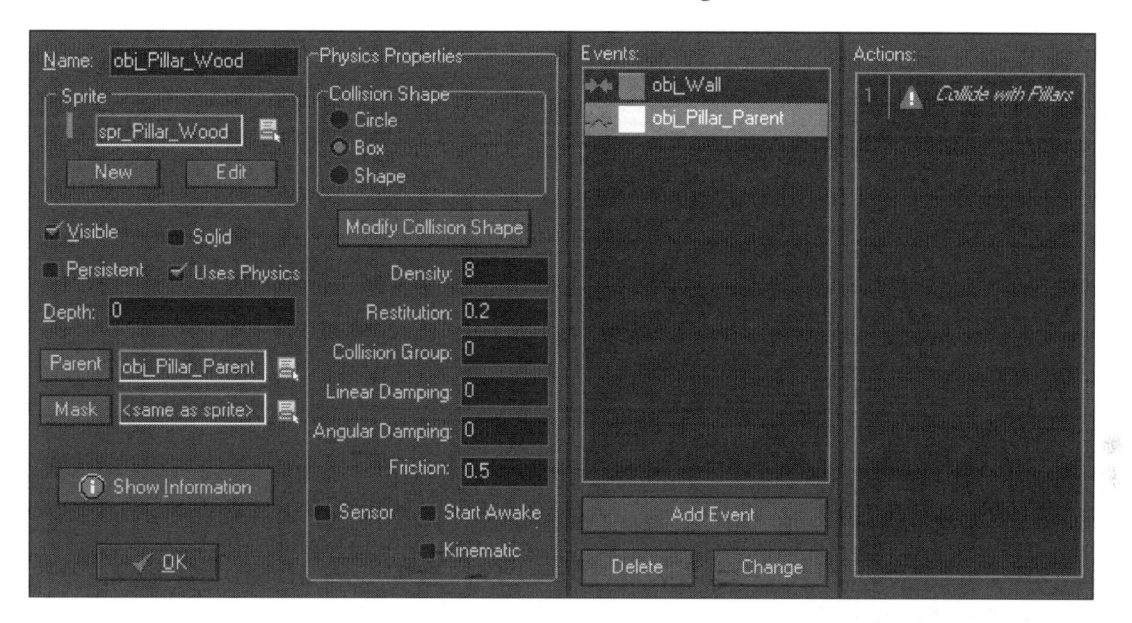

29. Our last Pillar, and the weakest one, is the one made out of Glass. Create a new Sprite, spr_Pillar_Glass, and load Chapter 6/Sprites/Pillar_Glass.png with **Remove Background** checked. Center the origin and click on **OK**.

30. Create a new Object, obj_Pillar_Glass, with its **Sprite** set to spr_Pillar_Glass.

31. Set the Parent to obj_Pillar_Parent.

32. Check **Uses Physics** and change the **Collision Shape** to **Box**.

33. Glass is the lightest material and we want it to move with very little force. Set the **Density** to 2.

34. We want the Glass to rattle a lot so we will set **Restitution** to 0.3.

35. The Glass should be very slick with a **Friction** value of 0.07.

36. As with the other Pillars, set the values for **Collision Group**, **Linear Damping**, and **Angular Damping** to 0, as we will not want the Pillar affected by them.

Toppling Towers

37. Finally, we need to add events for `obj_Ground` and `obj_Pillar_Parent` with comments attached for the collision detection to work. The final set up should look like the following screenshot:

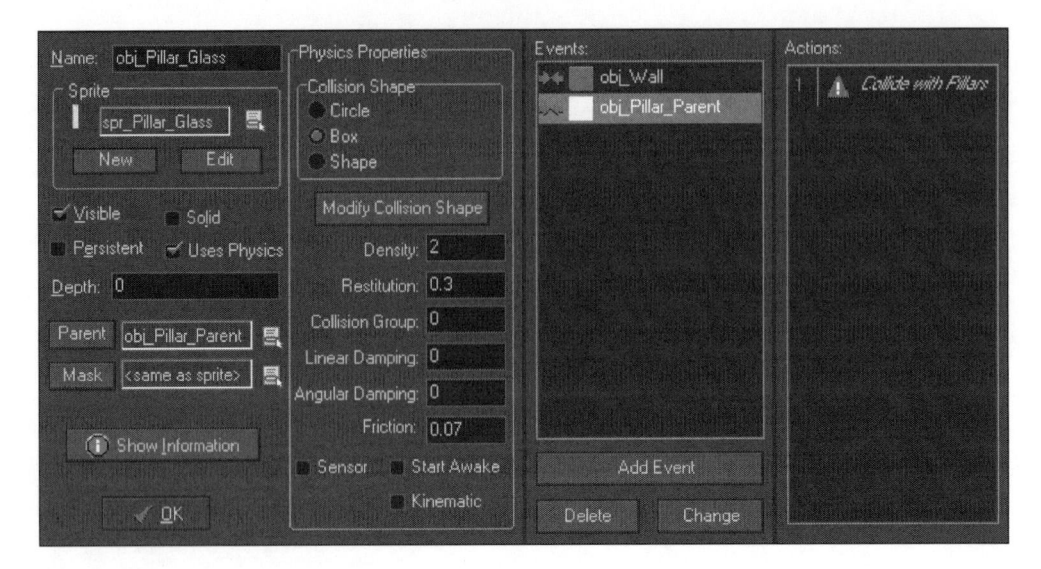

38. As we did with the other Pillars, create the remaining Glass pieces with the assets provided in `Chapter 6/Sprites/`.
39. Now that all the Pillars have been created, reopen Sandbox and place a few Pillars and some TNT. Run the Game and notice how the various materials react. The Glass will move easily while the Steel is fairly rigid. The Wood appears to react somewhere in between those two.

Breaking the Pillars into Debris

We have already created all the necessary objects for spawning Debris from the Pillars; we just need to write the functionality for the switch between the two. To do this, we will build a simple system that can be used by all Pillars. In this game we will only break apart the larger Pillars. The small Pillar and the Debris will be destroyed if enough force is applied.

1. We will start with the weakest object, the Glass Pillar, by initializing some variables. Create a new Script, `scr_Pillar_Glass_Create`, and apply this to a **Create** event in `obj_Pillar_Glass`.

    ```
    myDamage = 5;
    debris01 = obj_Debris_Glass_01;
    debris02 = obj_Debris_Glass_02;
    debris03 = obj_Debris_Glass_03;
    ```

The first variable we have will be used for the amount of damage a Pillar can take. In this case, the Glass Pillar requires at least five points of damage to break apart. Next we are setting variables for each piece of Debris that we will need to spawn.

2. Create a new Script, scr_Pillar_BreakApart with the following code:

```
if (abs(other.phy_linear_velocity_x) > myDamage || abs(other.phy_
linear_velocity_y) > myDamage)
{
    if (phy_mass <= other.phy_mass)
    {
        p1 =instance_create(x, y, debris01);
        p1.phy_speed_x = phy_speed_x;
        p1.phy_speed_y = phy_speed_y;
        p1.phy_rotation = phy_rotation;

        p2 =instance_create(x, y, debris02);
        p2.phy_speed_x = phy_speed_x;
        p2.phy_speed_y = phy_speed_y;
        p2.phy_rotation = phy_rotation;

        p3 =instance_create(x, y, debris03);
        p3.phy_speed_x = phy_speed_x;
        p3.phy_speed_y = phy_speed_y;
        p3.phy_rotation = phy_rotation;

        instance_destroy();
    }
}
```

We start by determining the velocity of the collision, so that it only applies to moving objects, not static ones. We are using a function called abs, which will ensure that the velocity we are given is always a positive number. This will make the comparison much easier, as we don't need to consider the direction of movement. If the colliding object is moving faster than the damage amount of the Pillar, we then check a second conditional statement comparing the mass of the two instances involved in the collision. We only want the Pillar to break apart if it is hit by something stronger than itself. It would not make any sense to have a Glass Pillar destroy a Steel Pillar. If a Pillar is hit by a heavier object, we then spawn the Debris. For each piece of Debris, we need to place it in the appropriate position based on the physics speed and rotation of the Pillar it is spawning from. Once we have created the Debris, we destroy the Pillar.

Toppling Towers

3. Add this script to the `obj_Pillar_Parent` event in `obj_Pillar_Glass`. We can remove the comment as it is no longer needed for the collision to work.
4. Reopen `Sandbox` and place a single instance of TNT, with a Glass Pillar and Steel Pillar on either side. It should look like the following screenshot:

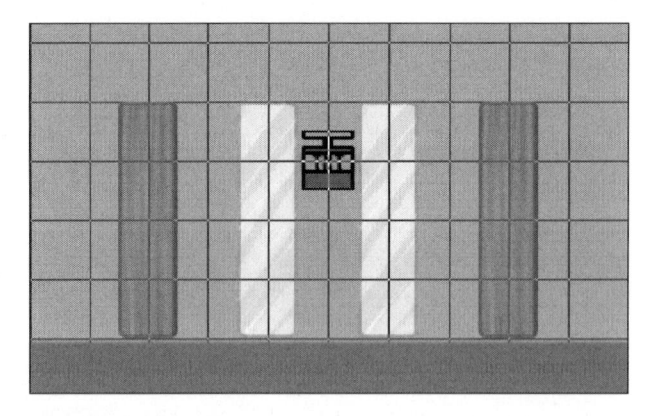

5. Run the game and explode the TNT. We should see the Glass Pillars push out to the side, collide with the Steel Pillars, and then break apart into a pile of Debris, like the following screenshot:

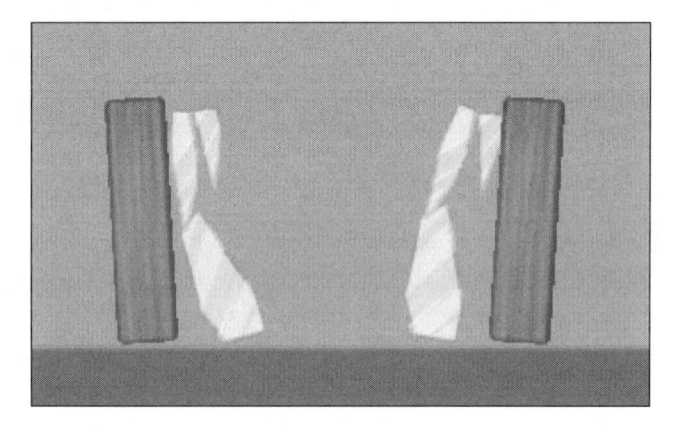

6. Let's move onto the Wood Pillar. Create a new Script, `scr_Pillar_Wood_Create`, and initialize the necessary variables. Add them to a **Create** event in `obj_Pillar_Wood`.

   ```
   myDamage = 16;
   debris01 = obj_Debris_Wood_01;
   debris02 = obj_Debris_Wood_02;
   debris03 = obj_Debris_Wood_03;
   ```

We have increased the required velocity of the damage to be applied in order for it to break apart. Glass is easy to shatter, while wood is not. We have also assigned the appropriate Debris to the Wood.

7. Remove the comment from the `obj_Pillar_Parent` and add `scr_Pillar_BreakApart` instead.
8. Reopen `Sandbox` and replace the Glass Pillars with Wood Pillars.
9. Run the game and explode the TNT. The Wood will move outwards, but will not shatter. This result is intended as we said we need more force to break it.
10. Add another instance of TNT below the one existing in `Sandbox`. This will apply more force when it is detonated.
11. Run the game. As can be seen in the next screenshot, this time the Wood Pillars move outwards and shatter on contact. The Steel Pillars will also be knocked over with this amount of force!

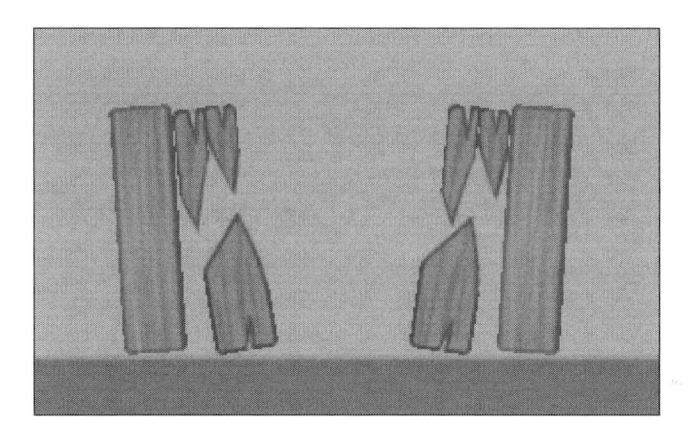

12. We only have the Steel Pillar remaining. We will set it up to function properly, though at this point we will not be able to test it, as there are no objects with more density than it. Create a new Script, `scr_Pillar_Steel_Create`, and add it to a **Create** event in `obj_Pillar_Steel`.

```
myDamage = 25;
debris01 = obj_Debris_Steel_01;
debris02 = obj_Debris_Steel_02;
debris03 = obj_Debris_Steel_03;
```

The same as before, we have increased the required velocity for damage and set the correct Debris to spawn.

13. We also need to remove the comment from the `obj_Pillar_Parent` and replace it with `scr_Pillar_BreakApart`.

14. We now have the Pillars breaking apart into smaller pieces when they are hit with enough force. Next, we need to destroy the small Pillars and the Debris when enough force collides with them. Create a new Script, `scr_Pillar_Destroy`, with the following code:

```
if (abs(other.phy_linear_velocity_x) > myDamage || abs(other.phy_linear_velocity_y) > myDamage)
{
    if (phy_mass < other.phy_mass)
    {
        instance_destroy();
    }
}
```

Similar to `scr_Pillar_BreakApart`, we check the velocity of the colliding object and then compare mass to see if it should be destroyed. Here is where the difference between density and mass becomes apparent. All of the Debris have the same density as the Pillar that spawned it, which means that the solidity is the same. However, the bigger the object is, the more mass it will have. This means that smaller Debris chunks can be destroyed by larger Debris chunks.

15. Apply this script to all small Pillars and Debris in their respective `obj_Pillar_Parent` events.

16. This script uses the same variables as the type of Pillar it is, which means that we need to initialize them. We can reuse the existing script to save us some time. For each small Pillar and Debris, add a **Create** event and apply the appropriate Pillar Create script, as in all Glass should have `scr_Pillar_Glass_Create` assigned.

17. Time to test this out. Reopen `Sandbox` and place two instances of Glass Pillars on top of the Wood Pillars, so that it looks like the following screenshot:

18. Run the game and explode the TNT. The Glass Pillars should shatter easily and most of the Debris will disappear very quickly. The Wood Pillars will also splinter a bit and most of its Debris disappears. The Steel Pillars will rock slightly, but remain undamaged.

Adding in the collision sounds

Everything is functioning, though a bit boring, due to the lack of sound. The Debris being destroyed so quickly is also not very satisfying. Let's fix both of these issues.

1. First we need to bring in some sounds. Create a new Sound, `snd_Shatter_Glass`, and load `Chapter 6/Sounds/Shatter_Glass.wav`. The default values will work, just make sure that **Kind** is set to **Normal Sound**. This effect will be for when the Glass breaks apart.

2. We also want a sound for when the Glass Pillars do not break. Create another new Sound, `snd_Impact_Glass` and load `Chapter 6/Sounds/Impact_Glass.wav`.

3. Repeat this process for the Wood and Steel sound effects.

4. We need to initialize some variables, so reopen `scr_Pillar_Glass_Create` and add the following at the end of the script:

   ```
   impact = snd_Impact_Glass;
   shatter = snd_Shatter_Glass;

   isTapped = false;
   isActive = false;
   alarm[0] = room_speed;
   ```

   We start by assigning variables to the `Impact` and `Shatter` sounds. We will only want to allow the impact sound to play a single time, so we have created the `isTapped` variable. The `isActive` variable and the alarm are going to be used, so that no sound is made when the game starts. When the physics system begins, all active instances in the world will have gravity applied, which will cause collisions. This in turn means that the impact sound will occur when nothing appears to be moving.

5. Reopen `scr_Pillar_Wood_Create` and `scr_Pillar_Steel_Create`, and add the same code with the appropriate sounds.

6. Now we can start implementing the sounds. Open `scr_Pillar_BreakApart` and insert the following line of code before the instance is destroyed:

   ```
   sound_play(shatter);
   ```

Toppling Towers

When the Debris spawns, we will play the Shatter sound a single time. Notice that we have given this sound a priority of 10, which means that if too many sounds need to be played, this sound will be chosen over lower priority sounds.

7. Still in the script, we need to play the impact sound if a collision occurs, but does not break the Pillar. We will add an `else` statement immediately after the instance is destroyed.

```
} else {
    if (!isTapped)
    {
        sound_play(impact);
        isTapped = true;
    }
}
```

If only a minor collision has occurred, we check to see if we have run the sound before. If we haven't, then we play the impact sound, with a low priority, and stop this code from executing again.

8. We only have one thing left to do in this script and that is to place all of the code into a conditional statement, so that it executes only if the instance is active. Add the check at the top of the script and place braces around all the existing code. When it is done, the whole script will look like the following:

```
if (isActive)
{
    if (abs(other.phy_linear_velocity_x) > myDamage || abs(other.phy_linear_velocity_y) > myDamage)
    {
        if (phy_mass < other.phy_mass)
        {
            p1 =instance_create(x, y, debris01);
            p1.phy_speed_x = phy_speed_x;
            p1.phy_speed_y = phy_speed_y;
            p1.phy_rotation = phy_rotation;

            p2 =instance_create(x, y, debris02);
            p2.phy_speed_x = phy_speed_x;
            p2.phy_speed_y = phy_speed_y;
            p2.phy_rotation = phy_rotation;

            p3 =instance_create(x, y, debris03);
            p3.phy_speed_x = phy_speed_x;
            p3.phy_speed_y = phy_speed_y;
```

```
                p3.phy_rotation = phy_rotation;

                sound_play(shatter);

                instance_destroy();
            } else {
                if (!isTapped)
                {
                    sound_play(impact);
                    isTapped = true;
                }
            }
        }
    }
}
```

9. We need to repeat this process for `scr_Pillar_Destroy`, so that the shatter sound is played on destruction, the impact sound on a light collision, and all of this when the instance is active. Here is the code in its entirety:

```
if (isActive)
{
    if (abs(other.phy_linear_velocity_x) > myDamage || abs(other.phy_linear_velocity_y) > myDamage)
    {
        if (phy_mass < other.phy_mass)
        {
            sound_play(shatter);
            instance_destroy();
        }       else {
            if (!isTapped)
            {
                sound_play(impact);
                isTapped = true;
            }
        }
    }
}
```

10. In order for the sounds to work, we need to make them active. Create a new Script, `scr_Pillar_Alarm0` and set `isActive` to `true`.

11. Rather than adding an alarm for every pillar and debris, we can just add an **Alarm 0** event to `obj_Pillar_Parent`. This will not cause any conflicts because the alarm will only be run once per instance and only changes a variable.

Toppling Towers

12. Run the game, explode the TNT and listen. We can hear the different sounds as the Pillars break apart and collide with each other. Also notice that there is more Debris now remaining. This is because there is now a one second delay before they can destroy themselves, which allows time for the Debris to escape any collision that happens upon creation.

Building the demolition equipment

We have everything we need to build towers, but this game is all about demolition. The player would become bored if all they had was TNT to destroy the towers. We are going to utilize some more physics functions and create some new equipment: a Wrecking Ball and a Magnetic Crane.

Creating a Wrecking Ball

Let's start with the Wrecking Ball as we have already built a large portion of it. We will utilize the Chain and Anchor and add a Ball to it.

1. Create a new Sprite, spr_WreckingBall, and load Chapter 6/Sprites/WreckingBall.png with **Remove Background** checked. Center the origin and click on **OK**.
2. Create a new Object, obj_WreckingBall, and apply the spr_WreckingBall as its **Sprite**.
3. We will want the Wrecking Ball to always be drawn in front of the chain that holds it. Set **Depth** to -100.
4. Check the box for **Uses Physics**. We do not need to change Collision Shape, as the Wrecking Ball is a circle.
5. We want this Wrecking Ball to be very powerful, so set **Density** to 50.
6. As it is such a heavy object and hanging from a chain, it should not be able to spin very much. To slow the rotation, set the **AngularDamping** to 5.
7. All other physics values for this object should be set to 0.
8. We are done building the Wrecking Ball, so now we need to add it to the Anchor and Chain. Reopen scr_Anchor_Create and add the following code at the end of the script:

    ```
    ball = instance_create(chain[9].x +24, y, obj_WreckingBall);
    physics_joint_revolute_create(chain[9], ball , chain[9].x,
    chain[9].y, -30, 30, true, 0, 0, false, false);
    ```

Here we are creating a Wrecking Ball at the end of the Chain, with a 24 pixel offset so it is positioned correctly. We then add a Revolute Joint between the last link in the Chain and the Wrecking Ball with a rotational limit of 30 degrees in either direction.

9. Next, we need to add the collision. We are not going to place the collision on the Wrecking Ball, as the existing scripts are going to look for variables that the Wrecking Ball will not have. Instead, we will start by reopening `obj_Pillar_Parent` and adding an `obj_WreckingBall` event, and attaching `scr_Pillar_Destroy`. As all Pillars and Debris are parented to the object, they will all respond to this event.

10. While this last step will work fine, it also means the large Pillars will be destroyed on contact as well. We want the large Pillars to always break apart first. We can still do this by reopening the three Pillars, `obj_Pillar_Glass`, `obj_Pillar_Wood`, and `obj_Pillar_Steel`, and add an `obj_WreckingBall` event with `scr_Pillar_BreakApart` attached. If a parent object and one of its children both have the same type of event, be it collision, step, or whatever, the child's event will be executed and the parent's event will be ignored.

> It is possible to execute both the parent event and the child event together by using the function `event_inherited()` in the child's event code.

11. Let's test this out. Reopen `Sandbox` and place an instance of `obj_Anchor` in the room, just off to the right of the existing Pillars. We can also remove the TNT as we do not need it for this test. The setup should look like the following screenshot:

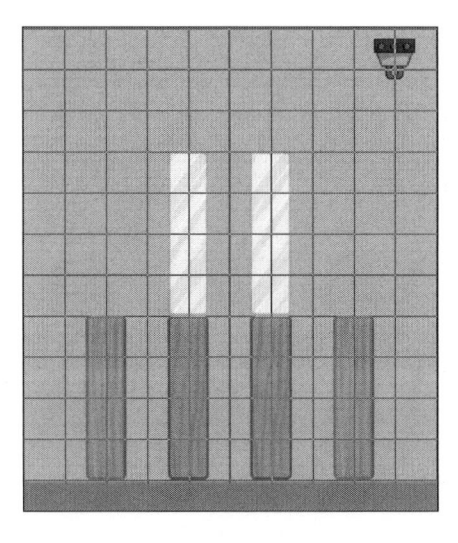

12. Run the game. We should see the Wrecking Ball swing down attached to the Chain and Anchor. When the Wrecking Ball collides with the Steel Pillar, the Pillar breaks apart, as do many of the other Pillars. Everything works correctly, but there is a bit of an issue. The Wrecking Ball falls immediately, when it should wait to be triggered. Let's fix all that.

13. In order for us to stop the Wrecking Ball from moving immediately, we need to deactivate from the World Physics. This is simply done by setting the `phy_active` variable to false for each instance we want to stop. Reopen `scr_Anchor_Create` and apply this change for the Wrecking Ball and every Chain. The entire script can be seen in the following code:

    ```
    for (i = 1; i < 10; i++)
    {
        chain[i] = instance_create(x+(i * 16), y, obj_ChainLink);
        chain[i].phy_active = false;
    }

    physics_joint_revolute_create(self, chain[1], self.x, self.y, 0, 0, false, 0, 0, false, false);

    for (i = 1; i < 9; i++)
    {
        physics_joint_revolute_create(chain[i], chain[i+1], chain[i].x, chain[i].y, -20, 20, true, 0, 0, false, false);
    }

    ball = instance_create(chain[9].x +24, y, obj_WreckingBall);
    ball.phy_active = false;
    physics_joint_revolute_create(chain[9], ball , chain[9].x, chain[9].y, -30, 30, true, 0, 0, false, false);
    ```

14. The Wrecking Ball and Chain will no longer move at the start, but we still need to be able to trigger it at some point. Create a new Script, `scr_Anchor_Activate`, and for testing purposes, attach it to a **Space** event under **Key Press**.

    ```
    for (i = 1; i < 10; i++)
    {
        chain[i].phy_active = true;
    }
    ball.phy_active = true;
    ```

    When this script is run, a simple `for` loop activates every Chain, and then the Wrecking Ball.

15. Run the game. The Wrecking Ball should be extended out to the right and static. When we hit the space key, the Wrecking Ball and Chain should become active and swing down, colliding into the tower. The collision itself is much higher on the tower, as the Chain is now fairly rigid with only a little elasticity. It looks like we are done!

Making a Magnetic Crane

Our third piece of demolition equipment will be a Magnetic Crane. This Crane will drop down and pick up any small Pillar and Debris made from Steel. It will then raise itself back up with whatever it has collected.

1. We will start by building the Magnet itself. Create a new Sprite, spr_Magnet, and load Chapter 6/Sprites/Magnet.png with **Remove Background** checked. Center the origin, and click on **OK**.

2. Create a new Object, obj_Magnet, and assign spr_Magnet as the **Sprite**.

3. Check the box for **Uses Physics** and set **Collision Shape** to **Box**.

4. We will want to make the collision area smaller, so that when it picks up objects, the effect appears more believable. Click on **Modify Collision Shape** and pull the sides in so that it looks like the following screenshot:

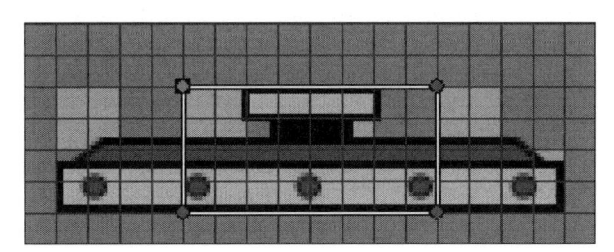

5. The Magnet needs to be quite heavy so that the other objects can't push it around. Set **Density** to 50.

6. Set all the other properties to 0, as we don't want them affecting the magnet's movement.

7. As our intention is for the magnet to only pick up the small objects made of Steel, we should change how the Steel Debris is parented. Currently, it is parented to obj_Pillar_Parent for collision purposes. We still need to be able to have that ability, but we want magnetic attraction to be unique to a few objects. To do this, we can parent the Debris to any object that has obj_Pillar_Parent as its parent. Let's set the Parent for all Steel Debris to obj_Pillar_Steel_Small.

[235]

8. We also need to add a variable to everything made of steel so that we know if it has been collected or not. Reopen `scr_Pillar_Steel_Create` and add the following line of code at the end of the script:

   ```
   isCollected = false;
   ```

9. Now we can make the script for the magnetic attraction. Create a new Script, `scr_Magnet_Step`, and attach it to a **Step** event in `obj_Magnet`.

   ```
   if (phy_active)
   {
       if (instance_exists(obj_Pillar_Steel_Small))
       {
           with (obj_Pillar_Steel_Small)
           {
               if (!isCollected)
               {
                   myMagnet = instance_nearest(x,y,obj_Magnet)
                   myDist = point_distance(phy_position_x, phy_position_y, myMagnet.x, myMagnet.y);
                   myDir = point_direction(phy_position_x, phy_position_y, myMagnet.x, myMagnet.y);
                   if (myDist < 200 && myDir > 60 && myDir < 120)
                   {
                       physics_apply_impulse(x, y, 0, -2000)
                   }
               }
           }
       }
   }
   ```

We start by seeing whether the magnet is active and can begin collecting scrap metal. Next, we check if there are any small Steel Pillars, or anything parented to it, in the world. If there are instances in existence, we apply code directly to them through a `with` statement. If the instance has not been collected, we find the nearest Magnet, see how far away it is, and in what direction. When checking for the X and Y coordinates of an object in a physics game, we need to use the `phy_position_x` and `phy_position_y` values to accurately know where they are in the world space. Next, we see if the instance is within the magnetic range, and whether it is underneath the Magnet. If it is, we apply a strong impulse upwards, which will make it move towards the Magnet.

10. Once a small Steel Pillar or Debris comes in contact with the Magnet, we want to consider it collected and to always move with it. To do this, we will dynamically create a joint to any instance that collides with the Magnet. Create a new Script, `scr_Magnet_Collsion`, and attach it to an `obj_Pillar_Steel_Small` event in `obj_Magnet`.

    ```
    physics_joint_prismatic_create(id, other, x, y, 0, 1, 0, 0, true, 0, 0, false, false);
    other.isCollected = true;
    ```

    Here we are making a Prismatic Joint with the magnet and the instance that collides with it. The first two parameters are the two instances that are to be joined, followed by where in the world they are connected. The fifth and sixth parameters are the direction it can move in, and in this case it is vertical only. The next three are the limits of the movement. We don't want it to move, so we set the min/max values to zero. The limits do need to be enabled, otherwise they won't lift with the Magnet. The following three are for whether there is a motor to move this joint. The final parameter is for collision with the objects which we want to avoid. Once the joint has been created, we then set the collected variable to `false`.

11. Next, we need to make a base for the Crane, which will function similar to the Anchor. Create a new Sprite, `spr_CraneBase`, and load `Chapter 6/Sprites/CraneBase.png` with **Remove Background** checked. Center the origin and click on **OK**.

12. Create a new Object, `obj_CraneBase`, and apply `spr_CraneBase` as the **Sprite**.

13. Check the box for **Uses Physics** and set **Collision Shape** to **Box**.

14. This object is meant to be static in the physics world, so we need to set the **Density** to `0`. All other properties can be left at their default values.

15. We will want the crane base to spawn the magnet and set the joint up. Create a new Script, `scr_CraneBase_Create`, and attach it to a **Create** event.

    ```
    magnet = instance_create(x, y+160, obj_Magnet);
    magnet.phy_active = false;
    crane = physics_joint_prismatic_create(id, magnet, x, y, 0, 1, -128, 128, true, 100000, 20000, true, false);
    ```

[237]

We are creating the Magnet well below the crane base and have deactivated it from the physics world. We then apply a Prismatic Joint between the two instances. This time we are allowing for 128 pixels of movement in a vertical direction. We are also running a motor, so that the Magnet can move up and down on its own. The maximum force the motor can apply is `100000` and we have the motor dropping the Magnet at a motor speed of `20000`. As you can see, the values we are using are extremely high and the reason for this is to make sure that the heavy magnet can lift plenty of Steel Debris.

16. As with the Wrecking Ball, we need to activate the crane base. Create a new Script, `scr_CraneBase_Activate`, and for testing purposes, attach it to the **Space** event under **Key Press**.

    ```
    magnet.phy_active = true;
    alarm[0] = 5 * room_speed;
    ```

    We want the magnet to drop down first, so we make it active in the physics world. We are using an alarm set for five seconds, which will raise the Magnet back up.

17. Create a new Script, `scr_CraneBase_Alarm0` and attach it to an **Alarm 0** event.

    ```
    physics_joint_set_value(crane, phy_joint_motor_speed, -20000);
    ```

    We are setting the value for the motor speed to go up at a value of `-20000`. Again, we are using a very large number to ensure it goes back up with the additional weight of the Pillar Debris.

18. The last thing we need to do for the Crane is to add a cable between the crane base and the magnet. For this we will simply draw a line between the two. Create a new Script, `scr_CraneBase_Draw`, and apply it to a **Draw** event.

    ```
    draw_self();
    draw_set_color(c_dkgray);
    draw_line_width(x, y, magnet.x, magnet.y-16, 8);
    ```

    Whenever a **Draw** event is used, it overrides the drawing of the default Sprite for the object. Therefore, we use `draw_self` to correct that override. Next we set a color to use, here we are using a default dark gray color, and then we draw an 8 pixel wide line between the crane base and the top of the magnet.

Chapter 6

19. All we need to do now is to add an instance of crane base to `Sandbox`. Place the instance off to the left-hand side of the existing Pillars. Also add a few instances of Debris and the small Steel Pillar as can be seen in the following screenshot:

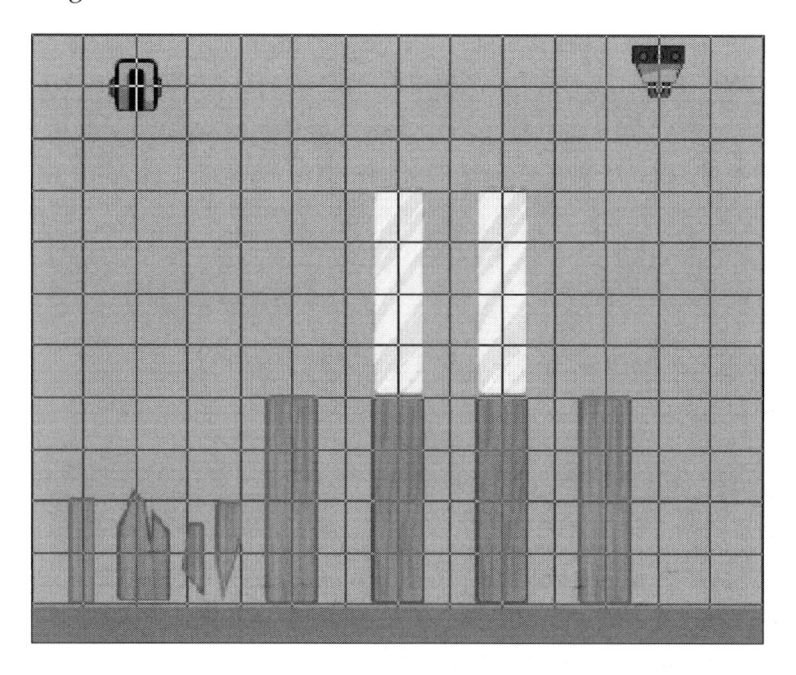

20. Run the game. The Magnet should be sitting in the air and we should notice the Debris shaking a bit as if there is some magnetic attraction occurring. When we hit space, the Magnet should drop down and collect a few pieces of Debris. After a few seconds, the Magnet will raise back up, taking the collected Debris with it. Also notice that none of the other Debris or Pillars are affected by the Magnet.

Completing the game

So far we have built a fun little toy, but it is not yet a game. We have no win or lose condition, no challenge, and no reward. We need to give the player something to do and challenge themselves with. We will start by implementing the win condition; remove all Pillars from a preset Zone. We will create some levels with a variety of Towers and Zones to clear. We will also create an Equipment Menu, so that the player can select what items they want to use and place them in the world.

Setting the win condition

The win condition for this game is to clear all Pillars and Debris from a specific Zone. The player will only be able to activate the equipment once and will have a small amount of time to clear the Zone. If they clear it, they win and move on. If it isn't cleared, they lose and they try again.

1. We will start by making a parent Zone that will have all the code, but is never actually placed into the world. Create a new Object, `obj_Zone_Parent`. There is no sprite to attach.

2. Create a new Script, `scr_Zone_Create`, and add it to a **Create** event.

   ```
   image_speed = 0;
   isTouching = true;
   ```

   We start by stopping the animation of the assigned sprite. All the Zones will consist of sprites with two frames of animation. The first frame will indicate collision and the second frame is the all clear signal. We also have a variable that we will use to identify if a Pillar or Debris is in contact with the Zone.

3. The Zone will need to constantly update whether it is clear of collision or not. Create a new Script, `scr_Zone_Step`, and attach it to a **Step** event with the following code:

   ```
   if (collision_rectangle(bbox_left, bbox_top, bbox_right , bbox_bottom, obj_Pillar_Parent, false, false))
   {
       image_index = 0;
       isTouching = true;
   } else {
       image_index = 1;
       isTouching = false;
   }
   ```

   Here we are using a function, `collision_rectangle`, to determine whether the Pillar parent is currently in contact with the Zone. We cannot use a collision event to check for contact, as we need to watch for the lack of collision to happen. We are using the bounding box parameters of the Sprite to determine the size of the collision area. This will allow us to have multiple Zone sprites with a variety of sizes without any additional code. If there is collision, we switch to the first frame of the animation and indicate that collision is currently happening. Otherwise, we switch to the second frame of animation and indicate that the Zone is currently free of collision.

4. Now that we have the parent Zone built, we can build the child Zones, which will be placed into the world. Create a new Sprite, `spr_Zone_01`, and load `Chapter 6/Sprites/Zone_01.gif` with **Remove Background** checked. Leave the origin at **X**: 0 **Y**: 0, so that collision will work correctly. Click on **OK**.

5. Create a new Object, `obj_Zone_01`, and apply `spr_Zone_01` as its **Sprite**.

6. We want the Zone to always be drawn behind the towers, so set **Depth** to 100.

7. Set Parent to `obj_Zone_Parent` and click on **OK**.

8. We have supplied a few more sprites in `Chapter 6` for variety. Repeat steps 4 to 6 with the appropriate naming conventions for the additional zones.

9. Open `Sandbox` and place an instance of `obj_Zone_01`, so that it covers some of the Glass Pillars only, as seen in the following screenshot:

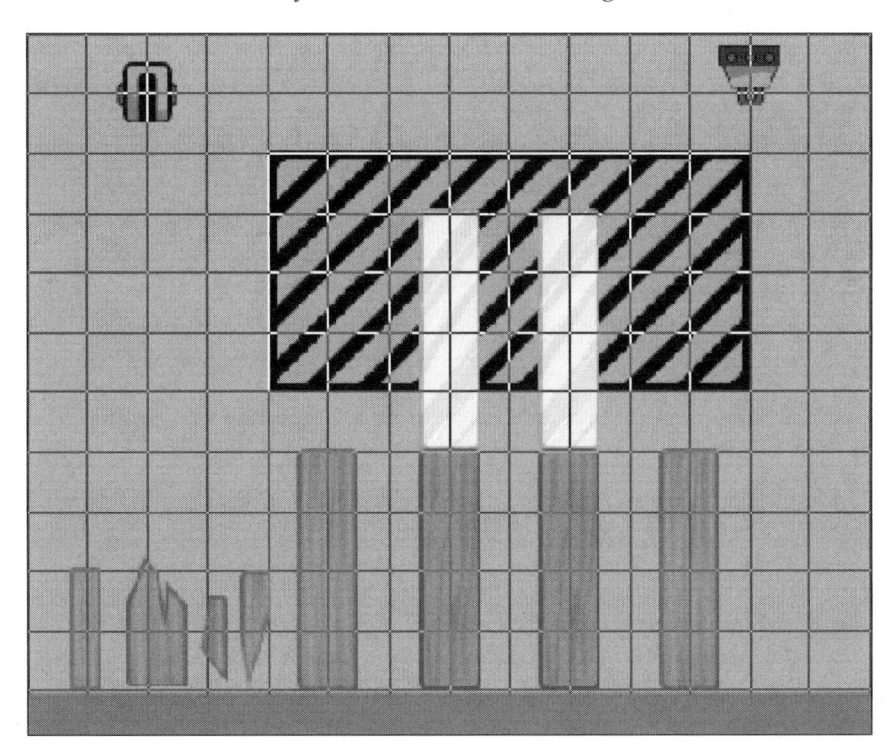

Toppling Towers

10. Run the game and activate the equipment. You should see the Zone remain red for as long as there are Pillars or Debris within it. Once it is clear, it will turn light blue, indicating that it is clear of collision.

11. Next, we need to create an Overlord to check for the win condition. Create a new Object and name it `obj_Overlord`.

12. Create a new Script, `scr_Overlord_Create`, and attach it to a **Create** event, so that we can initialize some variables.

    ```
    isTriggered = false;
    isVictory = false;
    ```

    We have two variables that we will be using. We will use `isTriggered` to check if the equipment has been activated or not. The `isVictory` variable will determine whether the win condition has occurred.

13. We are going to take the activation away from the individual pieces of equipment and place it into the Overlord. Reopen `obj_TNT`, `obj_Anchor`, and `obj_CraneBase`, and remove the **Space** event under **Key Press**.

14. Create a new Script, `scr_Overlord_Step`, and add it to a **Step** event in `obj_Overlord`.

    ```
    if (isTriggered)
    {
        if (instance_exists(obj_TNT))
        {
            with(obj_TNT) { scr_TNT_Activate(); }
        }
        if (instance_exists(obj_Anchor))
        {
            with(obj_Anchor) { scr_Anchor_Activate(); }
        }
        if (instance_exists(obj_CraneBase))
        {
            with(obj_CraneBase) { scr_CraneBase_Activate(); }
        }
        alarm[0] = 8 * room_speed;
        isTriggered = false;
    }
    ```

    This code will only execute if the variable `isTriggered` is `true`. If it is, we check to see if there are any instances of the TNT in existence. If there are instances, we use a `with` statement to run the activation script for each instance. We do the same for the Anchor and Crane Base. We also add an alarm set for eight seconds, which is when we will check for the win condition. Finally, we set `isTriggered` back to `false` so that this runs for the second time.

15. Let's activate the equipment. Create a new Script, scr_Overlord_KeyPress, and add it to a **Space** event under **Key Press**.

    ```
    isTriggered = true;
    ```

16. At some point we may want to have more than one Zone in a level that needs to be cleared. This poses a bit of a problem, in that we need to ensure that all Zones are clear while not knowing in what order we are going to check each Zone. What we need to do is have any Zone that has collision. Stop the checking process and set the win condition to false. Create a new Script, scr_WinCondition, with the following code:

    ```
    with (obj_Zone_Parent)
    {
        if (isTouching)
        {
            return false;
        }
    }
    return true;
    ```

    By using a with statement to check obj_Zone_Parent, we are able to look for all instances of that object and all of its children. We are going to use return statements here to help us exit the script. When a return is executed, the script will immediately stop and any code after it will not be run. If any instance has collision we return false; otherwise, if no instances have collision, we return true.

17. We can now use scr_WinCondition in our alarm event. Create a new Script, scr_Overlord_Alarm0, and add it to an **Alarm 0** event.

    ```
    isVictory = scr_WinCondition();
    if (isVictory)
    {
        if (room_exists(room_next(room)))
        {
            room_goto_next();
        }
    } else {
        room_restart();
    }
    ```

Toppling Towers

We start by capturing the returned `boolean` from `scr_WinCondition` in the `isVictory` variable. If it is `true`, we check to see if there is a room after the current room we are in. The order of rooms is determined by where they are placed in the Resource tree, with the next room being the one below it in the Resource tree. If there is a room, we go to it. If the win condition is `false`, we restart the room.

18. Reopen `Sandbox` and place a single instance of `obj_Overlord` anywhere in the room.
19. We can't test the win condition with only one room, so let's duplicate the `Sandbox` and name it `Sandbox_02`.
20. Rearrange the Pillars and equipment in the room so that you can tell that it is not the same room as Sandbox. Also move the Zone closer to the ground so that it guarantees the win condition will not happen, as shown in the following screenshot:

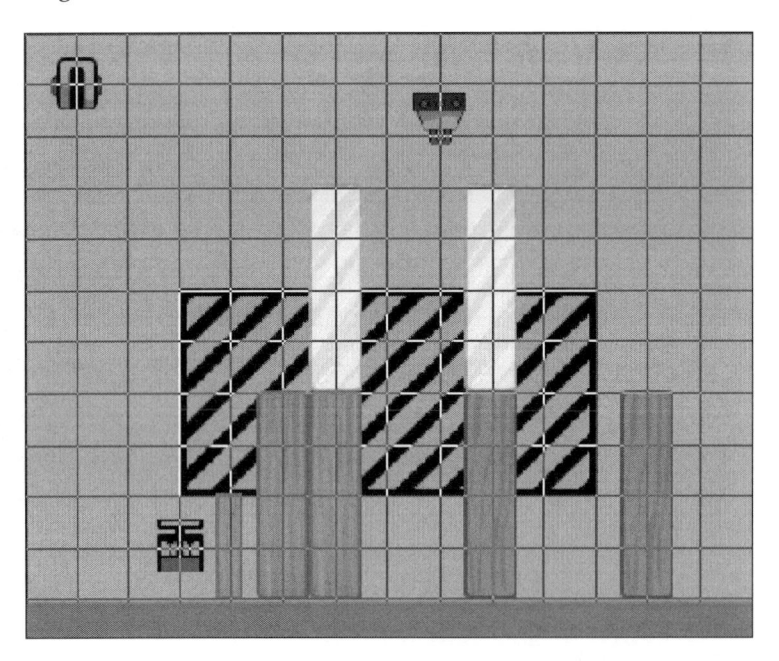

21. Run the game and press space. In the first room we should see some destruction clear the Zone and after a few moments, the room will switch over to `Sandbox_02`. When the equipment is activated this time, there will be some destruction, but there will still be Pillars and Debris in the Zone. After a few moments, this room will restart. The win condition works!

[244]

Creating the Equipment Menu

While we now have a win condition, there still isn't anything for the player to do. We are going to fix that by adding an **Equipment Menu**. This menu will be placed along the bottom of the gameplay screen and have selectable icons for the TNT, Wrecking Ball, and Magnetic Crane. When an icon is clicked it will create a placeable ghost version of the appropriate piece of equipment. To place the equipment, the player just needs to click somewhere in the world and the ghost will become the real item.

1. To build the Equipment Menu we are going to need several sprites. Create new sprites and load the appropriate files from `Chapter 6/Sprites/` for the following sprites with **Remove Background** unchecked. Leave the origin at **X**: 0 and **Y**: 0.
    - spr_Menu_BG
    - spr_Menu_TNT
    - spr_Menu_WreckingBall
    - spr_Menu_MagneticCrane

2. Create a new Object and name it `obj_Menu`. We will not apply a Sprite to this object.

3. We only need to initialize one variable to indicate when the menu is active. Create a new Script, `scr_Menu_Create`, and apply it to a **Create** event.
    ```
    isActive = false;
    ```

4. In this game we are going to require rooms of varying sizes, so that we can have tall or wide towers. This means that the menu will need to adapt to fit properly. This could be very frustrating except for the fact that we are going to set screen size to 640 x 480 at all times. If we use GameMaker's **Draw GUI** event, it ignores the world positioning and uses the coordinates based on the window size. Create a new script, `scr_Menu_DrawGUI`, and apply it to a **Draw GUI** event.
    ```
    draw_sprite(spr_Menu_BG, 0, 0, 400);

    menuItem_Zone = 32;
    menuItems_Y = 440;
    menuItem1_X = 40;
    draw_sprite(spr_Menu_TNT, 0, menuItem1_X, menuItems_Y);

    menuItem2_X = 104;
    draw_sprite(spr_Menu_WreckingBall, 0, menuItem2_X, menuItems_Y);

    menuItem3_X = 168;
    draw_sprite(spr_Menu_MagneticCrane, 0, menuItem3_X, menuItems_Y);
    ```

Toppling Towers

As we know that every room is going to be displayed at a resolution of 640 x 480, we start by drawing the background sprite at the bottom of the screen. We are going to use a variable, `menuItem_Zone`, to help with the mouse coordinates over the sprites. We will need to know exactly where the icon is placed when we code in the future, so we make variables for each menu item's coordinates and then draw the Sprite on the screen.

5. Reopen `Sandbox` and change the **Settings** of the room to **Width:** 800, **Height:** 600.
6. Under the **Views** tab, check the boxes for **Enable the use of Views** and **Visible When Room Starts**.
7. Change the **View In Room** to **W:** 800 **H:** 600. Do not change the values for **Port on Screen**. By doing this, we will be able to see the entire room and it will be displayed at the standard 640 x 480 resolution.
8. Now place a single instance of `obj_Menu` anywhere in the room.
9. Run the game. You should see the menu with the three icons at the bottom of the screen as shown in the following screenshot:

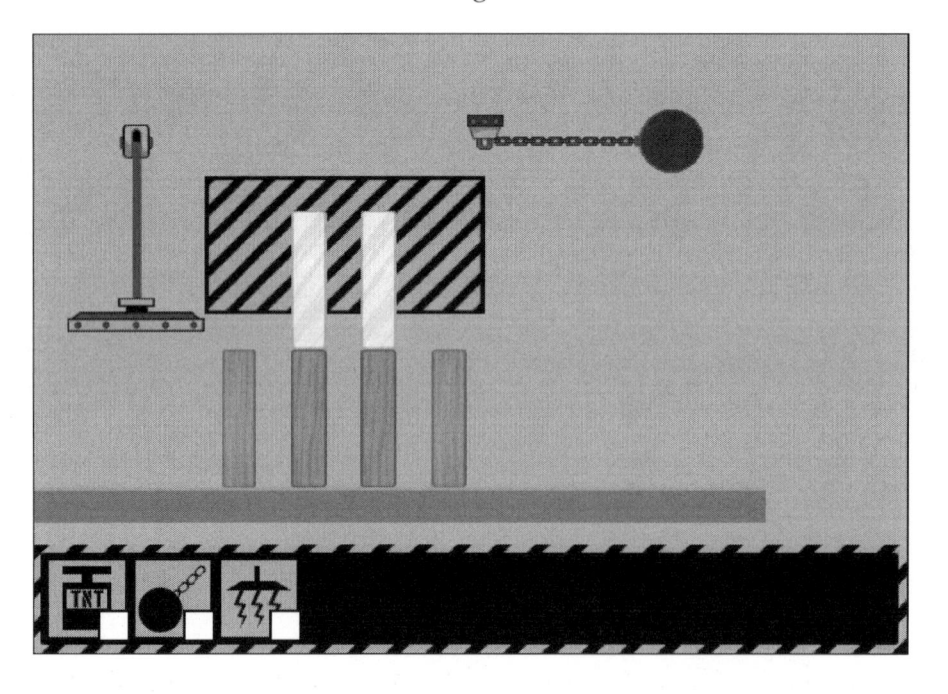

10. To make the menu functional we need to first create all the ghost objects. We do not need to bring in any new sprites, as we will use the existing sprites for each piece of equipment. Let's start by creating a new Object, `obj_Ghost_TNT`, and applying `spr_TNT` as the **Sprite**.

11. Create a new Script, `scr_Ghost_TNT_Create`, and apply it to a **Create** event with the following code:

    ```
    image_alpha = 0.5;
    myTool = obj_TNT;
    ```

    In order to differentiate the Ghost TNT from the real TNT, we start by setting the transparency to 50 percent. We are going to use some common scripts for all ghosts, so we will need a variable to indicate what this Ghost represents.

12. Next, we need to be able to move this object with the mouse around the room for placement. To do this we are going to write a Script that can be used by all ghosts. Create a new Script, `scr_Ghost_Step` and apply it to a **Step** event.

    ```
    x = mouse_x;
    y = mouse_y;
    ```

13. Create another new Script, `scr_Ghost_Released`, and add it to a **Left Released** event under **Mouse**.

    ```
    winHeight = window_get_height();
    winMouse = window_mouse_get_y();
    if (!place_meeting(x, y, obj_Pillar_Parent) &&  winMouse < winHeight - 64)
    {
        instance_create(x, y, myTool);
        obj_Menu.isActive = false;
        instance_destroy();
    }
    ```

    We don't want to be able to place the item down on top of the menu, or on top of other instances we are trying to destroy. To make this happen we first need to grab the height of the display area and the position of the mouse within the display. It is important to note that we cannot use the standard `mouseY` variable as it relates to the position within the world because we need to know its position on screen. We check to see if there is a lack of collision at the current location in the room with any Pillar, and that the mouse on screen is 64 pixels above the bottom, which ensures that it is above the menu. If this is all true, we create an instance of whatever item is to be placed, tell the Menu that it is no longer active and remove the Ghost from the world. We are now done with the Ghost TNT.

14. Up next is the Ghost Wrecking Ball. Create a new Object, `obj_Ghost_WreckingBall` and assign `spr_Anchor` as its **Sprite**.

15. We have some common scripts, so let's apply them quickly. Add a **Step** event, apply `scr_Ghost_Step`, and add a **Left Released** event under **Mouse** with `scr_Ghost_Released` attached.

Toppling Towers

16. Create a new Script, `scr_Ghost_WreckingBall_Create`, and add it to a **Create** event. All we need here is to initialize what item it will create when placed.

    ```
    myTool = obj_Anchor;
    ```

17. We can't build this exactly the same as the TNT, as the Wrecking Ball is comprised of several parts. For this Ghost we will need a **Draw** event and a new Script, `scr_Ghost_WreckingBall_Draw` with the following code:

    ```
    draw_set_alpha(0.5);
    draw_sprite(spr_Anchor, 0, x, y)
    for (i = 1; i < 10; i++)
    {
        draw_sprite(spr_ChainLink, 0, x + i * 16, y)
    }
    draw_sprite(spr_WreckingBall, 0, x + (9 * 16 + 24), y);
    draw_set_alpha(1);
    ```

    We start by setting the instance to half transparent so that it looks like a Ghost. We then draw the Anchor, run a `for` loop to draw the Chain, and then the Wrecking Ball is drawn at the end of the Chain. Finally, we need to reset the transparency back to full at the end of this code. It is critical that we do this, as Draw events affect everything that is drawn on screen. If we did not reset it, every object in the world would have half transparency.

18. Now for the Ghost Magnetic Crane. Create a new Object, `obj_Ghost_MagneticCrane`, and apply `spr_CraneBase` as the **Sprite**.

19. The same as for the other Ghosts, add a **Step** event and a **Left Released** event under **Mouse** and apply the appropriate scripts.

20. Create a new Script, `scr_Ghost_MagneticCrane_Create`, and initialize the necessary variable.

    ```
    myTool = obj_CraneBase;
    ```

21. Now draw the pieces. Create another Script, `scr_Ghost_MagneticCrane_Draw`, and add it as a **Draw** event.

    ```
    draw_set_alpha(0.5);
    draw_sprite(spr_CraneBase, 0, x, y)
    draw_set_color(c_dkgray);
    draw_line_width(x, y, x, y + 144, 8);
    draw_sprite(spr_Magnet, 0, x, y + 160);
    draw_set_alpha(1);
    ```

Chapter 6

In a similar manner as the Ghost Wrecking Ball, we start by setting the transparency to 50 percent. We then draw the crane base, draw a thick gray line and the magnet at the same position they would be when placed. We then set the transparency back to full.

22. The Ghosts are now all complete; we just need to spawn them. Reopen `scr_Menu_DrawGUI` and add the following code at the end:

```
if (!isActive)
{
    win_X = window_mouse_get_x();
    win_Y = window_mouse_get_y();
    if ((win_Y > menuItems_Y - menuItem_Zone && win_Y < menuItems_Y + menuItem_Zone))
    {
        if ((win_X > menuItem1_X - menuItem_Zone && win_X < menuItem1_X + menuItem_Zone))
        {
            draw_sprite(spr_Menu_TNT, 1, menuItem1_X, menuItems_Y);
            if (mouse_check_button_pressed(mb_left))
            {
                instance_create(menuItem1_X, menuItems_Y, obj_Ghost_TNT);
                isActive = true;
            }
        }
        if ((win_X > menuItem2_X - menuItem_Zone && win_X < menuItem2_X + menuItem_Zone))
        {
            draw_sprite(spr_Menu_WreckingBall, 1, menuItem2_X, menuItems_Y);
            if (mouse_check_button_pressed(mb_left))
            {
                instance_create(menuItem1_X, menuItems_Y, obj_Ghost_WreckingBall);
                isActive = true;
            }
        }
        if ((win_X > menuItem3_X - menuItem_Zone && win_X < menuItem3_X + menuItem_Zone))
        {
            draw_sprite(spr_Menu_MagneticCrane, 1, menuItem3_X, menuItems_Y);
            if (mouse_check_button_pressed(mb_left))
            {
```

Toppling Towers

```
                    instance_create(menuItem1_X, menuItems_Y, obj_
Ghost_MagneticCrane);
                    isActive = true;
                }
            }
        }
}
```

We start by checking if the menu is active or not. If a menu item is selected and hasn't been placed, the menu will be considered active. If we are able to select a menu item, we grab the mouse location on screen. We check the mouse location on screen, first with the Y coordinate and the Zone offsets to see if the mouse is on top of the Menu, then with the X coordinate and the Zone of each item. If the mouse is over the top of one of the icons, we redraw the sprite on the second frame of animation to indicate the hover state. We then check to see if the left mouse button has been pressed, and if it has, we spawn the appropriate Ghost item and the menu is now active. Now we can spawn TNT, Wrecking Balls, and Magnetic Cranes.

23. Run the game. We already have the menu on screen, but now when you hover over the icons, they should be highlighted. When you click on an icon, it creates the appropriate Ghost item, which will move with the mouse. When you click in the playable area, an instance of the item will be created and can be used.

Constructing the towers

We now have a working game and all that is left is to create some levels to play. We will build a few levels with a variety of different towers and room sizes to make sure all our code is working properly.

1. Create a new Room and in the **settings** tab, name it `Level_01`. Make sure this is moved to the top of the Rooms section of the Resource tree.
2. Open the **physics** tab, check the box for **Room is Physics World** and set the **Gravity** to **X:** `0` **Y:** `20`.
3. In the **objects** tab, select `obj_Ground` and place instances 64 pixels from the bottom and across the width of the room. The menu will take up the bottom 64 pixels, so we don't need to put any Ground down there.
4. Add single instances of `obj_Overlord` and `obj_Menu` in the area below the Ground instances. While technically they can go anywhere in the room, this will just keep things a bit more organized.

As this is the first level, let's make it easy for the player and only use Glass Pillars. Up to this point in the book, we have only been placing objects as they were created. When placing the Pillars, we can easily rotate them and place them in the world. To rotate an instance in the **Room Properties** editor, first place the instance in the room normally, and while it is still selected, change the **Rotation** value in the **objects** tab. There are options for scaling an instance, but we cannot use these in a physics simulation, as it does not affect the Fixture size.

5. Using only `obj_Pillar_Glass` and `obj_Pillar_Glass_Small`, construct a simple two story tower as seen in the following screenshot:

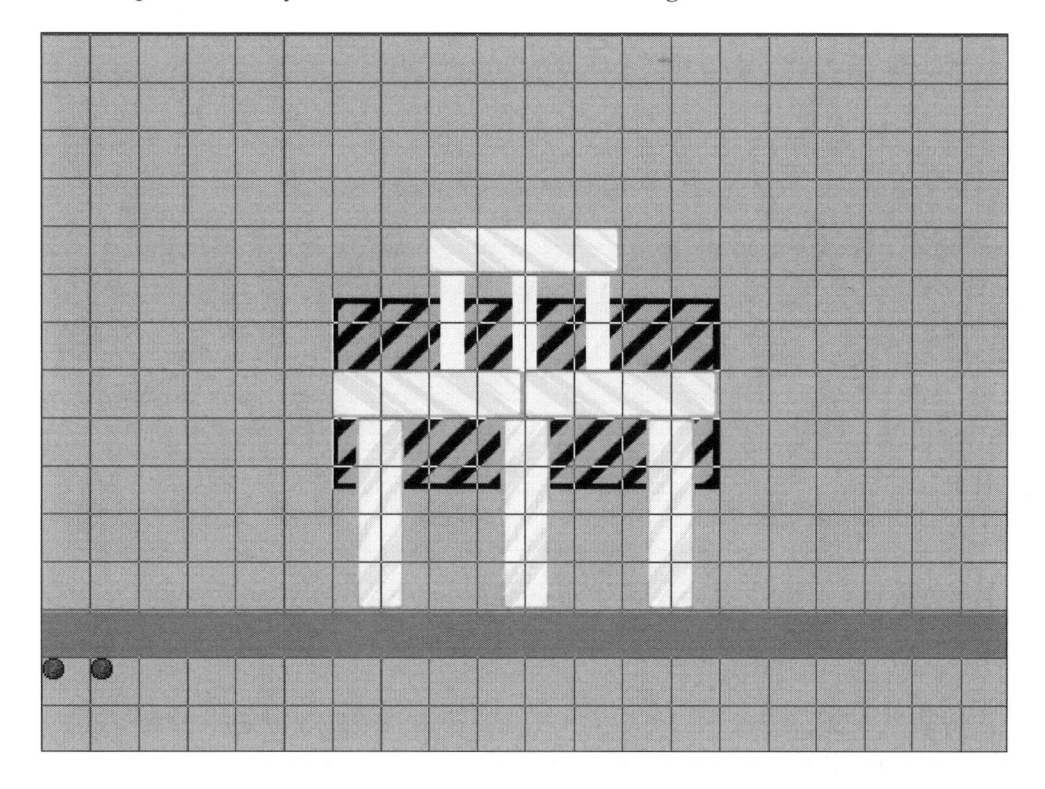

6. Finally, place a single instance of `obj_Zone_01` behind the tower and roughly in the center vertically. This room is now complete.

7. Let's build the final room meant for much later in the game, but this time much larger and with multiple zones. Create a new Room and in the **settings** name it `Level_12`, and change the **Width** to `1280` and **Height** to `960`.

8. In the Resource tree, move this room so that it is immediately after `Level_01`.

[251]

Toppling Towers

9. This room is now twice as big as `Level_01`, but we want to display it on screen at the same size. In the **views** tab, check the boxes for **Enable the use of Views** and **Visible When Room Starts**.

10. Change the **View In Room** to **W:** 1280 **H:** 960. Do not change the values for **Port on Screen**. Again, by doing this we will be able to see the entire room at the standard 640 x 480 resolution.

11. In the **physics** tab, check the box for **Room is Physics World** and set the **Gravity** to **X:** 0 **Y:** 20.

12. We will start by laying the ground down with `obj_Ground`. As the room is twice as large, our numbers need to double as well. The menu will display with a height of 64 pixels of screen resolution in this room, which means the Ground should be 128 pixels from the bottom.

13. Place single instances of `obj_Overlord` and `obj_Menu` in the area below the Ground instances.

14. As this level is meant to be a later level in the game, we can use all small and regular size pillars of all types. Build a couple of towers with varying heights and building materials.

15. Add an instance of `obj_Zone_01` behind each of the towers. An example of what the level could look like can be seen in the following screenshot:

[252]

16. Run the game. The first level should only need a few, well placed pieces of TNT to successfully destroy it. The next level should be much more difficult to complete, and requires all three types of equipment. The challenge now is to see how few pieces of equipment are needed to destroy everything. Have fun smashing things up as shown in the following screenshot:

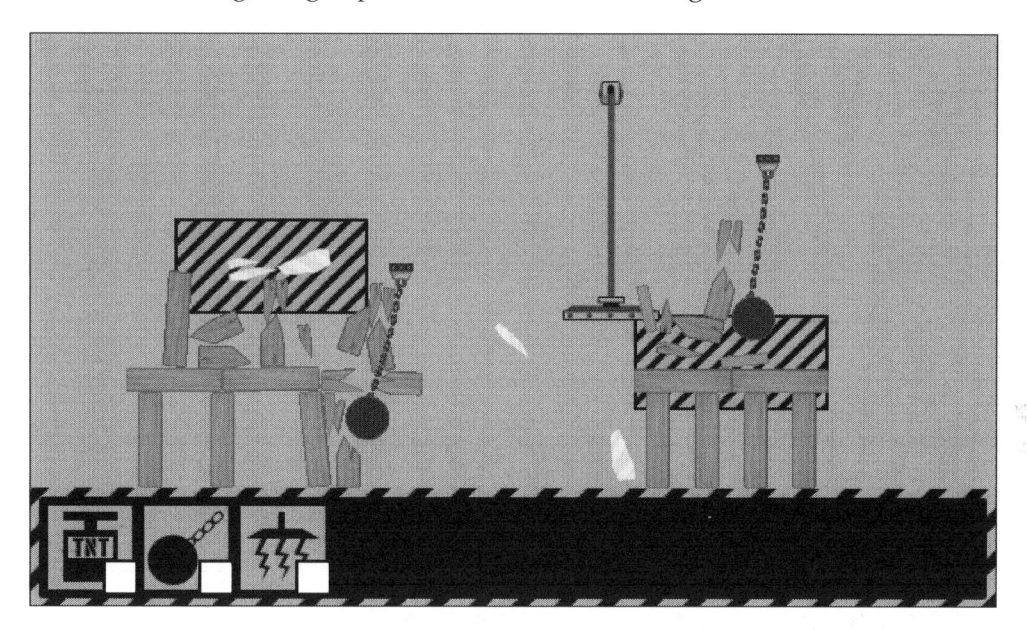

Summary

We covered a lot of material in this chapter. We started with the basics of using the Box2D physics system. We learned how to assign Fixtures to objects and what the different properties were that we could change. We created a Chain and Wrecking Ball that utilized Revolute Joints so each piece would rotate with the one preceding it. We built TNT and a Magnetic Crane that used Forces to move objects around the world. We also made Debris spawn from the large Pillars when they collided with heavier, stronger objects. Additionally, we learned about the Draw GUI event and the difference between a Sprite's location as represented in a room versus the location on screen. This allowed us to create a Menu that will display properly on screen no matter the size of the room.

We are going to continue to work on this game in the next chapter. We will create a store and inventory system so that the player has a limited amount of equipment and can purchase additional items. We will also dive into displaying dialog, so that we can add some basic story elements to the game to motivate the player to destroy more stuff!

7
Dynamic Front Ends

In the last chapter we built a tower toppling physics game where the player could use TNT, Wrecking Balls, and Magnetic Cranes to destroy towers made of Glass, Wood, and Steel Pillars. In this chapter we are going to build this game by implementing a Shop, a Score Screen, and Level Intro Dialog. We are also going to rework the HUD so that only the equipment that is available can be used to implement a countdown timer, and add buttons for restarting the level and going to the Shop. In order to accomplish all of this, we will spend some time looking at arrays and data structures for storing information and using global variables.

Setting up the rooms

In the last chapter we built two rooms, `Level_01` and `Level_12`, for testing the HUD and game difficulty. We now need to make rooms for all the levels in between those two, plus a few additional rooms for the Front End, Shop and Level Select:

1. Create a new Room for each level from `Level_02` to `Level_11`. Set the size of the rooms as follows:
    - `Level_02` – `Level_04` is set to **Width**: 640 and **Height**: 480
    - `Level_05` – `Level_08` is set to **Width**: 960 and **Height**: 720
    - `Level_09` – `Level_11` is set to **Width**: 1280 and **Height**: 960
2. Each room needs to have **Room is Physics World** checked in the **Physics** tab.
3. Make sure that **Views | Port on Screen** is set to **X**: 0, **Y**: 0, **W**: 640, and **H**: 480 so that each room will display properly on screen.
4. We have supplied backgrounds for each level which can be found in `Chapter 7/Backgrounds/`. Make sure that **Remove Background** is not checked.

Dynamic Front Ends

5. Each level should have a unique tower built from a variety of Pillars and ideally be made more difficult than the previous level. Start by placing the ground down in the room which requires a different Y coordinate depending on the size of the Room. The Y placement is indicated as follows:
   - `Level_02` – `Level_04`: **384**
   - `Level_05` – `Level_08`: **576**
   - `Level_09` – `Level_11`: **784**

6. Populate the levels with one instance of `obj_Overlord` and `obj_Menu` each. Each room should look something like the following screenshot:

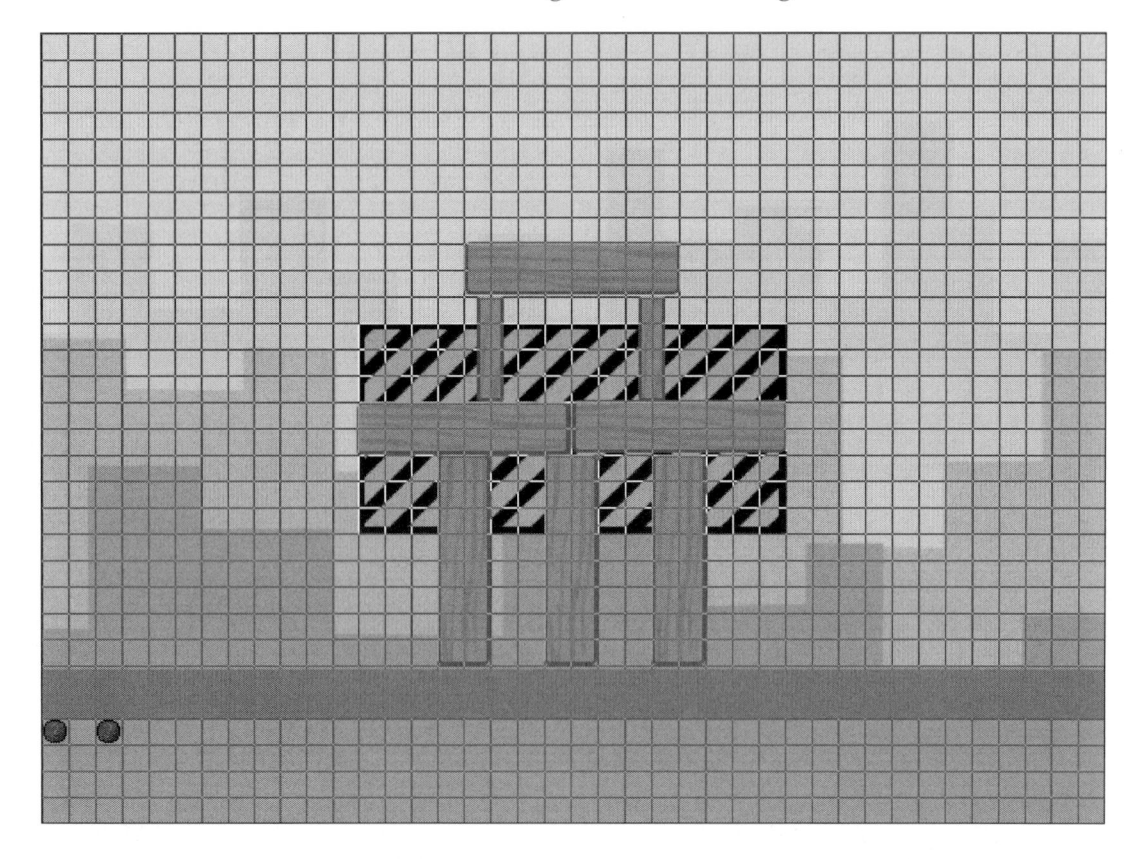

7. Once the levels have been built, we can move on to the Front End. Create a new Room and in the **Settings**, name it `MainMenu`, with a **Width** of `640` and **Height** of `480`. Move this to the top of the `Rooms` folder in the Resource Tree.

8. Create a new Background, `bg_MainMenu`, and load `Chapter 7/Backgrounds/BG_MainMenu.png`. Make sure that **Remove Background** is not checked.

9. In the **Room Properties | Background** tab, set **Background 0** to `bg_MainMenu`. The box for **Visible when room starts** should be checked. We are done with this room for now so click on **OK**.

10. We need two additional rooms for the Front End: `LevelSelect` and `Shop` with the appropriate backgrounds applied. The position in the Resource Tree does not matter. We now have all the rooms we will need for the game.

Initializing the main menu

The main menu is the very first screen the player will see and it consists of two objects: a button to start the game and a game initializing object with all the global variables:

1. Let's start with an object for initializing the game. Create a new Object and name it `obj_Global`.

2. Create a new Script called `scr_Global_GameStart`. We will be adding code to this as we go along, but for now we just need to initialize the score:
   ```
   score = 0;
   ```

3. Add an **Other | Game Start** event and apply `scr_Global_GameStart`. Click on **OK**.

4. Reopen `MainMenu` and place a single instance of `obj_Global` somewhere in the room.

5. We are going to be creating a few buttons, so let's build a parent object to run the common functionality of hover states. Create a new Object called `obj_Button_Parent`.

6. All buttons will have multiple frames of animation to be used for the hover states, so we need to stop them from playing. Create a new Script, `scr_Button_Parent_Create`, and attach this to a **Create** event with the following code:
   ```
   image_speed = 0;
   image_index = 0;
   ```

7. Create a new Script, `scr_Button_Parent_MouseEnter`, and attach it to a **Mouse | Mouse Enter** event with the code to change it to the second frame of animation:
   ```
   image_index = 1;
   ```

[257]

Dynamic Front Ends

8. We also need to reset this by creating another new Script, `scr_Button_Parent_MouseLeave` and attach it to a **Mouse | Mouse Leave** event:

   `image_index = 0;`

   The parent object is now complete and the setting should look like the following screenshot:

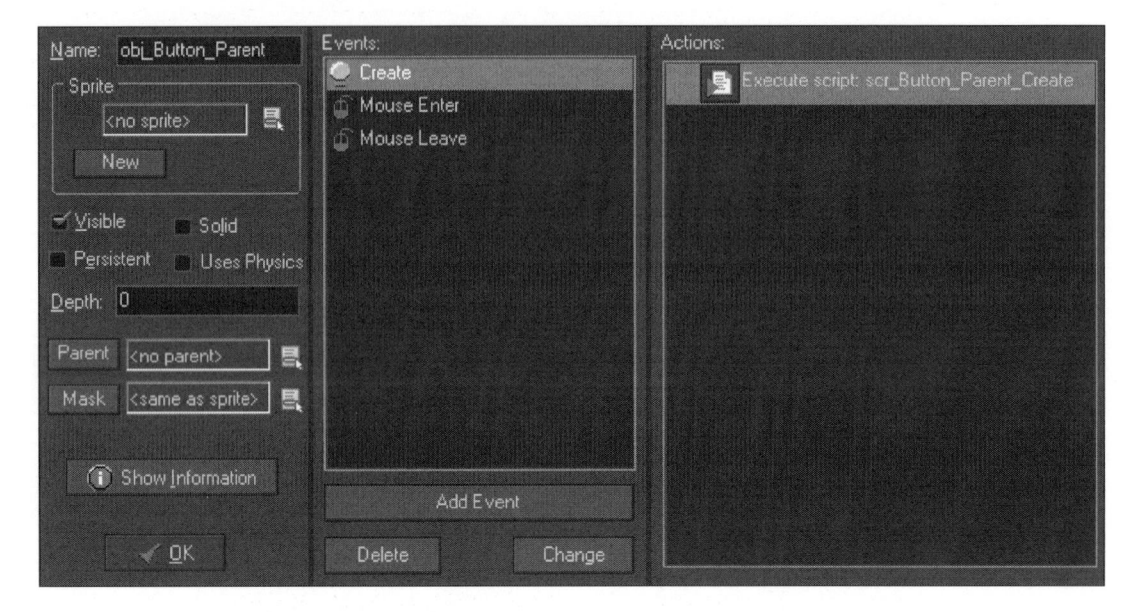

9. Next we can build the first real button. Create a new Sprite, `spr_Button_Start`, with **Remove Background** turned off, and load `Chapter 7/Sprites/Button_Start.gif`. **Center** the **Origin** and click on **OK**.

10. Create a new Object, `obj_Button_Start`, and apply `spr_Button_Start` as the **Sprite**.

11. Set the **Parent** to be `obj_Button_Parent` so that the hover states will function properly.

12. Since each button will do something different we need to give each button its own click event. Create a new Script, `scr_Button_Start_MousePressed`, and attach it to a **Mouse | Left Pressed** event with the following code to go to the room `LevelSelect`:

    ```
    room_goto(LevelSelect);
    ```

13. This button is now complete. Place a single instance of `obj_Button_Start` into `MainMenu` near the bottom of the screen at **X**: 320 and **Y**: 416. The Room should look like the following screenshot:

14. Run the game to make sure that it starts with `MainMenu` and that the **Start** Button functions as designed.

Selecting levels with 2D arrays

The next room we are going to build is `LevelSelect`. In this room there will be a button for going to the Shop and buttons for each level in the game, with only the first level unlocked at the start. As the player progresses, the buttons will unlock and the player will have access to all previous levels. To achieve this we will dynamically create buttons for each level in the game and use a 2D array to store all this information.

Dynamic Front Ends

A 2D array is just like the arrays we have already used in the book. It is a single static list of data but it allows for multiple values per row, like a spreadsheet. This is a very powerful tool at our disposal as it makes it much simpler to group several different elements together:

1. Create a new Script, `scr_Global_Levels`, and start by initializing some global variables:

   ```
   globalvar level, totalLevels;
   ```

   As we are always trying to simplify our code we can use an alternate method of declaring global variables with `globalvar`. This declaration method functions exactly the same way as `global`, but it will allow us to write `level` instead of `global.level`. While this will save us plenty of keystrokes, it is up to us to remember that it is a global variable as it is not as obvious.

2. Next we need to create a 2D array with one column holding the level and another with whether it is locked or not. Let's just add the first level:

   ```
   level[0, 0] = Level_01;
   level[0, 1] = false;
   ```

   To create a 2D array, you just need to place two numbers inside the brackets. The first number is for the row and the second for the column. Here we have only a single row that has two columns. The first column will hold the room name and the second column will be for whether that room is locked or not; in this case `Level_01` is unlocked.

3. There is one drawback in using simple arrays in GameMaker: Studio that there is no function to find out the size of the array. We need to know the size of this array so that we can dynamically create all the buttons. We already created a global variable to hold the total amount of levels; we just need to manually set its value. Let's add all the levels into the array, lock them, and set the `totalLevels` variable. Here is the complete script for all 12 levels:

   ```
   globalvar level, totalLevels;
   level[0, 0] = Level_01;
   level[0, 1] = false;
   level[1, 0] = Level_02;
   level[1, 1] = true;
   level[2, 0] = Level_03;
   level[2, 1] = true;
   level[3, 0] = Level_04;
   level[3, 1] = true;
   level[4, 0] = Level_05;
   ```

```
level[4, 1] = true;
level[5, 0] = Level_06;
level[5, 1] = true;
level[6, 0] = Level_07;
level[6, 1] = true;
level[7, 0] = Level_08;
level[7, 1] = true;
level[8, 0] = Level_09;
level[8, 1] = true;
level[9, 0] = Level_10;
level[9, 1] = true;
level[10, 0] = Level_11;
level[10, 1] = true;
level[11, 0] = Level_12;
level[11, 1] = true;
totalLevels = 12;
```

4. We need to initialize this array at the start of the game. Reopen scr_Global_GameStart and execute this script after the score variable.

   ```
   scr_Global_Levels();
   ```

5. Let's move onto building the button for going to the Shop. Create a new Sprite, spr_Button_Shop, and with **Remove Background** turned off, load Chapter 7/Sprites/Button_Shop.gif. **Center** the **Origin** and click on **OK**.

6. Create a new Object, obj_Button_Shop, and apply spr_Button_Shop as the **Sprite**.

7. This is a standard button so set the **Parent** to obj_Button_Parent.

8. The last thing we need to do to this object is to add a **Mouse | Left Pressed** event and apply a new Script, scr_Button_Shop_MousePressed with the code to switch rooms:

   ```
   room_goto(Shop);
   ```

9. We will draw some text onto these buttons which means that we need to bring in some fonts. We have supplied a font called Boston Traffic in this game, which is needed to be installed on your computer. To install this font on a Windows computer, right-click on Chapter 7/Fonts/boston.ttf and select **Install**. Then follow the directions when prompted.

Dynamic Front Ends

10. Back in GameMaker: Studio we need to create three new fonts: `fnt_Large`, `fnt_Medium`, and `fnt_Small`. All three will have a **Font** of `Boston Traffic`. Set the **Size** of `fnt_Large` to `20`, `fnt_Medium` to `16`, and `fnt_Small` to `10`.

11. Next we can move onto the buttons for selecting the levels. We will be dynamically creating these buttons and drawing a number on each one of them so that we only need a single art asset. Create a new Sprite, `spr_Button_LevelSelect`, and with **Remove Background** turned off, load `Chapter 7/Sprites/Button_LevelSelect.gif`. **Center** the **Origin** and click on **OK**.

12. Create a new Object, `obj_Button_LevelSelect`, and apply `spr_Button_LevelSelect` as the **Sprite**. These buttons cannot be parented to `obj_Button_Parent` as they require the ability to have a locked state, which will affect the hover states.

13. Since this button type is unique, we need to initialize some variables. Create a new Script, `scr_Button_LevelSelect_Create`, and attach it to a **Create** event.

    ```
    isLocked = true;
    myLevel = MainMenu;
    myNum = 0;
    image_speed = 0;
    alarm[0] = 1;
    ```

    We start by making all buttons locked by default. We set a default room for the room it should go to when clicked, and a number that we will draw on top. Finally we stop the sprite from animating and set an alarm for one step.

14. We are using an alarm so that we can ensure that the levels will properly display whether they are locked or not. Create a new Script, `scr_Button_LevelSelect_Alarm0`, and attach it to an **Alarm | Alarm 0** event:

    ```
    if (isLocked)
    {
        image_index = 2;
    } else {
        image_index = 0;
    }
    ```

    If the button is to be locked, we set the sprite to display the locked frame. Otherwise it is unlocked and we show the first frame.

Chapter 7

15. Create a new Script, `scr_Button_LevelSelect_MouseEnter`, and apply it to a **Mouse | Mouse Enter** event:

```
if (isLocked)
{
    exit;
} else {
    image_index = 1;
}
```

For the hover state of the button we first check to see if it is locked. If it is, we just exit the script immediately. If it is unlocked, we switch to the hover frame.

16. This same logic needs to be applied to when the mouse leaves the button. Create another new Script, `scr_Button_LevelSelect_MouseLeave`, and apply it to a **Mouse | Mouse Leave** event:

```
if (isLocked)
{
    exit;
} else {
    image_index = 0;
}
```

17. Next we will add a **Mouse | Left Pressed** event with a new Script, `scr_Button_LevelSelect_MousePressed`, attached with code to change rooms if it is unlocked only:

```
if (isLocked)
{
    exit;
} else {
    room_goto(myLevel);
}
```

18. Finally, we just need a new Script, `scr_Button_LevelSelect_Draw` that we can use to draw the button with the appropriate number on top. Add this to a **Draw | Draw** event:

```
draw_self();
draw_set_color(c_black);
draw_set_font(fnt_Large);
draw_set_halign(fa_center);
draw_text(x, y-12, myNum);
draw_set_font(-1);
```

[263]

Dynamic Front Ends

First we need to draw the sprite that has been applied to the object itself. Next we set the drawing color to black, set the font, and center align the text. We then draw the text held in the `myNum` variable, dropping it down a bit on the Y axis so that it centers vertically. Since we will be drawing a lot of text in this game, we should force the font to the default font by setting it to `-1` value. This will help prevent this font from affecting any other drawn font in the game:

1. We are now finished with the level selection button and the properties should look like the following screenshot:

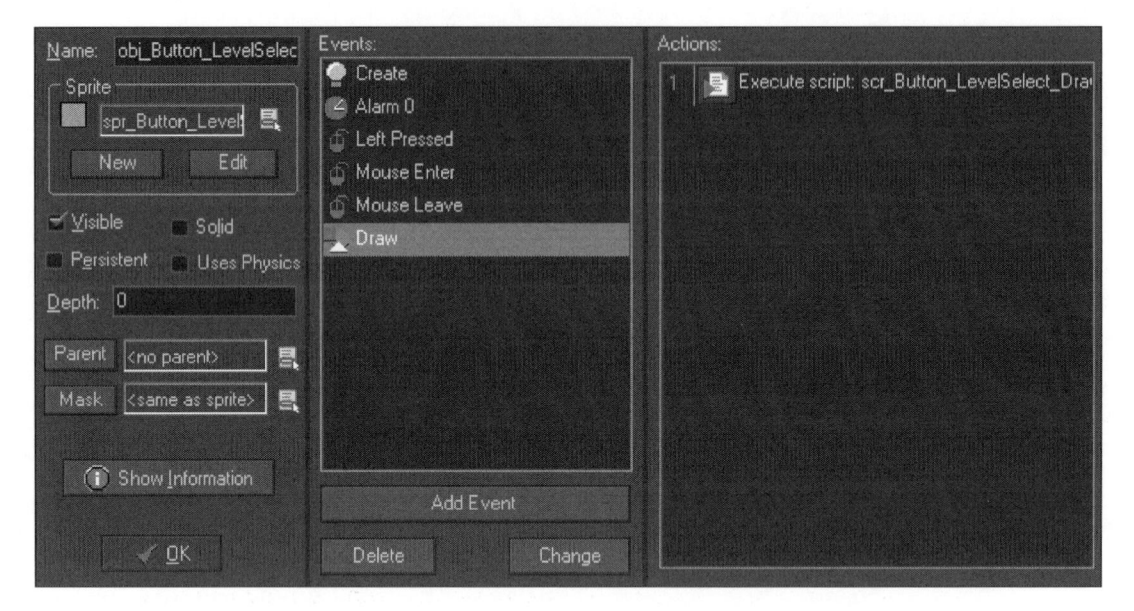

2. We now have all the components we need for a level selection screen, we just need to spawn everything. For this we will create a new Object, `obj_LevelSelect_Overlord`, to build the menu upon entering the room.

3. Add an **Other | Room Start** event and attach a new Script, `scr_LevelSelect_Overlord_RoomStart`, with the following code:

   ```
   column = 0;
   row = 1;
   for ( i = 0; i < totalLevels ; i++ )
   ```

```
{
    lvl = instance_create((72 * column) + 128, 80 * row + 128,
obj_Button_LevelSelect);
    lvl.myLevel = level[i, 0];
    lvl.isLocked = level[i, 1];
    lvl.myNum = (i + 1);
    column++;
    if (column > 5)
    {
        row++;
        column = 0;
    }
}
instance_create(320, 440, obj_Button_Shop);
```

We start by establishing variables for the row and columns that we will need for the layout of the buttons. We then run a loop starting at zero and run it for the total amount of levels we declared in the global variable `totalLevels`. Inside this loop, we first create an instance of `obj_Button_LevelSelect` and offset it in both horizontal and vertical directions with an additional 128 pixels of padding for a margin between the edge of the screen and the buttons. We then change the button's `myLevel` and `isLocked` variables by setting it according to the values in the `level` global array. Next we change the `myNum` variable to indicate what number will be drawn on the button. The last few lines of code are how we will limit the amount of columns and add additional rows of buttons. Every loop we increase the column count and once it passes five we reset it to zero. This will give us a row of six buttons. If we have more than six buttons, a new row will be created that can have another six buttons. This means we can add levels to the array later and they will be added into this menu automatically creating new rows for every six levels. Last but not least, we spawn an instance of the **SHOP** button at the bottom of the screen.

4. Open `LevelSelect` and place a single instance of `obj_LevelSelect_Overlord` somewhere in the room. This is all we need, and to do so click on the checkmark.

Dynamic Front Ends

5. Run the game. After clicking start game, you should end up in `LevelSelect` and it should look like the following screenshot. Only Level 1 is accessible at this point and the button is yellow. All the other buttons are gray, indicating that they are locked. Clicking on the button for **Level 1** will take you to that level and the **SHOP** button should take you to the Shop.

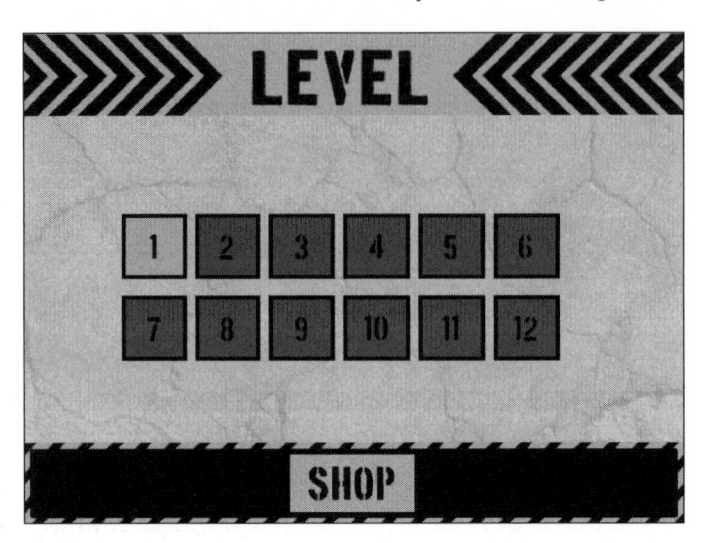

Preparing the Shop using data structures

The only room we have left to build is the Shop where the player will be able to purchase equipment to be used in each level. The room will consist of icons for each piece of equipment, a listing of the price, and a button to purchase the equipment. We will also have a display showing how much cash the player currently has and this will update as they spend money:

1. The first thing we need to do before we build anything is to establish some constants to make our code easier to read. Open the **Resources | Define Constants** editor and set values for the equipment: `TNT: 0`, `WRECKINGBALL: 1`, `MAGNET: 2`.

2. We will also need some constants that describe all the elements that comprise a piece of equipment. Add `SPRITE: 0`, `OBJECT: 1`, `AMOUNT: 2`, and `COST: 3`. When this is complete the settings in the editor should look like the following screenshot:

Name	Value
TNT	0
WRECKINGBALL	1
MAGNET	2
SPRITE	0
OBJECT	1
AMOUNT	2
COST	3

3. In order to stick with the color scheme of the game we will need to create a unique yellow color that we can access globally. Create a new Script, `scr_Global_Colors`, with this code:

   ```
   globalvar yellow;
   yellow = make_color_rgb(249, 170, 0);
   ```

   We create a global variable for our color and then use a function that has parameters for the amount of red, green, and blue to make our special yellow color.

4. Open `scr_Global_GameStart` and execute `scr_Global_Colors()`.

   To build a proper Shop and inventory system we need more control over the data than a static array allows. We need something more malleable and searchable. This is where **data structures** come in. Data structures are special dynamic structures similar to arrays, but with the ability to manipulate the data with specific functions for things such as shuffling or reordering the data. GameMaker: Studio comes with six different types of data structures, each with its own set of functions and benefits:

   - **Stacks**: This structure is last-in-first-out, meaning that each new piece of data is placed on top of the previous one and when it is read, the newest data is read first. Think of it like a stack of plates, where you are going to use the one last placed on the shelf.

   - **Queues:** This structure is first-in-first-out, meaning that each new piece of data is placed behind the one previous to it and when read, the oldest data is read first. Think of a line at a store, where the first person in line is going to be served first.

   - **Lists**: This structure is much more flexible. In this structure the data can be placed anywhere within the list and can be sorted, altered, and searched throughout. Think of this like a deck of cards, where they can be in any order which can be changed any time.

Dynamic Front Ends

- ○ **Maps**: This structure allows for information to be stored in linked pairs using keys and values, though it cannot be sorted and all keys must be unique. Think of a set of keys, where each key opens only the associated door.
- ○ **Priority Queues**: This structure is similar to a queue, but each value is assigned a priority level. Think of this like a line at a nightclub, where VIPs have a higher priority and are let in first.
- ○ **Grids**: This structure is the most robust and is similar to a 2D array. It has rows and columns, but it has many functions for sorting, searching, and manipulating the data. Think of a searchable airport departure schedule, where you can see all the planes, the companies, flight times, and so on, and sort it according to your preference.

We are going to start with a Grid data structure as we need several rows and columns of information for each item. Create a new Script, scr_Global_Equipment and write the following code to build the Grid:

```
globalvar equip;
equip = ds_grid_create(3,4);
ds_grid_set(equip, TNT, SPRITE, spr_Menu_TNT);
ds_grid_set(equip, TNT, OBJECT, obj_Ghost_TNT);
ds_grid_set(equip, TNT, AMOUNT, 1);
ds_grid_set(equip, TNT, COST, 100);
ds_grid_set(equip, WRECKINGBALL, SPRITE, spr_Menu_WreckingBall);
ds_grid_set(equip, WRECKINGBALL, OBJECT, obj_Ghost_WreckingBall);
ds_grid_set(equip, WRECKINGBALL, AMOUNT, 0);
ds_grid_set(equip, WRECKINGBALL, COST, 1000);
ds_grid_set(equip, MAGNET, SPRITE, spr_Menu_MagneticCrane);
ds_grid_set(equip, MAGNET, OBJECT, obj_Ghost_MagneticCrane);
ds_grid_set(equip, MAGNET, AMOUNT, 0);
ds_grid_set(equip, MAGNET, COST, 3000);
```

We start by declaring a global variable which we then use to hold the ID of a Grid. When creating a Grid we need to declare how many rows and columns it needs. For this game we have three rows for the pieces of equipment and each piece has four columns of data. We set the value for each Grid cell individually, so slot 0 is the sprite to use, slot 1 the object to spawn, slot 2 is for how many the player starts with, and finally, slot 3 is how much it will cost to purchase. We have done this for each piece of equipment and we (the player) will start the game with single TNT only.

5. Reopen `scr_Global_GameStart` and call this script. We now have all the equipment categorized and ready for the Shop.

6. Next we need to create an inventory for the player to track what equipment they have purchased. Since the player needs to add equipment to the inventory and will also use that equipment, we need a data structure that is easily mutable. We will use a List for this purpose. Create a new Script, `scr_Global_Inventory`, and start a List:

```
globalvar inventory;
inventory = ds_list_create();
ds_list_add(inventory, TNT);
```

We declare a global variable and then use it to hold the ID of the List we create. At the start of the game we have already established that the player will have some TNT, so that is all we need in the inventory.

7. Once again, call this script in `scr_Global_GameStart`. Here is the complete code:

```
score   = 0;
scr_Global_Levels();
scr_Global_Colors();
scr_Global_Equipment();
scr_Global_Inventory();
```

8. Now that we have all the data stored, we can move on to building the item menu. The first element we need to create is a purchase button. Create a new Sprite, `spr_Button_Buy`, and with **Remove Background** turned off, load `Chapter 7/Sprites/Button_Buy.gif`. **Center** the **Origin** and click on **OK**.

9. Create a new Object, `obj_Button_Buy`, and assign `spr_Button_Buy` as the **Sprite**.

10. This is a standard button so set the **Parent** to `obj_Button_Parent`.

11. Add a **Mouse | Left Pressed** event and apply a new Script, `scr_Button_Buy_MousePressed`, with the following code:

```
if (score > ds_grid_get(equip, myItem, COST))
{
    ds_grid_add(equip, myItem, AMOUNT, 1);
    score -= ds_grid_get(equip, myItem, COST);
    if (ds_list_find_index(inventory, myItem) == -1)
    {
        ds_list_add(inventory, myItem);
    }
}
```

Dynamic Front Ends

In order to purchase an item, we first need to check to see if the player has enough money. For this, we compare the `score` against the data held in the Grid we created. You will notice that we have a variable, `myItem`, that has not been initialized in the button itself. We will create that variable dynamically later, when we spawn the button. If the player can purchase the item, we increase the amount the player owns, and reduce the amount of money by the price of the item. Finally, we check to see if the player already has some of the item in their current inventory. If this is the first item of its type, we add it to the inventory List.

12. We are now ready to spawn everything in the room with a new Object called `obj_Shop_Overlord`.

13. Add an **Other | Room Start** event and attach a new Script, `scr_Shop_Overlord_RoomStart`, with the code for spawning the buttons needed in the Shop:

```
for ( i = 0; i < ds_grid_width(equip); i++ )
{
    buyButton = instance_create(512, (96 * i) + 152, obj_Button_Buy);
    buyButton.myItem = i;
}

instance_create(502, 440, obj_Button_Start);
```

We start by running a loop through each row of the equipment Grid so that we know how many buttons need to be created. We then spawn a purchase button which will be stacked vertically on screen. Next we pass the `myItem` variable that is used in the mouse pressed event. The last thing we do is create a start button in the lower right corner of the screen so that the player can go back to `LevelSelect` option.

14. We now have all the buttons placed, but we still need to draw all the other necessary information. Create a new Script, `scr_Shop_Overlord_Draw`, and add it to a **Draw | Draw** event:

```
draw_set_color(c_black);
draw_set_halign(fa_center);

for ( i = 0; i < ds_grid_width(equip); i++ )
{
    draw_sprite(ds_grid_get(equip, i, SPRITE), 0, 96, (96 * i) + 152);
    draw_set_font(fnt_Small);
    draw_text(116, (96 * i) + 166, ds_grid_get(equip, i, AMOUNT));
    draw_set_font(fnt_Large);
    draw_text(300, (96 * i) + 140, ds_grid_get(equip, i, COST));
}
```

First we need to set the font color to black and center-align the text. We then run a loop through the equipment Grid to draw each component. We first draw the proper sprite in the correct location to line up with the buttons. Here we use a small font to draw the amount of the item the player owns in the small space in the lower right corner of the sprite. We then change to a large font and display the price of the item.

15. The menu is now built but it is still missing an important piece of information; how much cash the player has. Add the following at the end of the script:

```
draw_set_color(yellow);
draw_set_font(fnt_Medium);
draw_text(96, 416, "Cash");
draw_set_font(fnt_Large);
draw_text(96, 440, score);
draw_set_font(-1);
```

We set the color to our special yellow color for the rest of this text. We set a medium font to display the word Cash and then change to a large font for the actual amount they have. Finally, we reset the font to default.

16. Open up Shop and place a single instance of obj_Shop_Overlord object somewhere in the room. We are done with this room so click on **OK**.

17. Run the game and go to the Shop. You won't be able to purchase anything at this point but you should see the icons, buttons, and information properly displayed. It should look like the following screenshot:

Rebuilding the HUD

Game development is an iterative process where elements are added in when they are needed and often reworked several times as features are implemented and feedback from users changes the direction of the project. Building a game in this fashion saves time because it allows us to get things done quickly, see the results, and adapt as we go. In the last chapter we were focused on functionality of the basic gameplay. We built a simple HUD that allowed us to spawn each piece of equipment with a click. However, we did not limit what equipment the player had access to, nor did it have the ability to restart the level or show a countdown timer displaying how much time was remaining to clear the Zone. We will need to fix all of this, plus we should allow the player to go to the Shop in case their supplies are running low. All of this can be done as follows:

1. We will start by adding some global variables. Create a new Script, `scr_Global_Gameplay`, and declare the necessary global variables:

   ```
   globalvar isGameActive, isTimerStarted;
   isGameActive = true;
   isTimerStarted = false;
   ```

   Here we initialize two variables that we will need to improve the functionality of the game. The variable `isGameActive` will be set to `true` at the start of each level to commence gameplay. It will also afford us the ability to display information at the end of the level while preventing the player from using the Menu. The `isTimerStarted` variable will be used for the countdown to clear the Zones.

2. Open `scr_Global_GameStart` and call this the script.

3. The Menu is also going to need some new variables. Open `scr_Menu_Create` and add the following code:

   ```
   timer = 10;
   isTimerStarted = false;
   menuItem_Zone = 32;
   menuItems_Y = 440;
   restartX = 468;
   shopX = 564;
   tempCost = 0;
   tempScore = 0;
   startEquip = ds_grid_create(3, 4);
   ds_grid_copy(startEquip, equip);
   ```

Chapter 7

The first variable is the amount of time the player will have for a countdown. Here we are going to give ten seconds for the Zone to be cleared. We then set the vertical location of the menu to be near the bottom of the screen. The next two variables are for the horizontal location of the Restart and Shop buttons. We need some temporary variables for holding the value of the equipment used and how much the player earns in the level as we don't want to change the global score unless the player wins the level. Finally, we create another Grid and copy the data from the `equip` Grid so that if the level is restarted we still have the original settings.

4. We will also want to make sure that the player is unable to play a level if they have no equipment in their inventory. If that happens we will want to automatically go to the Shop. At the very top of the script, add the following code:

```
if (ds_list_size(inventory) == 0)
{
    room_goto(Shop);
}
```

We check the size of the inventory and if it contains nothing we go to the Shop.

5. The previous draw script we used for the Menu functioned adequately for what we needed at the time. However, now that we have data structures, we can simplify the system and add new functionality. We will start by creating a new Script, `scr_Menu_Equipment`, for which we will need to accept some parameters:

```
slot = argument0;
item = argument1;

if (slot == 0) { myX = 40; }
if (slot == 1) { myX = 104; }
if (slot == 2) { myX = 168; }
```

We start by declaring two variables for the two arguments that must be supplied when calling this script. **Arguments** are just variables that pass information from a script or function when it is called. Here we will have a slot placement on the Menu and a declaration of what item is to be displayed in the slot. Since we have a predetermined amount of slots on our Menu to be three, we can check which slot is being passed and apply the appropriate horizontal offset.

[273]

Dynamic Front Ends

6. Next we will add the functionality for how the Menu equipment buttons work. Add the following code:

```
draw_sprite(ds_grid_get(startEquip, item, SPRITE), 0, myX,
menuItems_Y);
if (!isActive)
{
    if (win_Y > menuItems_Y - menuItem_Zone && win_Y < menuItems_Y
+ menuItem_Zone)
    {
        if (win_X > myX - menuItem_Zone && win_X < myX + menuItem_
Zone)
        {
            draw_sprite(ds_grid_get(startEquip, item, SPRITE), 1,
myX, menuItems_Y);
            if (mouse_check_button_pressed(mb_left) && ds_grid_
get(startEquip, item, AMOUNT) > 0)
            {
                instance_create(myX, menuItems_Y, ds_grid_
get(startEquip, item, OBJECT));
                ds_grid_add(startEquip, item, AMOUNT, -1);
                tempCost += ds_grid_get(startEquip, item, COST);
                isActive = true;
            }
        }
    }
}
```

Previously we had code similar to this for each piece of equipment. Now that we have the data structure, we can use the information to create all of the equipment dynamically. We start by drawing the sprite that is pulled from the local `startEquip` Grid. We then check to see if the Menu is active due to the player trying to place an item. We check for the mouse location on screen and see if it is hovering above the button and change to the appropriate frame of animation. If the button is clicked, we create the selected item, subtract one unit of the item from the Grid, add the value of the item to how much the player has spent, and make the Menu active.

7. We have drawn all the Equipment buttons, but we haven't displayed how many items the player has in their inventory. To fix this, add the following code to the end of the script:

```
draw_set_color(c_black);
draw_set_halign(fa_center);
draw_set_font(fnt_Small);
draw_text(myX + 20, menuY + 14, ds_grid_get(startEquip, item,
AMOUNT));
```

All we are doing here is setting the color, horizontal alignment of the text, and the font. We then draw the amount of units for each item in the lower right-hand corner as we did in the Shop.

8. Now that we have the improved and simplified Equipment button code, we can go back to `scr_Menu_DrawGUI` and remove all the old clunky code. Delete all the code except for the very first line that draws the menu background. Once it has been removed, add the following code to draw the Menu:

```
if (isGameActive)
{
    Win_X = window_mouse_get_x();
    Win_Y = window_mouse_get_y();
    for (i = 0; i < ds_list_size(inventory); i++)
    {
        scr_Menu_Equipment(i, ds_list_find_value(inventory, i));
    }
}
draw_set_font(-1);
```

We start by checking whether the global variable `isGameActive` is true or not. If it is true, we get the screen location of the mouse, so we have the proper information to place the menu correctly. We then run a loop for as many objects as the player has in the inventory, which will then execute the menu equipment script to draw all the buttons. At the very end of the script we once again set the font back to its default.

9. The HUD needs more than just buttons for the equipment. For a game like this we definitely need a button that allows the player to restart the level. Let's quickly create a new Sprite, `spr_Button_Restart`, and with **Remove Background** turned off, load `Chapter 7/Sprites/Button_Restart.gif`. **Center** the **Origin** and click on **OK**.

10. We do not need to create an object for this button as it is going to be drawn on the Menu. Create a new Script, `scr_Menu_Button_Restart`, and write the following code:

```
draw_sprite(spr_Button_Restart, 0, restartX, menuItems_Y);
if (win_Y > menuItems_Y - menuItem_Zone && win_Y < menuItems_Y + menuItem_Zone)
{
    if (win_X > restartX - menuItem_Zone && win_X < restartX + menuItem_Zone)
    {
        draw_sprite(spr_Button_Restart, 1, restartX, menuItems_Y);
        if (mouse_check_button_pressed(mb_left))
```

Dynamic Front Ends

```
        {
            room_restart();
        }
    }
}
```

Just as we did with the Equipment buttons, we start by drawing the button in its non-hovered state. We then check if the mouse is hovering over the button, and if it is, we change the animation to the hover state. If the button is clicked, we restart the room.

11. Reopen `scr_Menu_DrawGUI` and call this script after the loop that creates the buttons for the equipment.

12. We also need a button to allow the player to access the Shop. We can't use the button we previously created as we need it to be drawn on the menu, not spawned in the world. Luckily, we can use its sprite so all we need to do is create a new Script, `scr_Menu_Button_Shop`, with code similar to all the other menu buttons:

```
draw_sprite(spr_Button_Shop, 0, shopX, menuItems_Y);
if (win_Y > menuItems_Y - menuItem_Zone && win_Y < menuItems_Y + menuItem_Zone)
{
    if (win_X > shopX - menuItem_Zone*2 && win_X < shopX + menuItem_Zone*2)
    {
        draw_sprite(spr_Button_Shop, 1, shopX, menuItems_Y);
        if (mouse_check_button_pressed(mb_left))
        {
            room_goto(Shop);
        }
    }
}
```

Same as before, we draw the sprite and then check whether the mouse is hovering or not, making sure that we change the width to the larger size of this sprite. If the button is clicked, we go to the Shop.

13. Once again, open `scr_Menu_DrawGUI` and call this script immediately after the Restart button.

[276]

Chapter 7

14. We are almost finished with the HUD, we only have one very important piece of information we still need to show the player: How much time is left. This will be done completely with text, so all we need to do is create a new Script, scr_Menu_Clock:

    ```
    draw_set_color(yellow);
    if (isTimerStarted)
    {
        draw_set_font(fnt_Small);
        draw_text(320, 416,"COUNTDOWN");
        draw_set_font(fnt_Large);
        draw_text(320, 436, timer);
    } else {
        draw_set_font(fnt_Small);
        draw_text(320,416,"PRESS SPACE TO");
        draw_set_font(fnt_Large);
        draw_text(320,436,"DESTROY")
    }
    ```

    The background is black, so we will use the yellow color we created for all the text. If the global variable isTimerStarted is true, we draw the word "COUNTDOWN" in small letters and the amount of time remaining in a large font underneath it. If isTimerStarted is false, we then draw the text in a similar manner to indicate to the player what they are supposed to do.

15. Reopen scr_Menu_DrawGUI and call this script after the Shop button call. The completed script should look like the following code:

    ```
    draw_sprite(spr_Menu_BG, 0, 0, 400);
    if (isGameActive)
    {
        Win_X = window_mouse_get_x();
        Win_Y = window_mouse_get_y();

        for (i = 0; i < ds_list_size(inventory); i++)
        {
            scr_Menu_Equipment(i, ds_list_find_value(inventory, i));
        }
        scr_Menu_Button_Restart();
        scr_Menu_Button_Shop();
        scr_Menu_Clock();
    }
    draw_set_font(-1);
    ```

[277]

Dynamic Front Ends

16. To get the countdown started we need to activate it, which we can do in `scr_Overlord_KeyPress`. Add the following code:
    ```
    if (!isTimerStarted)
    {
        obj_Menu.alarm[0] = room_speed;
        isTimerStarted = true;
    }
    ```
    We check the `isTimerStarted` variable to see if it has been activated already or not as we only want it to happen once. If the timer has not started, it will turn on an alarm in the Menu in one second.

17. The last thing we need to do to get everything to work is to open `obj_Menu` and add an **Alarm | Alarm 0** event with a new Script, `scr_Menu_Alarm0`, attached.
    ```
    if (timer > 0)
    {
        timer -= 1;
        alarm[0] = room_speed;
    } else {
        obj_Overlord.alarm[0] = 1;
    }
    ```
    The Menu has a timer initialized for ten seconds and in this alarm we check to see if there is still time remaining. If there is, we reduce the time by one and reset the alarm for another second. This will repeat until time expires, in which case we tell the Overlord to run the victory condition alarm immediately.

18. The HUD is now controlling the time so we need to remove that functionality from the Overlord. Reopen `scr_Overlord_Step` and remove the line of code that sets the alarm.

19. Run the game and play the first level. The Menu has a single Equipment button of TNT, a Restart button, and a Shop button. Once you hit spacebar, the countdown timer will start ticking down until zero. When time expires the room will either restart or go to the next room based on whether the Zone is clear or not. The game should look like the following screenshot:

[278]

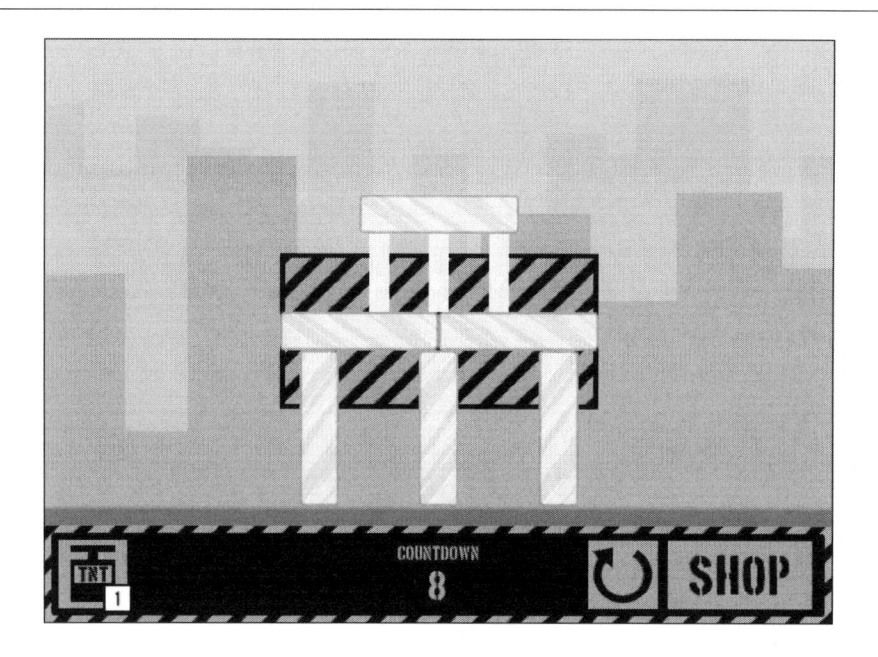

Adding risk and reward to destruction

So far there has been very little risk or reward in the game at all. We have added a Shop to the game where we can purchase items, but we are not yet able to earn any cash. We can use as much equipment as we want, as long as it is in our inventory, which means that there is no need for strategy. We need to add a Game Over Screen, if the player ever runs out of money or completes all the levels. We also need a Score Screen as currently the player has no idea how well they did so we will want to show that as well. It's time to add these features starting with rewarding the player points:

1. We will start with the Game Over screen. Create a new Room called `GameOver` and apply `bg_MainMenu` as its background.

2. Create a new Object, `obj_GameOver`, with no **Sprite** attached.

3. Upon creation we will create a variable that will contain the game over message and we will set an alarm for five seconds, which we will use to restart the game. Create a new Script, `scr_GameOver_Create`, with the following code and attach it to a **Create** event:

   ```
   gameOverText = "You ran out of money, better luck next time!";
   alarm[0] = 5 * room_speed;
   ```

4. Add an **Alarm | Alarm 0** event and then attach a new Script, `scr_GameOver_Alarm0`, and restart the game:

   ```
   game_restart();
   ```

Dynamic Front Ends

5. All that we have left to do is to draw the win/lose statement. Create a new Script, scr_GameOver_Draw, and attach it to a **Draw | Draw** event:

   ```
   draw_set_color(c_black);
   draw_set_halign(fa_center);
   draw_set_font(fnt_Large);
   draw_text(320, 280, "Game Over");
   draw_set_font(fnt_Small);
   draw_text(320, 320, gameOverText);
   draw_set_font(-1);
   ```

6. If it isn't still open, reopen GameOver and place a single instance of obj_GameOver somewhere in the room. We are now done with this and can close the room.

7. The next thing we will create is a new Object, obj_ScoreFloat, to display the points rewarded as each Pillar or Debris is destroyed.

8. Add a **Create** event with a new Script, scr_ScoreFloat_Create, and initialize two variables:

   ```
   fadeOut = 0;
   alpha = 1;
   ```

   We will have the score fade out over time, so we have a variable for triggering the fade out and one for the value of transparency which is currently set to full opacity.

9. Next we need to add a **Draw | Draw** event with a new Script, scr_ScoreFloat_Draw, to show the value on screen:

   ```
   y -= 1;
   fadeOut++;
   if (fadeOut > 60) { alpha -= 0.05; }
   if (alpha <= 0) { instance_destroy(); }
   draw_set_color(c_black);
   draw_set_font(fnt_Small);
   draw_set_alpha(alpha);
   draw_text(x, y, myValue);
   draw_set_alpha(1);
   ```

This object is not a part of the physics world, so we can manually move it vertically every frame. We increase the fadeOut variable and once it hits 60, we start to decrease the alpha variable by a small amount. Once alpha has hit zero, we destroy the instance so that it doesn't take up any memory. After that we set the color, font, and transparency values and draw the text. The myValue variable will be passed upon creation from the object that spawns it. Finally, we set the transparency back to full opacity; otherwise everything else in the entire room will fade out as well.

[280]

10. Now that we can display the score we need to spawn it and pass a value to it. Since we already know that each Pillar and Debris has a different mass, we can use that number to award points upon its destruction. Reopen scr_Pillar_BreakApart and insert the following code after the shatter sound is played but before the instance is destroyed:

```
scoreFloat = instance_create(x, y, obj_ScoreFloat);
scoreFloat.myValue = floor(phy_mass);
obj_Menu.tempScore += scoreFloat.myValue;
```

When the Pillar breaks apart it will spawn an instance of obj_ScoreFloat. We then set the displayed value to the rounded down amount of the object's total mass. Finally, we increase the Menu's tempScore by the same amount.

11. We need the Small Pillars and Debris to do the same, so open scr_Pillar_Destroy and insert the same code in the same place.

12. Run the game and destroy the Pillars in the first level. As each piece breaks, a number will float up signifying the value that it is worth. The floating numbers should fade out after a few seconds and should look something like the following screenshot:

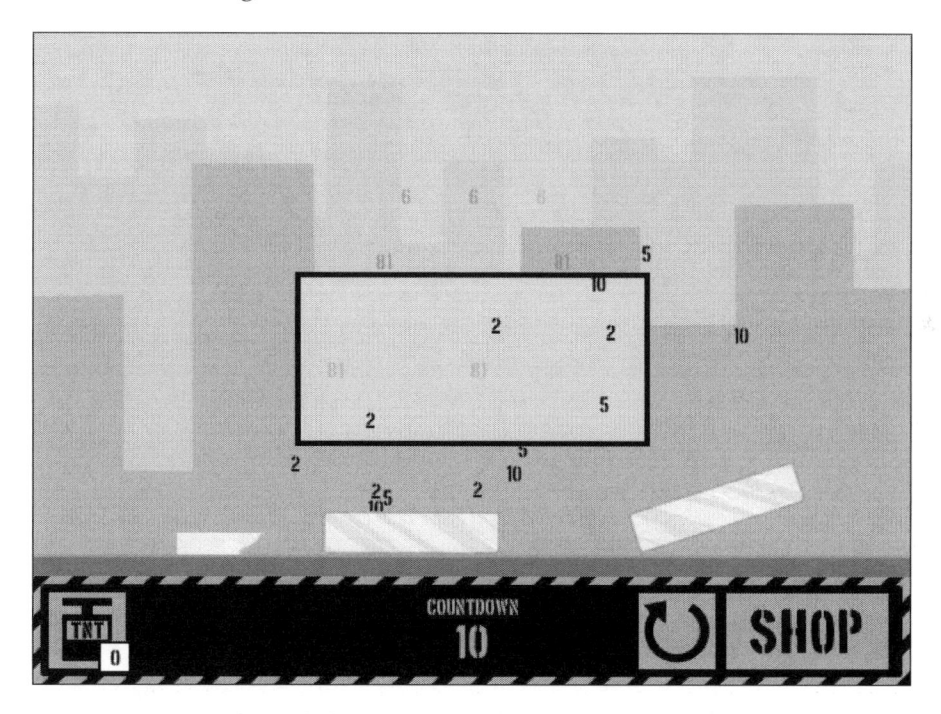

Dynamic Front Ends

13. All we need to do now is to make a Score Screen that sums up the damage and shows the total profit for the level. We will start by bringing in a few more sprites, spr_Screen_BG and spr_Button_NextLevel, both supplied in Chapter 7/Sprites/. Make sure not to **Remove Background** and to **Center** the **Origin** for both.

14. Let's create a new Script, scr_Menu_Button_NextLevel, with the functionality of this button:

```
if (isVictory)
{
    draw_sprite(spr_Button_NextLevel, 0, nextLevelX, menuItems_Y);
    if (win_Y > menuItems_Y - menuItem_Zone && win_Y < menuItems_Y
+ menuItem_Zone)
    {
        if (win_X > nextLevelX - menuItem_Zone && win_X <
nextLevelX + menuItem_Zone)
        {
            draw_sprite(spr_Button_NextLevel, 1, nextLevelX,
menuItems_Y);
            if (mouse_check_button_pressed(mb_left))
            {
                for(i = 0; i < totalLevels; i++)
                {
                    if (level[i, 0] == room)
                    {
                        level[i+1, 1] = false;
                        room_goto( level[i+1, 0] );
                    }
                }
            }
        }
    }
}
```

We only want the Next Level button to appear if the player successfully clears the Zones, so we check for that first. If the player has won the level, we draw the sprite and then check to see if the mouse is hovering over it. If the mouse is over the button and it is pressed, we run a quick loop through the level array to see what room we are currently in and unlock the next level. Finally we go to the room we just unlocked.

15. Now we are ready to create a new Object, obj_ScoreScreen, to display the Score Screen. Set the **Depth** to -100 so that it always draws on top of all other GUI elements.

[282]

16. Add a **Create** event with a new Script, `scr_ScoreScreen_Create` attached and initialize the following variables:

```
isGameActive = false;
obj_Menu.isActive = true;
isVictory = scr_WinCondition();
screenX = 320;
screenY = 200;
menuItem_Zone = 32;
menuItems_Y = 440;
restartX = 200;
shopX = 320;
nextLevelX = 440;
```

We don't want the player to play during this time, so we turn off the `isGameActive` variable and make the Menu active so that the Equipment buttons no longer function. Next we need to check if the player has been successful in order to know what to draw. The final seven variables are all for the placement of the various text and buttons we will be displaying.

17. Now to add a **Draw | Draw GUI** event with a new Script, `scr_ScoreScreen_DrawGUI` and we will start by drawing all the text we need:

```
draw_sprite(spr_Screen_BG, 0, screenX, screenY);

draw_set_color(c_black);
draw_set_halign(fa_center);
draw_set_font(fnt_Large);
draw_text(screenX, 60, room_get_name(room));
draw_text(screenX, 144, obj_Menu.tempScore);
draw_text(screenX, 204, obj_Menu.tempCost);
draw_text(screenX, 284, obj_Menu.tempScore - obj_Menu.tempCost);

draw_set_font(fnt_Medium);
draw_text(screenX, 120, "Damage Estimate");
draw_text(screenX, 180, "Equipment Cost");
draw_text(screenX, 260, "Total Profit");
draw_set_font(-1);
```

First we draw the background sprite. We then set the color, alignment, and font. We are using the largest font to draw the name of the room and the values for the amount of damage, the amount of equipment used, and the total profit. We then switch to the medium font to write the description of each value, placed above the number it corresponds to. We are done drawing text, so we set the font back to its default value.

Dynamic Front Ends

18. Now we just need to add the buttons into the script:

    ```
    Win_X = window_mouse_get_x();
    Win_Y = window_mouse_get_y();
    scr_Menu_Button_Restart();
    scr_Menu_Button_Shop();
    scr_Menu_Button_NextLevel();
    ```

    Just as we did with the Menu, we get the coordinates of the mouse on screen and then execute the scripts for the three buttons.

19. In order to activate the Score Screen, we need to reopen `scr_Overlord_Alarm0` and have it spawn an instance of `obj_ScoreScreen` instead of the code it currently runs. Remove all the code and replace it with the following code:

    ```
    instance_create(0, 0, obj_ScoreScreen);
    ```

20. Run the game and finish the first level. After the timer has run out, the Score Screen appears displaying the damage, the cost, and the profit. The in-game menu has disappeared and has been replaced by three buttons for replaying the level, going to the Shop, or the next level. It should look like the following screenshot:

21. There is one issue that we need to solve. While the screen says we have earned money, if we go to the Shop, there will be no cash available. This is because we haven't transferred the temporary values to the global values, which we will do in a new Script called scr_ScoreCleanUp:

```
with (obj_Menu)
{
    ds_grid_copy(equip, startEquip);
    ds_grid_destroy(startEquip);
    score += tempScore - tempCost;
    for ( i = 0; i < ds_grid_width(equip); i++)
    {
        e = ds_grid_get(equip, i, AMOUNT);

        if (e == 0)
        {
            inv = ds_list_find_index(inventory, i);
            ds_list_delete(inventory, inv);
        }
    }
}
```

When this script is executed, it will go into the Menu and copy the remaining equipment over to the global equipment values and then delete the temporary grid from memory. Next we increase the global score based on what occurred during gameplay. We then run a loop through the inventory looking for whether the player has run out of any items. If they have, we remove it from the inventory altogether.

22. If the player goes to the next level, we should pay them immediately. We should also check the score to make sure that the player has money. If they run out of money, then it is game over, otherwise they can go to the next level. Reopen scr_Menu_Button_NextLevel and replace the line of code where we switch rooms with the following:

```
scr_ScoreCleanUp();
if (score < 0)
{
    room_goto(GameOver);
} else {
    room_goto( level[i+1, 0] );
}
```

Dynamic Front Ends

23. If the player decides to go to the Shop, it becomes a bit trickier. The script we are calling is also used on the Menu, so we don't want it to change the data during gameplay. Reopen `scr_Menu_Button_Shop` and replace the line of code where we switch rooms with the following code:

    ```
    if (!isGameActive) { scr_ScoreCleanUp();}
    if (score < 0)
    {
        room_goto(GameOver);
    } else {
        room_goto(Shop);
    }
    ```

    Now the score will be transferred only if gameplay has stopped. We also check the score here for the game over state to decide what room to go to when clicked.

24. Everything should work properly now, so run the game and check to make sure that the score doesn't change when you go to the shop during gameplay.

Adding introductory text to each level

We have a good end to the levels, but the player may not be sure what to do. What we need is a bit of a story to sell the idea of destroying towers and explaining what it is the player needs to do in each level. To do this we will add a screen, much like the Score Screen at the start of each level:

1. We will need a button to start the level, which again will need to be drawn on screen. Create a new Script, `scr_Menu_Button_Start`, with some very familiar code:

    ```
    draw_sprite(spr_Button_Start, 0, startX, startY);
    if (win_Y > startY - start_ZoneHeight && win_Y < startY + start_ZoneHeight)
    {
        if (win_X > startX - start_ZoneWidth && win_X < startX + start_ZoneWidth)
        {
            draw_sprite(spr_Button_Start, 1, startX, startY);
            if (mouse_check_button_pressed(mb_left))
            {
                isGameActive = true;
                instance_destroy();
            }
        }
    }
    ```

[286]

All the standard button code is here, but when the button is clicked, we activate the gameplay and then destroy the Story screen object. The `start_ZoneWidth` and `start_ZoneHeight` variables used here haven't been initialized yet, but we will be doing that shortly.

2. Next we need all the text that we want to display for each level. For this we will want to use a Map data structure so that we can link the text to the level. Create a new Script, `scr_Global_Dialogue`, and write the dialog that we need:

```
globalvar dialogue;
dialogue = ds_map_create();
ds_map_add(dialogue, Level_01, "Welcome to Destruct! A tower toppling game.
# Let's start with some basic training. Here we have a glass tower that needs to come down. You have one stick of TNT to use to completely clear the Zone.
# Let's see what you can do.");
ds_map_add(dialogue, Level_02, "Temporary Dialogue for Level 02");
ds_map_add(dialogue, Level_03, "Temporary Dialogue for Level 03");
ds_map_add(dialogue, Level_04, "Temporary Dialogue for Level 04");
ds_map_add(dialogue, Level_05, "Temporary Dialogue for Level 05");
ds_map_add(dialogue, Level_06, "Temporary Dialogue for Level 06");
ds_map_add(dialogue, Level_07, "Temporary Dialogue for Level 07");
ds_map_add(dialogue, Level_08, "Temporary Dialogue for Level 08");
ds_map_add(dialogue, Level_09, "Temporary Dialogue for Level 09");
ds_map_add(dialogue, Level_10, "Temporary Dialogue for Level 10");
ds_map_add(dialogue, Level_11, "Temporary Dialogue for Level 11");
ds_map_add(dialogue, Level_12, "Temporary Dialogue for Level 12");
```

We make a new global variable and attach it to the Map data structure we create. For each entry we need to have a **Key** and a **Value** for that key. Here we use the name of each room as a key and write the dialog as the value. We need text for every room in the game so it doesn't error out, so we have temporary dialog for rooms 2-12 that you can replace with your own text. In the dialog for Level 01 we are using # which is a special character used to start a new paragraph. This will make large amounts of text a bit more readable.

3. Open `scr_Global_GameStart` and call this script.

4. We have all the art assets we need, but we do need a new Object, `obj_StoryScreen`, with a **Depth** of -100.

Dynamic Front Ends

5. Add a **Create** event and apply a new Script, `scr_StoryScreen_Create`, to initialize the variables:

```
isGameActive = false;
screenX = 320;
screenY = 200;
startY = 440;
startX = 320;
start_ZoneWidth = 128;
start_ZoneHeight = 32;
myText = ds_map_find_value(dialogue, room);
textLength = 0;
```

We stop gameplay and then set six variables for the location of the text we will be drawing. We then load up the text from the Map based on the room the player is currently in. The last variable we have, `textLength`, is going to be used for an inventory effect, where the text appears to be typed in over time.

6. Next we need to add a **Draw | Draw GUI** event with a new Script, `scr_StoryScreen_DrawGUI`, that draws everything:

```
draw_sprite(spr_Screen_BG, 0, screenX, screenY);
draw_set_color(c_black);
draw_set_halign(fa_center);
draw_set_font(fnt_Large);
draw_text(screenX, 60, string(room_get_name(room)));

draw_set_halign(fa_left);
draw_set_font(fnt_Small);
textLength++;
writeText = string_copy(myText, 1, textLength);
draw_text_ext(160, 120, writeText, -1, 320);
draw_set_font(-1);

win_X = window_mouse_get_x();
win_Y = window_mouse_get_y();
scr_Menu_Button_Start();
```

As we did with the Score Screen, we draw the background and set the color, alignment, and font for the title of the level. Next is the typewrite effect for the dialog to be shown on screen. We change the alignment and font for the dialog and start increasing the `textLength` variable by one step each. This value is what determines how many characters from the dialog need to be copied over to the `writeText` variable, which means that the text will grow over time. We are using the `draw_text_ext` function, which allows us to limit how wide the paragraph can be before it drops down a line, in this case 320 pixels. Once again at the end we get the mouse location for the start button to work.

7. All that is left for us to do is to spawn an instance of the Story screen in `scr_Overlord_Create`:

   `instance_create(0, 0, obj_StoryScreen);`

8. Run the game and go to the first level. The story screen appears and the dialog starts appearing one letter at a time and should look like the image below. When the **START** button is clicked, the gameplay starts as usual.

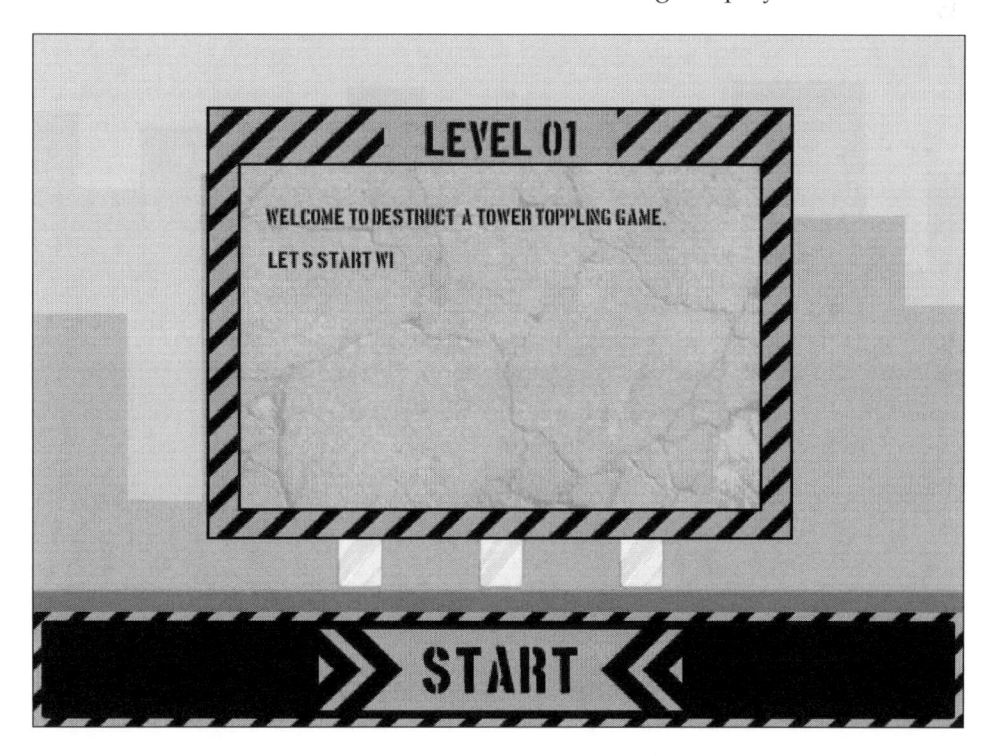

Saving the player's progress

Polish in games is not always about the visual embellishments. Sometimes it's also about adding smaller features that aren't immediately noticeable but can drastically improve the overall experience. Currently the game looks good and plays well, but if we close down the browser and return to play at a later time, we will need to start all over again. Players these days expect that they can come back to a game and continue from where they left off. In order to do this, we need to save the player's progress.

Understanding local storage

Whenever a game needs to save data the only viable option is to write the data to a file outside of the game itself. This poses a potential problem for web-based games as any file that needs to be downloaded will require the user to explicitly allow it. This would mean the player would know the name of the file and where it is located, which in turn would mean they could easily hack their own saved file. To get around this hurdle, HTML5 offers a solution known as **local storage**.

Local storage allows web pages, or in our case a game embedded into a web page, to save data within the browser itself. This is similar to internet cookies but with the benefit of being faster, more secure, and potentially able to store a lot more information. Since this data is saved in the browser, the user is not notified of the file being created or accessed; they cannot see the data easily and it is only accessible from the domain that creates it. This makes it perfect for saving our game data.

> There are only two ways to clear the saved data. Overwrite the data or clear your browser's cache. It is recommended that you always test games in a private browser mode to guarantee the save system is working properly.

Writing to local storage

For this game, we are going to save all the relevant data related to the levels unlocked, the amount of cash accrued, and the equipment purchased. To save the game data we are going to need to write to a file. GameMaker: Studio has two file formats that it can handle for HTML5 games: **Text files** and **Ini files**. Text files are useful for reading or writing large amounts of data and can be structured in any way you choose. Ini files are intended for smaller amounts of data and use a **section/key/value** structure. This structure breaks the data into separate sections and in each section there will be key/value pairs that look something like this:

```
[section]
key = value
[playerData]
playerFirstName = Jason
playerLastName = Elliott
```

Local storage requires all data to be in key/value pairs so that we will be using the Ini file system. It is possible to use the text file system, but for the little amount of data we need to save and the amount of extra coding it would take, it's not very beneficial:

1. The first thing any save system needs to do is to create a save file with the appropriate structure and settings desired. Create a new Script, scr_GameSave, and write the following code:

   ```
   theFile = argument0;
   ini_open(theFile);
   ini_write_real("Score","Cash", score);
   for (i = 0; i < totalLevels; i++)
   {
       ini_write_string("Levels", string("Level_" + i), level[i, 1]);
   }
   for ( j = 0; j < ds_grid_width(equip); j++ )
   {
       ini_write_real("Equipment",string("Equip_" + j), ds_grid_get(equip, j, AMOUNT));
   }
   ini_close();
   ```

Dynamic Front Ends

When we execute this script we will require the name of the file to be passed as an argument. We can then open the requested file, or if one is not found it will be created to open. Once the file is open we can write all of the necessary data. We start by writing to a `Score` section, with a key called `Cash` to set the value of score. We run a loop using the level array and in a `Levels` section we store each level and whether it has been unlocked or not. Next we run another loop, this time going through the equipment grid and writing how many of each item the player currently has in the game. Finally, after all the data has been written we close the file.

2. Saving a game is only useful if we actually load the data into it. Create a new Script, scr_GameLoad, so we can read from the file.

```
theFile = argument0;
if (!file_exists(theFile))
{
    scr_GameSave(theFile);
} else {
    ini_open(theFile);
    score = ini_read_real("Score","Cash", "");
    for (i = 0; i < totalLevels; i++)
    {
        level[i, 1] = ini_read_string("Levels", string("Level_" + i), "");
    }
    for ( j = 0; j < ds_grid_width(equip); j++ )
    {
        ds_grid_set(equip, j, AMOUNT, ini_read_real("Equipment",string("Equip_" + j), ""));
        if (ds_list_find_index(inventory, j) == -1 && ds_grid_get(equip, j, AMOUNT) > 0)
        {
            ds_list_add(inventory, j);
        }
    }
    ini_close();
}
```

We start by checking whether the file, as passed through the argument, exists. If the file is not found in local storage, such as the first time the game is run, we run the save script to initialize the values. If the file is found we open the save file and read the data into the game just as we saved it. We set the score, unlock the appropriate levels, and load the equipment. We also run through the inventory to ensure that all the equipment is available to the player.

[292]

3. We will want to load any game data at the start of the game. Open `scr_Global_GameStart` and add the following code at the end of the script:

```
globalvar saveFile;
saveFile = "Default.ini";
scr_GameLoad(saveFile);
```

We create a global variable for the filename so we can save our data easily later. We then pass the string to the load script. This code must be at the end of the script because we need the default values for our grids and arrays to have been initialized first.

4. The most logical place to start saving the game is after the player has completed each level. Open `scr_ScoreCleanUp` and just before the final brace, insert a call to `scr_GameSave`. The entire script is seen below:

```
with (obj_Menu)
{
    ds_grid_copy(equip, startEquip);
    ds_grid_destroy(startEquip);
    score += tempScore - tempCost;
    for ( i = 0; i < ds_grid_width(equip); i++)
    {
        e = ds_grid_get(equip, i, AMOUNT);

        if (e == 0)
        {
            inv = ds_list_find_index(inventory, i);
            ds_list_delete(inventory, inv);
        }
    }
    scr_GameSave(saveFile);
}
```

5. We also need to save the game when the player purchases Equipment in the Shop. Open `scr_Button_Buy_MousePressed` and insert the call to `scr_GameSave` just before the final brace.

6. Save the game and play the first few levels. After you have completed a few levels, refresh the browser. You should see that all your cash, equipment, and unlocked levels remain the same.

Dynamic Front Ends

Saving multiple game profiles

We now have a game that can save a player's progress, but no way of clearing the data if they want to replay the game. As we mentioned already, the only option for removing the data is to have the user clear their browser's cache or overwrite the data, both options having drawbacks. Most users won't want to clear their cache as it will remove all the data in local storage, not just the game data. Overwriting the data is problematic if multiple people want to play the game in the same browser. Having only a single save file becomes meaningless. We do have a third option available which is that we don't clear the data at all, but rather we create additional save files that can be loaded at any time. Our current save/load system is already prepared for us to have multiple user profiles, we just need to add an input system to capture the name of the user. We will keep the system fairly simple, placing it on the front end and limit the user names to a maximum of eight characters. When the player clicks the start button, it will load the proper profile before it switches rooms:

1. We will start by adding one more global variable for the player's name. Open `scr_Global_GameStart`, initialize the `playerName` variable, and set it to an empty string at the end of the script.

   ```
   globalvar playerName;
   playerName = "";
   ```

2. We will need to create a new Object, `obj_NameInput`, which we can use for tracking the player's input. It does not need a sprite since we will be drawing the text onto the screen.

3. Add a **Create** event with a new Script, `scr_NameInput_Create`, to initialize variables for the length of the string and how many characters have been typed.

   ```
   nameSpace = 0;
   nameMax = 8;
   ```

4. Next we will add a **Draw | Draw** event with a new Script, `scr_NameInput_Draw`, attached to draw the player's name as it is typed and a simple instruction telling the player to type in their name:

   ```
   draw_set_color(c_black);
   draw_set_halign(fa_center);
   draw_set_font(fnt_Small);
   draw_text(320, 280, "Type In Your Name");
   draw_set_font(fnt_Large);
   draw_text(320, 300, playerName);
   draw_set_font(-1);
   ```

5. Now that we have everything displayed on screen we need to gather the keyboard input. Add a **Key Press | Any Key** event and attach a new Script called `scr_NameInput_KeyPressed`.

```
if (nameSpace < nameMax)
{
    if (keyboard_key >= 65 && keyboard_key <= 90)
    {
        playerName = playerName + chr(keyboard_key);
        nameSpace++;
    }
}
```

We only want the name to be a maximum of eight letters, so we first check to see if there is still space available in the current name. If we can input another letter, we then check if the key that is being pressed is a letter. If a letter has been pressed, we add that letter to the end of the string and then indicate that another space has been used.

6. If we ran the game now we would be able to enter letters, but we have no ability to undo any letters. We can fix that with the following code:

```
if (keyboard_key == vk_backspace)
{
    lastLetter = string_length(playerName);
    playerName = string_delete(playerName, lastLetter, 1)
    if (nameSpace > 0)
    {
        namespace--;
    }
}
```

If the user presses *backspace*, we grab the length of the string to find out where the last space of the string is. Once we know that, we can then remove the letter at the end of the string. Finally we check to see if there are still letters remaining and if so, reduce the space count by one. This is needed so that we can't go into negative spaces.

7. Open `MainMenu` and place a single instance of `obj_NameInput` somewhere in the room, location does not matter.

[295]

Dynamic Front Ends

8. Save and play the game. In the front end you should be able to enter a name of up to eight letters and by clicking backspace, delete all those letters. It should look like the following screenshot:

9. The save system is now complete; all that is left to do is to load the data when the player clicks the **START** button. Since we use the **START** button in the Shop as well as the Main Menu, we will need to run a check to ensure we only load the game data at the beginning of the game. Open `scr_Button_Start_MousePressed` and before the room is changed, add the following code:

    ```
    if (room == MainMenu)
    {
        saveFile = string(playerName + ".ini");
        scr_GameLoad(saveFile);
    }
    ```

10. Save and play the game. Use your name and play the game, completing a few levels. Then refresh the page and enter a different name. When you get to the level selection, only the first room should be available.

11. Refresh the browser a second time and use your name once again. This time when you get to the level selection you should see all your unlocked levels. The save system works!

Summary

Excellent work! In this chapter we really rounded out the game experience by adding an entire front end, including a Shop and unlockable levels. We learned to use Grids, Maps, and List data structures to hold a variety of information. We rebuilt the HUD so that we could display more buttons, display only the available equipment, and built a basic countdown timer. We created a Score Screen to show the player how they fared in the level. We also created an introductory screen at the front of each level that utilized a simple typewriter effect that showed us how to manipulate strings. Finally, we added a save system that taught us about using local storage and allows us to have multiple player saves!

Overall we took the game from being a playable prototype to a fully fleshed out game with a beginning and end and plenty of risk and reward. In the next chapter we are going to continue to polish this game by taking a look at particle effects and adding them to the Pillar and Debris destruction. Let's get on with it!

8
Playing with Particles

Over the last two chapters we have built a robust physics-based game utilizing Joints, Fixtures, and Forces. We then added a full Front End that had a shop where the player could purchase equipment and unlockable levels. We also updated the HUD and implemented the Introductory and Score screens to round out each level. It feels almost like a complete game, but something is missing. The TNT blinks out of existence and the breaking of the Pillars just pops into view. In this chapter, we are going to solve this by adding a few particle effects to the game to help mask these changes. After this little bit of polish, our game will be ready for release!

Introducing particle effects

Particle effects are the decorative flourishes used in games to represent dynamic and complex phenomena, such as fire, smoke, and rain. To create a particle effect, it requires three elements: a **System**, **Emitters**, and the **Particles** themselves.

Understanding particle systems

Particle systems are the universe in which the particles and emitters live. Much like the universe, we cannot define the size but we can define a point of origin which all emitters and particles will be placed relative to. We can also have multiple particle systems in existence at any given time, which can be set to draw the particles at different depths. While we can have as many particle systems as we want, it is best to have as few as possible in order to prevent possible memory leaks. The reason for this is that once a particle system is created, it will remain in existence forever unless it is manually destroyed. Destroying the instance that spawned it or changing rooms will not remove the system, so make sure it is removed when it is no longer needed. By destroying a particle system, it will remove all the emitters and particles in that system along with it.

Playing with Particles

Utilizing particle emitters

Particle emitters are defined areas within a system from which particles will spawn. There are two types of emitters to choose from: **Burst** emitters that spawn particles a single time, and **Stream** emitters that spew particles continuously over time. We can define the size and shape of the region in space for each emitter, as well as how the particles should be distributed within the region.

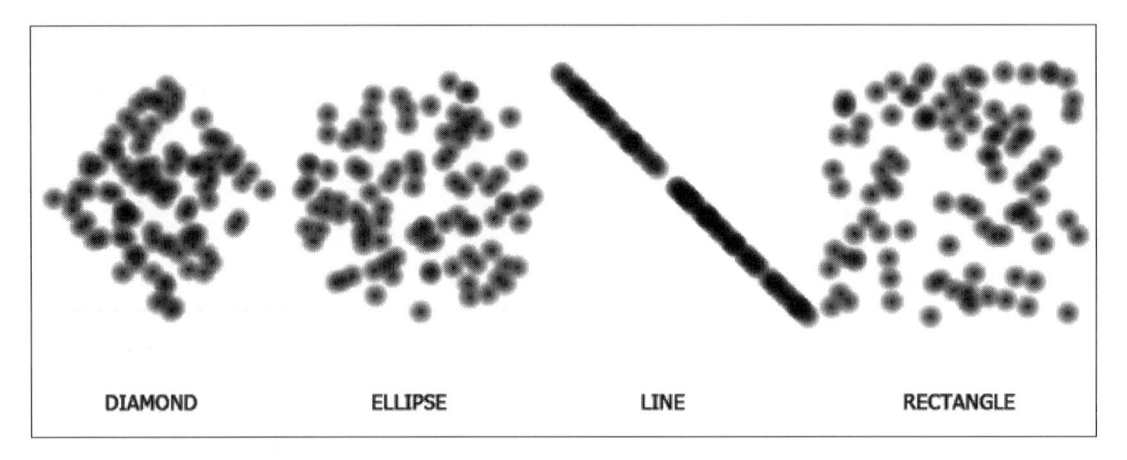

DIAMOND   **ELLIPSE**   **LINE**   **RECTANGLE**

When defining the region in space, there are four **Shape** options: DIAMOND, ELLIPSE, LINE, and RECTANGLE. An example of each can be seen in the preceding diagram, all using exactly the same dimensions, amount of particles, and distribution. While there is no functional difference between using any one of these shapes, the effect itself can benefit from a properly chosen shape. For example, only a LINE can make an effect appear to be angled 30 degrees.

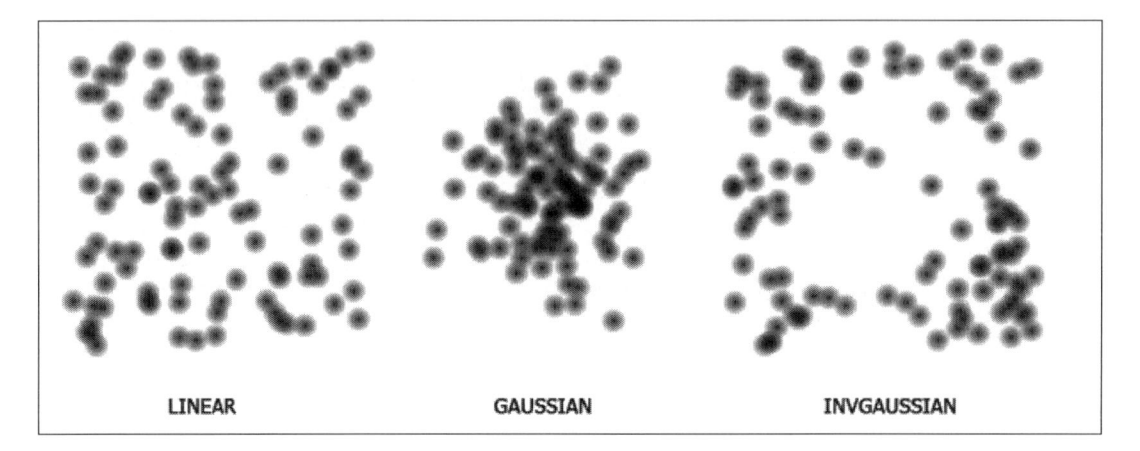

LINEAR   **GAUSSIAN**   **INVGAUSSIAN**

The **distribution** of the particles can also affect how the particles are expelled from the emitter. As can be seen in the preceding diagram, there are three different distributions. **LINEAR** will spawn particles with an equal random distribution throughout the emitter region. **GAUSSIAN** will spawn particles more towards the center of the region. **INVGAUSSIAN** is the inverse of GAUSSIAN, wherein the particles will spawn closer to the edges of the emitter.

Applying particles

Particles are the graphic resources that are spawned from the emitters. There are two types of particles that can be created: **Shapes** and **Sprites**. Shapes are the collection of 64 x 64 pixel sprites that comes built-in with GameMaker: Studio for use as particles. The shapes, as seen in the next diagram, are suitable for the majority of the most common effects, such as fireworks and flames. When wanting to create something more specialized for a game, we can use any Sprite in the Resource tree.

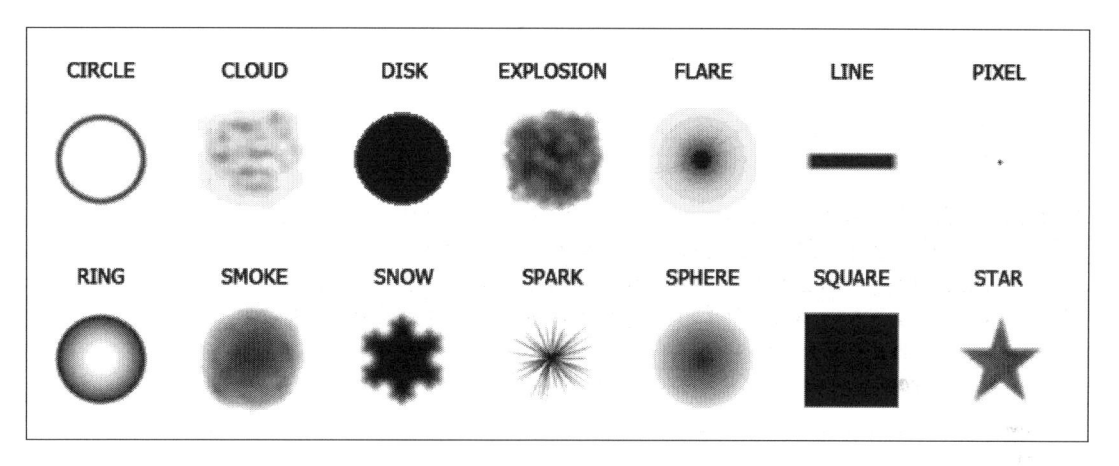

There are a lot of things we can do with particles by adjusting the many attributes available. We can define ranges for how long it lives, the color it should be, and how it moves. We can even spawn more particles at the point of death for each particle. There are, however, some things that we cannot do. In order to keep the graphics processing costs low, there is no ability to manipulate individual particles within an effect. Also, particles cannot interact with objects in any way, so there is no way to know if a particle has collided with an instance in the world. If we need this kind of control, we need to build objects instead.

Playing with Particles

> Designing the look of a particle event is generally a trial and error process that can take a very long time. To speed things up, try using one of the many particle effect generators available on the Internet, such as Particle Designer 2.5 by Alert Games found here: http://alertgames.net/index.php?page=s/pd2.

HTML5 limitations

Using particle effects can really improve the visual quality of a game, but when developing a game intended to be played in a browser we need to be careful. Before implementing a particle effect, it is important to understand potential problems we may encounter. The biggest issue surrounding particles is that in order for them to be rendered smoothly without any lag, they need to be rendered with the graphics processor instead of the main CPU. Most browsers allow this to happen through a JavaScript API called **WebGL**. It is not, however, an HTML5 standard and Microsoft has stated that they have no plans for Internet Explorer to support it for the foreseeable future. This means a potentially significant portion of the game's potential audience could suffer poor gameplay if particles are used. Additionally, even with WebGL enabled, the functionality for particles to have additive blending and advanced color blending cannot be used, as none of the browsers currently support this feature. Now that we know this we are ready to make some effects!

Adding particle effects to the game

We are going to build a few different particle effects to demonstrate the various ways effects can be implemented in a game, and to look into some of the issues that might arise. To keep things straightforward, all of the effects we create will be a part of a single, global particle system. We will use both types of emitters, and utilize both shape and sprite-based particles. We will start with a Dust Cloud that will be seen anytime a Pillar is broken or destroyed. We will then add a system to create a unique shrapnel effect for each Pillar type. Finally, we will create some fire and smoke effects for the TNT explosion to demonstrate moving emitters.

Creating a Dust Cloud

The first effect we are going to create is a simple Dust Cloud. It will burst outwards upon the destruction of each Pillar and dissolve away over time. As this effect will be used in every level of the game, we will make all of its elements global, so they only need to be declared once.

1. Open the Tower Toppling project we were previously working on if it is not already open.

2. We need to make sure that WebGL is enabled when we build the game. Navigate to **Resources | Change Global Game Settings** and click on the **HTML5** tab.

3. On the left-hand side, click on the tab for **Graphics**. As seen in the following screenshot, there are three options under **WebGL** in **Options**. If WebGL is **Disabled**, the game will not be able to use the GPU and all browsers will suffer from any potential lag. If WebGL is **Required**, any browser that does not have this capability will be prevented from running the game. The final option is **Auto-Detect** which will use WebGL if the browser supports it, but will allow all browsers to play the game no matter what. Select **Auto-Detect** and then click on **OK**.

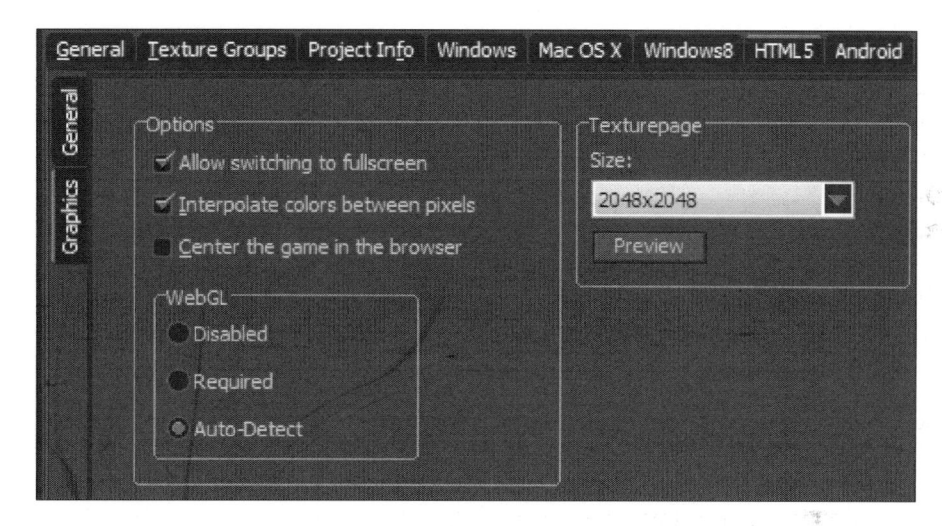

4. Now that we have WebGL activated we can build our effects. We will start by defining our particle system as a global variable by creating a new script called `scr_Global_Particles`.

   ```
   globalvar system;
   system = part_system_create();
   ```

5. The first effect we are going to make is the Dust Cloud which will be attached to the Pillars. For this we only need a single emitter which we will move to the appropriate position when it is needed. Create a global variable for the emitter and add it to the particle system with the following code at the end of the script:

   ```
   globalvar dustEmitter;
   dustEmitter = part_emitter_create(system);
   ```

Playing with Particles

6. For this particle, we are going to use one of the built-in shapes, `pt_shape_explosion`, which looks like a little thick cloud of dust. Add the following code to the end of the script:

    ```
    globalvar particle_Dust;
    particle_Dust = part_type_create();
    part_type_shape(particle_Dust, pt_shape_explosion);
    ```

    Once again we have made this a global variable, so that we have to create this Dust Cloud particle only once. We have declared only the shape attribute of this particle at this time. We will add more to this later once we can see what the effect looks like in the game.

7. We need to initialize the particle system with the other global variables. Reopen `scr_Global_GameStart` and call the particles script.

    ```
    scr_Global_Particles();
    ```

8. With everything initialized, we can now create a new script, `scr_Particles_DustCloud`, which we can use to set the region of the emitter and have it activate a burst of particles.

    ```
    part_emitter_region(system, dustEmitter, x-16, x+16, y-16, y+16, ps_shape_ellipse, ps_distr_gaussian);
    part_emitter_burst(system, dustEmitter, particle_Dust, 10);
    ```

    We start by defining a small area for the emitter based on the position of instance that calls this script. The region itself will be circular with a Gaussian distribution so that the particles shoot out from the center. We then activate a single burst of 10 dust particles from the emitter.

9. All we need to do now is execute this script from the destruction of a Pillar. Reopen `scr_Pillar_Destroy` and insert the following line of code on the line before the instance is destroyed:

    ```
    scr_Particles_DustCloud();
    ```

10. We need to add this effect to the breaking of the Pillars as well. Reopen `scr_Pillar_BreakApart` and insert the same code in the same spot.

11. Save the game and then play it. When the glass Pillars are destroyed, we should see thick white clouds appearing as shown in the following screenshot:

12. The particles are boring and static at this point, because we have not told the particles to do anything other than to look like the shape of a cloud. Let's fix this by adding some attributes to the particle. Reopen scr_Global_Particles and add the following code at the end of the script:

    ```
    part_type_life(particle_Dust, 15, 30);
    part_type_direction(particle_Dust, 0, 360, 0, 0);
    part_type_speed(particle_Dust, 1, 2, 0, 0);
    part_type_size(particle_Dust, 0.2, 0.5, 0.01, 0);
    part_type_alpha2(particle_Dust, 1, 0);
    ```

    The first attribute we add is how long we want the particle to live for, which is a range between 15 and 30 steps, or at the speed of our rooms, a half to a whole second. Next, we want the particles to explode outwards, so we set the angle and add some velocity. Both functions that we are using have similar parameters. The first value is the particle type for which this is to be applied. The next two parameters are the minimum and maximum values from which a number will be randomly chosen. The fourth parameter sets an incremental value every step. Finally, the last parameter is a wiggle value that will randomly be applied throughout the particle's lifetime. For the Dust Cloud, we are setting the direction to be in any angle and the speed is fairly slow, ranging only a few pixels per step. We also want to change the size of the particles and their transparency, so that the dust appears to dissipate.

Playing with Particles

13. Save the game and run it again. This time the effect appears much more natural, with the clouds exploding outwards, growing slightly larger, and fading out. It should look something like the next screenshot. The Dust Cloud is now complete.

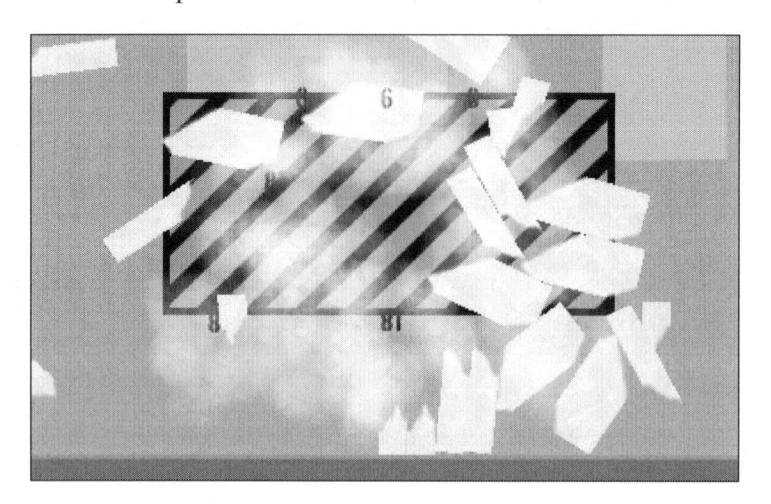

Adding in Shrapnel

The Dust Cloud effect helps the Pillar destruction appear more believable, but it lacks the bigger chunks of material one would expect to see. We want some Shrapnel of various shapes and sizes to explode outwards for each of the different types of Pillars. We will start with the Glass particles.

1. Create a new Sprite, `spr_Particle_Glass`, and with **Remove Background** checked, load `Chapter 8/Sprites/Particle_Glass.gif`. This sprite is not meant to be animated, though it does have several frames within it. Each frame represents a different shape of particle that will be randomly chosen when the particle is spawned.

2. We will want the particles to rotate as they move outwards, so we need to center the origin. Click on **OK**.

3. Reopen `scr_Global_Particles` and initialize the Glass particle at the end of the script.

   ```
   globalvar particle_Glass;
   particle_Glass = part_type_create();
   part_type_sprite(particle_Glass, spr_Particle_Glass, false, false, true);
   ```

   Once we have created the global variable and the particle, we set the particle type to be a Sprite. When assigning Sprites there are a few extra parameters beyond which resources should be used. The third and fourth parameters are for whether it should be animated, and if so, should the animation stretch for the duration of the particle's life. In our case we are not using animation, so it has been set to `false`. The last parameter is for whether we want it to choose a random subimage of the Sprite, which is what we do want it to do.

4. We also need to add some attributes to this particle for life and movement. Add the following code at the end of the script:

   ```
   part_type_life(particle_Glass, 10, 20);
   part_type_direction(particle_Glass, 0, 360, 0, 0);
   part_type_speed(particle_Glass, 4, 6, 0, 0);
   part_type_orientation(particle_Glass, 0, 360, 20, 4, false);
   ```

   When compared with the Dust Cloud, this particle will have a shorter lifespan but will move at a much higher velocity. This will make this effect more intense while keeping the general area small. We have also added some rotational movement through `part_type_orientation`. The particles can be set to any angle and will rotate 20 degrees per frame with a variance of up to four degrees. This will give us a nice variety in the spin of each particle. There is one additional parameter for orientation, which is whether the angle should be relative to its movement. We have set it to `false` as we just want the particles to spin freely.

5. To test this effect out, open up `scr_Particles_DustCloud` and insert a burst emitter before the Dust Cloud is emitted, so that the Glass particles appear behind the other effect.

   ```
   part_emitter_burst(system, dustEmitter, particle_Glass, 8);
   ```

6. Save the game and then play it. When the Pillars break apart, there should be shards of Glass exploding out along with the Dust Cloud. The effect should look something like the following screenshot:

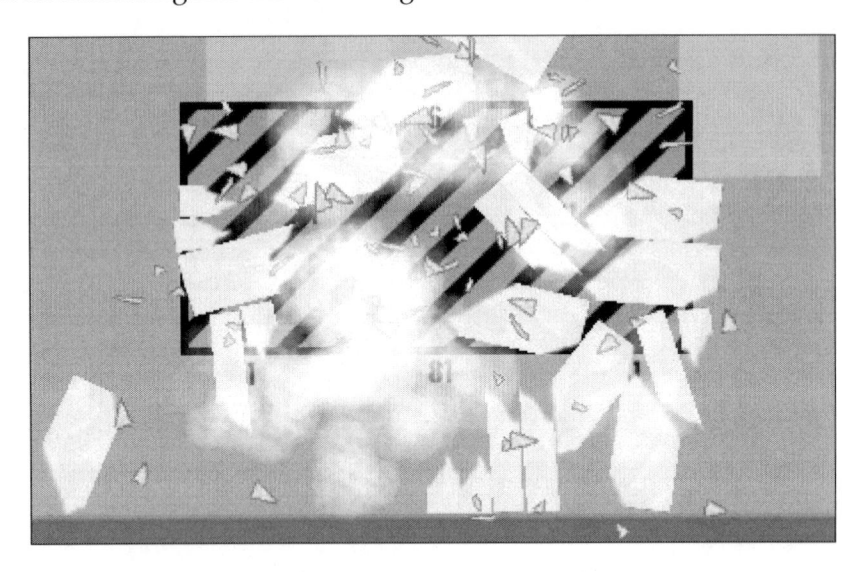

7. Next we need to create Shrapnel for the Wood and Steel particles. Create new Sprites for `spr_Particle_Wood` and `spr_Particle_Steel` with the supplied images in `Chapter 8/Sprites/` in the same manner as we did for Glass.

8. As these particles are global, we cannot just swap the Sprite out dynamically. We need to create new particles for each type. In `scr_Global_Particles`, add particles for both Wood and Steel with the same attributes as Glass.

9. Currently the effect is set to **Always create Glass particles**, something we do not want to do. To fix this we are going to add a variable, `myParticle`, to each of the different Pillars to allow us to spawn the appropriate particle. Open `scr_Pillar_Glass_Create` and add the following code at the end of the script:

```
myParticle = particle_Glass;
```

10. Repeat the last step for Wood and Steel with the appropriate particle assigned.

11. In order to have the proper particle spawn, all we need to do is reopen `scr_Particles_DustCloud` and change the variable `particle_Glass` to `myParticle` as in the following code:

```
part_emitter_burst(system, dustEmitter, myParticle, 8);
```

12. Save the game and play the game until you can destroy all the three types of Pillars to see the effect. It should look something similar to the following screenshot, where each Pillar spawns its own Shrapnel:

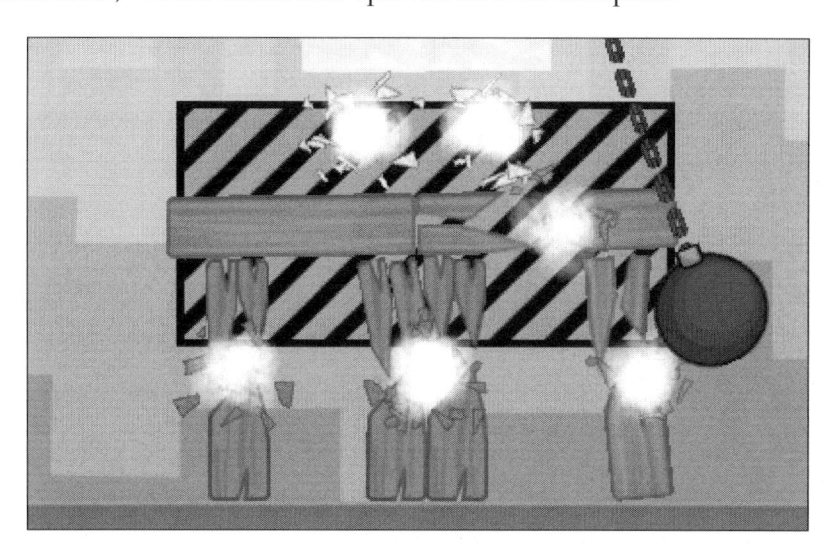

Making the TNT explosion

When the TNT explodes, it shoots out some TNT Fragments which are currently bland looking Sprites. We want the Fragments to be on fire as they streak across the scene. We also want a cloud of smoke to rise up from the explosion to indicate that the explosion we see is actually on fire. This is going to cause some complications. In order to make something appear to be on fire, it will need to change color, say from white to yellow to orange. As we have already mentioned, due to the fact that WebGL is not supported by all browsers, we cannot utilize any of the functions that allow us to blend colors together. This means that we need to work around this issue. The solution is to use several particles instead of one.

1. We will start by creating some custom colors so that we can achieve the look of fire and smoke that we want. Open scr_Global_Colors and add the following colors:

    ```
    orange = make_color_rgb(255, 72, 12);
    fireWhite = make_color_rgb(255, 252, 206);
    smokeBlack = make_color_rgb(24, 6, 0);
    ```

    We already have a nice yellow color, so we add an orange, a slightly yellow tinted white, and a partially orange black color.

Playing with Particles

2. In order to achieve the fake blending effect we will need to spawn one particle type, and upon its death, have it spawn the next particle type. For this to work properly, we need to construct the creation of the particles in the opposite order that they will be seen. In this case, we need to start by building the smoke particle. In `scr_Global_Particles` add a new particle for the smoke with the following attributes:

```
globalvar particle_Smoke;
particle_Smoke = part_type_create();
part_type_shape(particle_Smoke, pt_shape_smoke);
part_type_life(particle_Smoke, 30, 50);
part_type_direction(particle_Smoke, 80, 100, 0, 0);
part_type_speed(particle_Smoke, 2, 4, 0, 0);
part_type_size(particle_Smoke, 0.6, 0.8, 0.05, 0);
part_type_alpha2(particle_Smoke, 0.5, 0);
part_type_color1(particle_Smoke, smokeBlack);
part_type_gravity(particle_Smoke, 0.4, 90);
```

We start by adding the particle and using the built-in smoke shape. We want the smoke to linger for a while, so we set its life to range between a minimum of a second to almost two full seconds. We then set the direction and speed to be more or less upwards so that the smoke rises. Next, we set the size and have it grow over time. With the alpha values, we don't want the smoke to be completely opaque, so we set it to start at half transparent and fade away over time. Next, we are using `part_type_color1` which allows us to tint the particle without affecting the performance very much. Finally, we apply some gravity to the particles so that any angled particles float slowly upwards.

3. The smoke is the final step of our effect and it will be spawned from an orange flame that precedes it.

```
globalvar particle_FireOrange;
particle_FireOrange = part_type_create();
part_type_shape(particle_FireOrange, pt_shape_smoke);
part_type_life(particle_FireOrange, 4, 6);
part_type_direction(particle_FireOrange, 70, 110, 0, 0);
part_type_speed(particle_FireOrange, 3, 5, 0, 0);
part_type_size(particle_FireOrange, 0.5, 0.6, 0.01, 0);
part_type_alpha2(particle_FireOrange, 0.75, 0.5);
part_type_color1(particle_FireOrange, orange);
part_type_gravity(particle_FireOrange, 0.2, 90);
part_type_death(particle_FireOrange, 1, particle_Smoke);
```

Once again we set up the particle using the built-in smoke shape, this time with a much shorter lifespan. The general direction is still mainly upwards, though there is more spread than the smoke. These particles are slightly smaller, tinted orange and will be partially transparent for its entire life. We have added a little bit of upward gravity, as this particle is in between fire and smoke. Finally, we are using a function that will spawn a single particle of smoke upon the death of each orange particle.

4. The next particle in the chain for this effect is a yellow particle. This time we are going to use the FLARE shape, which will give a better appearance of fire. It will also be a bit smaller, live slightly longer than the orange particle, and move faster, spreading in all directions. We will not add any transparency to this particle so that it appears to burn bright.

```
globalvar particle_FireYellow;
particle_FireYellow = part_type_create();
part_type_shape(particle_FireYellow, pt_shape_flare);
part_type_life(particle_FireYellow, 6, 12);
part_type_direction(particle_FireYellow, 0, 360, 0, 0);
part_type_speed(particle_FireYellow, 4, 6, 0, 0);
part_type_size(particle_FireYellow, 0.4, 0.6, 0.01, 0);
part_type_color1(particle_FireYellow, yellow);
part_type_death(particle_FireYellow, 1, particle_FireOrange);
```

5. We have only one more particle to create this effect for, which is the hottest and brightest white particle. Its construction is the same as the yellow particle, except it is smaller and faster.

```
globalvar particle_FireWhite;
particle_FireWhite = part_type_create();
part_type_shape(particle_FireWhite, pt_shape_flare);
part_type_life(particle_FireWhite, 2, 10);
part_type_direction(particle_FireWhite, 0, 360, 0, 0);
part_type_speed(particle_FireWhite, 6, 8, 0, 0);
part_type_size(particle_FireWhite, 0.3, 0.5, 0.01, 0);
part_type_color1(particle_FireWhite, fireWhite);
part_type_death(particle_FireWhite, 1, particle_FireYellow);
```

Playing with Particles

6. We now have all the particles we need for this particle effect; we just need to add an emitter to spawn them. This time we are going to use a stream emitter, so that the fire continuously flows out of each Fragment. Since the Fragments are moving, we will need to have a unique emitter for each Fragment we create. This means it cannot be a global emitter, but rather a local one. Open `scr_TNT_Fragment_Create` and add the following code at the end of the script:

   ```
   myEmitter = part_emitter_create(system);
   part_emitter_region(system, myEmitter, x-5, x+5, y-5, y+5, ps_shape_ellipse, ps_distr_linear);
   part_emitter_stream(system, myEmitter, particle_FireWhite, 5);
   ```

   We create an emitter with a fairly small area for spawning with balanced distribution. At every step, the emitter will create five new Fire particles as long as the emitter exists.

7. The emitter is now created at the same time as the Fragment, but we need the emitter to move along with it. Open `scr_TNT_Fragment_Step` and add the following code:

   ```
   part_emitter_region(system, myEmitter, x-5, x+5, y-5, y+5, ps_shape_ellipse, ps_distr_linear);
   ```

8. As already mentioned we need to destroy the emitter, otherwise it will never stop streaming particles. For this we will need to open `obj_TNT_Fragment` and add a `destroy` event with a new Script, `scr_TNT_Fragment_Destroy`, which removes the emitter attached.

   ```
   part_emitter_destroy(system, myEmitter);
   ```

   This function will remove the emitter from the system without removing any of the particles that had been spawned.

9. One last thing we need to do is to uncheck the **Visible** checkbox, as we don't want to see the Fragment sprite, but just the particles.

10. Save the game and detonate the TNT. Instead of just seeing a few Fragments, there are now streaks of fire jetting out of the explosion that turn into dark clouds of smoke that float up. It should look something like the following screenshot:

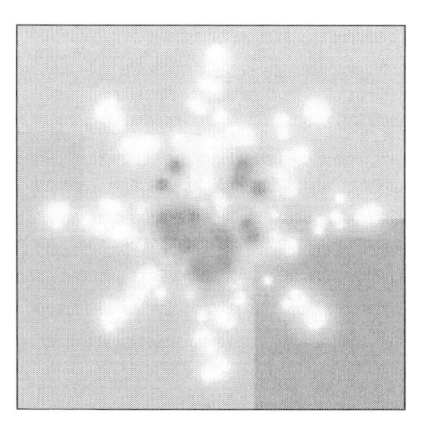

Cleaning up the particles

At this point, we have built a good variety of effects using various particles and emitters. The effects have added a lot of polish to the game, but there is a flaw with the particles. If the player decides to restart the room or go to the **SHOP** immediately after the explosion has occurred, the emitters will not be destroyed. This means that they will continue to spawn particles forever, and we will lose all references to those emitters. The game will end up looking like the following screenshot:

Playing with Particles

1. The first thing we need to do is to destroy the emitters when we leave the room. Luckily, we have already written a script that does exactly this. Open `obj_TNT_Fragment` and add a **Room End** event and attach `scr_TNT_Fragment_Destroy` to it.

2. Even if we destroy the emitters before changing rooms, any particles remaining in the game will still appear in the next room, if only briefly. What we need to do is clear all the particles from the system. While this might sound like it could be a lot of work, it is actually quite simple. As Overlord is in every level, but not in any other room, we can use it to clean up the scene. Open `obj_Overlord`, add a **Room End** event and attach a new Script, `scr_Overlord_RoomEnd`, with the following line of code:

   `part_particles_clear(system);`

   This function will remove any particle that exists within the system, but will not remove the particle type from memory. It is important that we do not destroy the particle type, as we would not be able to use a particle again if its type no longer exists.

3. Save the game, explode some TNT, and restart the room immediately. You should no longer see any particles in the scene.

Summary

We started the chapter with a complete game, and now we have added some spit and polish to really make it shine. We delved into the world of particles and created a variety of effects that add impact to the TNT and Pillar destruction. The game is now complete and ready to be released.

In the next chapter we are going to consider putting this game out on the Internet. We will cover uploading it to your own website, hosting it on Facebook, and submitting it to game portals. We will also take a look at using the various built-in developer services, such as analytics and advertising. Let's get the game out there!

9
Get Your Game Out There

After all the hard work, our game is ready to be released. In this chapter we are going to upload our game to a web server, so that it can be played on the Internet by anyone. We will look at how we can allow users to log into their Facebook account, and post the score of a level to their Facebook walls. We will also integrate Flurry analytics to track useful data that will allow us to understand how and where people are playing the game. Finally, we will briefly talk about earning money from games.

Releasing a game on your own site

In order for people to play the game, we need to get it up onto a website, preferably your own. This means we are going to need to find a place to host the website, export a final build of the game, and of course utilize an FTP program so that we can upload the game.

Creating the application

All throughout the book we have been testing and playing our games using GameMaker: Studio's built-in server emulator. It allows us to see how the game will perform as if it were on an actual website, but it is only accessible to the computer we are developing on. To upload the game to a website, we will need to build all the files into the proper HTML5 format.

1. Open the Tower Toppling game that we have been working on, if it isn't already open.
2. Before we create the final build, we should look at some of the options available. Navigate to **Resources | Change Global Game Settings**, and then go to the **HTML5** tab.

Get Your Game Out There

In the **General** subtab there are four sections of options as can be seen in the next screenshot. Looking at **HTML5 File Options**, it is possible to use a custom web page file and a custom loading bar if we want a specific layout or additional content on the page. Creating these files requires knowledge of HTML and JavaScript, and a code editor that supports these languages, both of which are outside the scope of this book.

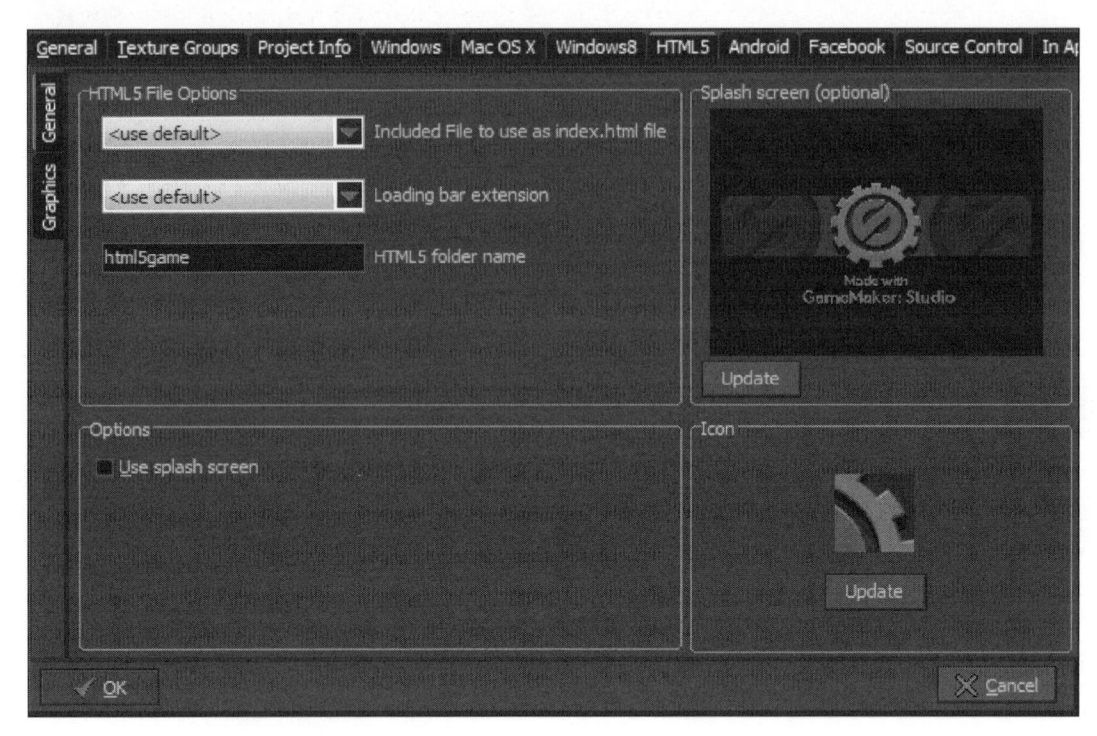

Splash screens are seen before the game is loaded and are actually embedded into the `index.html` code. It requires a PNG file that should be of the same size as the game area; if it is of a different size, it will be scaled to fit the proper dimensions. One drawback of using a splash screen is that the image will be drawn instead of the loading bar. As it is generally considered a best practice to always let the user know what is occurring, especially when it comes to the loading of data, we will not be adding a splash screen to this game.

When we compile the game, GameMaker: Studio will create a file named `favicon.ico` in the root directory with the icon set in the **Global Game Settings**. Users will see this icon in the browser tab along with the name of the page that the tab is showing; it is also visible when saving the page as a bookmark. The icon, a common feature of most websites, is a small image in the ICO format used for displaying a representative symbol of the website. Most image editors do not natively save out to ICO format and usually require a plugin to do so. Luckily, there are plenty of free websites that will convert any image into an icon for us. I personally prefer using `http://iconverticons.com/online/` because they accept most common image formats and convert into all the major icon formats including Windows, Mac, and web icons. Once we have a proper ICO file, we can then use it in our game.

1. Let's update **Icon** by clicking on **Update** and by loading `Chapter 9/Resources/Extras/GameIcon.ico`. Click on **OK**.

2. The game is now ready to be exported. Navigate to **File | Create Application** and save the game to a new folder called `Destruct` in the game project directory.

3. Click on **Save** and you will see the game compile and create all the files required to run your game. In the `Destruct` folder you should see two files and a folder. There is a `favicon.ico` file, and an `index.html` file which is the web page that will display the game. The folder, `html5game`, contains all the assets, such as all the sounds in both OGG and MP3 formats, a few PNG files starting with `index_texture` that contain all the graphics compiled into individual sprite sheets, and an `index.js` file that contains all the game functionality. There is also a `particles` folder that contains all the images used for the particle shapes.

Hosting the game

The game has been built; we just need a place to put it. There are many options available on the Internet for hosting a website for the game. These can range from free web hosting to owning a personal server and everything in between. Choosing a host can be very time consuming due to all the different packages available, the varying price-points, and what our overall intentions are. Every developer will need to consider things, such as how many people are expected to play the game, will more games be added in the future, and will the site have advertising on it, and so on. A free web hosting service might suffice if the game will only be shown to family and friends, but if the goal is to earn money from the game it is better to use some form of paid service. When selecting a provider, the main features we want to look for are: how much server space, the amount of bandwidth, FTP access, and maximum file size.

Additionally, you should ensure that the site allows MP3 files to be uploaded, as many free and a few paid sites do not allow this. Popular sites, such as www.godaddy.com and www.globat.com offer plenty of server space and bandwidth for a very affordable price that will suit most developers, or at least when they first start releasing games.

In order to move onto the next step, make sure you have secured web server space and that you have FTP access to it.

Uploading the game with FTP

To get our game onto the server we need to use an FTP client to transfer the files. There are many free downloadable FTP clients available, such as WinSCP, CuteFTP, and FileZilla. Some browsers can be used for FTP if the appropriate plugin is installed, such as FireFTP for Firefox. Some web hosting services even offer drag-and-drop FTP capabilities. For this project we will be using WinSCP which can be downloaded from http://winscp.net.

1. Download the WinSCP client and install it according to the instructions. When the **Initial user settings** page appears, select **Commander interface** as shown in the following screenshot:

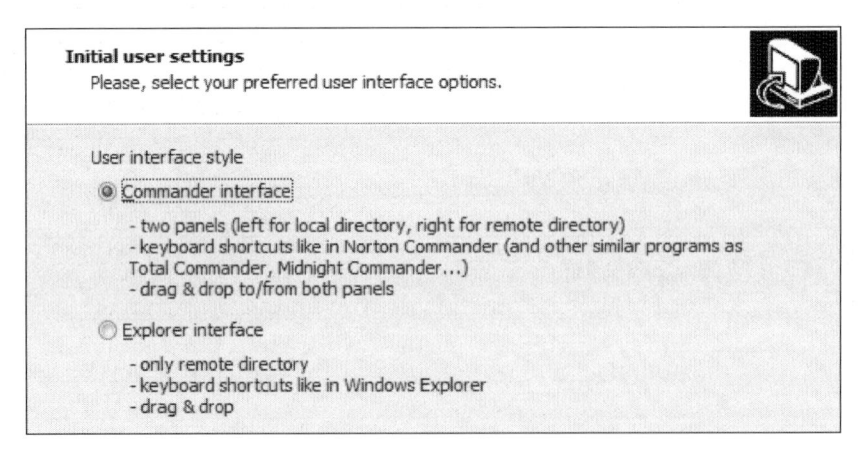

2. Run WinSCP.
3. As this is the first time we are accessing the website's FTP, we will need to click on **New** to create a new FTP session.

Chapter 9

4. We need to select a file protocol method by navigating to **Session | File Protocol** to transfer the files. The default is **SFTP (Secure FTP)**, but many hosting sites only allow for standard FTP access, so we will go with that. Navigate to **File Protocol | FTP**.

> Consult your hosting provider's documentation for instructions on how to configure your FTP connection.

5. Next we need to enter the server FTP address, often your website name, plus your username and password. It should look something like the following screenshot:

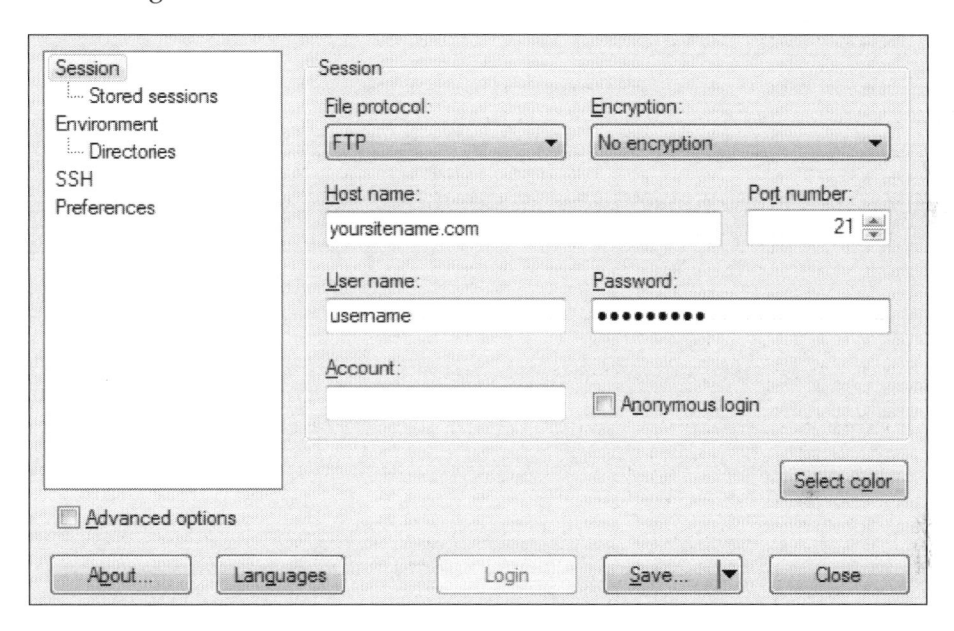

6. To make it easier to access the site in the future we can save these settings, including the password. Click on **Save**.

[319]

Get Your Game Out There

7. This will take us back to the login screen and we can now see the FTP connection in the **Stored sessions** list as shown in the next screenshot. To open a connection, we can double-click the site name, or select the site name and click on **Login**.

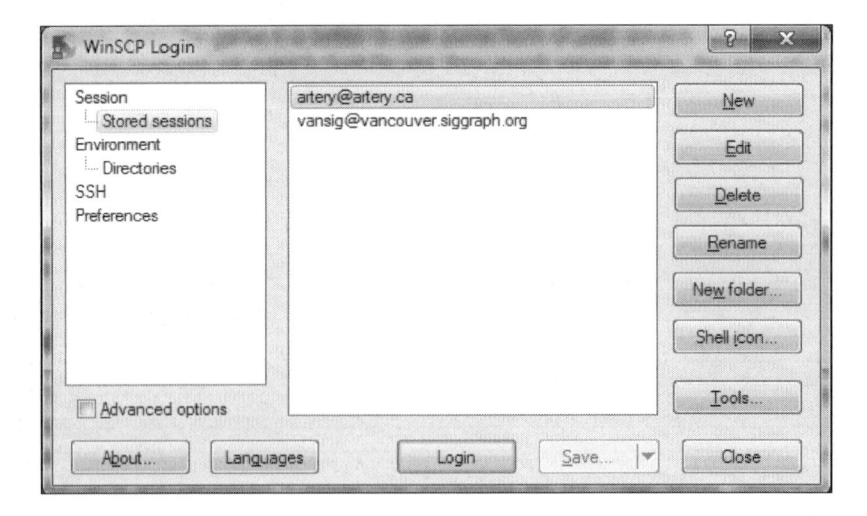

If all the information has been correctly entered, a directory window should open. As seen in the next screenshot, there are two panes with file directories. The left-hand side is the local drives of the computer and the right-hand side is the server directory. The server should be open to the root directory though it might be displayed as being in a folder called `www` or `public_html`. There likely is at least one file in the directory already, `index.html`, which would be the default page that is seen when people go to the domain.

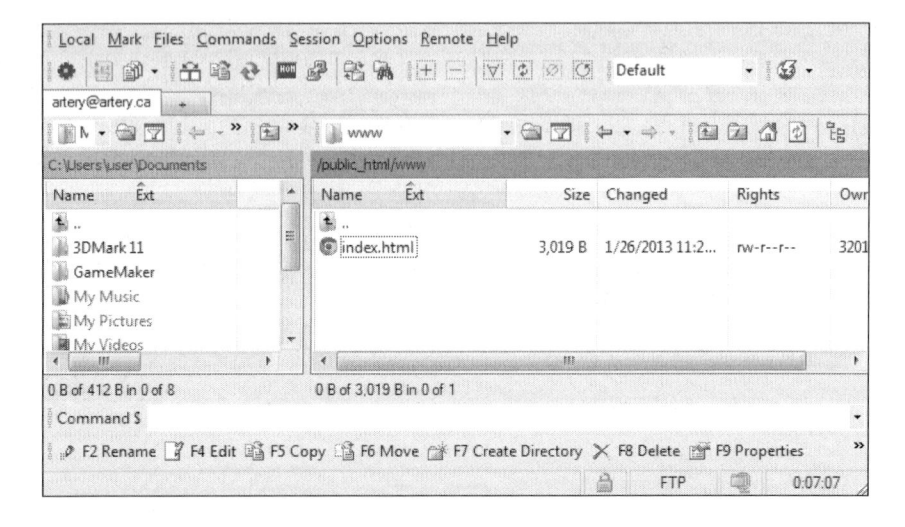

8. In the left panel, locate the `Destruct` folder where our game has been exported to. Drag the entire folder over to the right panel to transfer all the files to the server.

9. A pop-up dialog box will ask if we want to copy all the files over. Click on **Copy**. It may take a few moments to transfer everything over.

10. The game has now been uploaded and is accessible on the Internet. To access it, just open a browser and go to the website and the `Destruct` subdirectory, for example, `http://www.yoursitename.com/Destruct/`.

Integrating with Facebook

With the game now uploaded to a server it is available for anyone in the world to play it. They can play the game, that is, if they know about it. One of the most difficult challenges any developer faces is getting the word out about their product. One of the easiest ways to spread the news is through social media sites, such as Facebook. GameMaker: Studio makes this easy as the functionality for connecting with Facebook is already integrated. We are going to add a Facebook login button to the frontend of the game, and we will add the ability for the player to post their scores to their Facebook walls.

1. In order to use the Facebook functions, we need to have both a Facebook account and a Facebook developers' account. Go to `http://developers.facebook.com/` and log in. If you do not have a Facebook account, it will prompt you to create one.

2. Once we have logged in to the developers' page, we need to click **Apps** on the top menu bar. This will take us to the **Apps** page.

3. Next we need to click on the **Register as a Developer** button. This will open a registration dialog that we need to go through. First we will need to **Accept the Terms and Conditions**, and then we need to supply a phone number to **Verify the Account**. This must be a valid number, as it will send a text message that is needed for verification. Finish the process as instructed.

> Always read the Terms and Conditions *before* you agree to them and ensure that you fully understand what it is you are legally agreeing to.

4. Having completed the registration, we should find ourselves back on the **Apps** dashboard. There is a Create New App button close to the registration button. Click on it.

Get Your Game Out There

5. In the **Create New App** dialog box, as seen in the next screenshot, we need to enter an **App Name**. This name does not need to be unique so long as we don't have another app with the same name. There are a few rules about naming conventions that you can read by clicking on the **Facebook Platform Policies** link. The optional **App Namespace** is for integrating into Facebook a bit deeper with app pages and using Open Graph, a notification tool. We will not need an App Namespace so we can leave it blank. We also do not need **Web Hosting** and can click **Continue**.

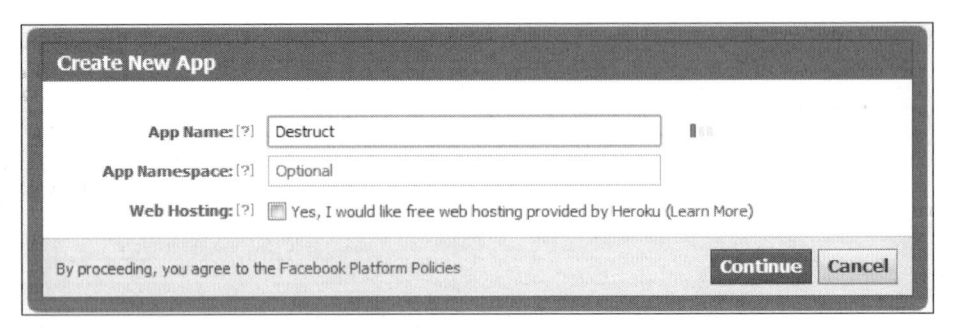

```
Create New App

       App Name: [?]  Destruct
  App Namespace: [?]  Optional
    Web Hosting: [?]  ☐ Yes, I would like free web hosting provided by Heroku (Learn More)

By proceeding, you agree to the Facebook Platform Policies          Continue  Cancel
```

> To learn more about Facebook Open Graph, App Namespaces, and more, check out the Facebook Developers API Documentation at https://developers.facebook.com/docs/reference/apis/.

6. The next step is a CAPTCHA security check. Follow the directions and click on **Continue**.

7. The app has now been created and we are on the **Basic Info** page. Here we can finish setting up how the game will be integrated into Facebook. Enter the base domain name of the game website in **Basic Info | App Domains**. This will allow the app to run on that domain and all subdomains. It should not include the `http://` or any other element beyond the name of the root site.

8. Under **Select how your app integrates with Facebook**, we need to select **Website with Facebook Login**, and then enter the exact URL where the game is located.

9. Click on **Save Changes** as we are done with the basic info. The settings should look like the following screenshot with the appropriate domain information entered for your site:

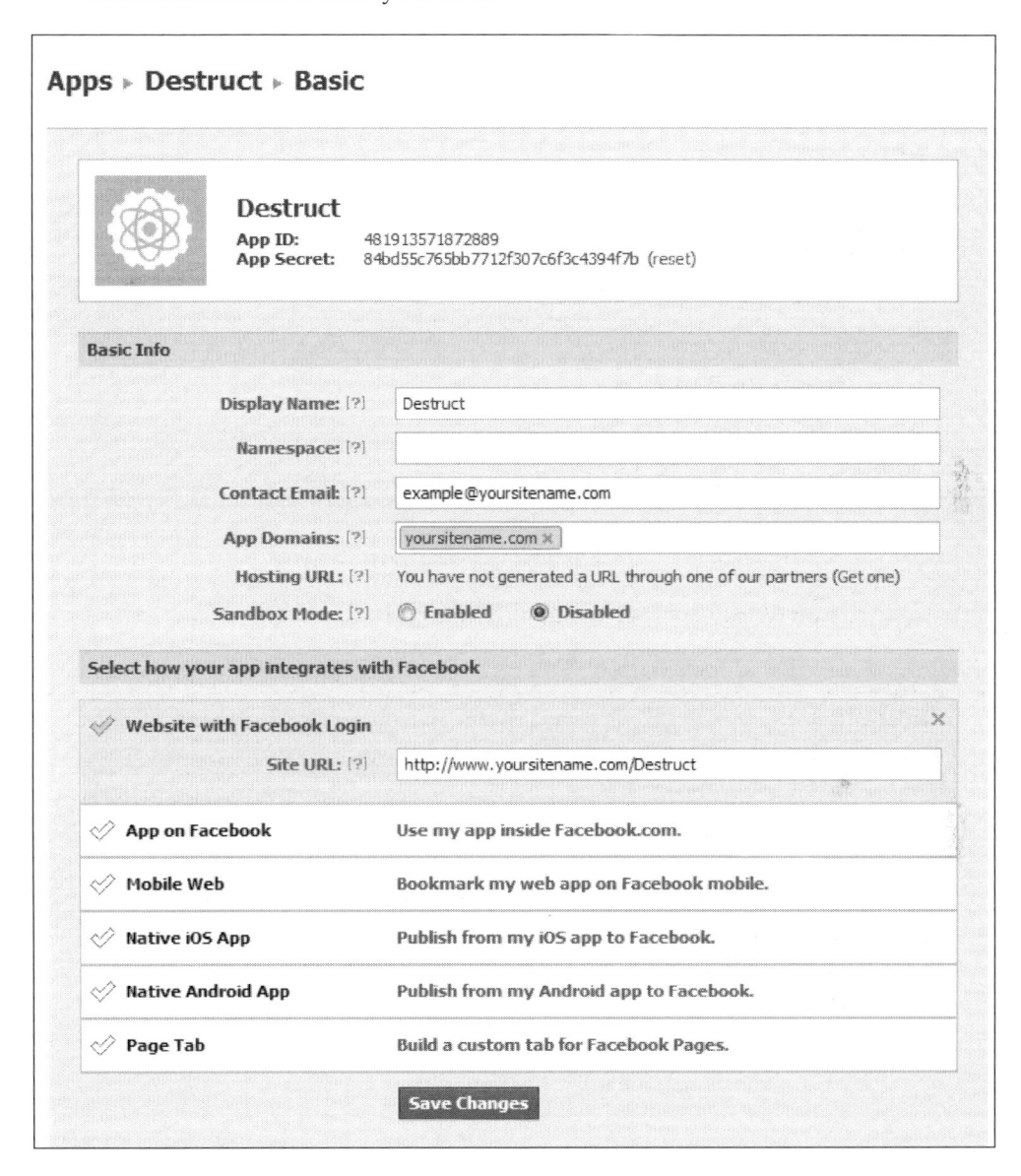

Apps ▸ Destruct ▸ Basic

Destruct
App ID: 481913571872889
App Secret: 84bd55c765bb7712f307c6f3c4394f7b (reset)

Basic Info

Display Name: [?]	Destruct
Namespace: [?]	
Contact Email: [?]	example@yoursitename.com
App Domains: [?]	yoursitename.com ×
Hosting URL: [?]	You have not generated a URL through one of our partners (Get one)
Sandbox Mode: [?]	○ Enabled ● Disabled

Select how your app integrates with Facebook

✓ **Website with Facebook Login**   ×
   Site URL: [?] http://www.yoursitename.com/Destruct

✓ App on Facebook	Use my app inside Facebook.com.
✓ Mobile Web	Bookmark my web app on Facebook mobile.
✓ Native iOS App	Publish from my iOS app to Facebook.
✓ Native Android App	Publish from my Android app to Facebook.
✓ Page Tab	Build a custom tab for Facebook Pages.

Save Changes

Get Your Game Out There

10. Before we get back into GameMaker: Studio, we need to copy **App ID:** from the top of the **Basic** page.

11. Reopen the game project and navigate to **Resources | Change Global Game Settings**.

12. Go to the **Facebook** tab, as shown in the next screenshot, check the box for **Use Facebook**, and then paste the ID we copied into **Facebook App Id**. Click on **OK**.

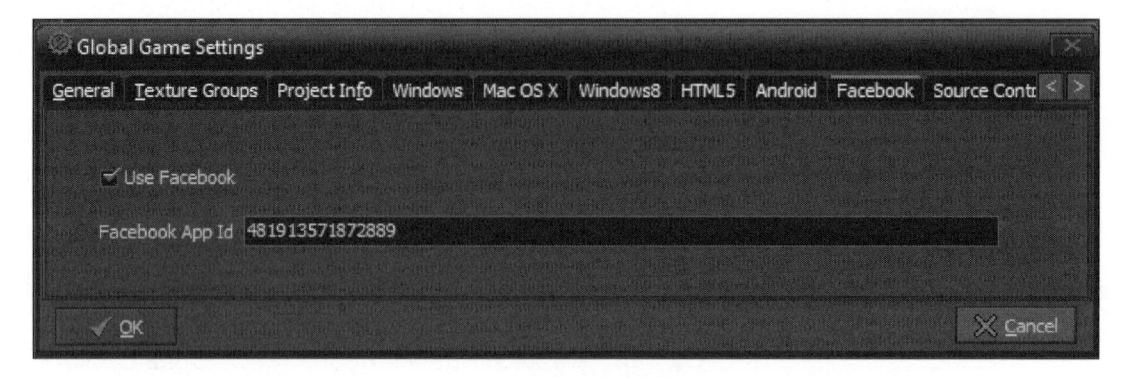

13. We now have access to the Facebook app; now we just need to initialize it. Create a new script, scr_Global_Facebook, with the following code:

```
facebook_init();
globalvar permissions;
permissions = ds_list_create();
ds_list_add(permissions, "publish_stream");
```

We start by initializing Facebook, and then we create a global variable for a ds_list that will contain all the permissions we want to be able to request from Facebook. In our case we are just asking to be able to publish to the Facebook wall of the logged in user. All the options that are available can be found on the Facebook Developers' site.

14. Open scr_Global_GameStart and execute the following line at the end:

```
scr_Global_Facebook();
```

Adding a Facebook login button

Now that we have Facebook active, we can implement it into the game. We will start by adding a login button.

1. Create a new Sprite, `spr_Button_FacebookLogin`, with **Remove Background** unchecked, load `Chapter 9/Resources/Sprites/FacebookLogin.gif`, and center the origin.

2. Create a new Object, `obj_Button_FacebookLogin`, attach the sprite we just created, and then set **Parent** to `obj_Button_Parent`.

3. Add a **Mouse | Left Pressed** event and attach a new Script, `scr_Button_FbLogin_MousePressed`, and have the user log in to Facebook.

   ```
   facebook_login(permissions);
   ```

4. Open `MainMenu` and add a single instance of the button below the **START** button.

5. Next, we need to let the players post to their walls. For this we will add another button to the score screen. Create a new Sprite, `spr_Button_FacebookPost`, with **Remove Background** unchecked, load `Chapter 9/Resources/Sprites/FacebookPost.gif`, and center the origin.

6. The score screen is all code, so we don't need a new object, but we do need to add code to the existing scripts. Open `scr_ScoreScreen_Create`, and add a variable for the Y placement, width offset, and height offset of the button.

   ```
   postfb_Y = 340;
   postfb_OffsetW = 64;
   postfb_OffsetH = 16;
   ```

7. Next we will create a new Script, `scr_Menu_Button_FbPost`, which will control the functionality.

   ```
   if (isVictory)
   {
       status = facebook_status()
       if (status == "AUTHORISED")
       {
           draw_sprite(spr_Button_FacebookPost, 0, screenX, postfb_Y);
           if ((win_Y > postfb_Y - postfb_OffsetH && win_Y < postfb_Y + postfb_OffsetH))
           {
               if ((win_X > screenX - postfb_OffsetW && win_X < screenX + postfb_OffsetW))
   ```

[325]

```
            {                   {
                    draw_sprite(spr_Button_FacebookPost, 1, screenX,
    postfb_Y);
                    if (mouse_check_button_pressed(mb_left))
                    {
                        myTitle = "Destruct";
                        myCaption = "Play this game at yournamesite.
    com"
                        myText = "I just destroyed the " + room_get_
    name(room) + " Towers playing Destruct!";
                        myImage = "http://yoursitename.com/Destruct/
    Thumbnail.gif";
                        mySite = "http://yoursitename.com/Destruct/"
                        facebook_post_message(myTitle, myCaption,
    myText, myImage , mySite, "", "");
                    }
                }
            }
        }
    }
}
```

We only want to post to Facebook if the player defeats a level, so we start by checking the win condition. We check the status of the Facebook connection, as we want to display the button only if the player is signed in. If the player is signed in, we draw the button on the screen and check to see if the mouse is hovering over it, as we did with all our other buttons. If the button is clicked, we create some variables for the message title, caption and text, an image, and a link back to the site. We then post a message to Facebook. The function also has two additional parameters that are for using more advanced Facebook actions, but we are leaving these blank.

> To see what advanced options are available, see the Facebook Developers' API Post page at `https://developers.facebook.com/docs/reference/api/post/`.

Chapter 9

8. In order to draw this on screen we need to reopen `scr_ScoreScreen_DrawGUI` and execute the script we just created:

    `scr_Menu_Button_FbPost();`

9. Save the game and click on **Create Application**. It is OK to overwrite the existing project files.
10. Open WinSCP and connect to the FTP server.
11. Transfer all the files over to the server. Click on **Yes to All** when prompted to confirm the overwriting of the files.
12. We also need to transfer over the image we want to include in the post. Open `Chapter_09/Resources/Extras/` and transfer `Thumbnail.gif` over to the server into the `Destruct` folder.
13. Open a browser and go to the game site. When the game loads up, we should see the new button just below the **START** button as shown in the following screenshot:

[327]

14. Click on the **Log Into Facebook** button. A pop-up window, like the next screenshot, should appear. If nothing happens, check to see if the browser has blocked pop ups and unblock it. When the pop up does appear, we just need to sign into our Facebook account.

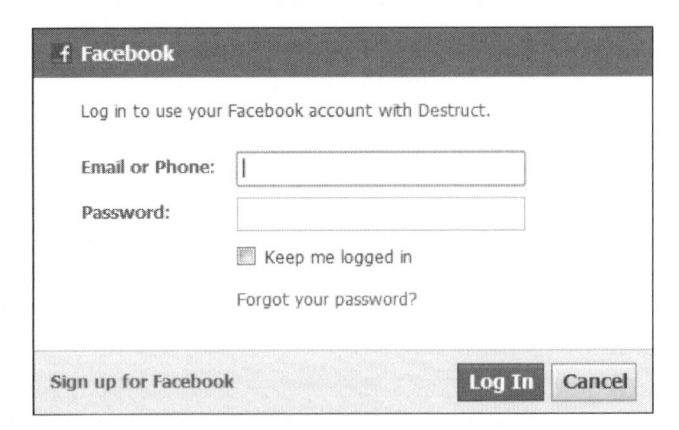

15. Play a level successfully. When the Score screen appears we should see the **POST TO FACEBOOK** button, as shown in the following screenshot:

16. Click on the button and then go to your Facebook page. We will see a new post that has been shared with the world, which will look like the following screenshot:

Congratulations! The game is now available for everyone to play and is being exposed to the world through Facebook. The goal for any developer is to create interesting games that everybody enjoys playing and is able to complete. But how do you know whether that is occurring? Are people getting stuck in the game? Is it too easy? Too hard? After all the hard work that went into making the game, it would be a shame to not know any of these answers. This is where analytics come in handy.

Tracking the game with Flurry Analytics

Analytics is the process of gathering and finding patterns within a set of data. This data can be any quantifiable action, such as a mouse click, and its related elements, such as what was clicked. This information allows developers to see how users are using their product. It is incredibly useful when creating games, because there are so many things that can be tracked.

We are going to implement Flurry Analytics, one of the two systems GameMaker: Studio has built-in and is the most robust. While it is possible to track anything and everything, it is generally better to focus on things that are most relevant to the user experience. For our game we are going to track each level's score, equipment used, and times played. We will only send this data out upon the player successfully completing a level. This will allow us to see how often each level is played, what equipment is used the most, the variation in scores, how hard each level is, and where people quit the game on average.

Get Your Game Out There

Setting up Flurry Analytics

In order to use Flurry Analytics, we need to have an account with the service, an application to send the data to, and have it activated in GameMaker: Studio. Once that has been done, a new build needs to be uploaded to the site and people need to play the game.

1. First, let's sign up for Flurry analytics. Go to http://www.flurry.com/ and sign up for a free account, following the site's directions.

2. Once the account has been set up and you have logged in, we should be on the developer home page. On the menu bar click on the **Applications** tab to go to the **Applications** page as shown in the following screenshot:

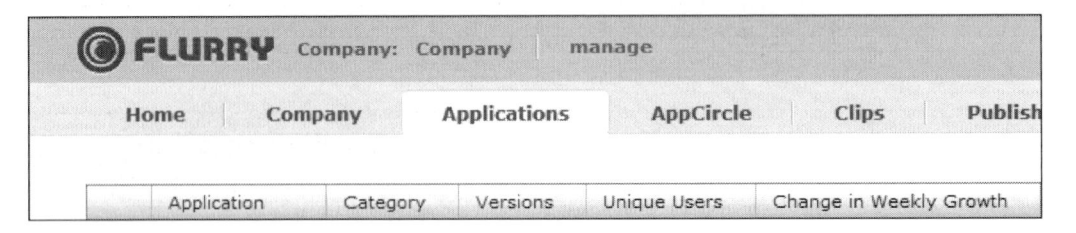

3. We don't have any application at this point, so we need to add one. Click on **Add a New Application**.

4. The next page asks for a platform to be selected. Click on the Java icon.

5. Next we need to add in some basic info for the application. As seen in the next screenshot, enter the name of the game, Destruct, and choose an appropriate category, in our case, **Games - Simulation** seems to fit best. Then click on **Create App**.

6. On the next page it asks how we want to integrate the SDK with a couple of options. GameMaker: Studio already has this integrated into the software, which means we can skip this step. Click on **Cancel** to finish this step and return to the **Home** page.

7. We should now see our application in **Application Summary**, as can be seen in the next screenshot. We need to get our application ID, so click on **Destruct**.

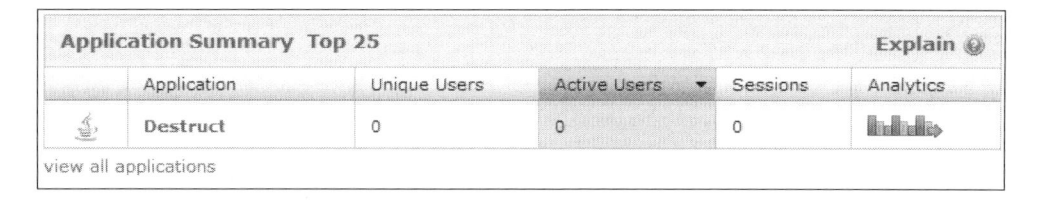

Application Summary Top 25				Explain
Application	Unique Users	Active Users ▼	Sessions	Analytics
Destruct	0	0	0	
view all applications				

8. Next, we need to navigate to **Manage | App Info** in the left menu to access the page with our application information. At the bottom of the list, as seen in the next screenshot, is the **API Key**. This key is needed to connect the game in GameMaker: Studio into this analytics app. Copy this key. We are done with this site for now.

App Name	Destruct edit
Category	Games - Simulation edit
SDK Version	No data received yet
Unique App ID	Click Here to Provide your Unique App ID Explain
API Key	MCCX5CRPQWV8YP4HG9QP

9. Reopen the project file and open **Global Game Settings**.
10. Click on the right arrow at the top of the **Global Game Settings** until you see the **Analytics** tab as shown in the next screenshot. Click on the **Analytics** tab.

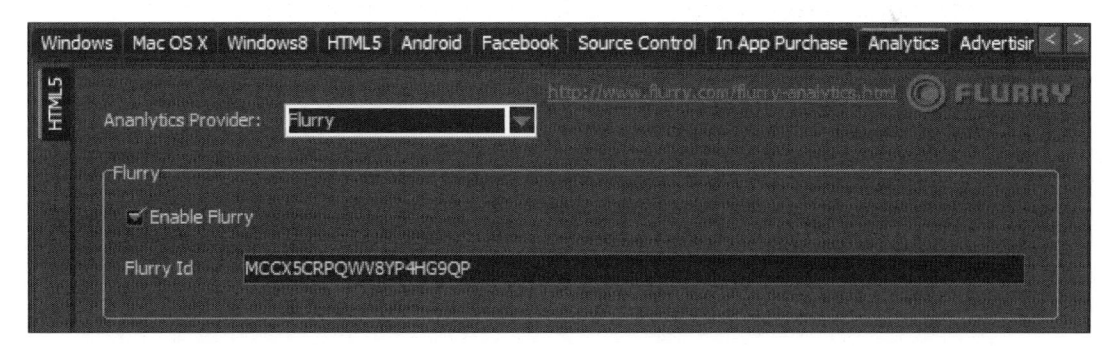

11. In the **HTML5** subtab, set **Analytics Provider:** to **Flurry**, check the box for **Enable Flurry**, and paste the API Key into **Flurry Id**. We now have everything set up and ready to output some data.

Get Your Game Out There

Tracking events in the game

Now that we can send out data we just need to implement it into the existing game. We need to add some bits of code into several scripts, plus create some new ones, in order to get useful, trackable information. We want to track the level being played, usage of each piece of equipment, how many times the level has been played, and the score of the level.

1. We already have constants for tracking the equipment (`TNT: 0`, `WRECKINGBALL: 1`, `MAGNET: 2`) that can be reused for tracking purposes. That leaves us needing some additional constants for the level, the attempts, and the score. Navigate to **Resources** | **Define Constants** and add `LEVEL: 3`, `ATTEMPTS: 4`, `LVLSCORE: 5`.

2. We need to keep this data in a grid accessible globally. Create a new Script, `scr_Global_Analytics`, and initialize values for the whole game.

   ```
   globalvar levelData;
   levelData = ds_grid_create(totalLevels, 6);
   for (i = 0; i < totalLevels; i++)
   {
       ds_grid_set(levelData, i, TNT, 0);
       ds_grid_set(levelData, i, WRECKINGBALL, 0);
       ds_grid_set(levelData, i, MAGNET, 0);
       ds_grid_set(levelData, i, LEVEL, level[i, 0]);
       ds_grid_set(levelData, i, ATTEMPTS, 0);
       ds_grid_set(levelData, i, LVLSCORE, 0);
   }
   ```

   We start by creating a global data structure that has six values for each level in the game. We run a loop to set the initial values for each piece of equipment, the level by grabbing the level name from the previously created level array, the amount of attempts, and the level score, all set to zero.

3. Reopen `scr_Global_GameStart` and execute this script.

4. Next, we need to insert some code to change these values for each level. We will start with tracking the attempts for each level. This is going to require changes to several scripts. The first one we will change is `scr_Button_LevelSelect_MousePressed`, where we need to add an attempt when the player selects a level. In the `else` statement, before we change rooms, add the following code:

   ```
   currentLevel = ds_grid_value_x(levelData, 0, LEVEL, totalLevels-1, LEVEL, myLevel);
   ds_grid_add(levelData, currentLevel, ATTEMPTS, 1);
   ```

[332]

We search through the levelData grid for the room that has been selected in order to find out what row we need to change. Once we have the row, we add one attempt to that level's data.

5. As we are tracking attempts, we need to insert the same code into `scr_Menu_Button_Restart` just before we restart the room.

6. Finally, we also need to add similar code to `scr_Menu_Button_NextLevel`, except we cannot use `myLevel` to find the room. Instead, we need to look ahead to the next room. Just before we change rooms, insert the following code:

   ```
   currentLevel = ds_grid_value_x(levelData, 0, LEVEL, totalLevels-1, LEVEL, level[i+1,0]);
   ds_grid_add(levelData, currentLevel, ATTEMPTS, 1);
   ```

7. With the attempts now being tracked, we can move onto tracking the rest of the desired data. Create a new Script, `scr_Level_Stats`, and update all the relevant stats.

   ```
   levelCompleted = ds_grid_value_x(levelData, 0, LEVEL, totalLevels-1, LEVEL, room)
   for (i = 0; i < ds_grid_width(equip); i += 1)
   {
       equipUsed = abs(ds_grid_get(obj_Menu.startEquip, i, AMOUNT) - ds_grid_get(equip, i, AMOUNT));
       ds_grid_set(levelData, levelCompleted, i, equipUsed);
   }
   levelScore = obj_Menu.tempScore - obj_Menu.tempCost
   ds_grid_set(levelData, levelCompleted, LVLSCORE, levelScore);
   ```

   We start by finding the row for the level that has just been completed. We then run a loop through the equipment to see how many were used in the level, by subtracting the remaining equipment from how many the player started with. To ensure we get a positive number we use the abs function which returns an absolute value. We also grab the final score of the level and update the grid.

8. We want to run this script only upon the successful completion of a level, and the easiest place to put this is into `scr_WinCondition`, just before the last line of code where we return a true value.

   ```
   scr_Level_Stats();
   ```

Get Your Game Out There

Sending the data to Flurry

The data is now properly updated each time the level is played and successfully completed. All we need to do now is send the data to Flurry. Flurry does not update in real time, but instead compiles the data several times a day. If we send bits and pieces of data individually throughout the entire play session, that data might be separated when it is compiled, resulting in anomalies. To help prevent this, we are going to send all the relevant data of every level each time we want to update. Flurry will recognize the changes and keep the data together.

1. Create a new Script, scr_Analytics_Send, and run a loop through all the level data and send it out.

    ```
    for (a = 0; a < totalLevels; a++)
    {
        levelName = room_get_name(ds_grid_get(levelData, a, LEVEL));
        levelScore = ds_grid_get(levelData, a, LVLSCORE);
        levelAttempt = ds_grid_get(levelData, a, ATTEMPTS);
        usedTNT = ds_grid_get(levelData, a, TNT);
        usedWB = ds_grid_get(levelData, a, WRECKINGBALL);
        usedMagnet = ds_grid_get(levelData, a, MAGNET);
        analytics_event_ext(levelName, "Level Score", levelScore,
    "Attempts", levelAttempt, "TNT Used", usedTNT, "WBalls Used",
    usedWB, "Magnets Used", usedMagnet);
    }
    ```

    In this loop, we start by grabbing the name of the room stored in the grid and all the values for each piece of data. Using the function analytics_event_ext we can send up to 10 different pieces of data to Flurry. The first parameter is the category of data, sent as a string, in this case we are using the name of the levels as categories. All the following parameters are key/value pairs with the name of the data we are tracking and its associated value.

2. We need to send an initial set of analytics upon the start of the game, so we can start with a clean slate. Reopen scr_Global_Analytics and send the data at the end of the script.

    ```
    scr_Analytics_Send();
    ```

3. We also need to send the data out upon completion of the level. Reopen scr_Level_Stats and send the data at the end of the script as well.

4. We are now finished implementing the analytics. All that is left is to put it up on the web. Save the game, click on **Create Application**, and upload the new version of the game to the server.

5. Play the game several times, making sure to use differing amounts of equipment and retrying levels each time. We want to have some basic data tracked, so we can see what it all means.

Understanding the Analytics

We are tracking several pieces of data, and Flurry will be compiling this information into event logs. We can see when a session has occurred and what happened during that play session. While this is somewhat useful, Flurry breaks things down even further on a global scale that will show us how each level is played on average. Let's take a moment to see what Flurry provides us with. Before we get started, it is important to know that Flurry Analytics are not updated in real time, and it may take a few hours before we see any data appear.

1. Log in to your Flurry account and go to your **Destruct** application page.
2. The very first statistic you will see on the **Dashboard** is the **Sessions** graph, as shown in the next screenshot. Here we can see how many times the game was played each day. There is also information, such as average duration of each play session, where in the world people are playing the game from, and so on.

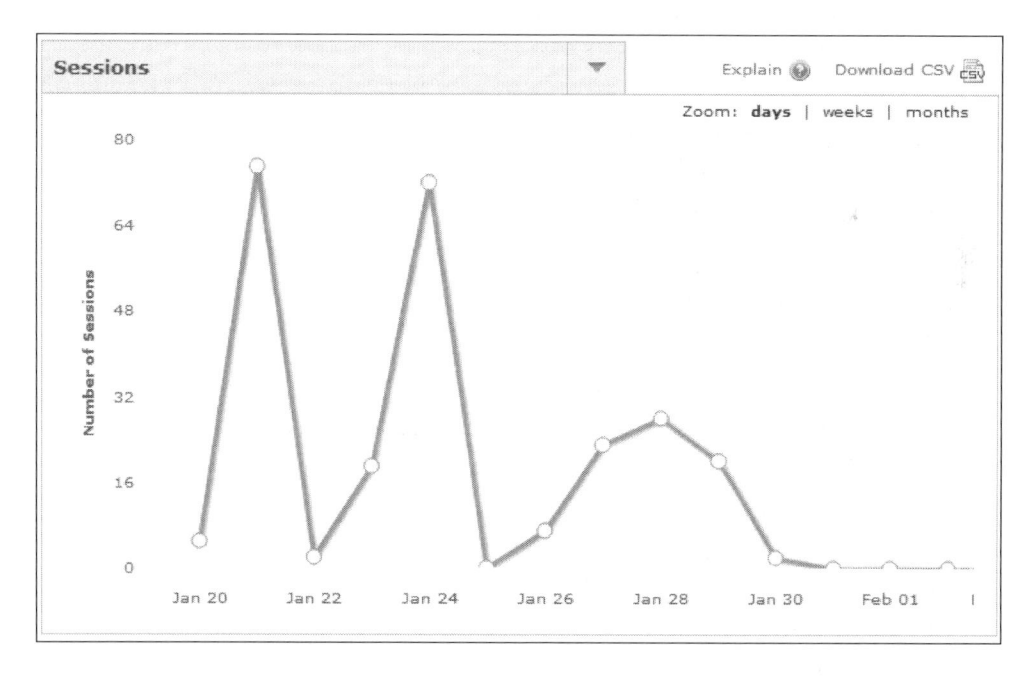

3. Click on **Events** on the left-hand side menu. The first option is the **Event Summary**, as shown in the following screenshot, which displays how often the level was played and the percentage of users that have completed this level per session.

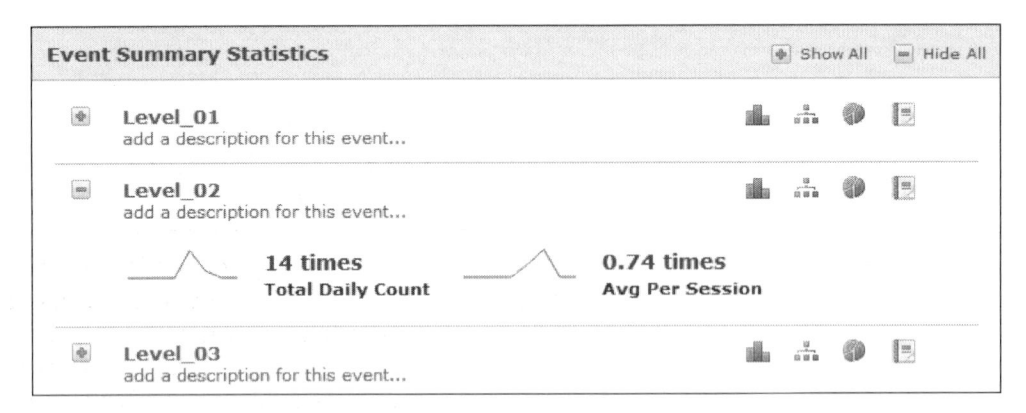

| Event Summary Statistics | Show All | Hide All |

Level_01
add a description for this event...

Level_02
add a description for this event...
14 times — Total Daily Count
0.74 times — Avg Per Session

Level_03
add a description for this event...

4. If we click on the little pie icon of a level, we will get a breakdown of the individual event parameters. Each parameter will show the total usage of all sessions. As can be seen in the following screenshot, one player used three pieces of TNT, another needed only two, and six players did not use any TNT at all.

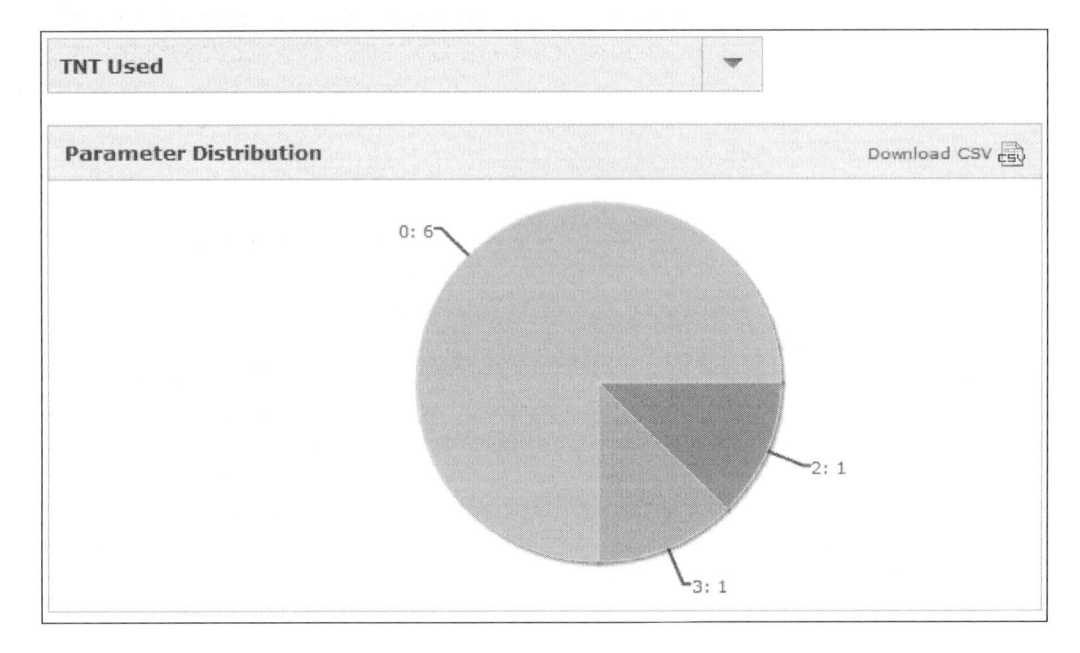

TNT Used

Parameter Distribution — Download CSV

0: 6
2: 1
3: 1

Having this type of information is incredibly valuable. Knowing where players stop playing the game can tell us where improvements can be made. Tracking what the player is using during the game lets us know if the game is balanced properly. The more useful data we can gather, the better we can apply the lessons learned to future games.

Making money with your games

Releasing a game is a fantastic accomplishment, but every developer at some point is going to want to earn some money from their efforts. The most common way to monetize a game is to place advertising on the site, but there are a few drawbacks with this when it comes to HTML5 games. The first problem is that the site will need a very high volume of traffic before enough clicks have accrued to earn any money. This affects the second problem, which is that advertising only works if people play the game on the specific site's web page. Unfortunately, other sites can embed HTML5 games through an **iframe**, which is a window inside a web page that allows content from another site to be displayed, and place their own advertising around it. This can be quite frustrating, as it means we are not earning money even though the game is running on our site. Happily, there are other ways to monetize a game, such as sponsorship.

Sponsors are game portals that will pay money to place their brand on a game. The branding is usually the sponsor's logo as the splash screen seen at the start of the game, but can also include things such as a button that links back to their site or what the Facebook post shows. The only downside to sponsorship is that there aren't many game portals that currently host HTML5 games, which means fewer potential offers. Looking to the future, expect more and more portals to jump onboard as HTML5 games mature and demand increases.

One of the best places to attempt to find sponsorship isn't a game portal at all, but rather a marketplace for all types of browser-based games. FGL, http://www.fgl.com, was originally created as a place to connect flash game developers with sponsors, but recently it has expanded into HTML5 and Unity games, as well as accepting games for iOS and Android devices. This marketplace allows developers to expose their game privately to sponsors and other game developers, gain feedback, and when ready, put the game up for bidding. Unlike a traditional auction house where the highest bid wins, the developer can choose which offer they prefer and can negotiate with bidders over the exact terms of the deal. There is no guarantee that a game will be offered any money, but if there is a chance to get money up front, this is where it will likely happen.

Summary

There we have it! In this chapter we covered a wide range of things. We started by uploading a game to a web server using an FTP client. We then integrated Facebook into the game, allowing players to log into their account and post level scores to their walls. We then implemented analytics using Flurry to track how players are playing the game. Finally, we briefly spoke about making money off our games through sponsorship.

Now that you have completed this book, you should have a very solid foundation to build your own games. We started by exploring the GameMaker: Studio interface and building the simplest of games. We took a look at creating art and audio so that we could improve the quality of our games. We then focused on using the GameMaker Language to code several games. We started with a simple side-scrolling shooter that demonstrated the basics of scripting. We then built upon that knowledge by creating an adventure game with multiple rooms and enemies on paths. We learned how to better structure our games and improve our scripting efficiency in our platforming boss fight. From there we moved onto using Box2D physics to create a simple tower toppling game, which we then polished into a full game with a full frontend, particle effects, Facebook integration, and Flurry Analytics.

GameMaker: Studio still has plenty more to offer and new features are constantly being added. It's up to you to use all of this acquired knowledge to make games of your own design. Have fun exploring the possibilities of the HTML5 platform and get your games out there. I wish you luck!

Index

Symbols

2D array
 about 260
 used, for selecting levels 259, 260
8-bit Collective
 URL 71

A

Adobe Photoshop
 about 50
 URL 50
analytics
 about 329
 using 335-337
angular damping 208
animated characters
 character movement, simplifying 120-124
 creating 120
 melee attack, implementing 124, 125
animated sprites
 about 65
 illusion of action 65
 looping 66-70
 sprite space, maximizing 66
animation system
 building 163-166
application
 creating 315-317
arguments 273
art assets
 manufacturing 49
artificial intelligence (AI) 133
audio
 manufacturing 71

audio APIst 8
audio file formats
 about 71
 MP3 71
 OCG 71

B

background images 24
background move
 adding 114, 115
background music, Sound Properties editor 28
Background Properties editor
 about 24
 used, for filling scene 24
backgrounds
 creating, with tilesets 54-65
BFXR
 URL 71
BMP format 50
boss battle
 about 179
 building 179
 Cannons, constructing 184-189
 giant LaserCannon, creating 190-194
 indestructible Gun, creating 179-183
 shielded Boss Core, creating 195-199
Box2D physics engine
 about 204
 working 204
Brawl
 about 119
 creating 140-145
bullet
 building 85, 86

firing 87
removing, from world 88
Burst emitters 300

C

canFire variable 175
Cannons
  constructing 184-189
character movement
  simplifying 120-124
child objects 88
classic platforming game
  boss battle, building 179
  creating 161
  player character, building 169
  room, setting up 177
  systems-based code, structuring 161
Coach
  about 119
  creating 146-155
coding conventions 78, 79
collectible
  about 29
  spawning, Time Line Properties
    editor used 38
collision forecasting system
  creating 166-168
collision group 207
collision_line function 150
collision sounds
  adding, in tower toppling game 229-231
consistency 74
constants 162
CSS3 (Cascading Style Sheets 3) 8

D

data
  sending, to Flurry 334
data object 28
data structures
  about 267
  grids 268
  lists 267
  maps 268
  priority queues 268

queues 267
stacks 267
debugging tools
  about 41
  HTML5 DEBUG console 42
  JavaScript code 45
  Windows version debugger 44
Debug Messages 42
debug version, JavaScript code 45
demolition equipment, tower toppling game
  building 232
  Magnetic Crane, creating 235-239
  Wrecking Ball, creating 232-234
density 207
Distance Joint 210
draw_text_ext function 289
Dust Cloud
  creating 302-306

E

else statement 151
Emitters 72
enemies, game
  Brawl, creating 140-146
  bringing to life 133
  Coach, creating 146-155
  constructing 88
  enemy parent, creating 88-90
  FloatBot 77
  FloatBot, building 91, 92
  Ghost Librarian, summoning 133-140
  SpaceMine 77
  SpaceMine, creating 93-96
  Strafer 77
  Strafer, creating 97-100
enemy parent
  creating 88, 89
Equipment Menu, tower toppling game
  creating 245-250
events
  about 79
  tracking, in game 332, 333
Exit object 129
explosions
  creating 115, 116

F

Facebook integration 321, 322
Facebook login button
  adding, to game 325
falloff 73
FGL
  URL 337
finishing details, adding
  background move 114
  explosions 115, 116
  game music 113
fixture
  about 205
  used, for defining properties 205-207
FloatBot
  about 77, 91
  building 91
Flurry
  data, sending 334
Flurry Analytics
  about 329
  implementing 329
  setting up 330, 331
Font Properties editor
  about 32
  text, writing 32-34
Force
  about 214
  applying, to objects 214-218
Freesound
  URL 71
friction 208
Front Ends
  rooms, setting up 255

G

game
  coding conventions 78, 79
  controlling, with Overlord 100
  debugging tools 41
  events, tracking 332, 333
  Facebook login button, adding 325-329
  finishing details, adding 113
  Ghost object, respawning 106-109
  hosting 317
  introductory text, adding to each level 286-289
  particle effects, adding 302
  releasing 337
  releasing, on website 315
  risk and reward, adding 279
  rooms, building 126
  rooms, navigating between 126
  rooms portal, creating 129
  running 23
  uploading, with FTP 318-321
  user interface, drawing 109-112
  win condition, setting up 105, 106
GameMaker Language 23, 78
GameMaker:Studio
  about 7
  animated characters 120
  animated sprites 65
  art assets, creating 49
  art assets, loading with Sprite Properties editor 12
  audio file formats 71
  audio, manufacturing 71
  code, introducing with Script Properties editor 23, 24
  collectibles, spawning with Time Line Properties editor 38-41
  complex movements, creating with Path Properties editor 35-37
  downloading 9
  features 7, 8
  Font Properties editor 32
  game objects, creating with Object Properties editor 14, 15
  game, running 23
  HTML5 Game Development 7
  image editor 53
  image file formats 50
  in-built Image Editor 53
  integrating, with Facebook 321-324
  interface 10
  layout 10
  noise, bringing with Sound Properties editor 27
  physics engine, building 203
  purchasing 9

resource editors 11
scene, filling with Background Properties
    editor 24-26
setting up 9
sprite sheets, importing 51, 52
tower toppling game, building 219
worlds, creating with Room Properties
    editor 20
GameMaker:Studio components
  Menu 10
  Resource tree 10
  Toolbar 10
  Workspace 10
game music
  adding 113
GAUSSIAN effect 301
Gear Joints 211
Ghost Librarian
  about 119
  summoning 133-140
Ghost object
  respawning 106-108
giant LaserCannon
  creating 190-194
GIF format 50
GIMP
  about 50
  URL 50
GM:S Audio engine
  about 72
  using 72, 73
Google Chrome 45
gravity
  creating 162, 163
grid data structure 268

H

heads-up display (HUD)
  about 109
  rebuilding 272-278
HTML5
  about 8
  testing 8
HTML5 DEBUG console
  about 42

using 42, 43
HTML5 limitations, particles effects 302

I

ICO format 317
iframe 337
image editor
  about 53
  backgrounds, creating with tilesets 54-65
image file formats
  about 50
  BMP 50
  GIF 50
  JPG 50
  PNG 50
in-built Image Editor 53
indestructible Gun
  creating 179-183
inheritance 88
INI files 291
instance_find function 148
introductory text
  adding, to each level 286-289
INVGAUSSIAN effect 301
isGameActive variable 272, 275
isLocked variable 265
isTimerStarted variable 272

J

JavaScript code
  about 45
  debug version 45
  obfuscated version 46
  using 45, 46
Joints
  about 210
  Distance Joints 210
  gear joints 211
  Prismatic Joints 211
  pulley joints 211
  Revolute Joints 210
  types 210
  used, for connecting objects 210
  working 211-213
JPG format 50

K

keyboard
  creating 169
keyboard_check_pressed function 125
keyframe 68

L

Legacy Sound engine 72
linear damping 208
LINEAR effect 301
list data structure 267
Listeners 72, 73
local storage
  about 290
  writing to 291-293
loop 73

M

Magnetic Crane, tower toppling game
  creating 235-239
map data structure 268
melee attack
  implementing 124-126
Menu 10
Microsoft Internet Explorer 9.0 45
motion planning functions 147
Mozilla Firefox 45
MP3 file format 71
mp_grid_create attribute 148
mp_potential_step function 150
multiple game profiles
  saving 294-296
myLevel variable 265
myNum variable 264

N

normal sounds, Sound Properties editor 27

O

obfuscated version, JavaScript code 46
obj_Bullet event 90
Object 11

Object Properties editor
  about 14
  player object, creating 16-19
  used, for creating game objects 14, 15
  wall object, creating 16
obj_Enemy_Parent 89
obj_Player event 89
OGG file format 71
Overlord
  about 28
  building 102-104
  used, for controlling game 28, 100
  wave of enemies, creating 101

P

parent object
  about 88
  creating 89
particle effects
  about 299
  adding, to game 302
  Dust Cloud, creating 302-306
  elements 299
  HTML5 limitations 302
  particles, cleaning 313, 314
  Shrapnel, adding 306-309
  TNT explosion, creating 309-312
particle emitters
  about 300
  Burst 300
  distribution 301
  GAUSSIAN 301
  INVGAUSSIAN 301
  LINEAR 301
  Shape options 300
  Stream 300
particles
  about 301
  applying 301
  cleaning 313, 314
particle systems 299
Path Properties editor
  about 35
  used, for creating complex movements 35, 37

persistent player
  teleporting 132, 133
physics engine
  about 203
  Forces, applying to objects 214-219
  objects, connecting with Joints 210-213
  physics world, activating 204, 205
  properties, fixing with Fixtures 205-210
physics properties
  angular damping 208
  collision group 207
  defining, with fixtures 205, 206
  density 207
  friction 208
  linear damping 208
  restitution 207
physics world
  activating 204, 205
Pickle
  about 50
  URL 50
Pillars and Debris, tower toppling game
  constructing 219-224
Pillars, tower toppling game
  breaking, into Debris 224-229
player character
  building 169-176
player object
  bulding 79
  bullet, building 85-87
  bullet, firing 87
  bullet, removing from world 88
  controlling 82-85
  creating 16-19
  player sprite, setting up 80, 81
player points
  rewarding 279
player sprite
  creating 13, 14, 80, 81
players progress, saving
  about 290
  local storage 290
  local storage, writing to 291-293
  multiple game profiles, saving 294, 296
PNG format 50
polish 76

priority queue data structure 268
Prismatic Joints 211
Pulley Joints 211
PyxelEdit
  URL 50

Q

quality bar
  consistency 74
  polish 76
  raising 74
  readability 75
queue data structure 267

R

readability 75
Reason
  URL 71
resource editors
  Background Properties editor 24
  Font Properties editor 32
  Object Properties editor 14
  Path Properties editor 35
  Room Properties editor 20
  Script Properties editor 23
  Sound Properties editor 27
  Sprite Properties editor 12
  Time Line Properties editor 38
Resource tree 11
restitution 207
Revolute Joints 210
risk and reward
  adding, to game 279-286
room portals
  creating 129-131
Room Properties editor
  about 20
  used, for creating worlds 20-22
rooms
  about 11
  navigating between 126
  persistent player, teleporting 132, 133
  setting up 126, 128, 177, 178
  Shop, preparing with data
    structures 266-271

rooms, HUD
  levels, selecting with 2D arrays 259-266
  main menu, initializing 257-259
  setting up 255-257

S

scr_Enemy_Collision_Bullet script 89
scr_Enemy_Collision_Player script 89
Script Properties editor
  about 23
  code, introducing with 23, 24
scr_Player_Attack_Alarm script 125
section/key/value structure 291
shape options, particle emitters 300
shapes 301
shielded Boss Core
  creating 195-199
Shrapnel
  adding 306-309
side scrolling shooter 77
Sonant
  URL 71
Sound Properties editor
  about 27
  background music 28
  collectible 29, 31
  game, controlling with Overlord 28, 29
  normal sounds 27
  used, for bringing noise 27
SpaceMine
  about 77, 93
  creating 93-96
splash screens 316
sponsors 337
spr_Bullet_SpaceMine script 93
Sprite 11, 301
Sprite Properties editor
  about 12
  player sprite, creating 13, 14
  used, for loading set assets 12
  wall sprite, creating 12, 13
Spriter
  URL 50
Spriters Resource
  URL 50

sprite sheets
  importing 51
stack data structure 267
startEquip Grid 274
Start object 129
Strafer
  about 77, 97
  creating 97-99
Stream emitters 300
systems-based code
  animation system, building 163-165
  collision forecasting system,
     creating 166, 167
  gravity, creating 162, 163
  keyboard, creating 169
  structuring 161

T

Text files 291
textLength variable 288
tileset 24, 54
Time Line Properties editor
  about 38
  used, for spawning collectibles 38-41
TNT explosion
  creating 309-313
Toolbar 11
totalLevels variable 260
towers, tower toppling game
  constructing 250-253
tower toppling game
  building 219
  collision sounds, adding 229-232
  demolition equipment, building 232
  Equipment Menu, creating 245-250
  Pillars and Debris, constructing 219-224
  Pillars, breaking into Debris 224-229
  towers, constructing 250-253
  win condition, setting 240-244

U

user interface, game
  drawing 109-112

V

Variables 79

W

wall object
　creating 16
wall sprite
　creating 12
waves of enemies
　creating 100, 101
WebGL 8, 302

win condition
　setting up 105, 106
win condition, tower toppling game
　setting 240-244
Windows version debugger
　about 44
　using 44
Workspace 11
Wrecking Ball, tower toppling game
　creating 232-235
writeText variable 289

[PACKT PUBLISHING] Thank you for buying HTML5 Game Development with GameMaker

About Packt Publishing

Packt, pronounced 'packed', published its first book "*Mastering phpMyAdmin for Effective MySQL Management*" in April 2004 and subsequently continued to specialize in publishing highly focused books on specific technologies and solutions.

Our books and publications share the experiences of your fellow IT professionals in adapting and customizing today's systems, applications, and frameworks. Our solution based books give you the knowledge and power to customize the software and technologies you're using to get the job done. Packt books are more specific and less general than the IT books you have seen in the past. Our unique business model allows us to bring you more focused information, giving you more of what you need to know, and less of what you don't.

Packt is a modern, yet unique publishing company, which focuses on producing quality, cutting-edge books for communities of developers, administrators, and newbies alike. For more information, please visit our website: `www.packtpub.com`.

Writing for Packt

We welcome all inquiries from people who are interested in authoring. Book proposals should be sent to `author@packtpub.com`. If your book idea is still at an early stage and you would like to discuss it first before writing a formal book proposal, contact us; one of our commissioning editors will get in touch with you.

We're not just looking for published authors; if you have strong technical skills but no writing experience, our experienced editors can help you develop a writing career, or simply get some additional reward for your expertise.

HTML5 Boilerplate Web Development

ISBN: 978-1-84951-850-5 Paperback: 174 pages

Master Web Development with a robust set of templates to get your projects done quickly and effectively

1. Master HTML5 Boilerplate as starting templates for future projects
2. Learn how to optimize your workflow with HTML5 Boilerplate templates and set up servers optimized for performance
3. Learn to feature-detect and serve appropriate styles and scripts across browser types

HTML5 Graphing and Data Visualization Cookbook

ISBN: 978-1-84969-370-7 Paperback: 344 pages

Learn how to create interactive HTML 5 charts and graphs with canvas, JavaScript, and open source tools

1. Build interactive visualizations of data from scratch with integrated animations and events
2. Draw with canvas and other HTML5 elements that improve your ability to draw directly in the browser
3. Work and improve existing 3rd party charting solutions such as Google Maps

Please check www.PacktPub.com for information on our titles

[PACKT] PUBLISHING

Responsive Web Design with HTML5 and CSS3

ISBN: 978-1-84969-318-9 Paperback: 324 pages

Learn responsive deisgn using HTML5 and CSS3 to adapt websites to any browser or screen size

1. Everything needed to code websites in HTML5 and CSS3 that are responsive to every device or screen size
2. Learn the main new features of HTML5 and use CSS3's stunning new capabilities including animations, transitions and transformations
3. Real world examples show how to progressively enhance a responsive design while providing fall backs for older browsers

HTML5 Mobile Development Cookbook

ISBN: 978-1-84969-196-3 Paperback: 254 pages

Over 60 recipes for building fast, responsive HTML5 mobile websites for iPhone 5, Android, Windows Phone, and Blackberry

1. Solve your cross platform development issues by implementing device and content adaptation recipes
2. Maximum action, minimum theory allowing you to dive straight into HTML5 mobile web development
3. Incorporate HTML5-rich media and geo-location into your mobile websites

Please check www.PacktPub.com for information on our titles

Printed in Germany
by Amazon Distribution
GmbH, Leipzig